CRITICALLY
SOVEREIGN

CRITICALLY
SOVEREIGN

Indigenous Gender, Sexuality, and Feminist Studies

JOANNE BARKER, EDITOR

DUKE UNIVERSITY PRESS
Durham and London · 2017

Printed in the United States of America on acid-free paper ∞
Designed by Courtney Leigh Baker
Typeset in Arno Pro and Trade Gothic by Westchester Publishing Services

Library of Congress Cataloging-in-Publication Data
Names: Barker, Joanne, [date] editor.
Title: Critically sovereign : indigenous gender, sexuality, and feminist studies /
Joanne Barker, editor.
Description: Durham : Duke University Press, 2017. | Includes bibliographical
references and index.
Identifiers: LCCN 2016048394 (print) | LCCN 2016050624 (ebook)
ISBN 9780822363392 (hardcover : alk. paper)
ISBN 9780822363651 (pbk. : alk. paper)
ISBN 9780822373162 (e-book)
Subjects: LCSH: Indians of North America—Historiography. | Indigenous
peoples—Historiography. | Sex role—Political aspects—United States—History. |
Feminist theory. | Queer theory. | Decolonization—United States. | Indigenous
peoples in literature.
Classification: LCC E76.8 .C75 2017 (print) | LCC E76.8 (ebook) | DDC 970.004/97—dc23
LC record available at https://lccn.loc.gov/2016048394

COVER ART: Merritt Johnson, *Waterfall Face Emergency Mantle for Diplomatic Security and Near Invisibility*, 2014, fabric, turkey wings, beads and spray lacquer.

TO ALL THE
murdered and missing
Indigenous women
and gender nonconforming
individuals.

TO THE
Grandmothers, Aunts, Sisters,
Mothers, Daughters, Friends, Lovers.
May all our relatives find
peace and justice.

Contents

Introduction
Critically Sovereign
JOANNE BARKER
1

I
Indigenous Hawaiian Sexuality and
the Politics of Nationalist Decolonization
J. KĒHAULANI KAUANUI
45

2
Return to "The Uprising at Beautiful Mountain in 1913"
*Marriage and Sexuality in the
Making of the Modern Navajo Nation*
JENNIFER NEZ DENETDALE
69

3
Ongoing Storms and Struggles
Gendered Violence and Resource Exploitation
MISHUANA R. GOEMAN
99

4

Audiovisualizing Iñupiaq Men and
Masculinities *On the Ice*

JESSICA BISSETT PEREA

127

5

Around 1978
*Family, Culture, and Race in
the Federal Production of Indianness*

MARK RIFKIN

169

6

Loving Unbecoming
The Queer Politics of the Transitive Native

JODI A. BYRD

207

7

Getting Dirty
*The Eco-Eroticism of Women in
Indigenous Oral Literatures*

MELISSA K. NELSON

229

Contributor Biographies
261

Index
263

CRITICALLY SOVEREIGN

JOANNE BARKER

A woman returned from the field to find a curious hole in the ground outside her lodging. She looked inside the hole, deep into the earth, and someone spoke to her from there. The woman asked who it was. "If anyone wishes to hear stories, let them come and roll a little tobacco or a bead, and I will tell them a story." So the people came, with tobacco and beads, and many stories were told. We do not know whether the stories are true, only that they tell us who we are. And they all begin with a giving of thanks.[1] *Wanishi* (Lenape). *Chin'an gheli* (Dena'ina). *Chokma'ski* (Chickasaw). *Nya:weh* (Seneca). Niawen/ *Niawen kowa* (Onyota'aka). *Ahéhee'* (Diné). *Mahalo* (Hawaiian). *Miigwech* (Anishinaabe). *Nyá:wę!* (Skarure). *Thank you* (English).

Contexts

It is a genuine challenge not to be cynical, given the relentlessness of racially hyper-gendered and sexualized appropriations of Indigenous cultures and identities in the United States and Canada: OutKast's performance at the

2004 Grammy Awards; the headdressed portraits of the reality TV star Khloe Kardashian, the singer Pharrell Williams, and the singer Harry Styles of the band One Direction;[2] Urban Outfitters' Navajo Hipster Panty and Victoria Secret's headdress-and-fringe lingerie fashion show; the supermodel and TV host Heidi Klum's "Redface" photo shoot; the *always already* corrupt tribal gaming officials of *Big Love, The Killing,* and *House of Cards;* the redface, song and dance, and tomahawk chop among sports fandom in Washington, Illinois, and elsewhere.[3] Everywhere.

It is also a challenge to take seriously the apologies that follow. Too often they are dismissive and defensive. Indigenous peoples are slighted for failing to respect the deep connection people claim with Indigenous cultures, as with Christina Fallin, daughter of the governor of Oklahoma, who was criticized for posing in a headdress for a portrait and insisted that "growing up in Oklahoma, we have come into contact with Native American culture institutionally our whole [lives].... With age, we feel a deeper and deeper connection to the Native American culture that has surrounded us. Though it may not have been our own, this aesthetic has affected us emotionally in a very real and very meaningful way."[4] Or Indigenous concerns are rejected as uninformed, as with Gwen Stefani, lead singer of the band No Doubt, who said in response to criticism that the headdress and buckskin she wore while engaging in sexual torture in the music video *Looking Hot* were sanctioned by "Native American experts in the University of California system." Or Indigenous people are written off as not understanding Indigenous identity at all, as when Johnny Depp responded to criticism of his blackbird-headed Tonto in the movie *The Lone Ranger* that he was "part Cherokee or maybe Creek." (He was adopted shortly thereafter by the Comanche Nation of Oklahoma.) Inherent in these various responses is the suggestion that Indigenous people are too sensitive, miss the point of the play, are easily duped by Hollywood glam, or are biased against those who are unenrolled or of mixed descent (not necessarily the same thing).

The insistent repetition of the racially gendered and sexualized image—of a particular kind of Indian woman/femininity and Indian man/masculinity— and its succession by contrite, defensive apologies laced with insult is neither a craze nor a gaffe. It is a racially gendered and sexed snapshot, a still image of a movingly malleable narrative of Indigenous womanhood/femininity and manhood/masculinity that reenacts Indigenous people's lack of knowledge and power over their own culture and identity in an inherently imperialist and colonialist world. There is something especially telling in how these instances occur most often in the public spaces of fashion, film, music, and politics. We seem to expect little from supermodels, actors, musicians, and elected officials (and their families), even as we make them fulfill our desires for money and power and our ideals about living in a democratic, liberal, and multicultural society. They make the perfect butt of our jokes even as (or because) they serve to disguise how their costumed occupations of Indigeneity reenact the social terms and conditions of U.S. and Canadian dominance over Indigenous peoples.

But Indigenous peoples miss none of the implications. Because international and state recognition of Indigenous rights is predicated on the cultural authenticity of a certain kind of Indigeneity, the costumed affiliations undermine the legitimacy of Indigenous claims to sovereignty and self-determination by rendering Indigenous culture and identity obsolete but for the costume. That this representation is enacted through racialized, gendered, and sexualized images of Indigenous women/femininity and men/masculinity—presumably all heterosexual and of a generic tribe—is not a curiosity or happenstance. It is the point. Imperialism and colonialism require Indigenous people to fit within the heteronormative archetypes of an Indigeneity that was authentic in the past but is culturally and legally vacated in the present. It is a past that even Indigenous peoples in headdresses are perceived to honor as something dead and gone. The modernist temporality of the Indigenous dead perpetuates the United States and Canada as fulfilled promises of a democracy encapsulated by a multicultural liberalism that, ironically, is inclusive of Indigenous people only in costumed affiliation. This is not a logic of elimination. Real Indigeneity is *ever presently* made over as irrelevant as are Indigenous legal claims and rights to governance, territories, and cultures. But long live the regalia-as-artifact that anybody can wear.

The relentlessness of the racist, sexist appropriations of Indigenous culture and identity and their work in rearticulating imperial and colonial formations has been shown up by the radical dance of Indigenous peoples for treaty and territorial rights, environmental justice, and women's and men's health and well-being within the Idle No More movement.[5] Idle No More originated in a series of e-mails exchanged in October 2012 by four women in Saskatoon, Saskatchewan—Nina Wilson (Nakota and Cree), Sylvia McAdam (Cree), Jessica Gordon (Cree), and Sheelah McLean—who shared concerns not only about the direction of parliamentary laws and energy development projects in Canada, but also about the need for a broader "vision of uniting people to ensure the protection of Mother Earth, her lands, waters, and the people."[6] In November of that year, the women organized a series of teach-ins to address the laws—at various stages of draft, vetting, and passage—and to strategize for the long term.[7] The laws included the Jobs and Growth Act (Bill C-45), which removed protections on fish habitat and recognition of First Nation commercial fisheries and vacated federal oversight over navigation and environmental assessment on 99 percent of Canada's waterways.[8] It also allowed government ministers to call for a referendum to secure land cessions by vote, nullifying their responsibilities to consult with Indigenous governments on land-cession proposals.[9] These types of deregulations were interconnected with Canada's free trade agreements with China in relation to multiple tar sands pipeline projects.[10] The laws undergirded and propelled the infrastructure necessary for Canada's expansive, unregulated energy development and revenue generation.[11] By the time the Jobs and Growth Act passed on December 4, 2012, Idle No More's actions had spread across Canada and into the United States, with Indigenous people demanding that Indigenous treaty and constitutional rights, including the right of consultation, be respected.

When the Canadian prime minister and Parliament continued to refuse meeting with Indigenous leaders outside the Assembly of First Nations process, a national day of action was called for December 10. In solidarity with Idle No More's objectives, Chief Theresa Spence of the Attawapiskat Nation initiated a liquids-only fast.[12] In a public statement, Spence declared, "I am willing to die for my people because the pain is too much and it's time for the government to realize what it's doing to us."[13] With international support, Spence agreed to attend a meeting that had been scheduled between Harper and representatives of the Assembly of First Nations on January 11, 2013, on the provision that Governor-General David Johnston, representing the Crown, agree to attend. When neither Harper nor Johnston could agree on the terms of the meeting, Spence and several other Indigenous leaders boycotted. On January 25, Spence acceded to concerns about her health and concluded her fast. In support, representatives of the Treaty Chiefs, the Assembly of First Nations, the Native Women's Association of Canada, the New Democratic Party, and the Liberal Party of Canada signed a thirteen-point declaration of commitment pledging to renew their efforts to oppose Bill C-45 and the bills that had not yet passed. They also outlined their demands of Harper and Parliament, including the need for transparency and consultation; a commitment to address treaty issues; an affirmation of Indigenous rights provided for by Canadian law and the "Declaration on the Rights of Indigenous Peoples"; a commitment to resource revenue sharing and environmental sustainability; and the appointment of a National Public Commission of Inquiry on Violence against Indigenous Women. These demands were echoed in solidarity actions in the United States, New Zealand, Australia, and throughout the world. In the United States, the actions also addressed the contamination of water by hydro-fracking, the multiply proposed tar sands pipelines from Canada to the Gulf of Mexico, and the gendered and sexualized violence against Indigenous communities within the energy industry's "man camps."[14]

This volume is engaged with ongoing political debates such as those instanced by cultural appropriation and Idle No More, about Indigeneity and Indigenous rights from the contexts of critical Indigenous gender, sexuality, and feminist studies. Three particular issues define the volume, with each essay operating as a kind of kaleidoscope whose unique turns emphasize different patterns, shadows, and hue and, thus, relationships between and within.

First, the volume is concerned with the terms and debates that constitute critical Indigenous gender, sexuality, and feminist studies. Contributors mark their own stakes within these debates by foregrounding the intellectual genealogies that inform her or his work. In doing so, many contributors engage feminist theories of heterosexism, sexism, and colonization, while others interrogate the terms of feminist theory in relation to gender and sexuality.

Second, the volume offers nation-based and often territorially specific engagements with Indigenous sovereignty and self-determination (what I term the "polity of the Indigenous"[15]). This is reflected by attention to the unique yet related ethics and responsibilities of gendered and sexed land-based epistemologies, cultural protocols and practices, governance histories and laws, and sociocultural relationships.

To be clear, locating Indigenous gender, sexuality, and feminist studies within and by Indigenous territories is not an essentialism of Indigeneity or a romanticization of Indigenous rights. No contributor claims that all Lenape, Dena'ina, Chickasaw, Seneca, Onyota'aka, Diné, Hawaiian, Anishinaabe, Skarure, or other Indigenous people are alike or that their perspectives and concerns can be reduced to "their nation" or "the land" as the only grounds on which they live and work. Further, it does not exclude Indigenous peoples whose territorial rights have been stripped from them; national and land-based knowledge and relationships are not predicated on recognition by the state. Rather, nations and territories provide the contexts necessary for understanding the social responsibilities and relationships that inform

Indigenous perspectives, political organizing, and intellectual theorizing around the politics of gender, sexuality, and feminism. Locating Indigenous gender, sexuality, and feminist studies within and by Indigenous territories holds the contributors—Indigenous and non-Indigenous—accountable to the specific communities to and from which they write as citizens or collaborators. This accountability is key to the theoretical reflection and methodological application of the protocols that (in)form Indigenous knowledge and politics.[16]

Third, the volume is concerned with the structure and operation of U.S. and Canadian imperialism and colonialism as related but unique state formations. The essays assume that gender and sexuality are core constitutive elements of imperialist-colonialist state formations and are concerned with the gendered, sexist, and homophobic discrimination and violence on which those formations are predicated.

I would not characterize these three particular issues as a necessarily distinct feature of this volume. Rather, the volume is an instance—a moment—within *ongoing* debates about Indigeneity and Indigenous rights within critical Indigenous gender, sexuality, and feminist studies. This instantiation has stakes in contributing to those debates in a way that emphasizes national, territorially based knowledge and ethical relationships and responsibilities to one another as scholars and to the communities from which and to which we write at the same time that it thinks through concrete strategies for political action and solidarity among and between Indigenous and non-Indigenous people against imperialist and colonialist state formations in the United States and Canada.[17]

In the remainder of the introduction, I orient the volume by considering some of the theoretical and methodological debates that have defined critical Indigenous gender, sexuality, and feminist studies. I begin with the institutionalization of the studies in the 1968–70 historical moment and then follow some of its routes through current scholarship. This is not meant to be definitive or comprehensive, but, with the three issues outlined above in mind, it is intended to provide a point of entry into the chapters that follow—to show something of the rich, diverse intellectual genealogies that define the studies and this volume's place within them.

The contributors examine a varied set of historical and current issues from multiple theoretical and methodological perspectives. These issues include the co-production of Native Hawaiian sexuality, belonging, and nationalism; the heteronormative marriage laws of the Navajo Nation; a U.S.-Canadian border town's experiences of violence against Indigenous women and environmental destruction by Hydro-Québec; the role of music and performance in Inuit processes of globalization and cosmopolitics; the heteronormativity of U.S. federal laws of 1978; the antimiscegenist erasure of Indigeneity within the U.S. Supreme Court's decision in *Loving v. Virginia* (1967); and, the eroticism of ecologically based relationalities. In their analyses, the contributors represent not only how critical sovereignty and self-determination are to Indigenous peoples, but the importance of a critical address to the politics of gender, sexuality, and feminism within how that sovereignty and self-determination is imagined, represented, and exercised.

The Studies

Critical Indigenous gender, sexuality, and feminist studies confront the imperial-colonial work of those modes of Indigeneity that operationalize genocide and dispossession by ideologically and discursively vacating the Indigenous from the Indigenous. Simultaneously, they confront the liberal work of those theoretical modes of analysis and the political movements from which they emerge that seek to translate Indigenous peoples into normative gendered and sexed bodies as citizens of the state. In these confrontations, the studies must grapple with the demands of asserting a sovereign, self-determining Indigenous subject without reifying racialized essentialisms and authenticities. They must also grapple with the demands of de-normalizing gender and sexuality against the exceptionalist grains of a fetishized woman-centered or queer difference. In their stead, the studies are predicated on *the polity of the Indigenous*—the unique governance, territory, and culture of Indigenous peoples in unique and related systems of (non)-human relationships and responsibilities to one another.[18]

Historically, though in very different ways in the United States and Canada, critical Indigenous studies (CIS); ethnic, critical race, and diaspora studies; and gender, sexuality, and feminist studies and fields of inquiry were established in the context of civil rights movements into higher education (first institutionalized as departments and programs in the 1968–70 moment). The movements challenged—not always in concert—the racism, sexism, homophobia, and capitalist ideologies of power and knowledge within university curricula; pedagogy; scholarship; and faculty, student, and staff representation. This is not to suggest that the intellectual work these movements represented did not exist before 1968; that they were always united in what they cared about or in how they were institutionalized; or that they did not confront racism, sexism, homophobia, and classism. Rather, because of how they were historically situated, they perceived themselves foremost in relation to civil rights matters. For instance, within CIS, fighting for the collective rights of Indigenous nations to sovereignty and self-determination in relation *to the state* was not considered the same fight as ethnic and critical race studies for citizenship, voting, and labor rights *within the state*.[19] Concurrently, within gender, sexuality, and feminist studies, perceptions about the relevance of race and class in understanding social justice and equity accounted for important differences in intellectual and pedagogical commitments. Notions of diversity and rights were not effortlessly reckoned across departments, programs, associations, or publishing forums. The differences resulted in part in compartmentalized histories of the formations and developments of CIS; ethnic, critical race, and diaspora studies; and gender, sexuality, and feminist studies and fields of inquiry. How they have informed one another frequently has been left out, limiting our understandings of how categories of analysis—or analytics—organize all manner of intellectual work (theoretically and methodologically), institutional formations (from curriculum to professional association), and community relationships and responsibilities.

INDIGENOUS

Critical Indigenous studies and its relationship to ethnic and critical race studies has distinct institutional histories in Canada and the United States. In Canada, the institutionalization of departments, programs, and the First Nations University resulted from constitutional and treaty mandates and federation agreements for Indigenous education. There was no institutionalization in Canada of ethnic, critical race, or diaspora studies, where fields of inquiry were located as emphases or specialties within disciplines such as history, sociology, anthropology, and literature. In the United States, however, CIS and ethnic, critical race, and diaspora studies were institutionalized concurrently out of the political struggles defining the 1968–70 historical moment. For CIS, the establishment of departments, programs, associations, and publishing forums originated with Indigenous activists' moving back and forth between their campuses (and their efforts to create CIS departments and programs) and the struggles of their nations for sovereignty and self-determination (such as the visible presence of Indigenous students at "fish-ins" in the Pacific Northwest in support of treaty-protected fishing rights). With ethnic, critical race, and diaspora studies, departments *et cetera* originated primarily with activists engaged in civil rights movements. These different origins are crucial for understanding how CIS distinguished itself from ethnic, critical race, and diaspora studies.

CIS distinguished itself through questions about Indigenous sovereignty, self-determination, and citizenship. Indigenous *peoples'* efforts to secure collective rights to sovereignty and self-determination as provided for within international and constitutional law was differentiated from the efforts of "minority" *people*—including immigrant and diaspora communities and their descendants—to claim citizenship and civil rights within their nation-states. This difference is germane to understanding the intellectual and political work of CIS, which directly builds on the unique histories and cultures of nations and often territorial-based communities to address current forms of oppression and think strategically through the efficacy of their unique but related anti-imperial and anticolonial objectives and strategies.[20]

In addition, CIS negotiated its scholarly and institutional relationship to various critical race, ethnic, and diaspora studies in the context of perceptions about and claims on who and what counts as Indigenous. For instance, claims of African origins and migrations in human and world history have been perceived to conflict with Indigenous knowledge and epistemologies about Indigenous origins in the lands of North America. Intellectual claims on the Pacific within Asian American studies similarly have been perceived to erase colonization by Asian states within the Pacific as well as the relevance of Indigenous sovereignty and self-determination in Hawai'i and the U.S.-occupied territories in the Pacific.

One of the consequences of these perceptions has been that CIS *curriculum* tends to focus on American Indian and Alaska Native peoples in the United States and on First Nation, Métis, and Inuit peoples in Canada, while CIS *scholarship* and political engagement is more engaged with Indigenous groups of North, South, and Central America; the Pacific; and the Caribbean.[21] The "balancing act" of perceived curricular and intellectual "territoriality"—and its implications for community relationships and engagements—was and remains a permanent feature of issues confronting CIS as a field of inquiry and in relation to program development, student recruitment, and faculty representation. It also serves as an example of the identificatory politics of Indigenous peoples both within scholarship, curriculum, and political work and in the context of processes of state formation.[22]

To put this in a slightly different way, how *Indigenous* includes or excludes Native Americans, American Indians, Alaska Natives, Native Hawaiians (Kanaka Maoli), South Americans, Central Americans, First Nation/Indians,

Métis, Inuits, Aborigines, or Maoris is not merely an academic question. It is a question about how these categories of identity and identification work to *include in* and *exclude from* rights to governance, territories, and cultural practice within international and constitutional law or contain or open possibilities of political solidarity against U.S. and Canadian imperialism and colonialism.

Consequently, whether or not a group or an individual identifies or is identified as legally and socially Indigenous implies all kinds of jurisdictions, citizenships, property rights, and cultural self-determinations that are *always already* entrenched within the legal terms and conditions of Indigenous relations to the United States and Canada as imperial-colonial powers. Identifying or being identified as Indigenous inextricably ties a person to the jurisdictional and territorial struggles of Indigenous peoples against the social forces of imperialism and colonialism. It is an act that simultaneously (un)names the polity of Indigenous governance, jurisdictions, territories, and cultures. As a consequence, the legal and political stakes of Indigenous identity and identification have been a core aspect of cis scholarship, curriculum, and community engagement. These stakes entail all kinds of social politics concerning the ethics and integrity of cis scholars' identifications and the scholarship that results. Nowhere have these politics been more raw than in gender, sexuality, and feminist studies, once predominately characterized by the cultural appropriation, misrepresentation, and exploitation of Indigenous cultures and identities.[23]

But cis criticisms of gender, sexuality, and feminist studies for cultural appropriation and exploitation have represented a knotted set of disconnects within cis for a number of reasons. For instance, many cis scholars have written, and enjoyed a receptive audience, within the studies even as (or because) they have sharply criticized feminism and feminists for collusion with imperialist, colonialist, and racist ideologies and practices. This is more curious as many of the same scholars have made these criticisms while located institutionally within women's studies departments (such as M. A. Jaimes Guerrero [Juaneño/Yaqui] of the Women's Studies Department at San Francisco State University) or published and circulated within gender, sexuality, and feminist professional forums (such as Haunani-Kay Trask [Kanaka Maoli], who is a frequent keynote speaker at women of color conferences).[24]

Another disconnect is in the way many cis scholars have criticized the marginalization of gender, sexuality, and feminism within cis. This includes critiques of how cis scholarship has frequently compartmentalized gender, sexuality, and feminism, bracketing them off from analysis of "more serious political" issues such as governance, treaty and territorial rights, or the law. Even the very well-respected Lakota legal scholar and philosopher Vine Deloria Jr., who wrote extensively about U.S. federal Indian law and politics only anecdotally addressed the politics of gender, usually by including a discussion of female creation figures or lone sketches of female leaders.[25] He never once wrote about sexuality or feminism.[26]

Another disconnect goes to the importance of gender, sexuality, and feminist studies in addressing the prevalence of sexism and homophobia within Indigenous communities.[27] Central to this have been claims that gender and sexuality are already respected forms of identity and experience within Indigenous cultures; thus, those issues do not need to be addressed within scholarship or political struggle. For instance, the Lakota activist, actor, and writer Russell Means claimed that the inherently matriarchal values that historically characterized tribal cultures made patriarchy and feminism unnecessary evils of "the West."[28]

One of the consequences of these disconnects has been that the core place of gender and sexuality in Indigenous sovereignty and self-determination has been minimized and deflected, contributing to and reflecting the disaggregation of race and racialization from the politics of gender and sexuality within CIS scholarship and within Indigenous sovereignty and self-determination struggles. As the essays in this volume show, gender and sexuality are permanent features of multiple, ongoing processes of social and identity formation within the United States and Canada. Their disarticulation from race and ethnicity or law and politics is a regulatory tool of power and knowledge. Such discursive practices suppress the historical and cultural differences that produce what gender and sexuality mean and how they work to organize history and experience. Similarly, feminism is shown to have multiple intellectual and political genealogies within Indigenous communities that need to be remembered, not for the sake of feminism, but for the sake of Indigenous knowledge and the relationships and responsibilities it defines.

GENDER, SEXUALITY, FEMINISM

In similar ways in the United States and Canada, the familiar history of gender, sexuality, and feminist studies is that the women's rights, gay rights, and feminist movements (not necessarily different or necessarily aligned) out of which the studies were established called for a women's and gay's liberation and civil rights equality that rested on essentialized notions of women and gay identity and experience. This essentialism has been narrated as *racializing* and *classing* gender and sexuality in such a way as to further a liberal humanist normalization of "compulsory heterosexuality," male dominance, and white privilege.[29] The studies it produced have been narrated as an unfortunate but ultimately necessary result of "strategic essentialism," with women's studies and LGBTQ studies serving to locate gender, sexuality, and feminism within an otherwise heterosexist patriarchal academy as a "fundamental category" of "analysis and understanding."[30] Gender studies and sexuality studies have been seen not only to make competing claims on radical feminist theory but also to offer critical insight on processes of subject formation in relation to the regulatory operations of discourse.[31]

These kinds of "wave" histories, of course, obfuscate the work of gender, sexuality, and feminism as categories of analysis and political coalition. They seem to do so primarily in two ways. First, they lend themselves to an ideology of socio-intellectual evolution. Gender, sexuality, and feminist studies *today* have moved past their troubled origins and evolved into a radical analytics, as is evident in their embrace of such methodologies as intersectionality and transnationality.[32] The presumptions of progress obscure those intellectual histories of gender, sexuality, and feminism that do not conform, such as erasing the role of nonwhite women in the suffrage movement.[33] Second, they serve to render equal and transparent—fully legible—all identificatory and regulatory aspects of the essentialisms of gender, sexuality, and feminism. If we understand *legibility* as that which has been accepted to be true—the essentialist origins of gender, sexuality, and feminism—numerous categories of analysis and understanding must be made *illegible*, such as Indigenous and Black women's feminisms.[34] As Judith Butler asks, "How can one read a text for what does not appear within its own terms, but which nevertheless constitutes the illegible conditions of its own legibility?"[35] This becomes important in understanding how debates over gender, sexuality, and feminism work. Specific points within the debates—the problematics of substituting "women" for "gender," the limits of the sex-gender and sex-sexuality paradigms, the operations of white middle-class heteronormativity, the politics of binaries such as male-female—actually serve not to make the issues clearer but to make illegible all kinds of other histories and analyses.[36] As Butler suggests, making these other histories and analyses illegible is, in fact, the condition on which the debates flourish.

One consequence of this is a reinscription of Eurocentric, patriarchal ideologies of gender, sexuality, kinship, and society that render historical and cultural difference unintelligible and irrelevant. A result of this reinscription is in how Indigenous genders, sexualities, and feminisms are used illustratively and interchangeably, not analytically, in debates about feminist theory and praxis.

For instance, as Biddy Martin argues, much work has been done in women's studies on separating anatomical sex (determinism) and social gender (constructionism). This separation has had consequences. First, it contributes to the notion of the stability and fixity of anatomical sex (what one is) and the malleability and performance of gender (what one does); the body and psyche are rendered virtually irrelevant to one's identity and experience.[37] Second, by reducing gender to one of two possibilities (man and woman), gender as a category of analysis stabilizes and universalizes binary oppositions at other levels, including sexuality, race, ethnicity, class, and nationalism.[38] "As a number of different feminists have argued," Martin writes, "the assumption of a core gender identity, now conceived as an effect of social construction, may also serve to ground and predict what biology, for constructionists, no longer can, namely, the putative unity or self-sameness of any given person's actual sex or gender."[39] In other words, we are at our core male or female and then made man or woman by society, and the equivalences are neatly proscriptive. Queerness, against the normativities that result, ends up standing in for the promise of a radical alterity of gender identity (performed) and a body-psyche utopia of sexual desire and pleasure.

These discursive formulations render little possibility for other understandings of gender and sexuality. For instance, Indigenous perspectives include those that insist on not equating biology and identity in understanding how the significance of gender and sexuality is reckoned in social relationships and responsibilities. Critical Indigenous studies scholars have uncovered multiple (not merely *third* genders or *two*-spirits) identificatory categories of gender and sexuality within Indigenous languages that defy binary logics and analyses. Within these categories, male, man, and masculine and female, woman, and feminine are not necessarily equated or predetermined by anatomical sex; thus, neither are social identity, desire, or pleasure.

But it is also true that some Indigenous perspectives see biology as core in relation to understandings of status, labor, and responsibilities, including matters of lineality (heredity), reproduction, and how relationships to not-human beings, the land and water, and other realities are figured. Further, matrilineality and patrilineality—not necessarily indicative of matriarchy or patriarchy—define social identities, relationships, and responsibilities in contexts of governance, territories, and cultures. Lineality would seem to indicate, then, an insistence on a biological relationship, but not one that ca-be used to stabilize gender and sexuality in the reckoning of social identity, desire, and pleasure.

These complicated matters have been translated within women's studies scholarship to make very different kinds of analyses, such as forcing "third genders" and "two-spirits" to fit within preexisting categories of sexual difference such as bisexuality, transsexuality, or queerness. Further, they have been mobilized in arguments that Western patriarchy and sexism are not natural or inevitable truths of human existence but particular social ills from which women ought to be liberated (as seen in Marxist feminist anthropology).[40] Consequently, Indigenous cultures and identities are used to illustrate the need and potential for women's and gay's liberation and equality, with Indigenous women and LGBTQ people serving as teachers of the metaphysical truths of universal womanhood or queerhood that transcend the harsh realities of capitalist, heteronormative, patriarchal sexism.

These representational practices suppress Indigenous epistemologies, histories, and cultural practices regarding gender and sexuality while also concealing the historical and social reality of patriarchy, sexism, and homophobia within Indigenous communities. Not only have gender, sexuality, and feminist studies not accounted for the great diversity of Indigenous gender and sexuality, but, ironically, they have either suppressed histories of gender- and sexuality-based violence and discrimination within Indigenous communities or championed the liberation of Indigenous women and LGBTQ people from "their men."

In the chapters that follow, contributors *defamiliarize* gender, sexuality, and feminist studies to unpack the constructedness of gender and sexuality and problematize feminist theory and method within Indigenous contexts. They do so by locating their analyses in the historical and cultural specificity of gender and sexuality as constructs of identity and subject formation. Each chapter situates itself within a specific intellectual genealogy—of CIS and of unique Indigenous nations and citizenships—and anticipates a decolonized future of gender and sexual relations, variously inviting and deflecting feminism as a means of getting there.

CRITICAL INDIGENOUS, GENDER, SEXUALITY, FEMINIST STUDIES
INSTITUTIONAL FOUNDATIONS, INTELLECTUAL ROOTS

Critical Indigenous gender, sexuality, and feminist studies emerge from histories of Indigenous writings that are much older than their institutionalization in the curriculum of departments and programs formed in the 1968–70 moment. These early writings provide nation-based and often territorially specific engagements with Indigenous sovereignty and self-determination that reflect their authors' commitments to the ethics and responsibilities of gendered and sexed land-based epistemologies, cultural protocols and practices, and national governance and laws. They also provide analyses of the structure and operation of U.S. and Canadian imperialism and colonialism as related but unique state formations predicated on gendered, sexist, and homophobic discrimination and violence.[41] But these early writings also exhibit "yawning gulfs in the archives," particularly of Indigenous female and nongender conforming authors.[42] That absence is especially stark in the context of the plethora of literature by English and French heterosexual women who were taken captive by Indigenous nations and the colonial families they either left behind or later rejoined.

In her crucial article on the politics of captivity narratives, "Captivating Eunice," Audra Simpson (Kahnawake Mohawk) addresses the raced and gendered politics of Indigenous kinship, recognition, and belonging in relation to Canada's regulation of Indigenous legal status and rights.[43] Through the story of Eunice Williams, the daughter of a Protestant minister, and her descendants, Simpson considers the politics of the kinship of a captive of the Kahnawake Mohawk and of her descendants as they are made the subjects of recent amendments to Mohawk membership criteria. Over time, Eunice and her descendants would be invested with the legal status and rights of "Indians" under the patrilineal provisions of Canada's Indian Act, but only as her sisters and their descendants would lose theirs:

> These forms of political recognition and mis-recognition are forms of "citizenship" that have become social, and citizenships that incurred losses, in addition to gains, and thus are citizenships I wish to argue, of grief. . . . The Canadian state made all Indians in its jurisdiction citizens in 1956; however, the marriage of Indian women to non-status men would alienate them from their reserves, their families, and their rights as Indians until the passage of Bill C-31 in 1985. Thus, one can argue that these status losses, and citizenship gains, would always be accompanied by some form of grief.[44]

Simpson argues that the grievability of Indigenous life under Canadian law is linked profoundly to "governability"—to the state's ability to regulate matrilineality out as a form of Indigenous governance, property, and inheritance.[45] Part of this regulation is reflected in the absence of Indigenous women from the early archives of colonial-Indigenous relations—literally *writing/righting* them out of history—as well as in the "mis-recognition" of their experiences and concerns in contemporary debates over Indigenous legal status and rights within Indigenous communities by the suppression of their grief and losses.

The emergence of suffragist writings and political organizing in the early 1800s addressed central questions of women's citizenship status and rights within the statehood posed by the formations of the United States and Canada. But the feminism of suffrage and the questions of equality and inclusion that it articulated were not an invited politic or organizing principle of Indigenous people. In particular, Indigenous women's dis-identifications with the feminism of suffrage, and thus of the state citizenship and electoral participation that it envisioned, contrasted their address to the specific struggles of their nations for sovereignty and self-determination, often co-produced by attention to their unique cultures.

In *Life among the Piutes* (1883), Sarah Winnemucca Hopkins (Northern Paiute) offered a personal account of Paiute history and culture as an impassioned plea for the U.S. government and its citizens to respect the humanity of Indigenous peoples and put an end to invasion and genocide.[46] In *Hawaii's Story by Hawaii's Queen* (1898), Liliuokalani (Kanaka Maoli) appealed to the moral principles of a Christian, democratic society to reconsider the justice of the annexation and respect the humanity of Hawaiians.[47] She asserted the immoral and illegal aspects of the actions of U.S. missionaries, in collusion with plantation owners and military officers, as an assault on true democracy and defended Hawaiian independence as a nation's right.[48] Zitkala-Ša (Yankton-Nakota Sioux) co-founded and worked with several Indigenous rights organizations, and wrote several articles and autobiographical accounts against allotment, boarding schools, and missionization as she recorded Lakota stories and songs.[49] E. Pauline Johnson (Six Nations Mohawk) was a performer and writer who published several poems and stories addressed to the lives of Indigenous people in tension with Canadian society.[50] In *Cogewea: The Half-Blood* (1927), Mourning Dove (Salish) told the story of a woman's difficult experiences living between Montana's white ranching community and the Salish and Kootenai tribes of the Flathead Indian Reservation.[51]

These writers and their contemporaries confronted the difficult place of feminism within modernist ideologies and discourses of social evolution and difference, as those ideologies and discourses were institutionalized not only within the academy and presses but in U.S. and Canadian federal, military, and economic policy. Laurajane Smith argues that modernist theories of Indigenous inferiority served to authorize the role and knowledge claims of empirical, evolutionary scientists in federal policy making to rationalize imperial-colonial objectives and even help direct programs.[52] Concurrently, imperial-colonial interests easily appropriated the allegedly empirical claims about Indigenous inferiority as a rationalization of genocide, dispossession, and forced assimilation efforts that served their capitalist ends.

Writing against these ideological and discursive workings, Indigenous writers narrated the relevance of their unique and related experiences as Indigenous peoples back onto their territories, their bodies, and with one another. As Mishuana Goeman (Tonawanda Seneca) argues, Indigenous writers "mediate and refute colonial organizing of land, bodies, and social and political landscapes."[53] Given the systemic sexual violence, criminal fraud, and forced removal that they confronted, the act of narration was a radical one, remapping Indigenous peoples back into their governance systems and territorial rights as culturally knowledgeable subjects refuting U.S. and Canadian narrations.

And yet, in complicated ways, they were acts often paired with an appeal to the liberal and evolutionary ideologies and discourses of modernity's civilization and Christianity.[54] As Mark Rifkin argues, the reinscription of the values of civilization and Christianity in Indigenous writings was often articulated through personal stories of romance, family loyalty, hard work, and social harmony.[55] These stories reinscribed white heteronormativity while remaining silent on Indigenous gender and sexual diversity. They were contrasted with stories of the rape, alcoholism, and fraud that characterized U.S. and Canadian relations with Indigenous peoples. In that contrast, Indigenous writers represented themselves and their communities as embodying and emulating the values of Civilization (humanism) and Christianity (morality) against the Savagery of U.S. and Canadian officials, military officers and troops, and local citizens. But by linking the righteousness of Indigenous sovereignty and self-determination to the measure of Indigenous Civilization and Christianity, do the writers legitimate the gendered, sexualized, and racialized normativities on which ideologies of Civilization and Christianity are based? Do they make Indigenous rights contingent on Indigenous societies' emulation of those ideological norms and social values that define an imperial-colonial, Civil-Christian society and advance racism, sexism, and homophobia?

Assuming that both Goeman and Rifkin are right, perhaps the questions are less about Indigenous writings being made to fit neatly together in some evolutionary metanarrative of oppositionality *or* assimilationism than they are about understanding the profound contestations and difficulties Indigenous peoples confront in having to constantly negotiate and contest the social terms and conditions of imperial and colonial imaginaries, policies, and actions. Since narrating Indigenous peoples back into their governance, territories, and cultures challenges the narrations and policies of U.S. and Canadian imperialism and colonialism, but claims to Civilization and Christianity potentially reaffirm imperial and colonial imaginaries and programs, the conflictedness within these significations indicates the (im)possibilities of effecting opposition, strategy, *or* conformity while honoring—as Simpson argues—the grievability of Indigenous lives and experiences.

By 1968–70, then, the issues confronting critical Indigenous gender, sexuality, and feminist studies were neither modest nor transparent. The diversity of gender and sexual identities had been addressed in the interim of suffrage and civil rights, especially by Indigenous scholars attempting to "correct" the gross ignorance and misrepresentation of empirical scholarship and its role in rationalizing imperial and colonial projects. For example, Beatrice Medicine (Standing Rock Lakota) and Ella Cara Deloria (Yankton Dakota) wrote extensively on Lakota women and paid attention, albeit sporadically, to non-heterosexual identities with a view to humanizing Indigenous people.[56] Similarly, Alfonso Ortiz (Tewa Pueblo) wrote to correct many of the errors within anthropological and historical writings about Pueblo culture and gender norms.[57] By 1968–70, critical Indigenous gender, sexuality, and feminist studies coalesced in curriculum and scholarship to affirm the polity of the Indigenous against U.S. and Canadian state formations configured through imperial and colonial practices of gendered-sexed based violence and discrimination.

In particular, *A Gathering of Spirit: Writing and Art by North American Indian Women*, edited by Beth Brant (Tyendinaga Mohawk); *Living the Spirit: A Gay American Indian Anthology*, edited by Will Roscoe; and *The Sacred Hoop: Recovering the Feminine in American Indian Traditions*, written by Paula Gunn Allen (Lebanese, Scottish, Laguna Pueblo), mark a foundational shift in the interdisciplinary circulation of Indigenous scholarship on the politics of gender, sexuality, and feminism.[58] Brant's *A Gathering of Spirit* was the first anthology of Indigenous women's writings and art.[59] It was published in 1983 as a special issue of *Sinister Wisdom*, a lesbian literary and art magazine. Reissued as an anthology by Firebrand Books in 1988 and by Women's Press in 1989, it included critical, creative, historical, and original writings, as well as art by women of many different gender and sexual identities from more than forty Indigenous nations in the United States and Canada.[60] It was offered as an affirmation of Indigenous cultural self-determination, as well as resistance against the misrepresentation and misappropriation of Indigenous genders and sexualities in the women's, LGBTQ, and feminist movements.

Roscoe, a gay rights activist and writer from San Francisco, offered *Living the Spirit* as the first collection addressed to sexual diversity and homophobia in Indigenous communities.[61] The book was organized mainly around the *berdache*, an anatomically male person who assumes the respected social status and responsibilities of a woman. The term and concept would be quickly problematized not only for its male-centric, pan-tribal generalizations but also for the way non-Indigenous gays romanticized its significance within their own movements for civil rights equality. But *Living the Spirit* did provide an important forum on the conflicted relationship between respect and prejudice in Indigenous LGBTQ people's historical experiences and lived realities.

The Sacred Hoop is often considered the first American Indian feminist study. In it, Allen analyzes Indigenous notions of gender and sexuality and the prominent role of women such as Spider Woman and Sky Woman in Indigenous peoples' creation stories. She situates this analysis within a critique of U.S. patriarchal colonialism's attempts to destroy Indigenous societies for being women-centered, "gynocratic" societies. These attempts, she argues, included genocide, land dispossession, and forced assimilation programs aimed at undermining women's roles and responsibilities within their nations and territories, as well as at eroding the cultural histories that figured those roles and responsibilities.

While Allen's "gynocratism" has been criticized for its "pan" generalizations of Indigenous cultures and identities, her work offers an important theoretical and methodological approach to Indigenous teachings that emphasizes historical, social, and cultural specificity. For instance, she maintains that when reading *Ceremony*, by Leslie Marmon Silko (Laguna Pueblo), one must have a solid understanding of Spider Woman teachings within Laguna Pueblo oral histories and social relations. Only then, she contends, can a reader appreciate Silko's work for its serious critique of U.S. imperialism and the long-term consequences of patriarchy, masculinity, and citizenship on Indigenous communities.

Further, *The Sacred Hoop* argues that there was a co-production of gender and sexuality in imperial and colonial projects. Allen maintains that imperialists tried to convert Indigenous peoples not only to their religious-capitalist worldviews but also to their sexist and homophobic ideologies and practices as a strategy of military conquest and capitalist expansion. She maintains that sustained sexual violence, particularly against Indigenous women, children, and non-heterosexually identified people, enabled colonial conquest and constituted the resulting state. In doing so, her work anticipates those focused on the legal and social articulations of violence against women, children, and LGBTQ people.[62]

But even as Brant's, Roscoe's, and Allen's books were issued, many Indigenous scholars (and) activists pushed back, particularly against the universalism and civil rights of feminist politics. For instance, Patricia Monture-Angus (Six Nations Mohawk) and Mary Ellen Turpel (Muskeg Lake Cree) rejected feminism's universalism of women's experiences and identities, as well as its generalizations of patriarchy as a social formation.[63] Similarly, M. A. Jaimes Guerrero, Theresa Halsey, Haunani-Kay Trask, and Laura Tohe (Diné) insisted that there is a fundamental divide between Indigenous sovereignty and self-determination and the mainstream women's or feminist movement's concerns for civil rights.[64] Giving primacy to the collective rights of Indigenous nations to sovereignty, they claim, negates the relevance of feminism, because feminism advances individualistic and civil rights principles. Therefore, feminism does not merely counter Indigenous women's concerns and is not only ignorant of Indigenous teachings about gender and sexuality, but it undermines Indigenous claims to the collective rights of their nations.

These arguments were linked in profound ways to Indigenous women's and LGBTQ efforts to redress sexism and homophobia within their communities and establish gender and sexual equality within federal and their own nations' laws. Many of these efforts strategically mobilized discourses of rights, equality, and feminism. In doing so, they experienced the retort of being *non-* or *anti-*Indigenous sovereignty within their communities. For instance, Indigenous women in Canada were criticized for inviting alliances with feminists to reverse the patrilineal provisions of an amendment to the Indian Act of 1876 for women who married non-band members and their children.[65] In the mid-1980s, several constituencies of Indigenous women and their allies—many of whom identified as Christian and feminist—secured constitutional and legislative amendments that partially reversed the 1876 criterion. But the amendments were not passed easily. Status Indian men dominated band governments and organizations and with their allies protested vehemently against the women and their efforts. They accused the women of being complicit with a long history of colonization and racism that imposed, often violently, non-Indian principles and institutions on Indigenous people. This history was represented for the men by the women's appeals to civil and human rights laws, and more particularly to feminism, to challenge the constitutionality and human rights compliance of the Indian Act, an act the men represented as providing the only real legal protection of Indigenous sovereignty in Canada. Demonized as the proponents of an ideology of rights based on selfish individualism, and damned for being "women's libbers" out to force Indigenous people into compliance with that ideology, the women and their concerns were dismissed as embodying all things not only *non*-Indian but *anti*-Indian. The women's agendas for legal reform were rejected as not only irrelevant but dangerous to Indigenous sovereignty. These dismissals perpetuated sexist ideologies and discriminatory and violent practices against women within their communities by normalizing men's discourses regarding the irrelevance of gender and the disenfranchisement of women in sovereignty struggles.[66]

The difficult place of gender, sexuality, and feminism within Indigenous claims to sovereignty and self-determination accentuates the historical and cultural contestations within Indigenous communities over issues of cultural tradition and authenticity. These contestations are entrenched within the ongoing work of modernism and liberalism at othering Indigenous difference to reason imperial and colonial designs, inclusions and exclusions, entitlements, and status and reputation. They are reflected in the continued efforts of Indigenous writers to re-narrate themselves and their communities back onto the land and into their bodies with one another in ways that respect their cultural teachings and challenge the violence and discrimination of racism, sexism, and homophobia within U.S. and Canadian state formations.

INTELLECTUAL ROUTES, CULTURAL FOUNDATIONS

The Lenape tell a story about how the Earth was created on the back of a turtle. An Old Man lived in a lodge in the middle of the people's village. He had a beautiful wife and daughter. For reasons no one quite understood, he became jealous and brooding. No one could cheer him up or figure out what was wrong, although everyone tried to talk him through it. One day, another man suggested that, perhaps, the Old Man wanted the rather large tree in front of his lodge pulled up and moved away. So the people, desperate to help, figured it was as good a reason as any and pulled up the tree. But in doing so, they created a large hole where the ground fell through.

The Old Man called his wife and daughter to come out of the lodge and look through the hole: "Come on, Old Woman, let's see what everybody is looking at!" He walked over to the hole with them and leaned far over to see inside. He stood by and exclaimed, "I have never seen anything like that!" He nudged his wife and daughter to look inside. "I am afraid," said the

Old Woman. He nudged her again and said, "You really must take a look. Don't be afraid. I am standing right here." So the Old Woman picked up her daughter and held her tight. She walked over to the hole and leaned far over to look through it. The Old Man grabbed at them and pushed them through the hole. The Old Woman grabbed at a nearby blanket and clump of huckleberries by the roots and soil as they fell through the hole and began to fly down through the clouds to the Earth below.

They were flying through the clouds when the Fire Serpent met up with them. "I am sorry that the Old Man tried to kill you. It is me that he is jealous of," the Fire Serpent said. He gave the Old Woman an ear of corn and a beaver. The other spirits watched and decided to hold council. "Who will look out for the Old Woman and her daughter?" they asked. After a long discussion, the good one—the Turtle—spoke up and said that she would do it. When the Old Woman and her daughter reached Earth, the Turtle raised her back so they would have a place to land.

Later, the Old Woman and her daughter wept as the Old Woman spread the dirt and berries around. The dirt kept getting bigger and bigger until the Earth was formed. Then the Old Woman planted the corn, and eventually the corn, trees, and grass grew tall. Then the Sun and the Moon and the Stars showed up to keep them company, and the Old Woman felt for the first time in a long time that she could stop weeping for herself and her daughter, for they were no longer alone.

I think of the current work within critical Indigenous, gender, sexuality, and feminist studies as our work together at re-creating the world we live in with our not-human relations and with the materials offered by the land and water. It is a world inhibited by jealousy, hate, competition, arrogance, and violence but it is also a world that can be remade. In the many kinds of labor that go into that remaking, we take responsibility for one another in humility, generosity, and love. Here, I will try to think through the work taking place at rebuilding (the resurgence) of the polity of the Indigenous and the work at rebuilding (the opposition) the structure and operation of U.S. and Canadian imperialism and colonialism.

By the 2000s, *settler colonialism* had become a core analytic within the studies on the structure and operations of state power. This is marked by the citational circulation of the work of Patrick Wolfe, particularly his *Settler Colonialism and the Transformation of Anthropology* (1999) and "Settler Colonialism and the Elimination of the Native" (2006).[67] Wolfe defines settler colonialism by his oft-cited differentiation between the structure and the event of invasion:

Positively, it erects a new colonial society on the expropriated land base—as I put it, settler colonizers come to stay: invasion is a structure not an event. In its positive aspect, elimination is an organizing principle of settler-colonial society rather than a one-off (and superseded) occurrence. The positive outcomes of the logic of elimination can include officially encouraged miscegenation, the breaking-down of native title into alienable individual freeholds, native citizenship, child abduction, religious conversion, resocialization in total institutions such as missions or boarding schools, and a whole range of cognate bicultural assimilations. All these strategies, including frontier homicide, are characteristic of settler colonialism.[68]

Recalling key arguments within critical race and feminist studies that understand racism and heterosexism as permanent features of state formation—such as Michael Omi and Howard Winant in *Racial Formation in the United States*, Cheryl I. Harris in "Whiteness as Property," and Aileen Moreton-Robinson in "Unmasking Whiteness"—Wolfe argues for the permanence of invasion as a racialized feature of the state formed after the empire's withdrawal.[69] He argues that settlers "[come] to stay," to build societies of their own on the lands of Indigenous peoples. Settlers are or provide their own labor and thus, unlike the empire's colony, do not perceive a need for the exploitation of Indigenous labor in the extractive accumulation of natural resources or agricultural use of lands. The "logic of elimination" as the "organizing principle" of the settler is about physical genocide, as well as how settler laws, policies, and practices are "inherently eliminatory" of Indigenous peoples and their cultures.[70] There is no postcolonial. The settler's permanence is in a constant state of the threat posed by the "counter-claim" of Indigenous territorial rights: the "native repressed continues to structure settler-colonial society."[71]

"Sexuality, Nationality, Indigeneity," Daniel Heath Justice (Cherokee Nation of Oklahoma), Bethany Schneider, and Mark Rifkin's special issue of GLQ; Scott Lauria Morgensen's *Spaces between Us*; and Rifkin's *When Did Indians Become Straight?* and *The Erotics of Sovereignty* mark one cluster of publications that pivot on settler colonialism as a modality of understanding the gendered and sexed politics of state formation, as well as the politics of white settlers' alliances with Indigenous peoples against settler colonialism.[72] Intending to further conversations between Indigenous and queer studies, they each provide critiques of the normative center of whiteness in queer studies that effaces the politics of "indigeneity and settlement," the normalization of heteropatriarchy within Indigenous studies concerning relationships between Indigenous nationhood and "settler governance," and the radical potential of Indigenous-queer alliances against the violently racialized sexisms and homophobias of settler politics and toward decolonization.[73]

An interrelated body of scholarship within the studies is paying attention to the conflicted work of racist ideologies of masculinity not only within the structure and operations of state power but also from the context of Indigenous social relations and cultural traditions. In *Native Men Remade*, Ty P. Kāwika Tengan (Kanaka Maoli) writes, "The formations of masculine and indigenous subjectivities as they develop within a historical context in which race, class, gender, and colonial domination—including global touristic commodification—have played major roles. As a consequence, many indigenous Hawaiian men feel themselves to be disconnected, disempowered, and sometimes emasculated."[74] To understand those experiences, Tengan focuses on how Hawaiian men have "remade" their identities through a personally ethnographic study of a group called the Hale Mua (Men's House). He examines their "transformations of self and society as they occur in practice through narrative and performative enactments."[75] He begins by examining the hyper-masculinist, patriotic nationalist discourse that pervades U.S. society and argues that these discourses reflect and inform the militarization and cultural exploitation of the Hawaiian Islands and people. Against these exploitations, Tengan argues that Hawaiian men and women reclaimed ceremonies in 1991 celebrating the legacy of King Kamehameha, who had united the islands in 1810. This reclamation inspired the formation of warrior societies charged with holding and transmitting ceremonial knowledge and practice. Out of this, the Hale Mua was formed. It consists mostly of middle-class men in military, business, and social-service jobs. Tengan analyzes how their efforts to confront their internalizations of racial and colonial violence and end cycles of abuse, incarceration, and community disintegration were articulated through Hawaiian traditions and practices.

Tengan's understanding of imperial-colonial formations as constituted by an emasculated Indigenous man, and the need for decolonization efforts to essentially remasculinize Indigenous men through available Indigenous traditions, inadvertently reifies heterosexist ideologies that serve conditions of imperial-colonial oppression. In doing so, Tengan's work represents the challenges confronting Indigenous men who rearticulate their cultures' teachings and practices as acts of decolonization to confront the social realities of heterosexism and homophobia. Getting at these difficulties and the potential for cultural reformation that they involve is Sam McKegney's edited volume *Masculindians*.[76] In interviews with several Indigenous scholars, artists, and activists (not necessarily mutually exclusive), the volume provides an important example of the struggles confronting Indigenous communities that need to (re)define Indigenous manhood and masculinity in a society predicated on the violent oppression and exploitation of Indigenous women and girls and the racially motivated dispossession and genocide of Indigenous peoples. Grounded by their respective polities, Indigenous interviewees discuss the need for better images of Indigenous men than those offered by the likes of Disney's Tonto (for instance), as well as the need to reclaim Indigenous teachings about the interdependence and power of men and women.

The calls to remember, empower, and rethink Indigenous gender and sexuality in the context of settler politics and masculinity resonate through the studies and their focus on cultural self-determination. For instance, in *Dancing on Our Turtle's Back*, Leanne Betasamosake Simpson (Michi Saagiig Nishnaabeg [Alderville First Nation]) emphasizes the need for Indigenous peoples to engage their unique cultural teachings in how they theorize and work against state oppression and for Indigenous empowerment: "[W]e need to engage in *Indigenous* processes, since according to our traditions, the processes of engagement highly influence the outcome of the engagement itself. We need to do this on our own terms, without the sanction, permission or engagement of the state, western theory or the opinions of Canadians. In essence, we need to not just figure out who we are, we need to re-establish the processes by which we live who we are within the current context we find ourselves."[77] Simpson argues that these traditions are not static, biblical dictates from the past, "rigidity and fundamentalism" understood to belong to colonial ways of thinking. Rather, they are living and lived and thus ever changing understandings of how to honor the unbroken importance of elders, languages, lands, and communities in Indigenous flourishment, transformation, and resurgence.[78] By engaging these teachings within processes of opposition to state oppression, Simpson maintains that ethical values of land-based relationships and responsibilities will ground practices of "self-actualization, the suspension of judgment, fluidity, emergence, careful deliberation and an embodied respect for diversity."[79]

Mindful of the state's claims to offering democratic inclusion through a liberal multiculturalism, and its commensurate call for resolution by inclusion and reconciliation, Simpson points to the relevance of Indigenous epistemologies and histories for reordering Indigenous governance, territories, and social relations.[80] This is interrelated with the dynamic work of scholars and activists such as Winona LaDuke (Anishinaabe [White Earth Reservation]) and Melissa K. Nelson (Anishinaabe [Turtle Mountain Chippewa]) on environmental justice.

In her foundational work in *All Our Relations*, LaDuke offers two central arguments.[81] One is that the biodiversity of the territories that constitute the United States and Canada and the cultural diversity of Indigenous peoples are inseparable. The other is that the U.S. and Canadian military and energy industries are deeply entrenched within Indigenous nations and lands—so much so, in fact, that it is impossible to extrapolate from them any meaningful understanding of the current contours of U.S., Canadian, or Indigenous politics.

These arguments are germane to understanding Indigenous decolonization projects in which Indigenous lands, ecosystems, and bodies are at stake, continually having to confront the consequences of the global military and energy industrial complexes through their cultural perspectives and practices. Those perspectives and practices, as Nelson argues in her introduction to *Original Instructions: Indigenous Teachings for a Sustainable Future*, have had to revitalize and reform in order "to thrive in this complex world during these intense times."[82] Recalling the work of Idle No More, Nelson's argument maintains that Indigenous peoples are survivors of a relentless and violent holocaust that continues today in the exploitation and destruction of their lands, resources, and bodies and that any viable strategy for decolonization must address the breadth of that oppression.

In these contexts, Indigenous peoples have taken on decolonization projects that include their minds and bodies in the remembrance and reform of their relations and responsibilities to the lands and ecosystems in which they live and to the other beings to whom they are related. This has included projects in the remembrance of their original teachings and personal accounts of their historical experiences and cultural values through multiple media of cultural production, including songs, dances, and artistry. For instance, *Without Reservation: Indigenous Erotica*, edited by Kateri Akiwenzie-Damm (Anishinaabe [Nawash First Nation]), and *Me Sexy: An Exploration of Native Sex and Sexuality*, edited by Drew Hayden Taylor (Ojibwa [Curve Lake First Nation]), represent an important eruption of writings about Indigenous sexuality, desire, and eroticism. Both disentangle issues of sex and sexuality from imperialism and colonialism by exploding the stereotypes of the sexualized Indian princess and the stoic or violent Indian warrior. They do so by offering empowered and nuanced stories of Indigenous gender, sex, and sexuality that are at once historical, cultural, land-based, humorous, erotic, and passionate.[83] They provide a rich array of personal stories and analyses addressed to histories of sexual violence against Indigenous peoples, the internalized violence within Indigenous families and sexed practices, and eroticism. They do so with an explicit aim to contribute to decolonization practices.

For instance, in Taylor's *Me Sexy*, Akiwenzie-Damm begins her essay, "Red Hot to the Touch," by addressing the absence of erotica by Indigenous writers. She attributes this to histories of sexual violence within residential schools and the "intergenerational trauma" it has caused. "I grieved about the violence and pain and lovelessness that had been forced onto our communities," she says, "but I also knew that we were so much more, that despite being victimized, we were not victims, that someone else's violence and hatred could never fully define us."[84] Juxtaposing an erotic story with her personal reflections on the importance of erotica for achieving "wholeness and joy," Akiwenzie-Damm describes how erotica provides a storied means to decolonization:

> I wanted to liberate myself. To decolonize myself. Not a victim, not a "survivor," not reactive, not forced into someone else's contorted image of who I was supposed to be, not confined, not colonized. Free. . . . What drove me to continue on this quest to bring the erotic back into Indigenous arts? Largely it was that I instinctively knew that the erotic is essential to us as human beings and that it had to take its rightful place in our lives and cultures before we could truly decolonize our hearts and minds.[85]

The importance of erotica in decolonization is evident not only in Akiwenzie-Damm's essay but throughout Taylor's *Me Sexy* and her edited volume *Without Reservation*. The collections record sexually rich stories of desire and passion. They address not only difficult histories of sexual violence but also the agency of sexual exploration and fun, emphasizing the multiple gendered-sexualized identities within Indigenous ways of knowing and being in the world grounded in Indigenous epistemologies. As the reproductive health rights activist Jessica Yee Danforth (Mohawk and Chinese), founder and executive director of the Native Youth Sexual Health Network, has said:

Sexuality is not just having sex. It's people's identities. It's their bodies. It's so many things. A lot of elders that I work with say that you can actually tell how colonized we are as a people by the knowledge about our bodies that we've lost. The fact that we need systems and institutions and books to tell us things about our own bodies is a real problem. If we don't have control over our bodies, then what do we have? If something like body knowledge no longer belongs to community and is institutionalized, then what does that really mean? . . . To place sexual health over here and land rights over there is a very colonial, imperial way of thinking. Environmental justice is over here, reproductive justice is over there. . . . What better way to colonize a people than to make them ashamed of their bodies?[86]

Current Indigenous movements such as those of Indigenous youth for reproductive rights, sexual and environmental justice, along with Idle No More, call for us to return to our polities—back onto our lands, into our bodies, in relationality and responsibility for one another. As Sarah Hunt (Kwagiulth [Kwakwaka'wakw Nation]) writes about Idle No More, "It is only through building stronger relationships with one another, across the generations and across differences in education, ability, sexuality, and other social locations," that we can rebuild Indigenous governments, territories, and relationships on a sovereignty and self-determination that will matter to the health and well-being of future generations.[87]

Indigenous Futurities: A Conclusion and Eight Essays

In *Live Long and Prosper (Spock Was a Half-Breed)*, Debra Yepa-Pappan (Jemez Pueblo and Korean) portrays an Indigenous woman in a jingle dress holding up her hand in what we know from the long-running *Star Trek* television and film series as the Vulcan sign for saying farewell: "Live Long and Prosper" (figure I.1).[88] Behind her are two tipis set on a lush green planet. On the tipis are *Star Trek* logos, suggesting either that the woman's people hold membership in the Federation or were recently visited by representatives of the Federation who gave her or them the emblems. (Tipi art can represent family lineage or historical events.) Flying back over the planet is the *Starship Enterprise*, past a bright star and its rings, out toward the edge of the system marked at the picture's top by the image of half a star. In an interview, Yepa-Pappan explained:

FIGURE I.1. Debra Yepa-Pappan, *Live Long and Prosper (Spock Was a Half-Breed)*, courtesy of the artist.

That's a digital image, so it's all digitally manipulated. That grew out of the stereotype series. "Indians live in tipis," it's my face placed on an Edward S. Curtis photograph of a Plains Indian woman with tee pees—a setting of tee pees behind her. I was invited to do a piece for a sci-fi western show with contemporary Native artists. So, I was thinking along the lines of stereotypes, I have another piece called "Indians say how," where I have my father putting his hand up in the stereotypical "how" pose. And I took that a step further and did the Vulcan salute. So it just grew from that, I took that piece and turned it into "Spock was a half breed." It was perfect because "Spock" is a half breed and I am a half breed. It bridges that gap because when people think about Indians they always put us in the past and in history. Here's this image that's very futuristic and there's the *Starship Enterprise* in the back, and its [*sic*] very contemporary. It brings that back that we are a part of today's society, that we do enjoy a series like *Star Trek* and science fiction. And we are not just a part of this historical, romantic past.[89]

Because of the vast systems and dimensions visited by the *Starship Enterprise*, the green grass does not necessarily signify Earth, although the Indigenous woman and tipis might. Was she visiting another planet? Were the Vulcans visiting her? Is she a Vulcan Indian? The mash-up of familiar images defamiliarizes their signification. Generatively, the picture's parenthetical "Spock Was a Half-Breed" suggests a link or similarity between Spock's Vulcan and human lineage and the woman's lineage. Both are mixed, maybe with each other. The parenthetical also recalls Spock's struggles in negotiating his Vulcan and human selves and the conflicted cultural expectations they signify. We are not sure what the woman's mix is, only that she is mixed. We can also be sure that Spock's "half-breed" identity does not bar him from having a future, so neither does the woman's. Indeed, Yepa-Pappan's work resituates Indigenous women and their communities in multiple possibilities of the past, present, and future in ways that refuse their foreclosure as historical relics or irrelevant costumes in the service of imperial formations and colonized identities.

Yepa-Pappan's provocations remind me of the work of Elle-Máijá Tailfeathers, who is Blackfoot from the Kainai First Nation (Blood Indian Reserve in Alberta) and Sámi from Norway. In her first short film, *Bloodland* (2011), Tailfeathers provides a graphic of an Indigenous woman dancing on the land who is captured by two male oil workers and taken to a cabin. She is tied down to a table, and the men torture her by drilling into her abdomen. She writhes in pain and screams as the blood oozes from her body. The images of her blood are juxtaposed with images of oil oozing from the land. As the credits roll at the end, the tribal chief and council and oil companies are acknowledged and thanked. At the symposium "Frack Off: Indigenous Women Lead Effort against Fracking" at the New School in New York on September 20, 2014, Tailfeathers explained the credits as owing to her forced revenue share in the decision by the Blood Reserve's chief and council to lease the band's lands for oil extraction. The decision was made without any consultation with the band's membership and included huge signing bonuses for the leaders.[90]

In a mixed style of film noir and graphic novel, Tailfeathers's second short, *A Red Girl's Reasoning* (2012), tells the story of Delia. The film opens by following a motorcyclist who is chasing a man running down an alley. Having cornered the man at a dead end, the rider stops and jumps off the motorcycle and removes the helmet to reveal an Indigenous woman (Delia). She beats up the man and afterward lights a cigarette. Her voiceover narration says, "I've been on this warpath for six long, lonely years. White boys have been having their way with Indian girls since contact. Forget what Disney tells you: Pocahontas was twelve when she met John Smith. It's pretty little lies like this that hide the ugly truth." The scene cuts to a bar where we learn that Delia has accepted another job to avenge another survivor. She allows a man to buy her a drink; he passes out and comes to in an abandoned warehouse, where Delia has tied him up and interrogates him. Finally, the man confesses to the rape and proceeds to make vulgar remarks about Indigenous women. Delia responds by pouring gasoline over his body and lighting a cigarette. We do not see the man set on fire, but we can imagine his fate.

The futures and otherworlds of Yepa-Pappan's and Tailfeathers's imaginations are ones in which Indigenous women defy the stereotypes and brutality of sexism and racism, resetting the proverbial stage of Indigenous (women's) self-determination. Situated within the intellectual genealogies partially mapped out here, they teach us to reimagine and reassert, refuse and wonder ourselves into better worlds than the ones made for us to live in by U.S. and Canadian imperialism and colonialism.

Perhaps most immediately, this volume is in conversation with "Native Feminisms: Legacies, Interventions, and Indigenous Sovereignties," the special issue of *Wicazō Ša Review* edited by Mishuana R. Goeman and Jennifer Nez Denetdale (Diné) published in Fall 2009, which includes articles by Lisa Kahaleole Hall (Kanaka Maoli), Luana Ross (Confederated Salish and Kootenai Tribes), Dian Million (Tanana Athabascan), Rayna K. Ramirez (Winnebago Tribe of Nebraska), Audra Simpson, and Sarah Deer (Muscogee [Creek Nation of Oklahoma]).[91] In their introduction, Goeman and Denetdale position the issue as a "study of Native women's lives and historical experiences" from the perspectives of "Native feminists . . . illuminating the workings of colonialism within our respective Native nations and communities and . . . reclaiming traditional values as the foundation for our lives and communities."[92]

While indebted to the issue's contribution, as noted at the beginning of this introduction, this volume is concerned with (1) the terms and debates that constitute critical Indigenous gender, sexuality, and feminist studies; (2) the nation-based and often territorially specific centrality of Indigenous sovereignty and self-determination; and (3), the structure and operation of U.S. and Canadian imperialism and colonialism as related but unique state formations. On the whole, the essays show how the politics of gender and sexuality are central to sorting out, from the context of Indigenous epistemologies, the challenges to Indigeneity and Indigenous rights posed within an imperial and colonial social formation. Individually, they offer unique emphases through many different narrative voices and styles. In doing so, they make a diverse set of critical and creative demands of readers within and outside of CIS and gender, sexuality, and feminist studies. The essays have been arranged in a sequence that, I hope, will best guide the reader through this diversity and set of demands.

The first two essays in the volume address all three concerns outlined earlier. In "Indigenous Hawaiian Sexuality and the Politics of Nationalist Decolonization," J. Kēhaulani Kauanui (Kanaka Maoli) examines the Hawaiian sovereignty movement in the early to mid-1990s to document practices of gender-based and sexuality-based exclusion, mis-recognition, and misrepresentation in order to provide context for reading the contemporary gestures of True Aloha, an indigenous social media group on Facebook that emerged in Fall 2013 to support the Hawaii Marriage Equality Act passed by the Hawai'i State Legislature in November 2013.[93] Kauanui argues that while there is indigenous cultural revitalization of Hawaiian concepts that may be considered part of broader cultural decolonization, the legislature's passage of the same-sex marriage bill is a form of settler-colonial continuity. Kauanui thereby engages all three of the volume's central issues to show how a critical gendered and sexed critique of the state's marriage laws undermine Hawaiian cultural self-determination and decolonization.

In "Return to 'The Uprising at Beautiful Mountain in 1913': Marriage and Sexuality in the Making of the Modern Navajo Nation," Jennifer Nez Denetdale examines an incident of Diné resistance to U.S. federal agents' attempts to criminalize and punish traditional forms of marriage and sexuality, including polygamy and non-heterosexuality. Denetdale shows how, over time, the Diné have come to conflate nation(hood) with family, marriage, and sexuality in ways that normalize the heteropatriarchy they once resisted.[94] As Kauanui, Denetdale engages all three of the volume's central issues to show how a critical gender- and sex-based critique of federal efforts to criminalize Diné marriage and sexuality provides a way to understand U.S. colonialism as a social formation and what its consequences have been for Diné resistance.

The next two essays in the volume are concerned primarily with providing a critical Indigenous feminist analysis of nation-based and territorially specific assertions of Indigenous sovereignty, considering how those assertions are undermined within U.S. and Canadian colonial state formations. To provide this analysis, the chapters' authors use specific texts in which to locate their broader analyses. In "Ongoing Storms and Struggles: Gendered Violence and Resource Exploitation," Goeman unpacks Linda Hogan's novel *Solar Storms* to understand the corporate production of the colonial spaces in which Indigenous peoples live and against which they tell their stories.[95] Goeman considers feminist theories of embodied trauma to argue that a mutually constitutive violence is committed against Indigenous lands, bodies, and memory by corporate-government polities to understand the role of that violence in reproducing colonialism. In "Audiovisualizing Iñupiaq Men and Masculinities *On the Ice*," Jessica Bissett Perea (Dena'ina [Athabascan]) provides a critical read of the gendered musical performances in the Iñupiaq filmmaker Andrew Okpeaha MacLean's *Sikumi* (2008) and *On the Ice* (2011) to understand the problematics inherent in how Iñupiat people have embraced processes of globalization, cosmopolitics, and musical modernities and how Inuit men and masculinities are (mis)recognized within those processes.[96] Both Goeman and Bissett Perea provide critiques of the structural, gendered violence of Indigenous women's and men's bodies that aim at thinking through decolonization as an oppositional refusal of colonial and colonized gendered identities that demands and anticipates territorial repatriation.

The next two essays of the volume engage critical Indigenous gender, sexuality, and feminist analyses in very different modalities to interrogate U.S. and Canadian law as a gendered and sexed apparatus of imperial-colonial formations, imaginaries, and desires. In "Around 1978: Family, Culture, and Race in the Federal Production of Indianness," Mark Rifkin argues that the apparent deviance of the U.S. Supreme Court decision in *Oliphant v. Suquamish* from a wave of federal affirmations of tribal self-determination in 1978 can be explained through the politics of Indianness.[97] He maintains that available ways to represent Indigenous peoples within federal law and policy are routed through the notion of "Indianness," understanding Indians less as fully autonomous polities than as a special kind of racially defined population. While not apparently about race, "family" and "culture" as employed within federal discourses depend on notions of reproductive transmission so that "Indian" appears to have non-racial content while the concept relies for its coherence on long-standing logics of racial genealogy. The apparent recognition of tribal difference on the basis of a shared, trans-tribal Indianness ultimately positions Native peoples as not quite political in ways that facilitate the ongoing assertion of plenary power over Native peoples and of the coherence and legitimacy of U.S. national space.

In "Loving Unbecoming: The Queer Politics of the Transitive Native," Jodi A. Byrd (Chickasaw) offers provisional thoughts on the collisions and collusions of queer theory and colonialism within critical Indigenous studies. She does so through a close reading of queer theory's *subjectlessness*, Samuel R. Delaney's short story "Aye, and Gomorrah," and the landmark U.S. Supreme Court ruling in *Loving v. Virginia* on antimiscegenation law.[98] She argues that Indigenous critiques of colonialism challenge social normativities in ways that are deeply misunderstood—or dismissed—by queer anti-normativity efforts. This misunderstanding inadvertently refutes an Indigenous analytics that insists on locating Indigenous bodies and desires in the contexts of Indigenous nations and territories, refiguring Indigenous analytics as merely advancing colonialism and its normativities. Examining how Indigenous analytics reject colonial formations and their ideological architects, Byrd unpacks the *Loving* decision to show how it reserves an Indigeneity that disavows Black-Indigenous lineage in favor of a liberal tale of whiteness—and queerness in subjectlessness—to protect the normativities of same-sex marriage that undergird a liberal colonial state.

The final essay of the volume is a provocation of Indigenous eroticism. Grounded in nation-based and territorially specific attention to Indigenous oral histories and literature (no pun intended), "Getting Dirty: The Eco-Eroticism of Women in Indigenous Oral Literatures," by Melissa K. Nelson, provides an account of the numerous stories of Indigenous women falling in love with nonhuman beings.[99] These "other-than-human" beings include animals, plants, stars, and even sticks and rocks from a diversity of gendered identities. Nelson explores what these stories reveal about women's desires and how these desires have been marginalized and subsumed under colonial social forces and Christian ideologies. Using a mixture of writing styles that include analytic essay, creative nonfiction, and personal narrative, Nelson examines the meaning of pansexual relations and how these stories are used by Indigenous women as inspiration for various activist movements, including movements for environmental justice, women's health and healing, and food sovereignty.

In their unique perspectives and approaches, the authors in this volume demonstrate the concerns within critical Indigenous gender, sexuality, and feminist studies over how critical sovereignty and self-determination are to Indigenous peoples. At the same time, they represent the importance within the studies of a *critical* address to the politics of gender, sexuality, and feminism within how that sovereignty and self-determination is imagined, represented, and exercised. It is not enough to claim you are sovereign as Indigenous, you must be accountable to the kinds of Indigeneity the sovereignty you claim asserts.

NOTES

1. John Bierhorts, *The White Deer and Other Stories Told by the Lenape* (New York: William Morrow, 1995), 17–18.

2. On Styles, see "Harry Styles Sparks 'Racism' Row after Posing in Native American Headdress," *Mirror*, March 14, 2014, http://www.mirror.co.uk/3am/celebrity-news /harry-styles-racism-row-after-3240238.

3. For fuller discussions of these and other examples, see the blog Native Appropriations: Examining Representations of Indigenous People, http://nativeappropriations.com.

4. Kristi Eaton, "Christina Fallin, Daughter of Oklahoma Governor Mary Fallin, Defends Headdress Photo," *Huffington Post*, March 7, 2014, http://www.huffingtonpost .com/2014/03/07/christina-fallin-headdress-photo_n_4921539.html.

5. Kino-nda-niimi Collective, ed., *The Winter We Danced: Voices from the Past, the Future, and the Idle No More Movement* (Winnipeg, MB: ARP Books, 2014).

6. Nina Wilson, Sylvia McAdam, Jessica Gordon, and Sheelah McLean, "Idle No More: Indigenous Brothers and Sisters Taking the Initiative for a Better Tomorrow," *Indian Country Today*, December 17, 2012, http://indiancountrytodaymedianetwork .com/article/idle-no-more-Indigenous-brothers-and-sisters-taking-initiative-better -tomorrow-146378.

7. Wilson et al., "Idle No More."

8. Canada is estimated to contain nearly 32,000 lakes and 2.25 million rivers; the bill lifted federal regulation over all but ninety-seven lakes and portions of sixty-two rivers.

9. CBC News, "Pam Palmater on Idle No More," CBC News, January 5, 2013, http:// www.cbc.ca/player/News/Canada/Audio/ID/2323100457.

10. Others include (1) the Family Homes of Reserve Matrimonial Interests of Rights Act (Bill S-2), which does not recognize First Nation bylaws that define matrimonial property law and allows for the indefinite transference of matrimonial property to non-members; (2) the First Nation Education Act, which would vacate federal funding for First Nation education, including funding provided by treaty, and incorporate provincial education laws into First Nation operations of reserve schools; (3) the First Nations Self-Government Recognition Bill (Bill S-212), which provides for the privatization of reserve lands by allotment. Lands will be divided into individual parcels and issued to status members, providing for the sale of unassigned lands to non–First Nation people and corporations; (4) the Safe Drinking Water for First Nations Act (Bill S-8), which overrides First Nation bylaws that protect safe drinking water and oversight of waste-water on reserve lands; (5) (Bill S-207), which will annul or destroy many First Nation treaty provisions. The Indian Act Amendment and Replacement Act (Bill C-428) repeals much of the Indian Act, including the rights of First Nations to pass bylaws; and (6) the First Nations Financial Transparency Act (Bill C-27), which forces First Nation governments to open up all of their business revenue records to be used in determining

federal funding of treaty and constitutional rights. It also provides that First Nation governments that do not make their business information public can lose federal funding.

11. "Oil Sands: A Complete Guide to All Projects Proposed, under Construction or up for Review," *Financial Post*, December 21, 2011, http://business.financialpost.com /2012/12/21/oil-sands-a-complete-guide-to-all-projects-proposed-under-construction -or-up-for-review/?__lsa=3596–4605>.

12. The Attawapiskat Nation has seen the exponential destruction of its lands and waterways by De Beers, the largest mining company in the world, whose local activities diverted public funds for transportation and housing and overwhelmed sewage systems. The Attawapiskats' modest sum of federal funding and mining shares have not translated into a significant improvement in their social infrastructure or overall quality of life on the reserve. Many live in tents without electricity or running water: see Winona LaDuke, "Why Idle No More Matters," *Honor the Earth*, http://www.honorearth .org/news/why-idle-no-more-matters; Chelsea Vowel, "Attawapiskat: You Want to Be Shown the Money? Here It Is." *Huffington Post*, December 6, 2012, http://www .huffingtonpost.ca/chelsea-vowel/attawapiskat-emergency_b_1127066.html. See also Alanis Obomsawin, director, *People of the Kattawapiskak River*, documentary, National Film Board of Canada, 2012.

13. Statement of Chief Theresa Spence, December 11, 2012, posted at http://www .attawapiskat.org. Several other Indigenous leaders—including Raymond Robinson (Pimicikamak Cree) of Manitoba—joined Spence on the fast in solidarity. See Audra Simpson, "Multicultural Settler Sovereignty," paper presented at the Native American and Indigenous Studies Annual Meeting, University of Saskatchewan, June 15–17, 2013; Audra Simpson, "The Chief's Two Bodies: Theresa Spence and the Gender of Settler Sovereignty," presentation, University of Winnipeg, March 14, 2014; Shiri Pasternak, "Blockade: Insurgency as Legal-Spatial Encounter," paper presented at the Native American and Indigenous Studies Annual Meeting, University of Texas, Austin, May 29–31, 2014.

14. See Idle No More's official webpage, at www.idlenomore.ca; Devon G. Peña, "Idle No More and Environmental Justice: Indigenous Women and Environmental Violence," *Environmental and Food Justice*, January 27, 2013, http://ejfood.blogspot .com; Sisters in Spirit Campaign website, http://www.sistersinspirit.ca/campaign.htm; Amnesty International, "Stolen Sisters: A Human Rights Response to Discrimination and Violence against Indigenous Women in Canada," October 4, 2004, http://www .amnesty.org/en/library/info/AMR20/003/2004; Amnesty International, "Maze of Injustice: The Failure to Protect American Indian Women from Violence in the USA," April 27, 2007, http://www.amnestyusa.org/our-work/issues/women-s-rights /violence-against-women/maze-of-injustice; United Nations Permanent Forum on Indigenous Issues Expert Group, "Combating Sexual Violence against Indigenous Women and Girls," United Nations Department of Economic and Social Affairs, January 20, 2012, http://www.un.org/en/development/desa/news/social/combating -violence-against-Indigenous-women-and-girls.html; Winona LaDuke, "Why the Violence against Women Act Is Crucial for Native American Women," *TruthOut* (for AlterNet), February 16, 2013, http://www.truth-out.org/news/item/14601-why-the -violence-against-women-act-is-crucial-for-native-american-women.

15. Joanne Barker, "Indigenous Feminisms," in *Handbook on Indigenous People's Politics*, eds. José Antonio Lucero, Dale Turner, and Donna Lee VanCott (New York: Oxford University Press), forthcoming; chapter available on-line at http://www .oxfordhandbooks.com/view/10.1093/oxfordhb/9780195386653.001.0001/oxfordhb -9780195386653-e-007. See also Joanne Barker, "Gender," in *The Indigenous World of North America*, ed. Robert Warrior (New York: Routledge Press, 2014).

16. Linda Tuhiwai Smith, *Decolonizing Methodologies: Research and Indigenous Peoples* (Chicago: Zed, 1999); Matthew Wildcat, Mandee McDonald, Stephanie Irlbacher-Fox, and Glen Coulthard, eds., "Learning from the Land: Indigenous Land-Based Pedagogy and Decolonization," *Decolonization* 3, no. 3 (2014): i–xv.

17. Eve Tuck and K. Wayne Yang, "Decolonization Is Not a Metaphor," *Decolonization* 1, no. 1 (2012): 1–40.

18. Barker, "Indigenous Feminisms."

19. David E. Wilkins and Heidi Kiiwetinepinesiik Stark, "Indigenous Peoples Are Nations, Not Minorities," in *American Indian Politics and the American Political System*, eds. David E. Wilkins and Heidi Kiiwetinepinesiik Stark (Lanham, MD: Rowman and Littlefield, 2010), 33–50. See also Vine Deloria Jr. and Clifford M. Lytle, *The Nations Within: The Past and Future of American Indian Sovereignty* (Austin: University of Texas Press, 1984).

20. See Vine Deloria Jr., *Behind the Trail of Broken Treaties: An Indian Declaration of Independence* (Austin: University of Texas Press, 1974).

21. Jack D. Forbes, "Black Pioneers: The Spanish-Speaking Afroamericans of the Southwest," *Phylon* 27, no. 3 (1966): 233–46; Jack D. Forbes, "Research Note: Hispano-Mexican Pioneers of the San Francisco Bay Region: An Analysis of Racial Origins," *Aztlán* 14, no. 1 (1983): 175–89; Jack D. Forbes, *Africans and Native Americans: The Language of Race and the Evolution of Red-Black Peoples* (Chicago: University of Illinois Press, 1993).

22. Chris Anderson, "Critical Indigenous Studies: From Difference to Density," *Cultural Studies Review* 15, no. 2 (2009): 80–100. See Winona Wheeler, "Thoughts on the Responsibilities for Indigenous/Native Studies," *Canadian Journal of Native Studies* 21 (2001): 97–104.

23. Kathryn Shanley, "Thoughts on Indian Feminism," in *A Gathering of Spirit: A Collection by North American Indian Women*, ed. Beth Brant (Ithaca, NY: Firebrand, 1984), 213–15.

24. M. A. Jaimes and Theresa Halsey, "American Indian Women: At the Center of Indigenous Resistance in North America," in *The State of Native America: Genocide, Colonization, and Resistance*, ed. M. A. Jaimes (Boston: South End, 1992), 311–44; Hauanui-Kay Trask, *From a Native Daughter: Colonialism and Sovereignty in Hawai'i* (Monroe, Maine: Common Courage, 1993).

25. For a few brief stories about Indigenous women's opposition to the Indian Reorganization Act of 1934, see Deloria and Lytle, *The Nations Within*. See also Vine Deloria Jr., "Identity and Culture," *Daedalus* 110, no. 2 (1981): 13–27.

26. See Jennifer Nez Denetdale, "'Planting Seeds of Ideas and Raising Doubts about What We Believe': An Interview with Vine Deloria Jr.," *Journal of Social Archaeology* 4, no. 2 (2004): 131–46. Denetdale attempted to solicit Deloria's remarks on the relationship between tribal nationalism and gender but was unable. His final editing of the text suppressed the record of that exchange. At the same time, it is important to acknowledge

that Deloria was supportive of women's issues, as shown in his refusal in May 2004 of an honorary doctor of humane letters degree from the University of Colorado, Boulder, because of how the university had handled sexual assault charges against its football players: James May, "An Interview with Vine Deloria Jr.," *Indian Country Today*, June 9, 2004, http://indiancountrytodaymedianetwork.com/ictarchives/2004/06/09/an-interview-with-vine-deloria-jr-93630.

27. For an address to the various confluences of homophobia and anti-feminisms, see Brian Joseph Gilley, *Becoming Two-Spirit: Gay Identity and Social Acceptance in Indian Country* (Lincoln: University of Nebraska Press, 2006); Jennifer Denetdale, "Securing Navajo National Boundaries: War, Patriotism, Tradition, and the Diné Marriage Act of 2005," *Wicazō Śa Review* 24, no. 2 (Fall 2009): 131–48.

28. Russell Means, "Comments on Patriarchy vis-à-vis Matriarchy," blog post, http://russellmeans.blogspot.com/2006/11/comments-on-patriarchy-vis-vis.html.

29. Angela Y. Davis, *Women, Race, and Class* (New York: Random House, 1981); Adrienne Rich, "Compulsory Heterosexuality and Lesbian Existence," *Signs* 5, no. 4 (1980): 631–60.

30. On "strategic essentialism," see Elaine Showalter's interview with Gayatri Spivak, "Women's Time, Women's Space: Writing the History of Feminist Criticism," *Tulsa Studies Women's Literature* 3, nos. 1–2 (1984): 29–43. On gender and feminism as categories of analysis, see Henry Abelove, Michèle Aina Barale, and David M. Halperin, eds., *The Lesbian and Gay Studies Reader* (New York: Routledge, 1993), xv: The quotes are from Judith Butler, "Against Proper Objects: Introduction," *Differences* 6 (1994): 1.

31. Joan Wallach Scott, "Feminism's History," *Journal of Women's History* 16, no. 2 (2004): 10–29; Joan Wallach Scott, "Deconstructing Equality-versus-Difference: Or, the Uses of Poststructuralist Theory for Feminism," in *The Postmodern Turn: New Perspectives on Social Theory*, ed. Steven Seidman (New York: Cambridge University Press, 1994), 282–98; Judith Butler and Elizabeth Weed, "Introduction," in *The Question of Gender: John W. Scott's Critical Feminism*, ed. Judith Butler and Elizabeth Weed (Bloomington: University of Indiana Press, 2013), 1–10.

32. See Kimberlé Crenshaw, "Mapping the Margins: Intersectionality, Identity Politics, and Violence against Women of Color," *Stanford Law Review* 43, no. 6 (July 1991): 1241–99.

33. Butler, "Against Proper Objects"; Davis, *Women, Race, and Class*.

34. Biddy Martin, "Sexualities without Genders and Other Queer Utopias," *Diacritics* 24, nos. 2–3 (1994): 104–21.

35. Judith Butler, *Bodies That Matter: On the Discursive Limits of Sex* (New York: Routledge, 1993), 37.

36. Joan Wallach Scott, "Gender as a Useful Category of Analysis," in *Gender and the Politics of History*, ed. Joan Wallach Scott (New York: Columbia University Press, 1988), 28–52; Joan Wallach Scott, "Gender: Still a Useful Category of Analysis?" *Diogenes* 57, no. 1 (2010): 7–14; Avtar Brah, *Cartographies of Diaspora: Contesting Identities* (New York: Routledge, 1996); Avtar Brah and Ann Phoenix, "Ain't I a Woman? Revisiting Intersectionality," *Journal of International Women's Studies* 5, no. 3 (2013): 75–86.

37. Martin, "Sexualities without Genders and Other Queer Utopias," 104.

38. Martin, "Sexualities without Genders and Other Queer Utopias."

39. Martin, "Sexualities without Genders and Other Queer Utopias," 104–5.

40. Such as the work of Eleanor Leacock, who wrote extensively within Marxist anthropology on the impact of capitalism on Indigenous communities in Canada: see Eleanor Leacock, *Marxism and Anthropology* (Montreal: McGraw-Hill, 1982).

41. The recently anthologized eighteenth-century writers Samson Occom (Mohegan), a Presbyterian clergyman, and William Apess (Pequot), a Methodist minister and politician, were sharply critical of the criminal fraud and religious hypocrisy that characterized U.S. and Canadian relations with Indigenous peoples over such issues as treaty rights, deforestation, the use of alcohol as currency, and violence against women: Joanna Brooks ed., *The Collected Writings of Samson Occom, Mohegan: Literature and Leadership in Eighteenth-Century Native America* (New York: Oxford University Press, 2006); Barry O'Connell, ed., *On Our Own Ground: The Complete Writings of William Apess, A Pequot* (Boston: University of Massachusetts Press, 1992).

42. Audra Simpson, "Captivating Eunice: Membership, Colonialism, and Gendered Citizenships of Grief," *Wicazō Ša Review* 24, no. 2 (2009): 106. See Leslie C. Green and Olive P. Dickason, *Law of Nations and the New World* (Lincoln: University of Nebraska Press, 1989): 141–241.

43. Simpson, "Captivating Eunice," 106.

44. Simpson, "Captivating Eunice," 124.

45. Simpson, "Captivating Eunice," 124.

46. Sarah Winnemucca Hopkins, *Life among the Piutes: Their Wrongs and Claims* (Reno: University of Nevada Press, [1883] 1994).

47. Liliuokalani, *Hawaii's Story by Hawaii's Queen* (Rockville, MD: Wildside, 2009).

48. Noenoe K. Silva, *Aloha Betrayed: Native Hawaiian Resistance to American Colonialism* (Durham, NC: Duke University Press, 2004).

49. Zitkala-Ša, *American Indian Stories* (New York: Dover, 2009).

50. E. Pauline Johnson, *Legends of Vancouver* (Vancouver: privately printed, 1911); E. Pauline Johnson, *The Moccasin Maker* (Toronto: William Briggs, 1913); E. Pauline Johnson, *Flint and Feather: The Complete Poems of E. Pauline Johnson* (Toronto: Musson, 1917).

51. Mourning Dove, *Cogewea, the Half-Blood: A Depiction of the Great Montana Cattle Range* (Lincoln: University of Nebraska Press, 1927).

52. Laurajane Smith, *Archaeological Theory and the Politics of Cultural Heritage* (New York: Routledge, 2004).

53. Mishuana R. Goeman, *Mark My Words: Native Women Mapping Our Nations* (Minneapolis: University of Minnesota Press, 2013), 3.

54. To understand how Civilization (science) and Christianity (religion) operate as linked discourses, see Clayton W. Dumont, *The Promise of Poststructuralist Sociology: Marginalized Peoples and the Problem of Knowledge* (Albany: State University of New York Press, 2008).

55. Mark Rifkin, *When Did Indians Become Straight? Kinship, the History of Sexuality, and Native Sovereignty* (New York: Oxford University Press, 2011), 6.

56. Beatrice Medicine and Patricia Albers, ed., *The Hidden Half: Studies of Plains Indian Women* (Lanham, MD: University Press of America, 1983); Beatrice Medicine, *Learning to Be an Anthropologist and Remaining "Native"* (Chicago: University of Illinois Press, 2001); Ella Cara Deloria, *Waterlily* (Lincoln: University of Nebraska Press, 2009).

57. Alfonso Ortiz, *The Tewa World: Space, Time, Being, and Becoming in a Pueblo Society* (Chicago: University of Chicago Press, 1972).

58. Brant, *A Gathering of Spirit*; Will Roscoe, ed., *Living the Spirit: A Gay American Indian Anthology* (New York: St. Martin's Griffin, 1988); Paula Gunn Allen, *The Sacred Hoop: Recovering the Feminine in American Indian Traditions* (Boston: Beacon, 1986). See also Walter L. Williams, *The Spirit and the Flesh: Sexual Diversity in American Indian Culture* (Boston: Beacon, 1992).

59. It would be followed a year later by the publication of *Mohawk Trail*, in which Brant examined her experiences as an urban lesbian Mohawk: Beth Brant, *Mohawk Trail* (Ithaca, NY: Firebrand, 1985).

60. Many other edited volumes followed, including Paula Gunn Allen, ed., *Spider Woman's Granddaughters: Traditional Tales and Contemporary Writing by Native American Women* (New York: Ballantine, 1990); Gloria Bird and Joy Harjo, eds., *Reinventing the Enemy's Language: Contemporary Native Women's Writing of North America* (New York: W. W. Norton, 1997); Christine Miller and Patricia Churchryk, eds., *Women of the First Nations: Power, Wisdom, and Strength* (Winnipeg: University of Manitoba Press, 1996); Karen L. Kilcup, ed., *Native American Women's Writing: An Anthology, circa 1800–1924* (Oxford: Blackwell, 2000); Sarah Carter, ed., *Unsettled Pasts: Reconceiving the West through Women's History* (Calgary: University of Calgary Press, 2005); Mary-Ellen Kelm and Lorna Townsend, eds., *In the Days of Our Grandmothers: A Reader in Aboriginal Women's History in Canada* (Toronto: University of Toronto Press, 2006); Sarah Carter and Patricia Alice McCormack, eds., *Recollecting: Lives of Aboriginal Women of the Canadian Northwest and Borderlands* (Edmonton, AB: Athabasca University Press, 2011); Connie Fife, *The Colour of Resistance: A Contemporary Collection of Writing by Aboriginal Women* (Winnipeg, MB: Sister Vision Press, 1993).

61. Many other publications followed, including Sue-Ellen Jacobs, Wesley Thomas, and Sabine Lang, eds., *Two-Spirit People: Native American Gender Identity, Sexuality, and Spirituality* (Chicago: University of Illinois Press, 1997); Will Roscoe, *The Zuni Man-Woman* (Albuquerque: University of New Mexico Press, 1992); Will Roscoe, *Changing Ones: Third and Fourth Genders in Native North America* (New York: Macmillan, 1998).

62. Allen, *The Sacred Hoop*, 194–208. See Luana Ross, *Inventing the Savage: The Social Construction of Native American Criminality* (Austin: University of Texas Press, 1998); Luana Ross, "Native Women, Mean-Spirited Drugs, and Punishing Policies," *Social Justice* 32, no. 3 (2005): 54–62; Sarah Deer, Bonnie Clairmont, Carrie A. Martell, and Maureen L. White Eagle, eds., *Sharing Our Stories of Survival: Native Women Surviving Violence* (Lanham, MD: AltaMira, 2007); Joanna Woolman and Sarah Deer, "A Critical Look at Child Protection: Protecting Native Mothers and Their Children: A Feminist Lawyering Approach," *William Mitchell Law Review* 40 (2014): 943–1158; Sarah Deer, *The Beginning and End of Rape: Confronting Sexual Violence in Native America* (Minneapolis: University of Minnesota Press, 2015); Barbara Perry, *Silent Victims: Hate Crimes against Native Americans* (Tucson: University of Arizona Press, 2008).

63. Patricia Monture-Angus, *Thunder in My Soul: A Mohawk Woman Speaks* (Halifax: Fernwood, 1995); Mary Ellen Turpel, "Patriarchy and Paternalism: The Legacy of the Canadian State for First Nations Women," *Canadian Journal of Women and Law* (1993): 174.

See Verna St. Denis, "Feminism Is for Everybody: Aboriginal Women, Feminism, and Diversity," in *Making Space for Indigenous Feminism*, ed. Joyce Green (Winnipeg, AB: Fernwood, 2007), 33–52; Luana Ross, "From the 'F' Word to Indigenous/Feminisms," *Wicazō Śa Review* 24, no. 2 (2009): 39–52.

64. Jaimes and Halsey, "American Indian Women"; Trask, *From a Native Daughter*; M. A. Jaimes Guerrero, "Civil Rights versus Sovereignty: Native American Women in Life and Land Struggles," in *Feminist Genealogies, Colonial Legacies, Democratic Futures*, ed. M. Jacqui Alexander and Chandra Talpade Mohanty (New York: Routledge, 1997), 101–21; Laura Tohe, "There Is No Word for Feminism in My Language," *Wicazō Śa Review* 15, no. 2 (2000), 103–10; Agnes Grant, "Feminism and Aboriginal Culture: One Woman's View," *Canadian Woman Studies* 14 (Spring 1994): 56–57.

65. Janet Silman, *Enough Is Enough: Aboriginal Women Speak Out* (St. Paul, MN: Women's Press, 1987).

66. Kathleen Jamieson, *Indian Women and the Law in Canada: Citizens Minus* (Ottawa: Advisory Council on the Status of Women/Indian Rights for Indian Women, 1978); Joyce Green, "Sexual Equality and Indian Government: An Analysis of Bill C-31 Amendments to the Indian Act," *Native Studies Review* 1, no. 1 (1985): 81–95; Jo-Anne Fiske, "Native Women in Reserve Politics: Strategies and Struggles," *Journal of Legal Pluralism and Unofficial Law* 30–31 (1990): 121–37; Jo-Anne Fiske, "Child of the State/ Mother of the Nation: Aboriginal Women and the Ideology of Motherhood," *Culture* 13 (1993): 17–35; Lilianne E. Krosenbrink-Gelissen, " 'Traditional Motherhood' in Defense of Sexual Equality Rights of Canada's Aboriginal Women," *European Review of Native American Studies* 7, no. 2 (1993): 13–16; Sharon McIvor, "Aboriginal Women's Rights as 'Existing Rights,' " *Canadian Woman Studies* 15 (Spring-Summer 1995): 34–38; Katherine Beaty Chiste, "Aboriginal Women and Self-Government: Challenging Leviathan," *American Indian Culture and Research Journal* 18, no. 3 (1994): 19–43; Karlen Faith, Mary Gottriedson, Cherry Joe, Wendy Leonard, and Sharon MacIvor, "Native Women in Canada: A Quest for Justice." *Social Justice* 17, no. 3 (1991): 167–89; Fiske, "Native Women in Reserve Politics"; Fiske, "Child of the State/Mother of the Nation"; Jo-Anne Fiske, "Political Status of Native Indian Women: Contradictory Implications of Canadian State Policy," *American Indian Culture and Research Journal* 19, no. 2 (1995): 1–30; Joan Holmes, *Bill C-31, Equality or Disparity? The Effects of the New Indian Act on Native Women* (Ottawa: Canadian Advisory Council on the Status of Women, 1987); Lilianne E. Krosenbrink-Gelissen, *Sexual Equality as an Aboriginal Right: The Native Women's Association of Canada and the Constitutional Process on Aboriginal Matters, 1982–1987* (Fort Lauderdale, FL: Saarbrucken, 1991); Lilianne E. Krosenbrink-Gelissen, "Caring Is Indian Women's Business, but Who Takes Care of Them? Canada's Indian Women, the Renewed Indian Act, and Its Implications for Women's Family Responsibilities, Roles and Rights," *Law and Anthropology* 7 (1994): 107–30; Wendy Moss, *History of Discriminatory Laws Affecting Aboriginal People* (Ottawa: Library of Parliament Research Branch, 1987), 1–29; Wendy Moss, "Indigenous Self-Government in Canada and Sexual Equality under the Indian Act: Resolving Conflicts between Collective and Individual Rights," *Queen's Law Journal* 15 (Fall 1990): 279–305; Val Napoleon, "Aboriginal Self-Determination: Individual Self and Collective Selves," *Atlantis* 29, no. 2

(2005): 31–46; Andrea Bear Nicholas, "Colonialism and the Struggle for Liberation: The Experience of Maliseet Women," *University of New Brunswick Law Journal* 43 (1994): 223–39; Bonita Lawrence, "Gender, Race, and the Regulation of Native Identity in Canada and the United States: An Overview," *Hypatia* 18, no. 2 (2003): 3–31.

67. Patrick Wolfe, *Settler Colonialism and the Transformation of Anthropology: The Politics and Poetics of an Ethnographic Event* (London: Cassell Wellington House, 1999); Patrick Wolfe, "Settler Colonialism and the Elimination of the Native," *Journal of Genocide Research* 8, no. 4 (2006): 387–409. See, e.g., Sherene H. Razack, *Race, Space, and the Law: Unsettling a White Settler Society* (Toronto: Between the Lines, 2002), Margaret D. Jacobs, *White Mother to a Dark Race: Settler Colonialism, Maternalism* (Lincoln: University of Nebraska Press, 2009), Lisa Ford, *Settler Sovereignty: Jurisdiction and Indigenous People in America and Australia, 1788–1836* (Cambridge, MA: Harvard University Press, 2010).

68. Wolfe, "Settler Colonialism and the Elimination of the Native," 388.

69. Cheryl I. Harris, "Whiteness as Property," *Harvard Law Review* 106 (1992): 1707; Michael Omi and Howard Winant, *Racial Formation in the United States: From the 1960s to the 1990s* (New York: Routledge, 1994); Aileen Moreton-Robinson, "Unmasking Whiteness: A Goori Jondal's [Aboriginal Woman's] Look at Some Duggai [White] Business," *Queensland Review* 6, no. 1 (1999): 1. See also Aileen Moreton-Robinson, *Talkin' up to the White Woman: Aboriginal Women and Feminism* (St. Lucia: University of Queensland Press, 2000).

70. Wolfe, "Settler Colonialism and the Elimination of the Native," 387.

71. Wolfe, "Settler Colonialism and the Elimination of the Native," 389–90.

72. Daniel Heath Justice, Bethany Schneider, and Mark Rifkin, eds., "Sexuality, Nationality, Indigeneity," GLQ 16, no. 1–2 (2010); Scott Lauria Morgensen, *Spaces between Us: Queer Settler Colonialism and Indigenous Decolonization* (Minneapolis: University of Minnesota Press, 2011); Mark Rifkin, *The Erotics of Sovereignty: Queer Native Writing in the Era of Self-determinism* (Minneapolis: University of Minnesota Press, 2012). See also Qwo-Li Driskill, Daniel Heath Justice, Deborah Miranda, and Lisa Tatonetti, eds., *Sovereign Erotics: A Collection of Two-Spirit Literature* (Tucson: University of Arizona Press, 2011); Scott Lauria Morgensen, "Theorising Gender, Sexuality and Settler Colonialism: An Introduction," *Settler Colonial Studies* 2, no. 2 (2012): 2–22.

73. Daniel Heath Justice, Mark Rifkin, and Bethany Schneider, "Introduction," GLQ 16, no. 1–2 (2010): 5–39.

74. Ty P. Kāwika Tengan, *Native Men Remade: Gender and Nation in Contemporary Hawai'i* (Durham, NC: Duke University Press, 2008), 3. See also Kim Anderson, Robert Alexander Innes, and John Swift, "Indigenous Masculinities: Carrying the Bones of the Ancestors," in *Canadian Men and Masculinities: Historical and Contemporary Perspectives*, eds. Christopher John Greig and Wayne Martino (Toronto: Canadian Scholars' Press, 2012): 266; Brendan Hokowhitu, "Tackling Maori Masculinity: A Colonial Genealogy of Savagery and Sport," *Contemporary Pacific* 16, no. 2 (2004): 259–84; Brendan Hokowhitu, "The Death of Koro Paka: 'Traditional' Māori Patriarchy," *Contemporary Pacific* 20, no. 1 (2008): 115–41; Brendan Hokowhitu, "Producing Elite Indigenous Masculinities," *Settler Colonial Studies* 2, no. 2 (2012): 23–48.

75. Tengan, *Native Men Remade*, 3.

76. Sam McKegney, ed., *Masculindians: Conversations about Indigenous Manhood* (Winnipeg: University of Manitoba Press, 2014). See also Lloyd L. Lee, *Diné Masculinities: Conceptualizations and Reflections* (CreateSpace Independent Publishing Platform, 2013).

77. Leanne Simpson, *Dancing on Our Turtle's Back: Stories of Nishnaabeg Re-creation, Resurgence and a New Emergence* (Winnipeg, MB: Arbeiter Ring, 2011), 17

78. Simpson, *Dancing on Our Turtle's Back*, 17, 19.

79. Simpson, *Dancing on Our Turtle's Back*, 20.

80. Elizabeth A. Povinelli, *The Cunning of Recognition: Indigenous Alterities and the Making of Australian Multiculturalism* (Durham, NC: Duke University Press, 2002); Dian Million, *Therapeutic Nations: Healing in an Age of Indigenous Human Rights* (Tucson: University of Arizona Press, 2013); Glen Sean Coulthard, *Red Skins, White Masks: Rejecting the Colonial Politics of Reconciliation* (Minneapolis: University of Minnesota Press, 2014).

81. Winona LaDuke, *All Our Relations: Native Struggles for Land and Life* (Boston: South End, 1999); Winona LaDuke with Sean Cruz, *The Militarization of Indian Country: From Geronimo to Bin Laden* (Minneapolis: Honor the Earth, 2011).

82. Melissa K. Nelson, ed., *Original Instructions: Indigenous Teachings for a Sustainable Future* (Rochester, VT: Inner Traditions, 2011), 14.

83. Kateri Akiwenzie-Damm, ed., *Without Reservation: Indigenous Erotica* (Cape Croker Reserve: Kegedonce Press, 2003); Drew Hayden Taylor, ed., *Me Sexy: An Exploration of Native Sex and Sexuality* (Madeira Park, BC: Douglas and McIntyre, 2008). See Chrystos, *Fire Power* (Vancouver: Press Gang, 1995); Deborah A. Miranda, "Dildos, Hummingbirds, and Driving Her Crazy: Searching for American Indian Women's Love Poetry and Erotics," *Frontiers* 23, no. 2 (2002): 135–49; Qwo-Li Driskill, Chris Finley, Brian Joseph Gilley, and Scott Lauria Morgensen, *Queer Indigenous Studies: Critical Interventions in Theory, Politics, and Literature* (Tucson: University of Arizona Press, 2011); Driskill et al., *Sovereign Erotics*.

84. Kateri Akiwenzie-Damm, "Red Hot to the Touch: WRi[gh]ting Indigenous Erotica," in *Me Sexy: An Exploration of Native Sex and Sexuality*, ed. Drew Hayden Taylor (Madeira Park, BC: Douglas and McIntyre, 2008), 109–10.

85. Akiwenzie-Damm, "Red Hot to the Touch," 112, 113.

86. Jessica Yee Danforth, "Our Bodies, Our Nations," in McKegney, *Masculindians*, 118–124.

87. Sarah Hunt, "More than a Poster Campaign: Redefining Colonial Violence," in Kino-nda-niimi Collective, *The Winter We Danced*, 192. See Bonita Lawrence and Enakshi Dua, "Decolonizing Antiracism," *Social Justice* (2005): 120–43.

88. Debra Yepa-Pappan, *Live Long and Prosper (Spock Was a Half-Breed)*, 2008. Artwork.

89. Alexandra Kelstrom, "Interview with Debra Yepa-Pappan," May 16, 2012, http://via.library.depaul.edu/cgi/viewcontent.cgi?article=1051&context=oral_his_series.

90. Elle-Máijá Tailfeathers, "Frack Off: Indigenous Women Lead Effort against Fracking," panel presented at the New School for Social Research, New York, September 20, 2014, https://www.youtube.com/watch?v=COCeQgZ94dY.

91. Mishuana R. Goeman and Jennifer Nez Denetdale, eds., "Native Feminisms: Legacies, Interventions, and Indigenous Sovereignties," *Wicazō Ša Review* 24, no. 2 (2009): 9–13.

92. Goeman and Denetdale, "Native Feminisms," 9.

93. J. Kēhaulani Kauanui, "The Politics of Blood and Sovereignty in *Rice v. Cayetano*," *Polar* 25, no. 1 (2002): 110–28; J. Kēhaulani Kauanui, "Precarious Positions: Native Hawaiians and U.S. Federal Recognition," *Contemporary Pacific* 17, no. 1 (2005): 1–27; J. Kēhaulani Kauanui, *Hawaiian Blood: Colonialism and the Politics of Sovereignty and Indigeneity* (Durham, NC: Duke University Press, 2008); J. Kēhaulani Kauanui, "Native Hawaiian Decolonization and the Politics of Gender," *American Quarterly* 60, no. 2 (2008): 281–87; J. Kēhaulani Kauanui, "Colonialism in Equality: Hawaiian Sovereignty and the Question of U.S. Civil Rights," *South Atlantic Quarterly* 107, no. 4 (2008): 635–50.

94. Jennifer Nez Denetdale, "Chairmen, Presidents, and Princesses: The Navajo Nation, Gender, and the Politics of Tradition," *Wicazō Ša Review* 21, no. 1 (2006): 9–28; Jennifer Nez Denetdale, *Reclaiming Diné History: The Legacies of Navajo Chief Manuelito and Juanita* (Tucson: University of Arizona Press, 2007); Jennifer Nez Denetdale, "Carving Navajo National Boundaries: Patriotism, Tradition, and the Diné Marriage Act of 2005," *American Quarterly* 60, no. 2 (2008): 289–94; Denetdale, "Securing Navajo National Boundaries."

95. Mishuana R. Goeman, "From Place to Territories and Back Again: Centering Storied Land in the Discussion of Indigenous Nation-Building," *International Journal of Critical Indigenous Studies* 1, no. 1 (2008): 23–34; Goeman, *Mark My Words*.

96. Jessica Bissett Perea, "The Politics of Inuit Musical Modernities in Alaska," PhD diss., University of California, Berkeley, 2011; Jessica Bissett Perea, "Pamyua's Akutaq: Traditions of Modern Inuit Modalities in Alaska," *MusiCultures* 39, no. 1 (2012): 7–41; Jessica Bissett Perea, "A Tribalography of Alaska Native Presence in Academia," *American Indian Culture and Research Journal* 37, no. 3 (2013): 3–28.

97. Mark Rifkin, *Manifesting America: The Imperial Construction of U.S. National Space* (Oxford: Oxford University Press, 2009); Rifkin, *When Did Indians Become Straight?*; Rifkin, *The Erotics of Sovereignty*.

98. Jodi A. Byrd, *The Transit of Empire: Indigenous Critiques of Colonialism* (Minneapolis: University of Minnesota Press, 2011); Jodi A. Byrd, " 'Been to the Nation, Lord, But I Couldn't Stay There: American Indian Sovereignty, Cherokee Freedmen and the Incommensurability of the Internal," *Interventions* 13, no. 1 (2011): 31–52; Jodi A. Byrd, "Follow the Typical Signs: Settler Sovereignty and Its Discontents," *Settler Colonial Studies* (2013): 1–4; Jodi A. Byrd, "Arriving on a Different Shore: U.S. Empire at Its Horizons," *College Literature* 2014, no. 1 (2014): 174–81.

99. Melissa K. Nelson, ed., *Original Instructions: Indigenous Teachings for a Sustainable Future* (Rochester, VT: Inner Traditions/Bear & Company, 2011); Melissa K. Nelson, "Protecting the Sanctity of Native Foods," in *State of the World 2013: Is Sustainability Possible?* ed. World Watch Institute (Washington, DC: Island Press, 2013), 201–9.

I

INDIGENOUS HAWAIIAN SEXUALITY AND THE POLITICS OF NATIONALIST DECOLONIZATION

J. KĒHAULANI KAUANUI

We put out a *kahea* [call] to our community to stand in support of ALL members of our *'ohana* [extended, intergenerational family] and in support of S[enate] B[ill] 1 and marriage equality.... We will not sit by idly and allow people to use Hawaiian culture and concepts to promote discrimination and replicate the very oppression that has been used against us for 200 years. Ua Mau ke Ea o ka 'Āina i ka Pono! The life of the land is perpetuated in justice! True Aloha does not discriminate. #truealoha—**"True Aloha" Facebook page,** https://www.facebook.com/truealoha/info

On October 31, 2013, the group True Aloha used social media to ask Kanaka Maoli (Native Hawaiians) to attend a rally at the State Capitol, under the banner "Aloha Does Not Discriminate," to support a proposal before the Hawai'i state legislature to legalize same-sex marriage. The announcement also called for Kanaka Maoli to wear their brightest *kīhei* (a rectangular cloth that rests over one shoulder, like a cloak) "in order to have a Kanaka Rainbow" and to bring *pū* (conch shells that are blown like trumpets in ceremonies and at public events), along with "signs that express true meanings

FIGURE 1.1. Marie Alohalani Brown, True Aloha Rally, courtesy of the photographer.

of ʻohana and aloha (love and more) and that support marriage equality for all."

The previous month, on September 9, Governor Neil Abercrombie announced that he would hold a special session on October 28 to consider the proposed Hawaii Marriage Equality Act. Tensions in the islands over the matter were heated, and there was even threat of a citizens' filibuster to block it.[1] In the midst of the statewide split over the issue, both proponents and opponents invoked Indigenous Hawaiian cultural models to their advantage, making for contested discourse regarding Kanaka Maoli tradition and sexuality. As part of that challenge, True Aloha was formed "to promote and support the authentic Hawaiian cultural value of aloha, which is an inclusive concept of love, compassion, and sympathy that does not discriminate against others."[2] In addition to those who attended in response, people all across the island of Oʻahu came together at the State Capitol in Honolulu to rally in support of the bill. They held signs that read "Kanakas for Equality" and "True Aloha Is Boundless = Marriage Equality for All" (which included the red-and-pink version of the Human Rights Campaign's equal sign logo[3]). On the flip side, those opposed to the bill held the Hawaiʻi state flag (also the Hawaiian Kingdom flag) and chanted, "Let us vote! Let us vote!" while some held signs with the plea, "Save Our ʻOhana!" Despite the division across Hawaiʻi, the legislature passed the bill on November 12, 2013.[4] In part to respond to the opposition, the law included a religious exemption, modeled after Connecticut state law, to protect religious groups and clergy who do not want to solemnize or participate in same-sex weddings.[5]

Notably, it was the 1990 Hawai'i case on same-sex marriage that set off passage of the Defense of Marriage Act (DOMA) in 1996. In the lawsuit, originally known as *Baehr v. Lewin* (later, *Baehr v. Miike*),[6] three same-sex couples argued that Hawai'i's prohibition of same-sex marriage violated the state constitution's equal rights amendment regarding gender. In 1993, the Hawaii State Supreme Court ruled in *Baehr v. Lewin* that refusing to grant marriage licenses to same-sex couples was discriminatory under the state's constitution. With regard to the couples involved in the Baehr case, the state was required to justify its position of opposing the marriages—to show that it had a "rational interest" in denying them this right.[7] Also in 1993, the same year the court ruled in *Baehr*, the U.S. Congress passed a joint resolution apologizing to the Hawaiian people for the 1893 overthrow, which acknowledged that "the indigenous Hawaiian people never directly relinquished their claims to their inherent sovereignty as a people or over their national lands to the United States, either through their monarchy or through a plebiscite or referendum." This development pushed the Hawaiian sovereignty question in a big way and added fuel to rapidly growing nationalist mobilization— critical context for the groups organizing during that period that weighed in on the issue of sexual diversity.

As the Hawai'i case moved through the courts, the U.S. Congress passed DOMA in 1996 as dozens of states and a number of tribal nations passed statutes and constitutional amendments banning same-sex unions.[8] By 1998, the passage of an amendment to the Hawaii state constitution allowed the state legislature to enact a ban on same-sex marriage, stating, "The legislature shall have the power to reserve marriage to opposite-sex couples."[9] That led to the dismissal of the case in 1999. Once taken out of the Hawaiian context, public discourse of Kanaka Maoli tradition and sexuality waned in some ways, and the same-sex marriage debate seemed to drop out of the Indigenous nationalist context.

In this chapter, I discuss nation-based accounts of Indigenous sovereignty and interrogations of the legal power of the settler state and foreground Indigenous criticism of the overarching colonial and gendered/sexualized power relations facing Kanaka Maoli within the Hawaiian sovereignty movement. Through a historical recollection of activist mobilizations, dialogues, and political struggle I draw close attention to the interrelationships and difficult dialogues that characterize Indigenous activist praxis. I reflect on the Hawaiian sovereignty movement during the early to mid-1990s to document some of the practices of exclusion, mis-recognition, and misrepresentation in that period to provide context for reading the contemporary gestures of True Aloha.[10] I offer a brief case study of a group of Kanaka Maoli bisexual, lesbian, gay, transgender, and *māhū* (BLGTM) individuals called Nā Mamo o Hawai'i,[11] which emerged in 1993 amid two, perhaps competing projects: the civil rights struggle for same-sex marriage in Hawai'i and the sovereign rights struggle for the restoration of a Hawaiian nation. Members of Nā Mamo courageously pushed Kanaka Maoli at large to consider all forms of decolonization, and their open reclamation of Indigenous practices with regard to sexual politics enabled a space to consider a more complex view of how people think about traditional Hawaiian norms with regard to sexuality and intimate unions. Moreover, they worked to challenge *haole* (white or foreign) oppression in this area of political organizing and erasure by both dominant gay activists in Hawai'i and Hawaiian sovereignty leaders.[12] Importantly, Nā Mamo was able to change the nature of sovereignty discussions by challenging long-held beliefs about the prevalence of same-sex sexuality in Hawaiian history. However, as I show, even when activists acknowledged that Hawaiian gender and sexual diversity is part of recognized traditions—and not a colonial import—that concession did not necessarily guarantee that the conversation was welcome. Too often, leaders admitted same-sex sexual traditions in Hawaiian culture as an excuse for nationalist exclusion.[13]

What follows here is a modest offering of the history of BLGTM recognition as it relates to Hawaiian sovereignty and an examination of some of the forms of cultural and political acknowledgment within the nationalist movement. I hope to provide insights as to the changing nature of debates about Hawaiian tradition during a very particular period of nationalist activism. After a brief historical background regarding Hawaiian history with regard to gender and sexuality and the transformation of Indigenous sovereignty, I provide an account of the early work of Nā Mamo in engaging Hawaiian sovereignty groups and recount a personal experience at a nationalist forum where I was invited to work alongside members who made an intervention that had a deeply ambivalent reception. I then return to the politics of True Aloha as the project and the state logics of marriage. In conclusion, I argue that while there is Indigenous cultural revitalization of Hawaiian concepts that may be considered part of broader cultural decolonization, the state legislature's passage of the same-sex marriage bill is a form of settler colonial continuity. In light of the unlawful U.S.-backed overthrow of 1893 and the annexation of an independent state in 1898, those in the Hawaiian nationalist movement contest the legitimacy of the so-called fiftieth state. Besides this form of imperialism wrought by occupation, the Hawaiian sovereignty question is bound up with the ongoing processes of settler colonialism.[14] In Hawaiʻi, same-sex marriage extends the colonial imposition of male-female marriage to the contemporary politics of assimilation and affirmation of U.S. occupation under the cover of inclusion in a multiracial liberal democracy in the "land of aloha."

Historical Background

Hawaiians had a range of models of gender and sexual diversity. For example, traditional ways to register interest in an enduring intimate relationship were called *awaiulu* (to bind securely, fasten, tie) or *hoʻao* (to stay until daylight).[15] The intimate relationships between *kane* (man) and *wahine* (woman) are sometimes referred to in the literature as "marriage," but that term does not correspond to Kanaka relationships. Both men and women were autonomous in all conjugal relations.[16] From the historical research of Lilikalā Kameʻeleihiwa and Noenoe K. Silva, respectively, it is clear that bisexuality was normative and that polygamy and polyandry also were not uncommon. In addition, there were distinct categories of same-sex sexual relationships, such as the *aikāne*, a same-sex intimate friendship that might include sexual relations.[17] There were also *māhū*, mentioned earlier, and the category of *punalua* to describe a situation in which two men were with the same woman or two women were with the same man.[18] High-ranking Hawaiian women and men held governing positions as paramount chiefs and lesser chiefs before the formation of the monarchy in the early nineteenth century. As Jocelyn Linnekin documents, women of all genealogical ranks were considered strong, autonomous within the context of an interdependent polity, and active agents. Historically, Kanaka women were "symbolically associated with land, valued as producers of high cultural goods, held a separate domain of female ritual and social power . . . and were points of access to rank, land, and political power."[19] The reformation of these Indigenous norms and practices was central to the nineteenth-century Western civilizing process, in which the bourgeois family was the model to be emulated.[20]

From 1795 to 1810, Kamchameha violently converted a Hawaiian society of multiple paramount island chiefs into a monarchy. The kingdom had strong Indigenous elements at the start, but by the 1840s it had become increasingly westernized. To gain access to the exclusive nineteenth-century Family of Nations, it was important for the kingdom to present itself as Christian.[21] This was made possible by the American Board of Commissioners for Foreign Missions' initiation of conversion through the first mission to Hawaiʻi, which began in 1820.[22] In this context, marriage itself was a colonial imposition, with coverture being a prime determinant of Hawaiian women's shift in status.[23] Based on English common law and operative in the United States at the time, after marriage a woman's separate legal existence was negated and brought under her husband's.

The representation of the nation as part of "civilized manhood" was crucial, especially for a Polynesian brown people considered irrational, savage (yet childlike), and oversexed. The acceptance of the kingdom by world powers necessitated an independent nation that displayed a masculine face, which served as a sign of modernity.[24] This major reorganization of social arrangements by Kanaka elites—male and female—to create new norms was a political strategy to fight Western racism, yet it necessitated a capitulation to that racism in the transformation of the Indigenous polity.

Favored Descendants?

From the start of Nā Mamo's existence, members drew from a range of Hawaiian symbols while working to secure a rightful place within various competing nationalist groups. They insisted on the recognition that their claims to these same-sex civil rights had a place within the same-sex legacies already identified within traditional Hawaiian cultural practices.[25] The nature of the terms in which Nā Mamo activists traced same-sex relations mark them as an integral part of "Indigenous tradition."

Within Nā Mamo's political discourse, genealogy was a central theme. For example, in an article on the group published in 1996 in the *Village Voice*, a co-founder, Kuʻumeaaloha Gomes, explained that King Kamehameha had had an *aikane* (male lover) named Kuakini, whom she identified as a high chief who later governed Hawaiʻi Island.[26] In relation to this history, she told how the group got its name: before going into battle, King Kamehameha called his warriors "nā mamo," meaning "favored descendants." Gomes's invocation of royal naming practices worked to insinuate members of the group within a particular Hawaiian lineage. It also exemplifies a central feature of Hawaiian genealogical practices, in which people trace ascent, selectively choosing their way upward. In other words, Nā Mamo insisted that Hawaiian same-sex legacies can be drawn on to bolster contemporary identities in terms of who Hawaiians are in the present, not just who they were in "ancient times." Within a Hawaiian ontological frame, genealogical precedence holds powerful sway in how the present is regarded, explained, and authorized.[27] As another co-founder, Noenoe Silva, stated in an interview, "Homosexuality wasn't a despised trait in ancient Hawai'i. It is part of our culture that the Christians have made our k[ū]puna feel ashamed about. But within our own families it's tacitly accepted—people aren't shunned from the family. Now maybe it's time for that side of our Hawaiian culture to come out of the closet and to say 'yes, we're part of the family.'"[28] Those affiliated with Nā Mamo made a point to claim a Native lineage for their work and in doing so attempted to secure a place in Hawaiian nationalist culture.

When asked about Hawaiian reception regarding differences when it comes to sexuality, many Kanaka Maoli leaders acknowledged that Hawaiians are mostly an accepting people. But their reception was limited: some leaders suggested that group members were being divisive by raising the "gay question" and thus threatening political unity. In asking what claims BLGTM Hawaiians had at the time within the multiple and competing sovereignty groups and citizenship models, Nā Mamo challenged Hawaiian sovereignty leaders to demonstrate their recognition. Gomes posed the challenge, "If we are creating these new nations, this new Hawaiian nation, and do not include homosexuals equally, then aren't we recreating the status quo?"[29] This was one of several direct calls to leaders asking them to delineate their groups' position statements with regard to bisexual, lesbian, gay, transgender, and māhū inclusion.

Soon after, Hawaiian sovereignty leaders responded to the call, with assistance from Susan Miller, in interviews published in a special issue of the gay magazine *Island Lifestyle*.[30] The first leader Miller interviewed was Kekuni Blaisdell, a longtime independence activist and the then-head of Ka Pākaukau, a coalition of organizations and individuals pursuing self-determination and independence. He answered questions about sexual politics in a way that acknowledged diverse Hawaiian legacies of varying forms of intimate expression. "It's not enough for sovereign organizations to say they don't discriminate," he argued. "In the plans for a new nation, sovereignty leaders must go beyond unwritten understandings with some type of formal policy to address how to recognize sexuality difference as an accepted part of the tradition of Kanaka Maoli."[31] Blaisdell clearly reminded us that "tolerance" is not enough; implicit acceptance is insufficient within the context of Hawaiian self-governance. In other words, he urged people to consider formal inclusion and to acknowledge the spectrum of sexual practices and identities as normative.

Miller next interviewed A'o Pohaku Kailala, the head of the Nation of Ku, another sovereignty organization. Pohaku stated, "Pre-Christianity, being gay was not a problem." When asked about her position on the inclusion of gays within the nation, Kaiala said, "I guess the time has come, since gay marriages and gays are becoming more open about their human rights. They have every right to fight for that. Hawaiians need to start looking at this and give support to other groups who are fighting for basic human rights. The Hawaiian movement is about basic human rights." Pohaku also openly acknowledged that one of her sons is gay and explicitly said, "Basic human rights for gays is also a cultural issue . . . and it is not our position to make this a moral issue. . . . That's why there needs to be more education."[32] Further, she stated, "For the Nation of Ku, we would have no reservation including anyone. We would love to take affirmative action. And I would love to work with gays or whoever [sic] chooses to work for the benefit of the nation."[33] Pohaku's use of the term "affirmative action" is important and highlights her proactive stance, especially since she also refers to human rights, which are more encompassing than civil rights. Interestingly, she notes that this is a "cultural issue," not a moral one, which seems to be her approach to affirming same-sex sexuality as a Hawaiian cultural norm.

Miller also interviewed Mililani Trask, then the *kia'āina* (governor) of Ka Lāhui Hawai'i, a Native initiative for Hawaiian self-government within existing U.S. federal policy. Trask asserted, "Hawaiian culture has always been very tolerant and incorporating of gay and lesbian practices. . . . Well, pretty much gay men's practices." But when specifically asked about Ka Lāhui's position on the matter, Trask responded, "I don't think our cultural perspective would be one that would be prejudicial, but it really hasn't come up in the nation."[34] Here, too, Hawaiian culture was mentioned as a way to suggest inclusion. But when asked how Ka Lāhui would protect Hawaiian civil rights in this area, Trask declared, "In this nation, the question is what are you going to do for your nation, not what is your nation going to do for you. . . . If they expect because they are gay or lesbian, that somehow they should have preferential rights—what do they want, preferential rights to land?"[35] Here Trask was more defensive about the group's policies, as demonstrated by her reappropriation of U.S. President John Kennedy's challenge, "Ask not what your country can do for you, but what you can do for your country." However, in a context in which various sovereignty groups—all claiming to represent the Hawaiian nation—were jockeying for membership, the key question for many Hawaiians at the time was, "What will *that* nation do for me?" Unfortunately, Trask's statement about protection seemed to distort the issue as "preferential rights" rather than a civil rights issue ensuring nondiscrimination—precisely the same argument neoconservatives use to dismiss Hawaiian sovereignty claims as a form of "racial preference." In another part of the interview, Trask articulated Ka Lāhui's position at the time: "Ka Lāhui is self-determination. . . . If people wish to marry each other they should be free to do so. We don't have a law saying men must marry women; men must marry men [or] when you have to get married. We don't have any of that; we don't impinge on private rights. All rights are guaranteed without regard to sexual preference. We've never had an incident in which it has been challenged."[36]

It seemed appropriate at the time that Ka Lāhui consider putting antidiscriminatory safeguards in place. However, the group never guaranteed antidiscrimination with regard to sexual preference in its constitution; it displaced the political critique and claims made by BLGTM Kanaka Maoli as one of "private rights" that are distinct from (and subordinate to) sovereignty.

In another, related case, the group Sovereign and Independent Nation-State of Hawai'i, led by Dennis "Bumpy" Kanahele, apparently considered asserting Hawaiian sovereignty over the issues of same-sex legal recognition. At a Hawaiian sovereignty panel I attended in early 1994, in Honolulu, another leader of the group, Kawehi Kanui, publicly announced that the leaders had mulled over whether to urge same-sex couples involved in the State Supreme Court case for gay marriage to allow the Hawaiian nation to marry them. The idea, she explained, was that the gay couples in the legal battle would then be affirming an Indigenous sovereign initiative instead of reaffirming the authority of the state. Yet when the group drafted its constitution, it also did not include "sexual orientation" in its antidiscrimination clause.[37]

Members of Nā Mamo claimed a Native lineage and in doing so attempted to secure a place in Hawai'i within the nationalist culture, where issues of belonging were fraught and contested. But these same genealogies were at times used to contain gay BLGTM identities. Hence, I suggest that merely marking same-sex sexuality as Indigenous terrain will not suffice as a de-colonial gesture, as we learn from this period.

After Reclaiming the Land Base?

In other group contexts, also during the 1990s, it was difficult to reach consensus on issues of sexuality and antidiscrimination. A similar issue came about through the gathering Puwalu 'Ekolu in the summer of 1996. Held at Puhi Bay, Hawai'i, Puwalu 'Ekolu was the third in a series of meetings at which the central agenda was to create an alternative to the state-sponsored "Native Hawaiian Vote" emanating from the Hawaiian Sovereignty Advisory

Commission (later renamed the Hawaiian Sovereignty Elections Council), established by the Hawai'i state legislature.[38] The council, whose members were appointed by the governor, was charged with determining, in part, "the will of the Native Hawaiian people to call a democratically convened convention for the purpose of achieving consensus on an organic document that will propose the means for Native Hawaiians to operate under a government of their own choosing."[39] Despite protests from Kanaka Maoli that this state-controlled process would violate the right of Indigenous self-determination, the council maintained that the state legislation "constitute[d] an exercise of expression of the will of the Native Hawaiian people without any commitment to the acceptance in the State of Hawai'i of such expression."[40] The Puwalu 'Ekolu challenged the state's authority but also focused on creating an alternative process to unite Kanaka Maoli on the political push for Hawaiian sovereignty.

The focus of this particular meeting of the Puwalu was *aloha 'āina* (love for the land) and *malama 'āina* (caring for the land). Those who attended the gathering were Hawaiians from a range of political backgrounds. Some represented sovereignty organizations, and others came as individuals, but all were committed to stopping the state's co-optation of our movement to restore Hawaiian self-governance and nation building. Members of Nā Mamo were the designated facilitators of the meeting. I was excited that Nā Mamo would play such a prominent role. At the meeting, Nā Mamo members asked me to join them to help facilitate the meeting. Gomes opened with a workshop on how we as Hawaiians could gain awareness about privileges so that we could hold a meeting at which all in attendance would feel empowered to speak, regardless of their skin color, class background, sexual orientation, or age. This was just the opening of what would be a very intense and demanding meeting.

By the third day it was time to finalize on paper the issues for which we had developed consensus. As we were wrapping up, Silva submitted a proposal that all printed material emanating from the meeting include a statement, at the beginning or end of the document, of antidiscrimination for BLGTM Hawaiians regarding all proposals put forth. Silva read the statement:

> We are Hawaiian, we belong to Hawai'i. Our 'āina permeates every part
> of us: the land is our ancestor, it is in our bones. It is our link to our past,
> our history, and our future well-being. All are linked to our relationship
> with our 'āina. Aloha 'āina is a familial relationship; that means that
> we resist all attempts to further separate any of us from our 'āina. Our

freedom to live in our land is linked to our freedom to determine how we live in our bodies, our freedom to live in relationships that may be *different from American culture*. Before colonization we lived in a society that accepted diversity, and now we want to propose support for ending discrimination against lesbians, gays, and bisexuals.[11]

Note the stress on the connection between the assertion of interconnectedness in relation to familial ties among Kanaka Maoli and to the land, a key difference from the settler colonial society. Nā Mamo wanted this statement of commitment that no one would be discriminated from land access because of one's sexual orientation and provided a potent cultural rationale for a claim to freedom from discrimination.

The overwhelming hostility from the participants was accompanied by an unyielding refusal to honor Nā Mamo's request. This was certainly a shock to me because Nā Mamo had played such a key facilitating role at the gathering and the entire meeting was premised on a commitment to antidiscrimination *among* Hawaiians—or so I thought, given that everyone willingly participated in the opening workshop that dealt with sexual orientation, among other issues. It was both fascinating and disheartening to see how those who had happily relied on Nā Mamo's labor had no interest in backing those who risked discrimination based on sexual orientation or non-binary gender status. Many of those with whom we camped, ate, sang, chanted, swam, and cried said the most offensive things without any self-consciousness. One person argued, "We don't need *that kind* of statement in our *palapala* [documents]," implying that an antidiscrimination statement would "look bad" to outsiders. Others suggested that the antidiscrimination sentiment could be implicitly assumed because we were Hawaiian. Another agreed, saying, "We take care of our own, so no need." A woman who (it turned out) was struggling with the fact that her daughter had come out as lesbian yelled, "We can't do *that!*" And several of the houseless Hawaiian men living on the beach argued, "If we start adding gay Hawaiians, we would have to say we won't discriminate against disabled and homeless Hawaiians— where would it end?" as though addressing multiple oppressions was what posed the dilemma.[42]

These issues of explicit acknowledgment and assurances of access were seen as outside the bounds of the central agenda for the gathering: aloha 'āina and malama 'āina. One other person argued that for a statement such as Nā Mamo's to be considered, we would need to wait until "after the land base" was reclaimed. Another participant said, "We're not discriminating against people. We all have māhū in our 'ohana, but we can't put that kind of statement on the paper because we're going to be sending it out to the media, and all the locals will see it." One person even went as far as to suggest that Hawaiians were so accepting that it would be like haole to write the statement out or delineate "special rights."

At this point, only two people spoke out: Silva and I. Silva pointed out a major contradiction that had emerged in their responses. On the one hand, they were saying that there was no problem with being gay and that they accepted that. But in the next breath they said that it was not OK to make this public and put it in print. I made the point that the suggestion that gay Hawaiians must wait until after the land base was like the dozens of social movements throughout the world in which women labor for their nationalist struggles but are informed by their male counterparts that they need to wait until "after the revolution" for their own liberation.[43] Needless to say, we both argued against a deferral.

Finally, two prominent leaders spoke out. Skippy 'Ioane stood up and reminded us all that it was Sunday morning, and none of us was at church. Many of us had fled church because it is oppressive to us as Hawaiians, he pointed out, discussing the connection between Christian missionization and colonial domination of Kanaka Maoli. Then Lilikalā Kame'eleihiwa stood up and reminded all of us that our ancestors' culture had no homophobia; homophobia was an import. With those two connected points spoken, things seemed to "click" among the group, and the vast majority reluctantly agreed to adopt the statement within the Puwalu Resolutions. However, in the end, the statement and minutes of the meeting were never publicly released.

Reflecting now, those who did not want the statement probably thought it was Nā Mamo's request that hindered our overall political project. But those who opposed the antidiscrimination clause not only managed to bring things to a standstill; they willingly risked alienating an entire group of people who had devoted their passion and labor to all Kanaka Maoli. Central to the Puwalu debate was the question of *who* would represent the *lāhui* (Nation/peoplehood). Implicit in the dispute were different understandings of the concepts of aloha 'āina and malama 'āina and what they might encompass. It was nothing less than a contest as to how the community—indeed, the nation—would be defined. Here a colonial and very American idea of normality was powerfully used to distinguish between public and private spheres, where the opposing Kanaka Maoli activists envisioned sovereignty as a specifically heterosexual formation.

To some degree, everyone who opposed the statement claimed same-sex practices within a Hawaiian genealogy rather than disowning them. In doing so, they claimed them as part of Indigenous tradition as they recognized that BLGTM Hawaiians were part of the "national community." Moreover, some specifically noted that "gay Hawaiians" can be found in all Hawaiian ʻohana. But they also asserted that there was no need for distinct protections from discrimination since, in this logic, culturally recognition is ample. This begs the question of who has the power to represent, and reveals the need to address the contradictions that arise from dominant unifying strategies such as what played out at the Puwalu gathering for enduring struggles for political self-determination.

These different leaders acknowledged that BLGTM Hawaiians are part of the "national community." Moreover, some specifically noted that gay Hawaiians can be found in all Hawaiian ʻohana, as well as in ancient histories. Rather than disowning LGBT status as "non-Hawaiian," they claimed it as part of Hawaiian culture. In other words, they look after their own *as Hawaiians* who are seen as falling under their (group's) jurisdiction. I suggest that this is a form of political containment enabled through the invocation of Native tradition—a tactic to efface or circumvent BLGTM Hawaiians' having another key point of identification outside the "Hawaiian community" unmarked as heterosexual. Lessons from this period show that mere recognition of the traditional presence of homoeroticism in Hawaiian society does not guarantee against the suppression of critical discussions of the oppression of BLGTM Hawaiian nationalists.

Nā Mamo supported the principle of equality within the context of fiftieth state debates about same-sex marriage, but their work exceeded state frameworks of civil rights as their affirmations of Hawaiian sovereignty called U.S. authority into question in the first place. Moreover, the critical interventions and calls to Indigenous organizations to be accountable to their constituents pushed the boundaries of Hawaiian nationalist understandings of inclusion within the body politics. Importantly, Nā Mamo's focus on decolonization far exceeded pointing to exclusions and insisted on reframing how Hawaiian history itself had been colonized with regard to same-sex sexuality and gender diversity and other forms of relating beyond heteronormativity and a gender binary. As an organization, Nā Mamo was defunct by late 1996. However, the legacy of the group's efforts provides lessons for today in terms of Hawaiian activism and issues of difference while offering analytics to read the contemporary period in terms of the broader context of state co-optation.

State Co-optation of "True" Aloha

The claim that same-sex marriage is a civil rights gain begs many questions, but here I want to focus on Hawaiian sovereignty and what is said to constitute customary Kanaka Maoli practice and even the concept of *aloha* itself. Settlers' romanticized notions of Hawaiian tradition complicate all of this without regard for ongoing nationalist contestation of U.S. authority *and* efforts to restore diverse sexual traditions as a central part of decolonization. A history of Christian conversion, wrought through a racist politics of colonial modernity, has shaped what is considered normative in Hawaiian contexts in the contemporary period.

Returning to the political context of 2013 regarding the contestation of the fiftieth state's legalization of same-sex marriage, True Aloha challenged the ways in which people distorted Hawaiian cultural concepts—such as ʻohana and aloha—for their own political ends in opposition to same-sex marriage.[44] As kuualoha hoʻomanawanui describes, the initiative developed in response to a paid television advertisement running when discussion of Senate Bill 1 began at the state legislature.[45] Titled "Perpetuating Hawaiʻi's Covenant with God," the ad features Collette Machado, board chair of the Office of Hawaiian Affairs, and at least one Hawaiian minister misrepresenting traditional Hawaiian values of aloha and ʻohana as derived from Christianity. In the spot, they claim "aloha" for "all people of Hawaiʻi" but ask viewers to oppose Senate Bill 1, asserting that allowing same-sex marriage would "affect our traditional sense of ʻohana." They are taking a position against same-sex marriage, they say, "for the sake of the children." The ad ends with the words *aloha ke akua* (God is love).[46] The misrepresentation of traditional Hawaiian values as rooted in Christianity surprised hoʻomanawanui and other Hawaiian educators and cultural practitioners. Some even claimed, counter to vast historical evidence, that Captain Cook introduced same-sex relations and other gender and sexual variances to Hawaiʻi. As hoʻomanawanaui points out, "Cultural values such as aloha are so often misappropriated, particularly through capitalism and tourism, that it is easy to forget its true complexity of meaning: love, compassion, sympathy, mercy, kindness, charity, to recall with affection (hence its allusion to the more simplified greetings "hello" and "goodbye" which don't carry such emotional attachment).... The 'True Aloha' movement began through social media with the intention of reclaiming the cultural root of aloha as reflective of all its meanings, applicable to everyone." The central purpose of the initiative was to remind everyone that "aloha does not discriminate." As hoʻomanawanui asserts, "Using the core value of aloha as a weapon against others is pure cultural hypocrisy."[47] Instead, aloha "is an important cultural value inclusive of traditional Hawaiian practices of fluid sexuality, sexual identity, and relationship statuses."

True Aloha highlighted (and drew on) de-colonial forms of cultural recovery. This reclamation is enabled by revitalization of the Hawaiian language, which empowers access to historical sources that illuminate the possibilities found within Indigenous customary practices revealing multiplicity in terms of gender and sexuality. True Aloha identified as "Inclusive of traditional Hawaiian values and practices of fluid sexuality, sexual identity, and relationship status such as: aikane, māhū, punalua, poʻolua, and hānai."[48] Here, note that aikane, māhū, and punalua are listed alongside two other concepts. Poʻolua (two heads) refers to a situation in which a child has two possible fathers—that is, when patrilineage was unclear, contested fatherhood was accommodated by having both men take responsibility for the child, who could then claim either one genealogy or both.[49] Hānai (to feed) is used to describe adoption or forms of foster parenting and often entails a child given to a grandparent, aunt, or uncle to raise.[50] In naming aikane, māhū, punalua, poʻolua, and hānai together, True Aloha offers a meaningful assertion of Hawaiian cultural concepts to call out homophobia, gender binarism, and heterosexism rooted in colonialism while advancing diverse models that together constitute the diversity of ʻohana.

True Aloha importantly confronted the distorted forms of cultural appropriation deployed by non-Kanaka, along with impoverished and limited understandings by some Christian Kanaka who opposed same-sex marriage. Clearly, these are very significant and laudable interventions—ones offered by respected allies—but because "marriage equality" is the primary frame of reference, these affirmations are easily co-opted into state logics in which marriage itself becomes the primary vehicle for the expression of aloha through assertions that the legalization of same-sex matrimony in Hawaiʻi is about the extension of that aloha. That same-sex marriage became the new symbol of "true aloha" is problematic when put forth as the new return to the old, especially since it is not just premised on "till death do us part" monogamy but also bonded to coercive regulation by the settler colonial state.[51] This is another version of state co-optation, but with an added element: contestation over precolonial Hawaiian sexuality and gender norms in the service of same-sex marriage, which itself can be understood as a marker of settler colonial continuity, given that heterosexual marriage itself was a colonial imposition.

Today, it seems that acknowledgment and inclusion are not the issue. Given the state moves to contain activism for Hawaiian sovereignty, co-optation is an ongoing problem. State containment arguably increased in the wake of the U.S. Congress's apology one hundred years after the US-backed overthrow of the Hawaiian Kingdom, as shown in the 1996 state imposition. This only increased after the U.S. Supreme Court's ruling in *Rice v. Cayetano* (2000), which found that Hawaiian-only elections (only Native Hawaiians could vote or run as candidates) of trustees for the Office of Hawaiian Affairs violates the Fifteenth amendment to the U.S. Constitution. These developments took place in the context of a broader backlash in response to Kanaka assertions of sovereignty, a backlash undergirded by an expansion of the New Right in Hawaii that framed Indigenous-specific political measures as "reverse racism" and "special rights." In the midst of these popular attacks, a state-driven proposal has been before the U.S. Congress for federal recognition of a Native Hawaiian governing entity since the ruling in *Rice*, which many understand as an attempt to contain Hawaiian national claims under international law. In the meantime, in 2011 the fiftieth state passed its own legislation to recognize a Native Hawaiian governing entity, presumably in anticipation of federal recognition.

But there are still competing projects under the banner of the "Hawaiian sovereignty movement," with the dividing line largely drawn between those who advocate for self-determination within U.S. federal policy on Indian tribes and those who oppose it based on a commitment to the restoration of a Hawaiian Kingdom independent from the United States. Within the latter projects, legal questions of sexual minorities are easily deferred, since most of them rely on the Kingdom constitution of 1864 as the legitimate governing document. Same-sex sexual activity, as well as all sexual activity outside heterosexual monogamous marriage, had been made illegal by that time under the 1823 and 1827 sumptuary laws promulgated by the high chiefs and reiterated by King Kamehameha III in the notification "No ka moe kolohe" (Concerning Mischievous Sleeping) of 1829.[52] This is not to say or to assume that those who support restoring an independent Hawaiian state would necessarily want to maintain the laws from that period, but the question of revising them hinges on restoration of the kingdom first. Hence, in 2013 Hawaiian nationalist groups did not enter the debates, although individual nationalists did (but not representing any particular group).[53]

Conclusion

These cases show that gender and sexuality present significant lines of tension in the Hawaiian sovereignty movement and that thinking with those histories demands support for decolonizing Indigenous gender and sexuality within Indigenous land-based sovereignty struggles and within theory in Indigenous studies.

In the movement, the political work is made up of more than legal strategies and histories. Kanaka Maoli are involved in a strengthening process of cultural renewal and reconstruction based on epistemological resources and forms of knowledge that hold meaning for their Indigenous identities, social roles, and relationships. In Indigenous contexts for decolonization, nationalist movements to restore sovereignty are always fraught with contradictions, given that the quest to reclaim particular cultural traditions is always selective. The political struggle as a whole has encouraged a rethinking of the past, in which different understandings of Hawaiian culture are mobilized in the quest for some form of Hawaiian recognition and self-determination.

In the 1990s, the same-sex marriage cases within the legal frame of the fiftieth state enabled a space for BLGTM Kanaka to raise the issue of sexual diversity within Hawaiian nationalist projects more broadly and, since a variety of Hawaiian groups were competing with one another to represent them, to question the bounds of explicit recognition in relation to initiatives garnering constituents. Nationalist developments have worked in relation to such ill-formulated notions of inclusion and, as a result, have worked to obscure institutional homophobia and exclusion that persist in defining meaningful citizenship.

Today, those advocating for the restoration of a Hawaiian nation would do well to consider gender and sexual oppression seriously as we pursue cultural and political decolonization and self-determination. Therefore, attending to these issues (while engaging in other forms of political work) is crucial to the collective survival of Kanaka Maoli as a people. The party line of Hawaiian sovereign belonging continues to be interrupted by BLGTM Kanaka Maoli who urge for a more thorough engagement with a politics of decolonization. A tension in the meanings of Hawaiian cultural inclusion could continue to produce a space for critical self-reflexivity about the meanings of national belonging. Such a shift, in any case, is in keeping with the open-ended historical period we are currently living through in relation to Hawaiian conceptions as to the structure that nationhood should take. Critical issues of decolonization must be raised and explored to the fullest to render those possibilities in the supplest form of which they are capable. The challenge is in linking those issues to the ongoing struggle for decolonization—a task that belongs to the entire lāhui.

NOTES

I thank Joanne Barker, who has served as a supportive editor and encouraged this work. Mark Rifkin and Melissa Nelson, fellow contributors to this volume, served as invaluable interlocutors as we workshopped our essays together as a subgroup. Their critical feedback was most helpful. I also express my gratitude to Lisa Kahaleole Hall, Scott Morgensen, and Noenoe K. Silva, who each read earlier drafts of parts of this essay and generously offered supportive engagement. *Mahalo nui loa.*

1. Before the bill's passage, same-sex couples in the state had been allowed to form civil unions since 2012, and they had been able to access recognition for "reciprocal beneficiary relationships" since 1997.

2. See https://www.facebook.com/truealoha/info.

3. For important critiques of Human Rights Campaign, see Derrick Clifton, "What's Behind Criticisms of Those Red Equal Signs in Your Facebook Feed?" *Huffington Post*, March 29, 2013, http://www.huffingtonpost.com/derrick-clifton/human-rights -campaign-same-sex-marriage_b_2973131.html; Eugene Wolters, "Why You Should Stop Caring about the HRC and Those Little Red Equal Signs," *Critical Theory*, April 7, 2013: http://www.critical-theory.com/why-you-should-stop-caring-about-the-hrc-and -those-little-red-equal-signs.

4. The bill was first introduced to the Hawaii (the 50th state government doesn't use the diacritical mark in its official name) House and Senate, but the state legislature adjourned without voting on the measure. Hence, the governor, who reportedly was emboldened by the U.S. Supreme Court rulings in *Hollingsworth v. Perry* (overturning Proposition 8 in the State of California) and *United States v. Windsor* (overturning the federal Defense of Marriage Act) of June 26, 2013, decided to hold the legislative special session that fall.

5. As reported, all of the twelve states that have passed laws legalizing same-sex marriage also protect religious groups and clergy who do not want to solemnize or participate in same-sex weddings. "Some states that have passed legislation have gone even further. For example, gay marriage laws in Maryland and Connecticut include language allowing religiously affiliated groups that provide adoption, foster care and similar social services to refuse to serve same-sex couples, as long as they do not receive any state funds for the program in question. Furthermore, the gay marriage statutes in these two states, as well as in New Hampshire, Rhode Island and Vermont, allow religiously affiliated fraternal societies, such as the Knights of Columbus, to refuse to provide insurance or other services to members who are married to a same-sex partner": David Masci, "States That Allow Same-Sex Marriage Also Provide Protections for Religious Groups and Clergy Who Oppose It," November 20, 2013, http://www.pewresearch.org /fact-tank/2013/11/20/states-that-allow-same-sex-marriage-also-provide-protections -for-religious-groups-and-clergy-who-oppose-it.

6. *Baehr v. Lewin*, 852 P.2d 44 Haw. 1993.

7. As the case moved through the state courts, the passage of an amendment to the state constitution in 1998 allowed the state legislature to enact a ban on same-sex marriage, stating, "The legislature shall have the power to reserve marriage to opposite-sex couples." That amendment led to the dismissal of the case in 1999.

8. The Defense of Marriage Act references not only states, as it's often represented in media and public discourse, but also tribal nations and U.S. colonies. Section 2 (Powers Reserved to the States) reads, "No State, territory, or possession of the United States, or Indian tribe, shall be required to give effect to any public act, record, or judicial proceeding of any other State, territory, possession, or tribe respecting a relationship between persons of the same sex that is treated as a marriage under the laws of such other State, territory, possession, or tribe, or a right or claim arising from such relationship." Here one can see how the U.S. federal government's plenary power functions over Native governing entities (federally recognized tribes) and island territories (the Commonwealth of the Northern Mariana Islands, Guam, American Samoa, the U.S. Virgin Islands, and Puerto Rico). Although the U.S. Supreme Court struck down DOMA on June 26, 2013, it is unclear how tribally recognized marriages (as just one example) will translate outside of their sovereign borders to states that legalize same-sex marriage.

9. Hawaii Constitutional Amendment 2, 1998.

10. Here I use the term "heterosexism" to mark the privileging of heterosexuality. The term can also be used to describe prejudice, discrimination, and other forms of subjugation against same-sex couples and ways of intimate relating. The term "homophobia" is often used to describe the irrational fear of homosexuality, but I use it here more broadly to encompass the many ways people marginalize same-sex sexual practices, as well as bisexual, lesbian, and gay identities. Similarly, I use the term "biphobia" to mark discrimination and other forms of oppression that specifically targets people who are bisexual. The term "queer" in this chapter is not used in any disparaging way. In communities around the globe, people are reclaiming it since it originated as a demeaning label.

11. The translation for *māhū* is complicated. The *Hawaiian Dictionary* defines the term as "homosexual, of either sex" or a "hermaphrodite" (an intersexed subject). Māhū is currently used more typically to refer to a biological man who "behaves" like a woman as a third gender: Mary Kawena Pukui and Samuel H. Elbert, *Hawaiian Dictionary*, rev. ed. (Honolulu: University of Hawaii Press), 1986.

12. At the same time, a lot of mainstream non-Indigenous gay media was promoting tourism to Hawai'i and a romanticized touristic notion of Hawaiian tradition as "gay-friendly," without regard to sovereignty struggles and the ongoing nationalist contestation of U.S. authority there. The cover of *Advocate*, for example, featured two white men in each other's arms each wearing floral lei and sarongs around their waist with no shirts, "island-style."

13. For another look at questions of Indigenous tradition in relation to same-sex sexuality, see Joanne Barker, *Native Acts: Law Recognition and Cultural Authenticity* (Durham, NC: Duke University Press, 2011). Barker offers a brilliant account of the early debates of same-sex marriage within the Navajo Nation and Cherokee Nation. She focuses on the fraught politics of marriage and sexuality in relation to legal rights and notions of cultural authenticity within Native communities that potentially reproduce

the injustices of sexism and homophobia (as well as ethnocentrism and racism) and that define U.S. nationalism, as well as Native oppression. She further documents how the tribal legislation bans on and defenses of them affirm the discourses of U.S. nationalism especially in their Christian and politically conservative forms.

14. As Patrick Wolfe argues, "Settler colonies were (are) premised on the elimination of Native societies. The split tensing reflects a determinate feature of settler colonization. The colonizers come to stay-invasion is a structure not an event": Patrick Wolfe, "Settler Colonialism and the Elimination of the Native," *Journal of Genocide Research* 8, no. 4 (2006): 387. Settler colonial policies push for the destruction of Indigenous societies and then impose assimilation programs on those who survive the process of systematic extermination and removal and become minorities in their own homeland. Because settler colonialism "destroys to replace," it is "inherently eliminatory": Patrick Wolfe, *Settler Colonialism and the Transformation of Anthropology* (London: Continuum International, 1999), 2.

Bringing settler colonialism and queer politics together, Scott Morgensen provocatively demonstrates how white settler colonialism is a primary condition for the development of modern queer politics in the United States. He traces the relational distinctions of "Native" and "settler" that define the status of being "queer," presenting a "biopolitics of settler colonialism" in which the imagined disappearance of indigeneity ensures a progressive future for white settlers. Through his ethnography with Radical Faeries, Morgensen documents non-Natives' appropriation of the concepts of traditional gender and sexual diversity of Native nations as their own patrimony, an attempt to indigenize or otherwise root themselves in a way that naturalizes settler colonialism: Scott Lauria Morgensen, *Spaces between Us: Queer Settler Colonialism and Indigenous Decolonization* (Minneapolis: University of Minnesota Press, 2011).

Mark Rifkin also provides a rich study of U.S. settler colonialism in relation to Native sexual and gender expression. He explores the complex relationship between contested U.S. notions of normality and shifting forms of Native peoples' governance and self-representation. Rifkin demonstrates both how white American discourses of sexuality have included Native peoples in ways that degrade Indigenous social formations and how Native intellectuals have written back to reaffirm their peoples' sovereignty and self-determination: Mark Rifkin, *When Did Indians Become Straight? Kinship, the History of Sexuality, and Native Sovereignty* (Oxford: Oxford University Press, 2011).

15. Pukui and Elbert, *Hawaiian Dictionary*, 26, 74, 34.

16. Jocelyn Linnekin, *Sacred Queens and Women of Consequence: Rank, Gender, and Colonialism in the Hawaiian Islands* (Ann Arbor: The University of Michigan Press), 1990.

17. "Aikāne relationships are defined in multiple ways throughout time and include devoted friends as well as lovers. The term is ambiguous, given that it describes a close relationship between people of the same gender (e.g, two men or two women) that may or may not include sexual intimacy": ku'ualoha ho'omanawanui, *Voices of Fire: Reweaving the Literary Lei of Pele and Hiiaka* (Minneapolis: University of Minnesota Press, 2014), 135–42; Noenoe K. Silva, "Pele, Hiiaka, and Haumea: Women and Power in Two Hawaiian Mo'olelo," *Pacific Studies*, 30, nos. 1–2 (2007): 159–81;

John P. Charlot, "Pele and Hi'iaka: The Hawaiian-Language Newspaper Series," *Anthropose* 93 (1998): 55–75.

18. Although ethnographic references to the punalua concept specifically mention heterosexual examples—two women with the same man or two men with the same woman—it seems possible, given the prevalence of bisexuality, that two women could have also been with the same woman or two men with the same man.

19. Because of the formative work of Lilikalā Kame'eleihiwa, as well as of Noenoe Silva, we can now identify strong female roles within Hawaiian cosmological traditions and among deities and chiefs in Hawaiian society. Kame'eleihiwa uses her background knowledge in Hawaiian language, chant, song, and prayer to restore a lost genealogy of female gods to their place in the Hawaiian cosmos and history: see Lilikalā K. Kame'eleihiwa, *Na Wahine Kapu/Divine Hawaiian Women* (Honolulu: 'Ai Pohaku Press, 1996); Noenoe K. Silva, *Aloha Betrayed: Hawaiian Resistance to American Colonialism* (Durham, NC: Duke University Press, 2004).

20. Sally Merry, *Colonizing Hawai'i: The Cultural Power of Law* (Princeton, NJ: Princeton University Press, 2000).

21. Noenoe K. Silva, "Talking Back to Law and Empire: Hula in Hawaiian Language Literature in 1861," in *Law and Empire in the Pacific*, ed. Donald Brenneis and Sally Engle Merry (Santa Fe, NM: School for American Research, 2004), 36.

22. Merry, *Colonizing Hawai'i*, 255.

23. Merry, *Colonizing Hawai'i*, 255. See also Patricia Grimshaw, *Paths of Duty: American Missionary Wives in Nineteenth Century Hawaii* (Honolulu: University of Hawaii Press), 1989.

24. Merry, *Colonizing Hawai'i*, 230; Silva, *Aloha Betrayed*.

25. Jonathan Goldberg-Hiller has also written about the Hawai'i debates over same-sex marriage in the 1990s, which includes a rich examination of the work of Nā Mamo, along with the historical and rhetorical claims regarding "traditional marriage" in the Hawaiian context with regard to the notions of place, Indigenous sovereignty claims, tensions with Christian values, and implications for coalition politics: Jonathan Goldberg-Hiller, *The Limits to Union: Same-Sex Marriage and the Politics of Civil Rights* (Ann Arbor: University of Michigan Press, 2002). For another treatment of the same-sex marriage debates in Hawai'i, though not pertaining to the work of Nā Mamo, see Robert J. Morris, "Configuring the Bo(u)nds of Marriage: The Implications of Hawaiian Culture and Values for the Debate about Homogamy," *Yale Journal of Law and the Humanities* 8 (1996): 105–59.

26. Angelo Ragaza, "Sovereignty and Sexuality in Hawaii: Aikāne Nation," *Village Voice*, July 2, 1996, 12–13.

27. By acknowledging the power of genealogical precedent, however, I am not advocating for a transhistorical notion of sexual identities. In his work on the politics of contemporary South Asian queers, Nayan Shah has written about how the searching for an "Indigenous tradition" and forms of "reclaiming the past" raises epistemological questions about what constitutes history. He warns against the presumption that sexuality is a definable and universal—and trans-historical—activity and flags this as a problem in "recovering the past" for those hoping to secure their identities as "timeless": Nayan

Shah, "Sexuality, Identity, and the Uses of History," in *Q & A: Queer in Asian America*, eds. David Eng and Alice Horn (Philadelphia: Temple University Press, 1998), 141–56.

28. Susan Miller, "Between Nations," *Island Lifestyle*, January 1994, 22.

29. Miller, "Between Nations," *Island Lifestyle*, January 1994, 22.

30. Susan Miller, "Native Gays Help Leaders Redefine Hawaiian Nation," *Island Lifestyle*, February 1994, 6–10.

31. Miller, "Native Gays Help Leaders Redefine Hawaiian Nation," 6.

32. Miller, "Native Gays Help Leaders Redefine Hawaiian Nation," 6.

33. Miller, "Native Gays Help Leaders Redefine Hawaiian Nation," 6–7.

34. Miller, "Native Gays Help Leaders Redefine Hawaiian Nation," 6–7.

35. Miller, "Native Gays Help Leaders Redefine Hawaiian Nation," 7–8.

36. Miller, "Native Gays Help Leaders Redefine Hawaiian Nation," 9.

37. The group's constituents ratified the constitution on October 9, 1994, as noted on Bumpy Kanahele's website, http://bumpykanahele.com. For text of the constitution issued on January 16, 1995, see http://www.hawaii-nation.org/constitution.html.

38. Pōkā Laenui recounts this development as an offshoot of the Sovereignty Advisory Council that was formed by the State Legislature the year before and included organizational representatives or individuals charged with the mandate "to develop a plan to discuss and study the sovereignty issue." That council submitted a report to the State Legislature describing the events of the overthrow, and the unresolved political issues stemming from it, and made suggestions on the state's taking further action on the issue. It concluded that a plebiscite should be called asking the Native Hawaiian people residing in the state whether an election of delegates should be held to propose a form of Native Hawaiian governance: Pōkā Laenui, "A Brief Introduction to the 'Aha Hawai'i 'Ōiwi (AHO)," October 8, 2010, http://www.nhconvention.org.

39. Hawaiian Sovereignty Advisory Commission, "Final Report," Honolulu, February 18, 1994, 2.

40. It did admit, however, that the process was inadequate to constitute a full expression of the rights of self-determination under international law: Hawaiian Sovereignty Elections Council, "Position on Plebiscite," January 1995, Anthony Castanha, "The Hawaiian Sovereignty Movement: Roles of and Impacts on Non-Hawaiians," August 1996, http://www.hookele.com/non-hawaiians/chapter3.html. The specific question that was eventually presented to Hawaiian voters by 1996 (in balloting done by mail) was, "Shall the Hawaiian people elect delegates to propose a Native Hawaiian government?" The vote was overwhelmingly in favor of such an election. The Ninth U.S. Circuit Court of Appeals lifted a temporary stay order on September 11, 1996, that cleared the way for the release of the voting results. The announcement of the outcome was delayed three times by a series of legal challenges, one of which was filed by Harold Rice, who later challenged Hawaiian-only voting in state elections for trustees to the Office of Hawaiian Affairs in a case that went before the U.S. Supreme Court (*Rice v. Cayetano*). In the case of the state "plebiscite" by the Hawaiian Sovereign Elections Council, Federal District Judge David Ezra ruled that the results could be released in the public interest and that they would not impede his ability to rule on the constitutional issues: See Carey Goldberg, "Native Hawaiians Vote in Referendum on Creating an Ethnic Government," *New York*

Times, July 23, 1996, http://www.nytimes.com/1996/07/23/us/native-hawaiians-vote
-in-referendum-on-creating-an-ethnic-government.html?pagewanted=all&src=pm.
See also "73 Percent Say Yes to Hawaiian Sovereignty: Supporters Say the Plebiscite
Is an Important Step toward a Native Hawaiian Government," *Honolulu Star-Bulletin*,
September 12, 1996, 1. For an account of the commission's work, see Anthony Castanha,
"A History of the Hawaiian Sovereignty Movement," in *The Hawaiian Sovereignty Move-
ment: Roles of and Impacts on Non-Hawaiians*, August 1996, http://www.hookele.com
/non-hawaiians/chapter3.html#fn25.

41. Emphasis added. The statement was reiterated by Noenoe Silva at a public event
titled Ka Leʻa O Ke Ola: A Forum on Kanaka Maoli Culture, Sexuality, and Spirituality that was sponsored by the American Friends Service Committee in 1998. The
forum was held at the Center for Hawaiian Studies of the University of Hawaiʻi (UH),
Mānoa. Co-sponsors of the forum included Nā Mamo o Hawaiʻi, the Marriage Project
Hawaiʻi, the Pacific Families Network, and a variety of UH organizations and programs,
including the Queer Student Union, the Center for Hawaiian Studies, Kuaʻana Student
Services, the Task Force on Sexual Orientation, and the Student Equity, Excellence, and
Diversity Office.

42. Here I purposefully use the term "houseless," since in Hawaiian vernacular it is
a political preference of the movement-affiliated Kanaka Maoli, which reminds people
that they are already at home, as in "homeland."

43. Political deferral for bisexual, lesbian, and gay rights has been a prominent feature
within many nationalist struggles.

44. According to kuʻualoha hoʻomanawanui, she co-administers True Aloha, which
was started by Trisha Kēhaulani Watson Sproat. They launched the Facebook page
to take a stand as straight allies, "especially when the ignorant conservative Christian
Kanaka started to try and re-define aloha in Christian-rooted ways": personal correspondence via email, April 23, 2015.

45. kuʻualoha hoʻomanawanui, "Living True Aloha," October 30, 2013, http://hawaii
independent.net/story/living-true-aloha.

46. To view the commercial, see https://www.youtube.com/watch?v=3yqMNt
CgxZw.

47. hoʻomanawanui, "Living True Aloha."

48. See https://www.facebook.com/truealoha/info.

49. Handy and Pukui, *The Polynesian Family System in Kaʻu, Hawaiʻi* (Rutland, VT:
Charles E. Tuttle Company, 1972), 56.

50. Pukui, *Nana I Ke Kumu: Look to the Source*, Volume 2 (Honolulu: Hui
Hanai 1972), 167.

51. Today, we see how same-sex marriage itself has overtaken broader queer political
organizing, and Hawaiʻi is no exception. As Dean Spade and Craig Willse argue, "Same-
sex marriage advocacy has accomplished an amazing feat—it has made being anti-
homophobic synonymous with being pro-marriage. It has drowned out centuries of
critical thinking and activism against the racialized, colonial, and patriarchal processes
of state regulation of family and gender through marriage": Dean Spade and Craig
Willse, "Marriage Will Never Set Us Free," Organizing Upgrade, September 6, 2013,

http://www.organizingupgrade.com/index.php/modules-menu/beyond-capitalism
/item/1002-marriage-will-never-set-us-free.

It is important to highlight the importance of queer critique in challenging these state logics. I am inspired by the work of Against Equality, an online archive and publishing and arts collective that focuses on critiquing mainstream gay and lesbian politics. As its mission statement states, "The collective is committed to dislodging the centrality of equality rhetoric and challenging the demand for inclusion in the institution of marriage, as well as the two other prongs of the 'holy trinity': the US military, and the prison industrial complex via hate crimes legislation": see http://www.againstequality .org. I should add that the ways the U.S. military and the prison-industrial complex pervade the everyday lives of Hawaiians needs more scholarly and political attention.

For another look at the impact of the marriage equality movement on queer politics, including the issue of normalization, see Mary Bernstein and Verta Taylor, eds., *The Marrying Kind? Debating Same-Sex Marriage within the Lesbian and Gay Movement* (Minneapolis: The University of Minnesota Press), 2013.

52. See Merry, *Colonizing Hawai'i*; Jonathan Kay Kamakawiwo'ole Osorio, *Dismembering Lāhui: A History of the Hawaiian Nation to 1887* (Honolulu: The University of Hawaii Press, 2002), 11, 13.

53. In all fairness, this may simply be because the fiftieth state governor called for a special session, providing little lead time for hearings, which moved very rapidly.

2

RETURN TO "THE UPRISING AT BEAUTIFUL MOUNTAIN IN 1913"

Marriage and Sexuality in the Making of the Modern Navajo Nation

JENNIFER NEZ DENETDALE

In 2010, the *Gallup Independent*, a border-town newspaper, published a brief article on the so-called Navajo Uprising at Beautiful Mountain in 1913.[1] The narrative recounts how the Indian agent at the Shiprock agency in the northeastern region of the Navajo reservation discovered that a Diné man named Hatalii Yazi, or Little Singer, was a polygamist. Following federal Indian mandates that outlawed Native traditional practices, the Indian agent was intent on forcing his Navajo wards to comply. The Indian agent sent his Navajo policemen to Beautiful Mountain, approximately fifty miles from Shiprock, to arrest Little Singer, and when the men discovered his absence, they brought his three wives and their children into the agency. Little Singer and his male relatives traveled to Shiprock to retrieve their women and instead became embroiled in a conflict with the authorities. After the confrontation, Little Singer and his kin fled with the women and children back to their homes at Beautiful Mountain. The Indian agent had been away. When he returned and learned about the events and the women's escape, he insisted that the Navajo men be taught to abide by American law and order.

The article, published in 2010, includes a photograph of Fort Wingate, which had been established in Navajo territory to announce American claims to the Southwest in the nineteenth century. According to the caption, the fort was intended to provide defense for Americans and New Mexicans against Navajo "marauders" and closed in 1912, the year before the Navajo "revolt" in 1913. Perhaps if the fort had stayed open, the article intimates, then Navajos might not have dared to rebel. Not surprisingly, the accompanying story reiterates frontier accounts of white settlers' fears about Indigenous violence, even though by the late nineteenth century Indigenous peoples had been reduced to dependence on the largesse of the U.S. government. Histories of the United States reinscribe American narratives as exceptional when those narratives present the treatment of and relationships to Indigenous peoples as bastions of democracy, freedom, and cultural diversity, which the U.S. then generously extends to Indigenous peoples such as the Navajos. In her study of the United States as empire, Amy Kaplan argues that the United States legitimizes its domain by disseminating its cultural values through literature and travel writing to reinforce Manifest Destiny through the domestication of the foreign.[2] In much the same way, discursive practices present the United States as benevolent in its claims to the Southwest. In these narratives about the peaceful takeover of the Southwest from Mexico, Navajos are presented as the savage and unruly ones who must know the authority of the United States for peace to reign in the region. After the Americans destroyed Navajo military power in 1863, Navajos became their charges who had to be brought into the modern world of the early twentieth century. Histories of Navajos, then, are written within the framework of what is called "New Indian history" and focus on the steady and peaceful incorporation of the Navajo into the U.S. polity; at the same time, they offer that under colonial assaults, Navajos have managed to retain a significant amount of cultural tradition. Indeed, it is the retention of culture that distinguishes tribal peoples such as the Navajo from their non-Indian counterparts and supports Native peoples' claims to sovereignty status in relation to the United States even as indigenous peoples continue to insist that their claims rests on their presence on lands since creation.[3]

The uprising at Beautiful Mountain has interested Navajo studies scholars, many of them schooled in American historiography, who have mostly presented it as an isolated moment of rebellion in a landscape of otherwise peaceful coexistence with whites. This sort of reading of Navajo rebellion points to the ongoing project of incorporating Navajos into the American cultural and political body by emphasizing points of contact between the United States and Navajos, centering Native subjects' responses to colonial invasions and assaults as evidence of Native resiliency and agency and as a process of learning how to communicate across cultures peacefully.[4] American-centered narratives also focus on the processes through which Navajos were incorporated into the United States as citizens as a movement from "traditional" to "modern," but always with retention of Navajo cultural markers. If there were points of violence, chaos, resistance, defiance, and miscommunications in these white-Navajo relationships, then sympathetic, well-intentioned whites worked with Navajo "cultural brokers" and together they brought about a measure of understanding and renewed harmony across race. Further, a focus on "race" as the center for analysis elides indigenous peoples' efforts to realize self-determination as citizens of their own, distinctive tribal nations.[5] These American narratives, termed "New Indian history," present the United States as an exceptional nation-state that shows the rest of the world the meaning of freedom, liberty, and democracy.[6]

New Indian histories sanitize and make benign the history of U.S. Indigenous peoples, thereby making it difficult for Indigenous peoples' grievances against the United States to be taken seriously. Further, New Indian history has disguised federal Indian policies as assimilation rather than part of a history of genocidal practices that was and is intended to eliminate them as Indigenous peoples.[7] Angela Cavender Wilson (now known as Waziyatawin) takes many Indigenous studies scholars to task for their failure to interrogate settler colonialism as the source of Native nations' and peoples' struggles. She writes, "Many [scholars] have assisted in our colonization and the perpetuation of our oppression in myriad ways, including celebrating the myth of Manifest Destiny, making light of the genocide and terrorism experienced by our people, and holding firm to a progressive notion of history that forever locks our people's past and our 'primitive' existence into a hierarchy where we occupy the bottom."[8]

New Indian history is a construction of the U.S. past, present, and future that sustains the structures of violence that shape Native nations, communities, and families. Crucial to interrogating colonial constructions—as discursive practices and materially—is to become critically conscious of how federal Indian policies such as the Courts of Indian Offenses of 1883 and the mandate to inculcate Indigenous children with American values are actually policies of ethnic cleansing that have shaped our lives as Indigenous and Diné people.[9] Generations of exposure of Indigenous children to Western education have resulted in an uncritical acceptance of Indigenous-U.S. relations as multicultural narratives that purport to have incorporated Indigenous peoples successfully as American citizens. Thus, the institutions of American education, the legal system, and others have limited our visions of what is possible in realizing sovereignty, for as Waziyatawin argues, as Indigenous peoples "we have difficulty imagining living in a state of freedom. This is perhaps the most profound impact of colonialism in our lives. It reveals a limitation in thinking so severe that it prevents us from reclaiming our inherent rights as Indigenous Peoples of this land, even in our dreams."[10] In line with Waziyatawin's definition of colonialism, Patrick Wolfe's explication of the logics of settler colonialism, which refers to the erection of a new colonial society on an expropriated land base, indicates how the elimination of the Native is systemic, and that colonial invasion "is a structure not an event," indicating that colonialism is ongoing.[11] Waziyatawin's and Wolfe's scholarship illuminates the workings of American colonialism on the Diné Nation and the projects to eliminate Diné by destroying all facets of Diné life that did not conform to the American values of inclusion and diversity. Further, Eve Tuck and K. Wayne Yang sustain the stance of critical Indigenous studies that our project is to reclaim lands and territories and that all settler colonial projects intend to continue practices of dispossession and disenfranchisement.[12] More and more, Indigenous scholarship is addressing specifically how settler colonialism has transformed gender in our tribal societies, and indigenous feminisms and queer indigenous studies illuminate how it has reconfigured tribal nations and societies as heterosexual patriarchies. Indigenous feminist and queer analysis demonstrates how the spaces of the domestic and intimate are also sites of colonial surveillance and control, thereby gendering settler colonialism.

Decolonizing Indigenous nations and communities requires scrutinizing the intersections of settler colonialism, tribal nations, and gender because every facet of Navajo life came under the purview of federal policy makers, including the domestic sphere. Decolonization necessarily employs gender as a category of analysis if Indigenous nations are ever to return to their own traditional principles as their foundations. This chapter, then, revisits the uprising at Beautiful Mountain through the lens of decolonization and anticolonial struggles and draws on the intersections of settler colonialism, Indigenous feminist theorizing, and queer Indigenous theorizing to illuminate the processes by which our tribal nations have become heteronormative patriarchies, thereby raising questions about how we as indigenous peoples can move in the direction of tribal sovereignty and self-determination that insist on the participation of all of our citizens.[13] As Ann Laura Stoler argues, constructs of the imaginary in which intellectualism is used to validate and legitimize nations and communities built on the asymmetries of race, class, and gender have been a crucial part of the colonial project; these processes profoundly transformed Indigenous societies in ways that have undermined women's places in their societies, devalued their authority, and rendered almost invisible gender roles beyond the heterosexual. Stoler points out that colonial states had an investment in a sentimental education, in the rearing of the young, and in affective politics: "Colonial regimes policed the cultural protocols and competencies that bounded their 'interior frontiers' and in monitoring those boundaries they produced penal and pedagogic institutions that were often indistinguishable—orphanages, workhouses, orphan trains, boarding schools, children's agricultural colonies—to rescue young citizens and subjects in the making."[14] Further, queer Native studies illuminates the processes through which Native peoples naturalize heterosexuality and patriarchy so that we have seemingly forgotten different forms of relating to one another across gender, marriage, and sexuality.[15]

The uprising at Beautiful Mountain provides an example of how federal Indian policies are intended to eliminate the Diné as Diné by transforming the Navajo nation into a heterosexual patriarchy, even as the Navajo remain matrilineal and LGBTQ people assert k'é as the foundation by which they belong to their people and the land. K'é is the traditional Navajo concept of how we belong to relate to each other based on kinship. We are all related to each other and those relationships require us as Diné to treat each other with respect. In 1863, in the aftermath of the U.S. pacification of the Diné—when they were no longer seen as a physical threat—the war on them shifted to domestic, spiritual, and political terrains. The so-called uprising offers an opportunity to understand the early reservation period as a site of ongoing resistance and challenges to American colonialism, for in fact, on Navajo and Hopi lands, Indian agents were often met with physical resistance from Navajo and Hopi who refused American ideology around family, children, marriage, sexuality, spirituality, and education. Through American educational, cultural, and legal institutions, the Diné were transformed into citizens of both the United States and tribal nations as heteronormative nuclear family units in which Diné citizens appeared to differ only slightly from their non-Indian American counterparts. Further, as my analysis of the Beautiful Mountain incident will reveal, modern settler nations such as the United States value only those aspects of Indigenous knowledge, culture, and practice that do not threaten the structure of heteronormative patriarchy; simultaneously, settler nations such as the United States distance themselves from their genocidal pasts with Indigenous peoples.[16] My examination also illuminates how

American multicultural narratives elide the transformation of Diné and their practices of polygamy, once deemed "traditional," to positions as always heterosexual and monogamous. These declarations of a heterosexual nation are found in tribal resolutions across several decades and were sanctioned again in the passage of the Diné Marriage Act in 2005.[17]

As I examine the processes by which Indigenous peoples were incorporated into the settler nation that is the United States, critical questions emerge about how the Diné have embraced a framework that conflates nation with family, marriage, and sexuality to normalize heteropatriarchy. Importantly, as tribal nations grapple with the relationships among modernity, nation, and tradition, the past is often invoked in ways that render Native traditions as fixed in an authentic past; they are then used as a standard against which to measure ourselves.[18] As I have shown in earlier publications, it becomes difficult to transform our nation and communities and move toward justice when we consistently reinscribe colonial values of heteronormativity, because we then fail to see how cultural traditions have shifted in ways that allow for some of our citizens to belong less than others.[19] For example, as Deborah Miranda, Joanne Barker, Scott Morgensen, and Mark Rifkin show, the assimilation of Indigenous peoples into the U.S. polity is actually the workings of biopolitics that transformed Indigenous peoples into nuclear families that privileged heteropatriarchy.[20] Further, re-creating the Diné as a heteropatriarchy depended on the use of brutality and violence by the colonial authorities, for, as Morgensen argues, "The terrorizing sexual colonization of Native peoples was a historical root of the biopolitics of modern sexuality in the United States."[21] In particular, Barker's analysis of Native tradition and authenticity shows how tribal nations' responses to contemporary issues around family, gender, marriage, and sexuality have been influenced by static notions of culture and authenticity so that we often do not behave to one another in a responsible or ethical manner. As Barker asserts, "Healthy, vibrant Native nations and communities—and meaningfully rich traditional teachings and practices—cannot result from social and interpersonal relations based on disrespect, indifference, discrimination, hate and violence."[22]

The transformation of the Diné into seemingly willing citizens not only of the United States but also of their native nation occurred through institutions that regulated and surveilled their traditional practices in arenas that ranged from governance and education to health, marriage, and sexuality.[23] Although Indigenous resistance or challenge to colonial authority is most often represented as moments in isolation, in fact Indigenous peoples continued to challenge colonial authorities. As Philip Deloria observes, in the late nineteenth century, after Indigenous peoples had been militarily defeated and removed to reservations, Indian resistance came to be categorized as "uprisings," "rebellions," and "outbreaks," which reflected "a fear of Indian people escaping the spatial, economic, political, social, and military restrictions placed on them by the reservation regime."[24] Diné often refused to comply with American federal policies intended to reproduce them as willing citizens of the state, and the narrative of the uprising at Beautiful Mountain exposes both the resistance against American insistence that Diné would readily acquiesce to white assumptions about citizenship, property, and how a nation should be gendered and the ways in which American exceptionalism is reinscribed as the inevitable incorporation into the American body.[25] Further, an examination of the uprising opens space to consider how Navajo traditional practices around family, marriage, and sexuality have been transformed under colonialism in ways that naturalize the heteropatriarchy of nationhood.

The Narrative of the Uprising

Several articles and references in book chapters published on the uprising position the episode as an isolated point of Navajo resistance to colonial rule amid what is often presented as an era of relative stability. In 1863, Navajos, like many other indigenous people who stood in the way of white American settlement on their lands and with news of possible valuable natural resources in their territories, were subjugated by the American military and removed to a reservation, the Bosque Redondo, far from their homeland.[26] At the Bosque Redondo prison camp from 1863 to 1868, Navajo prisoners were subjected to American policies intended to transform them into the image of White American citizens. All aspects of Navajo life came under American scrutiny, from their justice and governance systems to the domestic. These efforts, now known as ethnic cleansing, coerced Navajos into conformity with American heterosexuality, in which patriarchy was privileged. Indeed, the Native Queer studies scholar Mark Rifkin argues that the Indian Reorganization Act was introduced in 1934 to end the federal assault on Native traditions, but the act in fact continued to structure Native lives into forms and institutions acceptable to white American sensibilities.[27] The 1913 episode, then, can be seen as part of the process of shaping the conditions of Navajo political formations and practices such as marriage, sexuality, and family.

According to the standard narrative, Navajo began to enter modernity only with John Collier's draconian 1930s and 40s policies to reduce their livestock by 50 percent, thus forcing them into a wage economy.[28] After 1863, the Diné came under American colonial rule and saw their freedoms and autonomy almost completely destroyed. From the earliest declarations of war on the Diné and then to more subtle kinds of terrorism, General James Carleton's call to force Navajo conformity to American law and order echoes across a hundred years of federal Indian mandates.[29] In 1863, Carleton declared, "[The Diné] understand the direct application of force as law. If its application be removed, that moment they become lawless. . . . The purpose now is never to relax the application of force with a people that can no more be trusted than you can trust the wolves that run through the mountains."[30] It was at the Bosque Redondo reservation that the Diné began to experience the erosion and disappearance of their ways of life, including their philosophies and customs around family, marriage, and sexuality. Federal officials extinguished the traditional leaders' authority and power; they forced the leaders to answer to them and attempted to transform the Diné from a pastoral people with a flexible political system into village-dwelling, self-sustaining people organized into nuclear households with a man as the head.[31] Navajo traditional leaders were expected to enforce established Anglo-American forms of criminal law. Seven criminal offenses—murder, theft, absence from or refusal to work, destruction or loss of tools, destruction of the reservation's trees or farm produce, the missing of curfews, and absence from the reservation without permission—were outlined for the Diné and punishable by fines, hanging, whipping, imprisonment, and hard labor.[32] Raymond Austin notes, "Although some military officers expressed reservations about applying Anglo-American laws of punishment to the Navajo prisoners, they nonetheless saw it as imperative to the overall process of civilizing the Navajo people."[33]

The Indian Offenses Act adopted by the federal government in 1883 also applied to Navajos and had two significant impacts: (1) it authorized the federal government to take jurisdiction over major crimes in Indian Country; and (2) it criminalized Indigenous ceremonies, traditions, and the speaking of Indigenous languages. Thus, given the provisions in the Treaty of 1868 and the Indian Offenses Act, Indian agents, educators, missionaries, and others were intent on eradicating any and all Navajo thought and practices that did not conform to American values. Navajos and other Natives often challenged U.S. authority over them, and the uprising at Beautiful Mountain was but one of several events in which Navajos and Hopis challenged U.S. authority in the early twentieth century. As Indigenous studies scholars have demonstrated, a crucial part of the process of "civilizing" Native peoples included the use of terrorizing violence, which acted as a mode of social control by subjecting Navajo society to the new moral order. Transforming Navajos from people enmeshed within a matrilineal system that included polygamy and recognized genders beyond the binaries of feminine and masculine into American citizens required force and coercion. As Deborah Miranda has proved, sexual violence historically has been integral in colonial projects in which the imposition of European gender relationships on Native communities has been central to the remaking of our nations and communities. U.S. federal officials and other policy makers reshaped the domestic and intimate spaces of Navajo so that they conformed to American national expectations.[34]

In 1913, William T. Shelton, also known as Nat'aani Nez (Tall Leader), the Indian agent at Shiprock, New Mexico, learned from one of his Navajo policemen that another Navajo, Little Singer, had three wives. Reportedly, the Navajo who divulged the information to Shelton had been involved in a dispute with Little Singer. Shelton was one of those zealous government officials who was determined to stamp out all Indigenous customs and practices that did not conform to U.S. ideology about family, marriage and sexuality. Previously, Shelton had reacted quickly and with force when he saw any signs of Navajo resistance. For example, in 1907, following reports that the medicine man Ba'áliilii and his followers were stirring up trouble in Aneth, Utah, and whites feared an imminent Navajo uprising, Shelton called in the U.S. Cavalry. J. Lee Correll characterizes Shelton as a "puritanical disciplinarian who would tolerate no opposition to his arbitrary and autocratic methods."[35]

According to Davidson McKibbin's recounting of the 1913 incident, when Shelton discovered that Little Singer had three wives, he "order[ed] an agency policeman, a Navaho, to bring in the four for questioning. . . . [Shelton] found himself with [the] three wives but no husband. The policeman couldn't locate the husband, but the man's father came into Shiprock and told Shelton that he would bring in his son for questioning." On the morning of September 17, while Shelton was in Durango, Colorado, on a horse-stealing case involving Indians from his reservation, eleven Indians, including the husband of the three women, rode into the agency armed with revolvers and rifles. They threatened the Indian policemen, located the women, thrust aside school employees who tried to talk to them, and drew their weapons in a threatening manner, frightening women and children. One Indian policeman was hit on the head with a quirt. They then galloped to a nearby trading post, where the white traders talked them out of further violence.[36]

Incensed at the display of nonconformity, Shelton immediately wired his superior for support and demanded that the men be arrested and punished for their criminal behavior. McKibbin notes that Shelton's first report presented the Navajo men as violent desperados who were incapable of reason.[37]

Local and regional newspapers quickly picked up the story and played to whites' fears about Navajo violence. In response to the exaggerated newspaper accounts, Father Anselm Weber, a Franciscan priest who had lived among the Navajos for at least two decades, responded with his own report, titled, "Navajos on the Warpath?"[38] A longtime advocate of Navajos who worked tirelessly to secure land for Navajos who had returned to traditional residences that fell outside the original 1868 treaty reservation, Weber believed that settling Navajos into communities rather than living in extended family units scattered across their homeland would lead to their conversion to Catholicism.[39]

In an account of the incident he wrote in his journal in January 1914, and of which a revised account was published in 1919, Weber ridiculed depictions of Navajo resistance that emerged in national and local newspapers. He wrote,

> Many blood-curdling accounts about the Navajo "uprising" were published of late in the papers of the country. Fifteen hundred strong—thus ran the reports—armed with the latest high-power guns, well supplied with ammunition and food for the winter, they were defying the U.S. Government in their natural stronghold on top of Beautiful Mountain, N.M. They had threatened to raid the Shiprock Agency, to burn the Agency saw mill, and to kill the Indian traders—so the papers stated—they were charged—in the press—with murder, larceny, jail-breaking, polygamy, rioting, assault: women had taken refuge at the Agency to protect themselves against the brutality of their husbands, etc.

Newspaper accounts also claimed that once the men had rescued the women and fled the agency, they "had a victory dance and when word of this became public, there was an outcry from people, including residents of Gallup, for the U.S. Army to take action."[40]

Father Weber conjures up all of the images of warlike savage Indians who, if unrestrained, will attack, scalp, and kill white settlers and rape the white women. The cited number of 1,500 Navajos involved in the revolt was later called an exaggeration. Weber then gives his purpose for putting his fingers to the typewriter: "To vindicate the good name of the Navajo tribe against false and grossly exaggerated reports, I have decided to place the facts before the readers of your esteemed paper." Weber goes on to describe the assistance he provided to the Navajo men, whom he successfully persuaded to give themselves up to American authorities.

Even though Navajo military might had been destroyed by the end of 1863 and more than ten thousand Navajos were subjected to U.S. violence so thoroughly that the experience remains in the collective Navajo memory to the present, in the early twentieth century federal officials and New Mexican settlers continued to raise the specter of violent Navajos who could rampage at any moment. Certainly, Shelton's first telegrams to Washington, DC, warned of a Navajo insurrection and the need to punish the "recalcitrant" Navajos as a lesson to others who might be considering rebellion. The power of the discourse of Indian violence and the threat to white settlement continued to influence how Native peoples would be treated into the early twentieth century. As Deloria notes, expectations of Indian violence shifted after the massacre at Wounded Knee in 1893 and gave way to expectations of a "new, rebellious brand of Indian warfare—the outbreak."[41] "Outbreak," "rebellion," and "uprising," which became key words in representing Indian violence, suggest how U.S. colonial administrators negotiated the period in which they sought to exert complete control over Native peoples: "uprising" reflects the colonial power's fear that Navajos were escaping the "spatial, economic, political, social, and military restrictions placed on them by the reservation regime" by positioning them as "a pocket of stubbornness in the midst of the sweep of the American empire" and thereby providing yet another opportunity to re-create the structures to regulate and surveillance them.[42]

Once Shelton issued a warrant for eleven Navajo men, including Little Singer and his father, General Scott traveled from El Paso, Texas, to Gallup, New Mexico, where he met 380 soldiers detailed from Fort Robinson, Nebraska. Father Weber and the Navajo leaders Chee Dodge and Frank Walker met with the offending Navajo men several times. In his brief narrative of the episode, Peter Iverson notes several incidents of Navajo rebellion as part of the early reservation period and interprets them as Navajo responses to adaptation and incorporation of American ways. Of the men who intervened in the affair to bring about a peaceful resolution, Iverson asserts, the Indian agents were the instigators while the "heroes" were Chee Dodge and Weber.[43] Weber, Dodge, and Walker attended a ceremony because they expected the Navajo men they were seeking to be present. Weber estimated that at least two thousand Navajos were in attendance, including Little Singer, who was one of the dancers. Weber references an instance in which Chee Dodge gave a "splendid speech against polygamy and against such occurrences as had happened at Shiprock."[44] Of course, most likely because of his position as a leader recognized by the United States and as a man of considerable wealth, little or no attention is paid to the fact that Dodge himself was a polygamist. In a biographical essay, the Navajo studies scholar David Brugge notes that Dodge was married to eight Navajo women and had at least six children. Brugge explains to readers that Dodge's polygamist practices were within Navajo standards for marriage, for at least six of the women were either sisters or related by clan.[45] One of his daughters, Annie Dodge Wauneka, was one of the few women elected to the Tribal Council, on which she served for more than a decade.[46]

After several weeks, and with the interventions by Father Weber and Navajo leaders recognized by the federal government, the eleven Navajo men were compelled to give themselves up to American justice and be tried in Santa Fe. The men were charged with a number of infractions, including horse stealing and rioting. At issue was the Navajo men's refusal to submit to the Indian agent's authority. Just as the Lakota learned from Wounded Knee that the use of force would be absolute if they ever again resisted American authority, the Navajos were assured of the American potential for violence toward them. In their efforts to "reason" with the resistant Navajos, American colonial authorities raised the specter of the 1863 war on the Navajos. Further, the Navajo leaders who worked with Weber to bring about a peaceful resolution called for restraint and pointed to the all-out war on Navajos in the midnineteenth century.

As the colonial authorities consulted with one another about how to deal with Little Singer and his men, they believed that Navajos should not be allowed to challenge or resist their laws or policies. For example, Weber recalled an incident in 1905 in which the Indian agent Reuben Perry learned about a Navajo man who was accused of an attempted rape that was taken care of according to Navajo justice. When Perry insisted that the matter be tended to through American justice, the Navajo men forced him to accept their terms. After being forced to agree, Perry reported feeling "overcome by the fear that the Indians were lying in wait for him and would shoot him from their hiding places."[47] In an effort to understand what had transpired between himself and the Navajo men, Perry consulted with other White American authorities and Navajo leaders acknowledged by the federal government. "He realized that he would have to teach these Indians a lesson or give up his office," according to Weber.[48] Weber added his own thoughts on possible Navajo rebellion if Perry's authority was subverted: "It would work for our good if Mr. Perry's authority were upheld. The agent must demonstrate to the Indians that the government and the army stood behind him and upheld his honor; otherwise the orderly relations on this reservation would be at an end; otherwise everything would be in an uproar."[49] Several years later, in 1913, Shelton would also be determined to remind Navajos that they must submit to American law and order.

In response to Shelton's insistence that the Indians respect the authority of the American colonial state, Brigadier-General Hugh L. Scott arrived in Gallup from Fort Bliss, in El Paso, Texas, where he was met by U.S. troops from Fort Robinson, Nebraska. Scott met with two Franciscan priests and Navajo leaders, including Dodge, all of whom warned him that sight of the U.S. Army could cause a "possible outbreak." Scott reassured the concerned men that "the troops would be employed merely to point out to the Navahos the intent of the government," and "Scott intended no trouble, but wanted the Indians who had refused to surrender to note that the government meant business."[50] Scott parlayed with the "recalcitrant" Indians for two days and even shared Thanksgiving dinner with them (mutton was substituted for turkey). At different times, the men insisted that they had done nothing wrong and that Shelton was harsh and mean-spirited. They explained their positions regarding the women. They had gone into the agency hoping to meet with Shelton and especially to look into the welfare of the women and children. They aired their grievances and charged that the policemen took sexual liberties with female prisoners. They also complained that the Indian agent often threatened them and took them prisoner for the slightest infractions, and that prisoners often stayed a year and provided labor for Shelton's school or in his garden or farm. Indeed, in his narrative, Weber transmitted the Navajo men's outrage at Shelton's use of them as slave labor and, in another section, made positive remarks about Shelton's efforts to make the agency successful: "We spent the afternoon in seeing and admiring the magnificent school-plant at Shiprock, the ideal garden, the school—and stock farm. We also visited the irrigation project in course [sic] of construction which will irrigate a large area of land. Shiprock is a monument to the ability and energy of Mr. Shelton, its founder and up-builder."[51] The Navajos' valid complaints about being used as slave labor and the sexual abuse of their women by Shelton's staff is therefore silenced and placed outside legal and cultural protections when Weber lauds the Indian agent's prowess at making a previously barren place yield fruit.[52]

To speak on their behalf, the Navajo men selected Bizhoshi Biyi', a son of Bizhoshi ("Bizhoshi Biyi'" translates as "Bizhoshi's son"), who then related to Scott the list of events that had led to the men being pursued by Shelton and then by the U.S. Army. Scott expressed concern but was adamant that the men acquiesce to American authority. He used threats that brought forth images of the Long Walk and incarceration at the Bosque Redondo. To the assembled Navajos he said, "I have got over three hundred soldiers out there; I do not want them to come here. They will not come unless I call them; I don't want to call them; I don't want to fight you. Some of my soldiers have never seen an Indian; they would not know you from my friend Charley Mitchell here; they might kill innocent people. They would not know a man from a woman; they might kill some of your women and children."[53] Scott pressed the Navajo men about the cost of continued resistance by asking them how much they valued their women and children. General Scott repeated the official American point of view: "They had a perfect right to go to Shiprock and see Mr. Shelton about those women prisoners, but that it had been very wrong to take them away as they had done. Mr. Shelton represented the U.S. Government; they might like him or they might not like him, but as long as he was their Agent, they had to obey him as the representative of the Government."[54] He went on to explain to the men the "absolute necessity of (American) law" for their protection and for peace.[55] Under the threat of violence toward their families, women, and children, the men agreed to surrender. They beseeched Weber and the Navajo leaders to accompany them to Santa Fe, where they were to stand trial. Nine of the men were tried for rioting. The U.S. attorney refused to issue a warrant for polygamy against Little Singer. Weber noted, "[The U.S. attorney] was of the opinion that the Indians ought to be educated to a certain standard of morality before being prosecuted in the courts for such offenses." Because of issues related to the logistics and costs of returning to Santa Fe and to avoid having to wait months for another court hearing, the Navajo men agreed to plead guilty to the charge of rioting.

After hearing from Weber and Dodge, who spoke on behalf of the prisoners, the judge lectured the guilty men for approximately thirty minutes, saying, "If they [the Indians] obeyed the law, all white people would be their friends and help them; if they disobeyed the law, they would have to be punished. They had been right in some things and wrong in others: they had had a perfect right to go and see Mr. Shelton about the women prisoners. Every man, white, red or black, had a right to protect his family."[56] The judge then went to the crux of the matter: the men should not have taken away Shelton's prisoners, and they should have surrendered immediately to the military. He then delivered the sentences: two of the men, Little Singer and Niduhullin Binalli, were sentenced to serve thirty days in a Gallup jail (Binalli was sentenced for having quirted the policeman while reacquiring the women). The other five men were sentenced to serve ten days in the Gallup jail.

After their sentencing, according to Weber, the Navajo men were elated at the judiciousness of the American justice system, and before departing for their jail cells in Gallup, they went to the judge and shook his hand. Weber, like the U.S. attorney and the judge, was of the opinion that it did no good to punish Indians for polygamy because they were untutored in the ways of civility and thus could not understand the gravity of their transgressions. Like the other authorities who meted out American values, Weber believed that constant lectures on the merits of Catholicism and American governance and education were the methods to bring the Navajos into the American fold. However, Shelton was furious, for he had continually insisted that an example be made of the Indian men so Navajos would learn to answer to their colonial rulers. The narrative of the uprising, then, becomes a focal point for attempts by both non-Navajos and Navajos to restore some measure of stability across cultures, and, in a larger context, their efforts indicate that after cross-cultural communication, "reasonable" Navajos and non-Indians were able to persuade "unreasonable" and "recalcitrant" Navajos to acquiesce to American authority. This sort of reading suggests that Navajos were successfully incorporated into the American national body—to become similar, but not the same, for the Diné could become Americans only in the lower echelons of the U.S. nation. As Deloria argues, the resurgence of categories such as "violent Indians" allowed for the reproduction of grossly asymmetrical social, political, legal, and economic relations between Native peoples and dominant American society.[57]

The initial reason for the event revolved around polygamy and the Indian agent's determination to abolish the practice. However, that charge was not answered by the judicial authorities. Although primary and secondary sources provide a glimpse of Navajo practices around polygamy, the women were never heard from directly; nor was there any attention given to the initial charge of polygamy. Rather, the narratives about the uprising suggest that the meaning of the rebellion and how it ends—peacefully and with the men agreeing that American justice is just—is about the Navajo turn from tradition to modernity and their agreement regarding the superiority of American values to Navajo values.

Navajo studies scholars point out that Little Singer's marriage to three Navajo women followed custom. Iverson notes that the women were related to one another and that Little Singer had followed Navajo customs regarding marital practices within a matrilineal system.[58] According to

Weber's narrative, one of the elder men in the group, Bizhoshi, who was the father of Little Singer and Bizhoshi Biyi', related that the men "did not want to take the women home; they only wanted to take them to a store just outside of the Agency grounds, buy provisions for them, since they had not had any meat since their arrest, and await the return of Mr. Shelton."[59] The men's efforts to ensure the safety of the women reaffirmed Navajo values around matrilineality, family, and marriage, even as the men faced colonial power that intended to erase their interdependence within an extended kin network based upon clans.[60] These accounts of Navajo marriage and sexuality practices are common in non-Indian observations and mark the Diné as "different" and "exotic," as well as "savage" and "uncivilized."[61] Rather than seriously considering how matrilineality and kinship structured family, marriage, and sexuality for the Diné, "uprising" narratives are imbued with American expectations of nation and family.[62] However, as studies are beginning to acknowledge, Navajo society was organized around matrilineal clans in which women were, and still are, central to social, economic, political, and spiritual organization of the people and their nation.[63]

The Uprising and the Modern Navajo Nation

The uprising offers a window to reflect on the making of the modern Navajo nation in ways that illuminate how Navajo values and tradition conflate and complement American values that privilege heterosexuality and patriarchy as normative, for the narrative is also about the birth and establishment of the Navajo nation as a modern entity. While most studies of tribal nations and self-determination still do not center gender as analysis, feminist critiques illuminate how nations are gendered.[64] Once the Diné were militarily defeated and subjected to brutal and humiliating treatment, and with the signing of a final treaty with the United States, they started to be depicted as on the road to nationhood. As Iverson offers in his history of the Diné return from the Bosque Redondo reservation in 1868:

> Previously, the Navajos had had things in common culturally, but politically there had been little centralization. They had lived in widely scattered locations, and authority was vested solely in local headmen. Their allegiances and frames of references were based on a far more limited area. But now things would be altered. They had gone through the common crucible of the Long Walk experience. Now, through the treaty of 1868, they would be returned to a portion of their old home country, but they

would return to a reservation with strictly defined borders. Their political boundaries had been established: the Navajo Nation had begun.[65]

The image of a crucible—of people overcoming incredible odds—is common in American history narratives. According to this type of historical narrative, after surviving genocidal policies of extermination, Navajos agreed to become Americans and then citizens of their own nation. Their choices seemingly affirm the United States' narratives about itself as a liberal nation that embraces cultural diversity and peaceful coexistence with tribal nations within its boundaries.[66] However, when the uprising is viewed through the lens of Indigenous feminism and queer Indigenous studies, questions arise about the conflation of nation building and development, which includes Navajo progress toward Western ideals that privilege the nuclear family unit as normative. To the contrary, the uprising indicates that where "modern states claim legitimacy on the grounds that the rule of law established through their agency has led to enduring social peace, in fact terrible atrocities have been committed on populations that threatened existing perceptions of nation unity and security by the agencies of the state."[67] Further, the uprising illuminates that colonial imposition of order meant "sovereignty as a tentative and always emergent form of authority grounded in violence that is performed and designed to generate loyalty, fear, and legitimacy from the neighborhood to the summit of the states."[68]

Once the Navajos were under American colonial rule, the knowledge collected about them through annuities counts; census records; and marriage, birth, and baptismal records were used as technologies of surveillance intended to transform them from enemies of the U.S. state into American subjects. As Deloria has argued, "Reservation administrators had long sought to transform Indian people from conquered enemies into colonial subjects who were—and who saw themselves as—part of the American state." A shift occurred from all-out wars on Indigenous people: where once they had been militarily defeated by the United States, now they were subjected to "civil" kinds of violence to create "perfected Natives" who would never be treated as equals, but who would be relegated to the lower echelons of American society. Simultaneously, as a result of exposure to federal Indian policies, which are still termed "assimilation" but fit the definitions of ethnic cleansing, Navajos became self-regulating and policed Navajo national boundaries where heterosexual patriarchy was and still is privileged.

Shelton's vow to enforce federal mandates around family, marriage, and sexuality form part of a pattern in which colonial authorities paid close attention to Navajo behavior and practices to transform them into American citizens, among whom heterosexuality and nuclear family units are privileged. Documents indicate a transition in Navajo marriage customs that began with Navajos' coming under military rule in the 1860s and continued under Indian agents who enforced federal policy around family, marriage, and sexuality. In the early reservation era, from 1868 into the 1890s, Indian agents at the forts expressed dismay when non-Indian traders took on Navajo practices of polygamy. They banned these "squaw men" from the posts because they were seen as modeling immoral behavior before the agents' colonial subjects. For example, in 1873, the federal inspector William Vandever reported on the state of the Fort Defiance, Arizona, post. He complained about the "immoral employees at the agency who were cohabiting with Indian women," among other infractions.[69] The agent in charge of the post, William F. Arny, agreed with Vandever's complaints and dismissed non-Indian men who were not only married to Navajo women but also practiced polygamy. Arny "was convinced that his objective to lead the Indians to a Christian life could not be attained if the Indians were continually subjected to the influence of the immoral men at the agency."[70] The Navajo sense of justice for transgressions also alarmed white American authorities and was seen as aberrant and savage.[71]

The episode of the uprising was just one part of concerted and ongoing efforts to press Navajos into conformity with American ideology around domestic matters. For example, a file titled "Relative to the Policy of the Indian Office in Dealing with Plural Marriages, Divorces, and Other Customs of Unallotted Indians," at the National Archives and Records Administration in Washington, DC, contains correspondence with Washington, DC, from a number of Indian agents on the Navajo reservation expressing alarm about plural marriages and the marriages of young girls to older men. Charles H. Dickson, superintendent at the Leupp School on the Arizona side of Navajo land, wrote, "One of the most distressing conditions which the Government has to contend with on the Navajo Reservation is the moral laxity of the Indians regarding marriage and divorce."[72] Dickson went on to urge that "Indian custom marriages" be "discouraged in every way possible." Another set of letters provides information on the case of Joe Williams, a Diné who was involved with a woman who had a daughter and whereupon he took his stepdaughter as a second wife. Williams was also involved with a third woman. The issue came to the attention of the agent after complaints about how property was being divided after the death of the first wife. About this case the agent wrote, "Every effort is being made to have the Indians marry and divorce according to the law of the land."[73] Of course, the law referred to was American law.

In 1936, the white researcher Richard Van Valkenburgh wrote a report on Navajo common law that provides a perspective on traditional Navajo practices around gender. He noted that property was individually owned and not gender-specific. "Contrary to popular belief that the female owned all tangible property," he observed, "there is no sex discrimination in ownership." He provided a table to prove his point and wrote about the procedure for divorce that the husband simply took his personal property and left the hogan (home). Division of property upon the death of a family member followed clan rules. Children from polyandrous marriages, he observed, were "members of their mother's clan, and ha[d] the same status as other children. There is no such word as 'bastard' in the Navajo language."[74]

By 1940, the Navajo Tribal Council had passed Resolution No. CJ-2–40, which defined marriage as between one man and one woman and set up the procedures for issuing licenses and recording tribal custom marriages. An amendment to the resolution stated in no uncertain terms that plural marriages were unlawful. The Navajo Tribe began regulating marriage by establishing marriage laws, including the requirement that couples who had been married according to traditional custom also obtain licenses.[75] After July 18, 1944, consummated plural marriages were declared void, and both parties were subject to fines not to exceed thirty dollars and imprisonment for terms not to exceed thirty days. In 1944, General Superintendent J. M. Stewart sent a letter to Commissioner of Indian Affairs John Collier apprising him of the state of marriage and family among Navajos in which he stated that it was older Navajos who were raising objections to plural marriage because younger Navajo men were using the practice to gather girls into their hogans and live with them simultaneously, "with no provision or thought for the future welfare of the girls or their offspring." He noted that plural marriages were on the wane. In the same time period, Thomas Dodge, the son of Chee Dodge, reported, "The vast majority of the Navajo people have always opposed plural marriages. It is being stamped out gradually by public opinion and disfavor." In 1944 and 1945, the Navajo Tribal Council passed resolutions outlawing plural marriages, and marriage between a man and a woman was codified into tribal law.[76] Under American colonial rule, Native peoples faced constant condemnation of relationships that fell outside of the binaries of heterosexuality. Recognition of multiple genders was considered sexual transgression.[77] Violence was shown to Navajos, as the uprising narrative depicts, if they did not conform to American practices around gender, family, marriage, and sexuality and was so thorough that any variation in Navajo practices outside nuclear family units, heterosexuality, and monogamy appeared to have passed.[78]

By 1968, the conflation of Navajo values with American ones around gender and domesticity were evident in the year-long celebrations of the Navajos' return from their Bosque Redondo prison camp in 1868. Naming the centennial celebrations "A Hundred Years of Progress," tribal leaders encouraged the Navajo people to reflect on the meaning of the years from 1868 to 1968. The word "Progress" was deployed to encourage Navajos to think about how they might also acquire the American dream and enter the modern era. Through a number of cultural mediums, including fairs, essay contests, and publications, "A Hundred Years of Progress" was attached to the development of Navajo natural resources, including water, coal, and uranium—all of which supported the idea that development would create the modern Navajo family. The *Navajo Times*, established in 1958, was also instrumental in deploying messages about Navajos' entering a modern era by presenting Navajo families as heterosexual nuclear units.[79] The publication *Navajo: A Century of Progress, 1868–1968* suggested that the previous one hundred years had seen the Navajos enter America modernity through the establishment of their own government based on American democratic principles—even as those principles were imposed on them via the Indian Reorganization Act of 1934 (never mind that the Navajo Tribal Council voted against that act) and, further, that the development of their natural resources would allow Navajos to enjoy the benefits of American life, including access to electricity, running water, and other modern conveniences. Money from development projects would offer nuclear families opportunities to build Western-style homes with living rooms, kitchens, and multiple bedrooms. One black-and-white photograph from *Navajo: A Century of Programs* particularly captured my attention and shows a Navajo nuclear family—a husband and wife with a toddler and an infant swaddled in a cradleboard—sitting in a buckboard. At the back of the buckboard is a barrel that most likely contains water for household use. The husband is speaking to another Navajo man who is standing near the wagon; in the background, behind the family, is a gigantic electric power line.[80] The line is taking electricity from the reservation to power urban areas such as Phoenix and Tucson. One senses the family's hope to be included in the American dream. By 1968, then, Navajo tribal leaders were asserting national sovereignty through a modern vision of nationhood. Their consciousness of nationhood was shaped by American values of democracy, including notions of the gender binary of heterosexuality. Significantly, the question of tradition and modernity surfaced, for tribal nations were, and still are, placed within impossible situations of demonstrating their authenticity as tribal peoples according to standards for authenticity and tradition created by non-Indians in the nineteenth century. As Joanne Barker points out, these expectations of Indigenous peoples to remain "traditional" are "entrenched within the theoretical paradigms of social evolution and cultural assimilation." These paradigms have produced problematic notions of Native culture and identity that fix standards for measuring perceived changes within the terms of a whole cascade of binaries and hierarchies that assume authenticity and inauthenticity.[81]

In 2005, the Navajo Nation continued its move toward returning to traditional principles as the foundation of government, as reflected in policies and legislation intended to revalue these principles. Raymond Austin, a former Navajo Supreme Court justice who is now a law professor at the University of Arizona, published a study of the Navajo Nation's use of Navajo traditional principles in its judicial system. Discussing the court's involvement in legal issues around domesticity, family, and marriage, Austin confirmed that marriage traditionally is between one man and one woman. "Another traditional practice, although not prevalent, was when a man supposedly had 'more than one wife,'" he wrote. "The two or more 'wives' were usually sisters." At the same time that he noted plural marriages as "traditional" at one time, he argued that polygamy was not, and is not, "traditional": "Using a traditional analysis, the assertion that a Navajo man can be married to two women simultaneously is inaccurate because by custom a man could not marry another woman in a traditional wedding ceremony while he was married to his present wife." He continued, "The man said to have 'two wives' usually carried on an extramarital relationship with the second woman, and because he could not marry her in a traditional ceremony, she was not legally his wife under Navajo common law."[82] Austin reasoned that because it was customary for a person to have only one "traditional wedding ceremony" in his or her lifetime, then all other marriages—plural or successive—were not legitimate or valid. Thus, Austin conflates "traditional" marriage with the custom of having only one "traditional" marriage ceremony performed. His statement that a man who was married to two women was actually involved in an extramarital relationship simply does not bear out in documented cases of polygamy. Austin's illumination of how Diné traditional principles around gender, marriage, and family thus raise questions about tradition as static and unchanging. Further, Austin's claim that traditional Navajo marriages take place between one man and one woman belies a history of polygamy and raises questions about the intertwined processes of modern American and Navajo nation building and how the Diné have come to accept American values of nation and gender as "traditional." Contrary to his arguments that marriage practices have not changed over time, it is perhaps more productive to consider how the meaning of "tradition" has shifted, particularly in relationship to the imposition of Western democratic principles in the making of the modern Navajo nation.

On April 22, 2005, the Navajo Nation Council passed the Diné Marriage Act by a vote of 67–0, with two abstentions.[83] The act is the Navajo version of the American ban on same-sex marriage. According to its sponsor, Council Delegate Larry Anderson of Fort Defiance, the purpose of the law is simply to "promote strong families and strong family values, not discriminate."[84] The resolution was vetoed by President Joe Shirley Jr., who said the issue was not of primary concern to Navajo citizens. After mounting a campaign, the council easily overrode the veto, 62–14 (twelve delegates abstained or were absent during the vote). In her discussion of Native sexuality and tradition, Barker points out that many people, native and non-Native, were surprised to learn that tribal nations such as the Navajo Nation and the Cherokee Nation would engage in national debates and state propositions that ban same-sex marriage, which was contrary to the expectation that tribal governments would offer support for same-sex marriage rights.[85]

Anderson's call for an affirmation of Navajo family values as nuclear in composition and of marriage defined as between a man and a woman surfaced while the American public was debating same-sex marriage as states brought anti-gay marriage provisions to the ballot.[86] Navajos publicly debated the issue and raised questions about whether traditional Navajo society had once recognized genders beyond the feminine-masculine binary. Drawing on creation narratives in which the nádleehí, a third gender, played an important role in primordial times, the Navajo gay, lesbian, and transgender community and its allies argued that Navajos and other Natives had long recognized and revered same-sex-oriented people, but that generations of exposure to Western ideology had erased memories of multiple genders in our societies.[87] Traditionalists argued that the role of the nádleehí, who technically is a person with both female and male sexual organs, was not sexual but a spiritual person who brought about reconciliation between the two sexes.[88] Calling the proposed legislation discriminatory, students at Diné College in Tsaile, Arizona, formed a gay-straight alliance. They hoped not only to challenge such narrow definitions of Navajo sexual relationships and family but also to bring attention to their experiences as Navajo gay, lesbian, and transgender people.[89] In concert with actions happening in other tribal nations, including the Cherokee Nation's refusal to recognize same-sex marriage, the debates around the proposed legislation challenged "compulsory heterosexual" norms, claimed the humanity of those outside of heterosexual as normative, and asserted non-heterosexual human and civil rights. In particular, debates about gender and tradition exposed the silences around the discrimination and hate Navajo gays, lesbians, and transgender people experience in our communities. More recently, Alray Nelson, an openly gay Navajo who has lived much of his life in the Navajo Nation, formed the Coalition for Navajo Equality to repeal the Diné Marriage Act. As Nelson and other Navajo queer people and their allies maintain, they, like many other Diné, have a deep and abiding respect for Diné traditional ways and are simply seeking inclusion and acceptance in their nation.[90]

Conclusion

Violence over the Land, Ned Blackhawk's study of colonial violence and Indigenous peoples, indicates that violence has been integral to the conquest of Indigenous peoples across colonizers and time.[91] With the military defeat of Indigenous peoples seen as completed by the end of the nineteenth century, federal Indian policy makers began anew their terrorizing violence on Indigenous peoples through legal, cultural, social, and religious institutions to force conformity with the values of a heterosexual patriarchy. In much the same way, the processes of colonialism have meant the remaking of the Diné in the image of the white man, but without the full benefits and entitlements accorded white male citizens. The imposition of U.S. authority over the Diné not only included efforts to remake Navajo individuals into citizens who embrace American heterosexual patriarchy; it also resulted in the creation of a Navajo Nation that was formed to privilege heterosexual patriarchy as normative. My analysis of the "Uprising at Beautiful Mountain" and what scholars choose to retell about the event highlights the ways in which the narrative is presented within American exceptionalism. The account is interpreted within American historiography in ways that minimize the level of violence and coercion that was used to transform Navajos into American citizens, or colonial subjects. A closer look at the rebellion raises questions about the nature of technologies of surveillance and the institutions used by the Americans to transform Natives into their own version of heteronormative nations and community. Finally, the uprising narrative gives us pause about the possibilities for decolonization at a time that tribal nations and leaders face problems whose foundations lie in the legacy of U.S. colonialism. As Diné and Indigenous peoples, we should take stock of how we internalize colonial values, often as tradition, so we can move toward true sovereignty and what that means for all of our Native citizens. Although illuminating how Indigenous nations have naturalized patriarchy may seem a daunting task, I am heartened by emerging critical Indigenous scholarship, including the work of Audra Simpson. In *Mohawk Interruptus*, she names the ways in which Indigenous nations and their citizens reject the "gift of recognition" by refusing to embrace settler nations' institutions because they intend to legitimize Indigenous dispossession and disavow the violent means through which Indigenous peoples have been colonized and remade in ways intended to mimic their colonizers.[92] To refuse the gifts of liberalism, democracy, and freedom on the settler nation's terms means affirming traditional principles that acknowledge the authority and power of women and queer people in ways that recognize our commitment to tribal sovereignty, and it expresses once again inclusion, acceptance, and belonging on age-old principles of k'é. As I endeavor to bridge the space between my nation and academia, I am profoundly affected by the persistence of my people's wisdom, of the women and the queers who steadfastly affirm their love of the land, the natural world, and all beings.

NOTES

1. Bill Donovan, "The Last Uprising: 1913 Navajo Insurrection," *Gallup Independent*, December 10, 2010, 1. In this essay Navajo words are spelled according to each author and source used. If there was no source, I used a current Navajo dictionary.

2. Amy Kaplan, *The Anarchy of Empire in the Making of U.S. Culture* (Cambridge, MA: Harvard University Press, 2005).

3. Vine Deloria Jr. and Clifford M. Lytle, *The Nations Within: The Past and Future of American Indian Sovereignty* (Austin: University of Texas Press, 1984); David E. Wilkins and Heidi Kiiwetinepinesiik Stark, "Indigenous Peoples are Nations, Not Minorities," in *American Indian Politics and the American Political System* (Lanham, MD: Rowman and Littlefield, 2010), 33–50; Lloyd L. Lee, "The Future of Navajo Nationalism," *Wicazō Śa Review* (Spring 2007): 53–68; Lloyd L. Lee, "Reclaiming Indigenous Intellectual, Political, and Geographical Space: A Path for Navajo Nationhood," *American Indian Quarterly* 32, no. 1 (Winter 2008): 96–109.

4. For examples of Native historiography, see Colin Calloway, *New Directions in American History* (Norman: University of Oklahoma Press, 1992); Donald L. Fixico, *Rethinking American Indian History* (Albuquerque: University of New Mexico Press, 1997). Recent publications show both a persistence of New Indian history methodology and an ongoing challenge to New Indian history by Native historians: see, e.g., Albert L.

Hurtado, ed., *Reflections on American Indian Past: Honoring the Past, Building a Future* (Norman: University of Oklahoma Press, 2008). Challenges to entrenched methods of doing Native history are in James Riding In and Susan A. Miller, eds., *Native Historians Write Back: Decolonizing American Indian History* (Lubbock: Texas Tech University Press, 2011).

5. Scott Richard Lyons, *X-Marks: Native Signatures of Assent* (Minneapolis: University of Minnesota Press, 2010).

6. Perhaps one of the most powerful voices to name the United States a settler nation is the Dakota historian Waziyatawin. For examples, see Waziyatawin, *What Does Justice Look Like? The Struggle of Liberation in the Dakota Homeland* (St. Paul, MN: Living Justice, 2008); Waziyatawin Angela Wilson, *Remember This! Dakota Decolonization and the Eli Taylor Narratives* (Lincoln: University of Nebraska Press, 2005).

7. Bonita Lawrence, "Rewriting Histories of the Land: Colonization and Indigenous Resistance in Eastern Canada," in *Race, Space, and the Law: Unmapping a White Settler Society*, ed. Sherene H. Razack (Toronto: Between the Lines, 2002): 21–46.

8. Angela Cavender Wilson, "Reclaiming our Humanity: Decolonization and the Recovery of Indigenous Knowledge," in *Indigenizing the Academy: Transforming Scholarship and Empowering Communities*, eds. Devon Abbott Mihesuah and Angela Cavender Wilson (Lincoln: University of Nebraska Press, 2004), 79.

9. Francis Paul Prucha, ed., *Documents of United States Indian Policy* (Lincoln: University of Nebraska Press, 2000), 158–60, 179–80. The historian Gary Anderson argues that American Indians experienced not "genocide" but, rather, "ethnic cleansing." In the sections in which he discusses the experiences of the Navajo under American colonialism, Anderson declares that the term "genocide" does not apply, because the majority of Navajos survived incarceration at the Bosque Redondo at Fort Sumner from 1863 to 1868: see Gary Clayton Anderson, *Ethnic Cleansing and the Indian: The Crime That Should Haunt America* (Norman: University of Oklahoma Press, 2014): 240–41. See also Roxanne Dunbar-Ortiz, *Indigenous Peoples' History of the United States* (Boston: Beacon, 2015).

10. Waziyatawin, "Colonialism on the Ground," n.d., http://unsettlingamerica .wordpress.com/tag/waziyatawin.

11. Patrick Wolfe, "Settler Colonialism and the Elimination of the Native," *Journal of Genocide Research* 8, no. 4 (2006): 388, 390.

12. Eve Tuck and K. Wayne Yang, "Decolonization Is Not a Metaphor," *Decolonization: Indigeneity, Education, and Society* 1, no. 1 (2012): 7.

13. In the past ten years or so, publications on Indigenous feminist and queer theorizing have energized Indigenous studies: For examples, see Joanne Barker, *Native Acts: Law, Recognition, and Cultural Authenticity* (Durham, NC: Duke University Press, 2011); Mishuana Goeman, *Mark My Words: Native Women Mapping Our Nations* (Minneapolis: University of Minnesota Press, 2013); Jennifer Denetdale and Mishuana Goeman, eds., "Native Feminisms: Legacies, Interventions, and Indigenous Sovereignties," *Wicazō Śa Review* 24, no. 2 (Fall 2009): 9–13; Qwo-Li Driskell, Chris Finley, Brian Joseph Gilley, and Scott Lauria Morgensen, eds., *Queer Indigenous Studies: Critical Interventions in Theory, Politics, and Literature* (Tucson: University of Arizona Press, 2011).

14. Ann Laura Stoler, "Tense and Tender Ties: The Politics of Comparison in North American History and (Post) Colonial Studies," in *Haunted by Empire: Geographies of Intimacy in North American History*, ed. Ann Laura Stoler (Durham, NC: Duke University Press, 2006), 43.

15. See, e.g., Mark Rifkin, *When Did Indians Become Straight? Kinship, the History of Sexuality, and Native Sovereignty* (New York: Oxford University Press, 2011).

16. Elizabeth A. Povinelli, *The Cunning of Recognition: Indigenous Alterities and the Making of Australian Multiculturalism* (Durham, NC: Duke University Press, 2002).

17. Diné Marriage Act, 2005, Resolution of the Navajo Nation Council, CAP-29–05, April 22, 2005, http://www.navajocourts.org/Resolutions/29–05%20Marriage%20Act.pdf.

18. Barker, *Native Acts*, 20.

19. Jennifer Nez Denetdale, "Chairmen, Presidents, and Princesses: The Navajo Nation, Gender, and the Politics of Tradition," *Wicazō Ša Review* 21, no. 1 (Spring 2006): 9–44; Jennifer Nez Denetdale, "Carving Navajo National Boundaries: Patriotism, Tradition, and the Diné Marriage Act of 2005," *American Quarterly* 60, no. 2 (June 2008): 289–94; Jennifer Nez Denetdale, "Securing the Navajo National Boundaries: War, Patriotism, Tradition, and the Diné Marriage Act of 2005," *Wicazō Ša Review* 24, no. 2 (Fall 2009): 221–41.

20. Deborah M. Miranda, "Extermination of the Joyas: Gendercide in Spanish California," GLQ 16, nos. 1–2 (2010): 253–84; Deborah M. Miranda, *Bad Indians: A Tribal Memoir* (Berkeley, CA: Heyday, 2013); Barker, *Native Acts*; Scott Lauria Morgensen, *Spaces between Us: Queer Settler Colonialism and Indigenous Decolonization* (Minneapolis: University of Minnesota Press, 2011); Rifkin, *When Did Indians Become Straight?*

21. Scott Lauria Morgensen, "Settler Homonationalism: Theorizing Settler Colonialism within Queer Modernities," GLQ 16, nos. 1–2 (2010): 105–6.

22. Barker, *Native Acts*, 227.

23. Philip J. Deloria, *Indians in Unexpected Places* (Lawrence: University of Kansas Press, 2004).

24. Deloria, *Indians in Unexpected Places*, 20–21.

25. Rifkin, *When Did Indians Become Straight?* 183.

26. Jennifer Nez Denetdale, *Reclaiming Diné History: The Legacies of Chief Manuelito and Juanita* (Tucson: University of Arizona Press, 2007); Jennifer Denetdale, *The Long Walk: The Forced Navajo Exile* (New York: Chelsea House, 2007).

27. Rifkin, *When Did Indians Become Straight?* See in particular chapter 4, "Allotment Subjectivities and the Administration of 'Culture': Ella Deloria, Pine Ridge, and the Indian Reorganization Act."

28. Richard White, *The Roots of Dependency: Subsistence, Environment, and Social Change among the Choctaws, Pawnees, and Navajos* (Lincoln: University of Nebraska Press, 1983); Marsha Weisiger, *Dreaming of Sheep in Navajo Country* (Seattle: University of Washington Press, 2009).

29. In the aftermath of the attack on the United States on September 11, 2001, Indigenous scholars such as Jeannette Writer (Cherokee) argued that Indigenous peoples

have experienced terrorism at the hands of the United States and that U.S. violence against its Indigenous peoples continued to be denied and ignored: see Jeannette Writer, "Terrorism in Native America: Interrogating the Past, Examining the Present, Constructing a Liberatory Future," *Anthropology and Education Quarterly* 33, no. 3 (2002): 1–14; Jodi A. Byrd, *The Transit of Empire: Indigenous Critiques of Colonialism* (Minneapolis: University of Minnesota Press, 2011).

30. James Carleton to Lorenzo Thomas, September 6, 1863, cited in Lawrence Kelly, *Navajo Roundup: Selected Correspondence of Kit Carson's Expedition against the Navajo, 1863–1865* (Boulder, CO: Pruett, 1970), 56–57.

31. Raymond D. Austin, *Navajo Courts and Navajo Common Law* (Tucson: University of Arizona Press, 2009), 3.

32. Austin, *Navajo Courts and Navajo Common Law,* 4.

33. Austin, *Navajo Courts and Navajo Common Law,* 4.

34. Miranda, "Extermination of the Joyas." See also Andrea Smith, *Conquest: Sexual Violence and American Indian Genocide* (Cambridge, MA: South End, 2005); Morgensen, "Settler Homonationalism," 108–9.

35. J. Lee Correll, *Bai-a-lil-le: Medicine Man or Witch?* (Window Rock, AZ: Research Section, Navajo Parks and Recreation, 1970), 7.

36. Davidson B. McKibbin, "Revolt of the Navaho, 1913," *New Mexico Historical Review,* no. 4 (October 1954): 261.

37. McKibbin, "Revolt of the Navaho," 264–71.

38. Anselm Weber, "Navajos on the Warpath?" in *The Navajo as Seen by the Franciscans, 1898–1921: A Sourcebook,* ed. Howard M. Bahr (Lanham, MD: Scarecrow Press, 2004) (hereafter, Bahr), 366–85. The original is in "Indian Office/Navajo/Hostile Indians," record group (RG) 48, Department of the Interior, Office of the Secretary, CCF, 1907–1936, 5–1, Navajo, E-L, box 1254, National Archives and Records Administration (hereafter, NARA), Washington, DC.

39. Robert L. Wilken, *Anselm Weber, O.F.M.: Missionary to the Navaho: 1898–1921* (Milwaukee: Bruce Publishing, 1955).

40. Wilken, *Anselm Weber, O.F.M.;* Weber, "Navajos on the Warpath?" (Bahr), 367.

41. Deloria, *Indians in Unexpected Places,* 20–21.

42. Deloria, *Indians in Unexpected Places,* 26–27.

43. Iverson, *Diné: A History of the Navajos,* 108.

44. Weber, "Navajos on the Warpath?"

45. David M. Brugge, "Henry Chee Dodge: From the Long Walk to Self-Determination," in *Indian Lives: Essays on Nineteenth- and Twentieth-Century Native American Leaders,* ed. L. G. Moses and Raymond Wilson (Albuquerque: University of New Mexico Press, 1985), 95–98.

46. Carolyn Niethammer, *I'll Go and Do More: Annie Dodge Wauneka, Navajo Leader and Activist* (Lincoln: University of Nebraska Press, 2001).

47. Howard M. Bahr, "The Navajo Trouble of 1905," in Bahr, *The Navajo as Seen by the Franciscans,* 233.

48. Bahr, "The Navajo Trouble of 1905," 233.

49. Bahr, "The Navajo Trouble of 1905," 234.

50. McKibbin, "Revolt of the Navaho," 272–73.

51. Weber, "Navahos on the Warpath?" 15.

52. Sheila Gill's study of how Canadian White settler law privileges and empowers its subjects, thereby disavowing the evidence of injustice against Indigenous peoples, has been very helpful in the development of my analysis of the uprising: see Sheila Dawn Gill, "The Unspeakability of Racism: Mapping Law's Complicity in Manitoba's Racialized Spaces," in Razack, *Race, Space, and the Law*, 157–83.

53. Weber, "Navajos on the Warparth?" (NARA), pt. 2 to November 19, 1910.

54. Weber, "Navajos on the Warparth?" (NARA), pt. 2 to November 19, 1910.

55. Weber, "Navajos on the Warparth?" (NARA), pt. 2 to November 19, 1910.

56. Weber, "Navajos on the Warpath?" 284, in Bahr.

57. Philip J. Deloria, *Playing Indian* (New Haven, CT: Yale University Press, 1999).

58. Iverson, *Diné*, 110–11.

59. Weber, "Navajos on the Warpath?," n.p.

60. Mark Rifkin argues that in the face of colonial violence intended to destroy traditional forms of kinship and family, Native peoples found ways to both challenge colonial authority and to reaffirm traditional values: see *When Did Indians Become Straight?*, 116.

61. Jennifer Nez Denetdale, "Representing Changing Woman: A Review Essay on Navajo Women," *American Indian Culture and Research Journal* 25, no. 3 (2001): 1–26. Carol Sparks argues that the earliest American observers of Navajos were confounded by Navajo gender roles because they did not fit neatly into Western categories of gender: see Carol Douglas Sparks, "The Land Incarnate: Navajo Women and the Dialogue of Colonialism, 1821–1870," in *Negotiators of Change: Historical Perspectives on Native Women*, ed. Nancy Shoemaker (New York: Routledge, 1995).

62. See, e.g., Mark Rifkin, "Romancing Kinship: A Queer Reading of Indian Education and Zitkala-Sa's *American Indian* Stories," GLQ 12 (2006): 27–59.

63. See, e.g., Dana E. Powell and Dáilan J. Long, "Landscapes of Power: Renewable Energy Activism in Diné Bikéyah," in *Indians and Energy: Exploitation and Opportunity in the American Southwest*, ed. Sherry L. Smith and Brian Frehner (Santa Fe, NM: School for Advanced Research Press, 2010), 231–62; Bennie Klain, dir., *Weaving Worlds*, Trickster Films, 2008. In both of these works, Navajo women are presented as authorities on cultural knowledge and practice. As the head of extended family households that revolve around matrilineally centered clans, Navajo women make decisions concerning land use, livestock, and the economics around their families.

64. For the most part, studies of Native nations and governance ignore nation building and gender. For examples, see Deloria and Lytle, *The Nations Within*; David E. Wilkins and K. Tsianina Lomawaima, *Uneven Ground: American Indian Sovereignty and Federal Law* (Norman: University of Oklahoma Press, 2002); Miriam Jorgensen, ed., *Rebuilding Native Nations: Strategies for Governance and Development* (Tucson: University of Arizona Press, 2007). Works that have informed my understanding of nation and gender include Nira Yuval-Davis, *Gender and Nation* (Thousand Oaks, CA: Sage, 1997); Chandra Talpade Mohanty, Ann Russo, and Lourdes Torres, eds., *Third World Women and the Politics of Feminism* (Bloomington: Indiana University Press, 1991); Anne McClintock, Aamir Mufti, and Ella Shohat, eds., *Dangerous Liaisons: Gender, Nation,*

and Postcolonial Perspectives (Minneapolis: University of Minneapolis Press, 1997); Ann Laura Stoler, *Carnal Knowledge and Imperial Power: Race and the Intimate in Colonial Rule* (Oakland: University of California Press, 2002); Lee Maracle, *I Am Woman: A Native Perspective on Sociology and Feminism?* (North Vancouver, BC: Write-On Press, 1988); Barker, *Native Acts*; Rifkin, *When Did Indians Become Straight?*; Morgensen, *Spaces between Us.*

65. Peter Iverson, *The Navajo Nation* (Westport, CT: Greenwood, 1981), 10.

66. Jennifer Nez Denetdale, "Discontinuities, Remembrances, and Cultural Survival: History, Diné/Navajo Memory, and the Bosque Redondo Memorial," *New Mexico Historical Review* 82, no. 3 (Summer 2007): 305–6.

67. Veena Das, "Violence, Gender, and Subjectivity," *Annual Review of Anthropology* 37 (2008): 284; Thomas Blom Hansen and Finn Stepputat, "Sovereignty Revisited," *Annual Review of Anthropology* 35 (2006): 297.

68. Thomas Blom Hansen and Finn Stepputat, 297.

69. Norman J. Bender, *"New Hope for the Indians": The Grant Peace Policy and the Navajos in the 1870s* (Albuquerque: University of New Mexico Press, 1989), 101.

70. Bender, *"New Hope for the Indians,"* 102.

71. For example, Martha Blue documents an episode in Navajo history that is commonly known as the "Witch Purge of 1878." In 1878, one of the signers of the 1868 treaty was accused of witchcraft, and other leaders, including the headman Manuelito, meted out Navajo justice to a number of men accused of witchcraft. Blue argues that an examination of the episode through Navajo oral history illuminates Navajo sensibilities of traditional conflict management, which embodies information gathering and exchange, mobilization of kin networks, instructive and creative speech in a public setting, and restoration of harmony: see Martha Blue, *The Witch Purge of 1878: Oral and Documentary History in the Early Navajo Reservation Years* (Tsaile, AZ: Navajo Community College Press, 1988). Richard Van Valkenburgh also sheds light on Navajo justice for crimes such as murder: see Richard Van Valkenburgh, "Notes on Navajo Common Law," ms., Ayer Modern MS Kimball, Newberry Library, Chicago, box 24, folder 230.

72. Charles H. Dickson to Acting Commissioner, Department of Interior, Office of Indian Affairs, Washington, DC, 1912, "Relative to the Policy of the Indian Office in Dealing with Plural Marriages, Divorces and Other Customs of Unallotted Indians," letter, RG 75, Records of the Bureau of Indian Aaffairs, CCF, 1907–1939, Leupp. 2932–1911–11 to 26106–1923–11, NARA, box 1, PI-163 E-121 HM 2000.

73. Dickson to Acting Commissioner.

74. Van Valkenburgh, "Notes on Navajo Common Law."

75. Austin, *Navajo Courts and Navajo Common Law*, 160.

76. Austin, *Navajo Courts and Navajo Common Law*, 160.

77. Morgensen, "Settler Homonationalism," 115.

78. Morgensen, "Settler Homonationalism," 114–15.

79. Benedict Anderson argues that newspapers were instrumental in fomenting a national consciousness of belonging: Benedict Anderson, *Imagined Communities: Reflections on the Origin and Spread on Nationalism* (New York: Verso, 1991).

80. Charles Wilkinson argues that Navajo and Hopi natural resources were developed to build the infrastructure of the Southwest. Navajo and Hopi natural resources built

urban areas such as Los Angeles, Las Vegas, Phoenix, Tucson, and Albuquerque: see Charles Wilkinson, *Fire on the Plateau: Conflict and Endurance in the American Southwest* (Washington, DC: Island Press, 2004). See also John Redhouse, "Geopolitics of the Navajo Hopi Land Dispute (Redhouse/Wright Productions, 1985): 1–35.

81. Barker, *Native Acts*, 196–97.

82. Austin, *Navajo Courts and Navajo Common Law*, 160.

83. Pamela G. Dempsey, "Navajo Nation Officially Bans Same-Sex Marriage," *Gallup Independent*, April 23, 2005.

84. "Diné Debate Gay Marriage," *Gallup Independent*, January 17, 2005, 5.

85. Barker, *Native Acts*, 196.

86. Barker, *Native Acts*, 189.

87. Sue-Ellen Jacobs, Wesley Thomas, and Sabine Lang, eds., *Two-Spirit People: Native American Gender Identity, Sexuality, and Spirituality* (Urbana: University of Illinois Press, 1997).

88. My assertion here is based on my conversations with many Diné, including medicine men, many of whom also provided multiple meanings about who nádleehí are; their places in traditional creation narratives; and their connections to contemporary concerns around Navajo gay, lesbian, and transgenders. Some have insisted that the nádleehí did not serve a sexual function, while others claim that during the Separation of the Sexes (a creation story), the nádleehí went with the men who moved away from the women after an argument about which was the superior sex. The nádleehí performed domestic duties for the men and served as sexual partners. They were instrumental in bringing about a reconciliation between the men and the women.

89. Cindy Yurth, "Gay-Straight Alliance Sets Agenda," *Navajo Times*, April 20, 2006, C5.

90. Massoud Hayoun, "Navajo Group Aims to Undo Law Banning Gay Marriage," Al Jazeera America, December 30, 2013, http://america.aljazeera.com/articles/2013 /12/30/navajo-aim-to-undothedinedoma.html; National Public Radio, "States May Recognize Same-Sex Marriage, but Navajo Nation Won't," transcript, January 9, 2014, http://www.npr.org/templates/transcript/transcript.php?storyId=261048308; Alysa Landry, "Same-Sex Marriage Unrecognized in Navajo Culture, but for How Long?" *Indian Country Today*, February 2, 2014, http://indiancountrytodaymedianetwork.com /2014/02/13/same-sex-marriages-unrecognized-navajo-culture-how-long-153512?page =0%2C1.

91. Ned Blackhawk, *Violence over the Land: Indians and Empire in the Early American West* (Cambridge, MA: Harvard University Press, 2006).

92. Audra Simpson, *Mohawk Interruptus: A Political Life across the Borders of Settler States* (Durham, NC: Duke University Press, 2014).

3

ONGOING STORMS AND STRUGGLES

Gendered Violence and Resource Exploitation

MISHUANA R. GOEMAN

Some people see scars and it is wounding they remember.

To me they are proof of the fact that there is healing.—**Linda Hogan**, *Solar Storms*

In Linda Hogan's novel *Solar Storms,* the elder Dora-Rouge asks, "How do conquered people get their lives back?"[1] This is not only a pivotal question within the novel but an important question that resounds throughout indigenous communities and is an appropriate trajectory of political inquiry for developing Native feminisms. This question moves us beyond intervention into the colonial order and into creating new possibilities for social justice. Hogan fashions the small community of Adam's Rib, situated on the border waters between the United States and Canada, through the narrative of the confused, angry, and scared seventeen-year-old Angel Jensen. This imaginary place, and the actual one from which Hogan draws inspiration, is formed through years of unabated colonization, and the people, homes, and land reflect the impact of these historical and ongoing moments of destruction and settler accumulation. Angel's return to the village intersects the personal with these larger narratives of colonization. While the tale is fictional, the generations of women's narratives in the text of the gendered and sexualized processes of colonization correspond to nonfictional communities in border waters between Canada and the United States. Angel returns to the Adam's Rib twelve years after the state removed her from the community, a removal that resulted from a brutal, cannibalistic attack by her mother that scars Angel for life. The event of violence does not begin with Angel, however, and as we move through the life stories of her mother, Hannah, and grandmother, Loretta, we begin to witness the connections between colonization and generations of violence. The events of violence on these women's bodies set up the various structures in the text, such as dispossession, subjugation, erasure of cultural and political rights, and, most important, land theft. The pain of these individual women and what we witness through the stories and tellings of memories that unravel as we proceed through the story not only affect the body of individual Native women; Native women's bodies also become the conduit of possible violence that reinforces settler structures of violence. The story that unravels the past, present, and future interconnects generations of witnessing violence that occurs at the level of interpersonal violence, of violence directed at specific communities, and of state violence that transpires against all humans and nonhumans.

I propose that we examine spatial injustice and Native feminist practices in the weaving of this story that enable us to delve more deeply into the ways that gendered and sexualized violence has multiple connections that spread out on vertical and horizontal scales. It builds from an individual's story in a particular place to a story that entangles multiple generations of stories and journeys through temporalities and spaces. Angel's arrival in the village after her long absence and dislocation through child protective services intersects the personal with larger narratives of colonization and neoliberal models of settler nation-states. While Angel Jensen's narrative is a fictional tale, this non-anthropocentric plot reflects the gendered and sexualized processes of colonization that are foundational to settler states and have greatly affected the nonfictional tribal communities composed of Cree and Naskapi peoples of the Canadian Subarctic. By applying an Indigenous feminist praxis that connects humans, nonhumans, and land in symbiotic relationships, a reading of *Solar Storms* can raise questions about the various scales of social justice. Many settler discourses (and Native discourses affected by settler notions of time and space) proceed with the conception of body-contained and land-contained entities, following what Noelani Goodyear-Ka'opua terms "logics of containment": "Containment can manifest in geographic forms as reservations or small school spaces, in political forms as legal-recognition frameworks that seek to subsume sovereignty within the settler state's domestic laws, and in ideological forms . . . that allows a sprinkling of Indigenous history and culture only to maintain its marginality."[2] Through Hogan's language and work with these three generations of women, we see a wrestling to find a place in which the spatial and temporal are not controlled solely by settler discourse and bodies and lands become conduits of connection rather than impermeable entities.

I suggest that we take a cue from Hogan and think of the various scales of space, starting with the body. The body operates at three scales throughout the novel: the individual bodies of Angel, Hannah, and Loretta (protagonist, mother, and grandmother, respectively) and of the community that stands in for the social body; the individual and her relationship to the land that literally sustains us; and the social body of the Native community and the national bodies of the United States, Canada, and Quebec. Rather than thinking of these scales as disconnected, we need to think of the social processes that "freeze" them. The social processes that freeze the scales, according to Neil Smith, is an exertion of colonial control over space. "The construction of scale is not simply a spatial solidification or materialisation of contested social forces and processes," Smith says. "Scale is an active progenitor of specific social processes. . . . Scale demarcates the sites of social contest, the object as well as the resolution of contest."[3] That place is produced as different from other places is useful in thinking through how settler power and spatial scales operate. As Smith contends, it is advantageous to think of "the criteria of difference not so much between places as between different kinds of places."[4] Here I examine the language of scale not by privileging difference but, rather, by examining Indigenous forms of connections, such as defining different uses of land or different desires for the uses of land and water. Colonial logics of difference relegate who is expendable (Indigenous populations) and who is given priority (settlers). It is a violent use of the scalar form in which the Indigenous bodies are made absent or disinterred to lands now renamed and domesticated. Hogan upsets the scale based on difference, however, and asserts a scale based on connection, thus collapsing the settler scale that separates humans, lands, animals, and so on. Indigenous bodies and sense of being are tied to a sense of place.[5] The different kinds of places conceived in the novel map colonial power relations even as they position power relations as unstable. The language used to declare areas as settler properties and territorial jurisdictions are often referred to in temporal gestures or in the language of a need to develop these "unused" lands that could provide benefits for the majority non-Native populations.

Violence Written on the Body

Individual bodies of the Wing family represent acts of violence or events of colonialism but are also tied to the destruction of the environment around them. In addition, in thinking of the body as private or impermeable, we elide an examination of the structures that mark embodied experiences. In examining the settler operation of the expendable body, particularly the bodies of Angel, Hannah, and Loretta Wing, I aim to add a discussion of embodied experiences, which are always gendered, to theories in settler colonial studies. Settler colonialism, driven by a devouring of land, focuses on the structures put in place through what Patrick Wolfe has determined is a logic of elimination.[6] If the aim of settler colonial studies is to confront colonial structures, it must consider an investigation of embodied practices in settler societies beyond the way that settler knowledge represents the indigenous as absent. Settler colonial theory needs also to be accountable to how bodies move through spaces and the scales of space set up through imposed criteria—or a logic of containment. Furthermore, embodied practices must move beyond a notion of the body as individual, private and moving independently as a fixed entity. Instead, the body is often written on in both historical and geographical ways. As the symbolizing in *Solar Storms* demands, we must account for the embodied experiences of Native people—that is, Native feminism must examine how a highly regulated Native individual body is situated in a broader social, political, and economic systems of meanings, as well as how that body's experience in the world becomes an important ontological origin. In thinking of the body as a geography connected to other geographies under the structures of settler colonialism, we can uproot it from narrowly defined colonial scales.

Over the year in which the novel takes place, Angel learns of her past, the history of Adam's Rib, and where she fits in her multilayered Native community, which is like many others: composed of Native people who originated in the area and those who found themselves sharing land and indigenous principles as various Native diasporas occurred during settler occupation and environmental destruction. We arrive at the temporal and spatial point in the novel at which Angel seeks to regain a place and connection at Adam's Rib and to her community. The removal by the state and the attack by her mother scar Angel physically and literally, and it is this embodied scar that manifests as a meeting point of violence on which the novel's plot is mapped. As in many situations, Native people have come together in this community that is built on the past, present, and their hopes for the future. Angel's immediate family and tribal members either have been killed through various processes of colonization or are dispersed.

We come to find out that as a young child and young woman Hannah faced extensive physical and sexual abuse at the hands of colonizing men who repeatedly molested and raped her. She is one of the lost and eventually becomes a nomadic figure in the border waters region. Throughout the novel, Hannah and Loretta are subtly referred to at times as among the boat sex workers; though not named, this is a mode of exploitation of Native women and children that still exists in this borderland of Canada and the United States.[7] In one of the first-person accounts, Bush, Angel's adoptive mother, tells Angel about the first time she was able to get Hannah to undress. After Hannah has removed the clothes she has stolen from clotheslines and houses in Adam's Rib, Bush notices that, "beneath all the layers of clothes, her skin was a garment of scars. There were burns and incisions. Like someone had written on her. The signatures of torturers" (99). While this poignant passage evokes empathy with the small girl, it also alludes to history—that of the physical terror Natives have gone through and that of the terror of the written word. The metaphor of signatures written across the body of the young girl stands in for treaties, laws, and the signing away of land. Bush says, "All I could think was that she was the sum total of ledger books and laws. Some of her ancestors walked out of death, out of a massacre. Some of them came from a long trail of dying, people sent from their world, and she was also the child of those starving and poisoned people on Elk Island" (101). This abuse results in Hannah's detachment disorder, and she is unable to engage the life forces around her, human and otherwise. These are the "original sins," the colonial abuses that led to the displacement of Angel into the foster system. Throughout the text, Hogan refers to gendered colonial violence as original sin, a play on and twist of biblical connotations that run throughout the text. Unfortunately, this aspect of the story also roots itself in the real story of colonization as the historic and present consequences of sex trafficking in the region that is just now being brought to light in scholarship. Hogan creates an awareness of the scale of bodily injustice, although Native communities often through their lived experiences have long been aware of Aboriginal and First Nations girls targeted for sexual violence. The bodies of Native women often provide the documentation of gendered forms of violence as they become marked through colonial dispossession, sex work that opens them to increased levels of violence, and targeting for death.[8] Hannah and Loretta—Angel's mother and grandmother, respectively—embody a history of colonization. Their bodies bear the scars.

Dora-Rouge, Agnes, Husk, and Frenchie work to break the cycle by taking Angel in as an infant and welcoming her home when she returns as a teen. Her return accompanies a tale in which she (and the reader) learn not only about why the state removed her and sent her to Oklahoma, but also about what set up the context of removal. Unlike tales of relocation through public policies (such as termination and relocation) or urban-reserve/ation dichotomies, the reader recognizes a gradual unfolding of dispossession through resource extraction in generations of Angel's family. The gendering and sexualization of colonial entanglements structure the novel, as noted in the naming of the protagonist Angel and the place name of Adam's Rib; the naming reflects the gendering of colonization as Christianity disrupted matrifocal societies and replaced them with Western knowledge systems. As depicted in the novel, however, this is not complete, by any means, and the ongoing pressure of domestication or death of lands and bodies is a theme taken up throughout. For instance, Angel's removal, like that of many Native children, is a result of the state's imposing forms of domesticity through policy, forms that do not recognize alternative family or kinship formations that are not based on direct biological descent. The story that unravels the past, present, and future addresses the misrecognition of knowledge systems and connects generations of witnessing violence that occurs at both the level of interpersonal violence and state violence.

The narrative of *Solar Storms* deals precisely with the consistently traveling body of Angel Jensen. The prologue begins with Angel's childhood departure and the ceremony that her adopted parent, Bush, throws for her. In the ceremony, Bush, who had traveled years earlier from Chickasaw homelands, comes to find her place in the community by reminding the community of "the map inside ourselves" (17). Thus, Angel's departure also reflects on the movement of others in the community, or community movement. Often in thinking of Native diasporas we think of the individual body traveling and being lost to the community as such, rather than thinking also of community mobility. In relation to the suspect ceremony Bush performs, Hogan states, "Maybe it reminded us that we too had made our own ways here and were ourselves something like outcasts and runaways from other lands and tribes to start with" (17). As Angel arrives via ferry and bus as "summer was walking away into the arms of autumn," she watches out over the moving fog, steps off the boat, and is reminded that "even land was not stable" (23, 29).

The linking of moving bodies, moving temporalities, and moving lands, as well as the scale evoked through the narrative, an interesting investigative lens in American Indian studies, a field is politically driven by the seeming stability of History (capital H intended) and statist conceived territory. In many ways, the novel reflects on what it might mean to think of Native peoples as becoming and belonging in movement rather than as stable and unchanging identities.

Bodies of Water, Bodies of Land

Yet while we have the personal story of Angel and her family, the novel also engages in the larger vertical and horizontal scales of colonialism. A Native feminist practice that kindles a new look at the historical and Native futurities, or the vertical, and the connections among peoples and places out from a specific event, or the horizontal, is a powerful key to disrupt processes of spatial injustices that rely on the cooptation of both axes to ensure settler regimes. In the novel, the vertical and horizontal converge in the settler states' ongoing devouring of Native land and bodies. Hogan situates the novel against a backdrop of the completion of the actual Hydro-Québec project that floods the boundary waters where the characters in the novel have formed their community. In 1970, Quebec Province drew up plans for what is known as the Hydro-Québec project to dam three major rivers that traveled to James Bay. Inuit and Cree communities, who practiced a subsistence way of life passed down through generations, fought as legal battles raged over Aboriginal claims to the territory. The electricity produced by damming the rivers provided power to the United States and built an economic base for Quebec Province, whose desire to become a nation-state independent from Canada was put well before the safety and life of Indigenous peoples.

Conceptions of Native peoples in isolated areas, defined by dominant standards as impoverished, depends on generations of settler rhetoric used to create notions of *different* space; these notions played an important role in this widely debated political issue.[9] Native people were dismissed in disputes over the damming; the temporalization of the Cree and Inuit as relics of the past and efforts to minimize their numbers resulted in a large percentage of Canadians' demanding that First Nations put aside their land rights for the good of Quebec. Through this forced displacement, much as Hogan depicts in the novel, Cree and Inuit villages were made absent from the space of the nation. The plant, animal, and human destruction of life was immense; the dams caused twelve thousand kilometers of land to be submerged under water, resulting in a steep rise in mercury poisoning that, in turn, led to the demise of fish and wildlife, as well as of Cree and Inuit ways of life. Hogan's story is set in the climax of these events and thus provides a poignant lens for understanding the spatialized relationship between the nation-state and Indigenous people and how to demand spatial justice.[10] By spatial justice, I am thinking through both a model of material redistribution that ensures the life of Native peoples and forms of spatial justice that concentrate on dismantling the settler state's decision-making process, which poses the everyday threat of Indigenous dispossession. In this settler model of redistribution and spatial injustice, Cree people's land, resources, and ways of life are infringed on and continue, while those in mainstream United States and Quebec/Canada continue to receive capital and electricity. While the novel takes place temporally when the real flooding of Cree land began, in the novel Hogan uses this instance to demonstrate how colonial power continues to pose a threat. This threat is not fictional, however, and most recently the state led by the Canadian government of Stephen Harper presented legislation that seeks to extend its settler authority over tribal lands and waters to cut protections especially for waterways. Indigenous communities are the ones most affected as the state garners their resources to redistribute to China. Although *Solar Storms* is set temporally in the 1970s, it contains much insight into future effects as Canada and the United States continue to override treaty rights and practice unethical resource development. These redistributions of resources demand justice. Like the fictional Angel, many Native people continue to be left fragmented and in chaos from such mass-destruction of the human and nonhuman, and, like Angel, the reliance on memory and story ensures survival.

Angel's moments of self-discovery intensify when she and her relatives embark on a season-long canoe trip to the north, the place of her origins, to fight against the hydroelectric dams being built on Cree lands. In this way, Hogan entangles the political story of Hydro-Québec and environmental disaster that reconfigures the rivers, land, food supply, and community relationships with that of the young woman's coming-of-age narrative. This story, however, is tied to other personal journeys that widen out from a variety of scales both temporal and spatial. The reasons for this treacherous trip vary depending on the individual: Angel is going because she is seeking answers from Hannah, her estranged mother who currently lives at the site of the destruction; Bush, the woman who saves Angel as a child, is Chickasaw, but her fight for Fur Island off of Adam's Rib emboldens her to become politically active against the flooding and damming of the northern rivers, which threatens the island's, and her, existence; Angel's paternal great-grandmother, the elderly Dora-Rouge, desires to return home to her memories and relatives to die where she was born; and Angel's paternal grandmother, Agnes, goes out of familial obligation. The intergenerational thread that ties these motives together began before Angel's time with the first wave of colonization that set in motion the historical (re)mappings of people and places.[11]

The women who embark on this journey fight not only to stop the flooding of their Cree neighbors to the North, but also to defend their own world as environmental exploitation changes the local landscape and colonialism continues unabated to form unjust geographies. The environmental devastation caused by the damming of rivers too often has caused Native land dispossession in the settler states, such as Quebec and New York, and the nation-states of Canada and the United States, the boundary area in which the novel takes place. Linking this impact to interpersonal forms of violence is necessary in an effort to seek a spatial justice that encompasses notions of settler colonialism that operate at various scales. Edward Soja reckons that adhering an understanding of the spatial to that of justice, with initial ties to the legal and new meanings that have come to stand in for equality and fairness in various aspects of life outside the law, is "effective in providing an organizational and motivational adhesive . . . that can encourage and maintain heterogeneous and pluralistic association and coalition building."[12] In a community such as Adam's Rib, and in other Native communities, this idea is useful especially in the specific context of settler colonialism, which relies on unjust geographies to maintain itself. The flooding of Cree land threatens to change the community at Adam's Rib as the chain reaction of environmental impact occurs. Through the reverse retracing of the ancestors' journey from Adam's Rib to the north, the women realize that the water levels have already risen; that those animals and plants that have not drowned are now trapped on small plots of land; and that the places of their ancestors are almost buried already under "angry" water. This personification of water continues through the book, emphasizing the nonhuman and the need to treat water and land also as beings that need respect. There is much symbolizing here as this threat to all forms of life are repeated again and again. Hogan continually reminds us that there is no differentiation between the threat to the human and that to the non-human. We rely on water to sustain life. The course of water, land, history, and culture has violently changed with colonial altering, and so have the lives of these women yet again. Indigenous scales of spatial justice include a consideration of all bodies: the human, the land, the water. The women do not necessarily find what they expect in this journey, but each learns that the answers to Dora-Rouge's question about how to heal and cope with displacement are not easy and often have surprising consequences.

Generational Violence

By addressing what happens at the scale of the body in the novel in its horizontal and vertical contexts, I examine how spatial embodiments operate in the context of settler colonialism as experienced in these three generations of women. As Judith Butler states, the body is a "cultural locus of gender meanings."[13] Furthering the logic of the body as a cultural locus, I contend that Native women's bodies, as markers against territorial appropriation, Indigenous futurities and contestations of colonial politics, are a locus of gendered colonial meanings and a site of contest. Exploring generations of the body in place in *Solar Storms* enables an understanding of colonial formations.

Loretta, Hannah, and Angel are descendants of the Elk Island people. Stories and testimonies of Native people around the turn of the century make up the collage of events embedded in Hogan's narrative that reflect the atrocities that took place to humans and the land during resource extraction. Loretta, Angel's grandmother, was one of the few Elk Island people to survive a winter in which the starvation of her community was so severe that the people ate the poisoned deer left out to kill the wolves. Settlers were hunting what little game was left after various waves of resource exploitation, and they did not want to compete with wolves. In rash but typical settler fashion, they did not measure the implications of leaving out poison and neglected to consider the connection between humans and nonhumans. Such intentional neglect is ongoing and foundational to settler accumulations. The ingestion of cyanide by the wolves and by her people have left its sweet-smelling mark on Loretta and on the following generations; it is the terror of starvation and slow death that has formed Loretta's relationships with the world. This embodied experience marked her as one who becomes a cannibal through starvation. The story and the trauma do not end in the individual body of Loretta but become intergenerational violence: Loretta and her daughter Hanna Wing are open wounds that embody the mental and physical destruction of colonization, they are a "meeting place," and it is this cycle that Angel begins to break.

The generational bodies of women stand in for the unspeakable acts of a gendered colonial process; for this reason, I address Angel's, Hannah's, and Loretta's embodiment of historical settler colonization through the intergenerational violence they face and the physical scars on their bodies. Maria Yellow Horse Brave Heart defines historical trauma as a "cumulative emotional and psychological wounding, over the life span and across generations, emanating from massive group trauma experiences."[14] In her clinical study, Brave Heart lists an array of unhealthy responses that form through the experiences of historical trauma, many of which we see manifested in the context of the community at Adam's Rib.[15] Interestingly, Joe Gone, who is also a psychologist, rigorously intervenes in regard to the concept of American Indians' historical trauma, citing the ahistoricism and generalizing of the American Indian experience both temporally and culturally and the need to think through the complexity of various situated traumas. Using the first-person account of a Gros Ventre woman captured during a war with the Piegan, he attempts to unpack the issues in simply stating that trauma somehow travels genetically through the generations that arise:

> I strongly object, however, to the essentialist implications that many or most Contemporary A[merican] I[ndian]s are traumatized—wounded, weakened, disabled—by history, and that many or most AI experiences of colonization—including adjustment to and resilience in the face of these processes—were more uniform than diverse in terms of their past impacts on indigenous communities throughout North America. Moreover, I worry that locating the sources of AI distress in past generations displaces vigilant attention—and resultant action—from the ongoing structural inequalities that systematically disadvantage Indian Country today.[16]

Gone's use of first-person narrative, in an as-told-to genre, becomes the touchstone of his argument precisely because it advocates specificity, and his analysis of whether we should consider dysfunction solely as intergenerational trauma is an important consideration. I propose that if we examine *Solar Storms* as a specific narrative in time and in place, we can address the relationships and scales as I have outlined them here without eroding the political or present responsibilities of Native individuals and communities. Furthermore, by acknowledging the role of storytelling in the novel to address historical trauma, we can heed the Native feminist Dian Million's proposition in relation to why felt theory, in particular Native women's stories, are significant: "It seems inherent in 'doing history' that histories are positioned, and histories that do not understand their own positioning cannot answer to those conditions they perpetuate that require silencing that which by its nature is a contra-histoire: the voice that is always an alterNative historical interpretation of 'what happened.' Those whose subjective history this is must speak it . . . because of this history that continuously haunts our storied bodies and lands."[17] The key to reconciling the conflation in historical trauma rests in the stories that haunt, which we must engage, because "to 'decolonize' means to understand as fully as possible the forms colonialism takes in our own times."[18]

While others have proposed examining American Indians' historical trauma in *Solar Storms,* the pitfalls outlined by Gone still need to be considered. The "shifting and unstable" natures of historical and cultural contexts are at issue in the novel as rivers, animals and humans move across various backdrops and even dimensions in the case of Dora-Rouge; if historical and cultural elements are always shifting, we must be careful not to apply a "myopic projection of what appear to be contingent."[19] *Solar Storms* provides a way to mark the intimacy with which the trauma manifests itself in the struggle of interpersonal relationships by examining how colonial events set up the structures of Angel's lived experience. Addressing traumatie specificity in relation to scale is a more complex way to consider the impact of history on our bodies, both physically and mentally, without slipping into issues of the "recentness" of the trauma and its endless reverberations through subsequent generations.

Regenerative Structures of Violence

From the smell of cyanide passed down through generations to the maps of scars they share, these women embody history in the flesh. Adam's Rib, a name that evokes the link among women, history, and colonization, renders an image of the creation of hierarchies based on conceptions of the body in Christianity. According to Christian doctrine, women were made from the rib material of the first man, Adam. Civilizing the Indian was a large part of colonization, and one of the main methods of erasure was to Christianize the Indian and to change bodily and sexual practices of tribal communities, which often had multiple genders based on roles performed rather than biological organs.[20] Through the legislation of gendered criminality that relied on Christian doctrines, women in many Native communities lost much control over their social lives and practices and control over their bodies. Naming the town Adam's Rib, itself a component of settler mapping and naming that implicates the gendering processes of colonization, is a profound metaphor that links Western creation narratives and history intimately together. The Chicana feminist Cherríe Moraga first formed the phrase "theories of the flesh" to speak about her particular location as a light-skinned, mestiza, queer woman. For Moraga, as for Hogan, knowing the history of the production of her body and understanding how history affects her movements in the world is a vital component in the struggle for liberation and freedom. In the seminal *A Bridge Called My Back*, which addresses issues of women of color, Moraga writes: "The materialism in this book lives in the flesh of these women's lives: the exhaustion we feel in our bones at the end of the day, the fire we feel in our hearts when we are insulted, the knife we feel in our backs when we are betrayed, the nausea we feel in our bellies when we are betrayed, or even the hunger we feel between our hips when we long to be touched."[21]

In *Solar Storms*, the body feels the brute force of colonization, and these material impacts are necessary in a discussion about how to heal from the wounds inflicted and still experienced in place. Through the name Adam's Rib given to this small community, we can focus a discussion on the materiality of the body and the struggle for the colonized to get their lives back. Within women-of-color feminist theorizing, especially as explored in Chicana feminism,[22] theories of the flesh address history at the level of the materiality of the body—also an important step for Native women. The scars on Angel's face have remained a question for her, and she goes to Adam's Rib to discover how she became scarred. Hogan asks throughout the novel: how do bodies remember colonization and its processes, and how do we disrupt the recurring discourses that stem them? Furthermore, how do we reclaim the body that continues to be structured through the violence of settler colonialism?

Native people, however, already have many of these stories or theories of the flesh in place. For instance, Hogan frames Loretta and Hannah as a Windigo, a cannibalistic creature once human who is forged through starvation and the cold, through the Cree stories of the elder Agnes, who reflects on having found Hannah washed up on the shore of Adam's Rib and being pulled toward the "magnetic center of what I feared." Agnes relates, "Old stories . . . of the Cree began to play across my mind, stories about the frozen heart of evil that was hunger, envy, greed, how it had tricked people into death or illness or made them go insane" (13). The naming of this imbalance through stories provides an alternative to a historical trauma that begins with colonization; the fact that stories exist about dissociative and destructive violence differs from the common theories that correlate colonial historical trauma. Native peoples' stories attest to the fact that, at times, individuals and the world are out of balance, and we needed ways to bring the world into harmony always.

The self-determination in the story of Hannah and Loretta as a form of Windigo deftly weaves colonialism into a tribal narrative without privileging the event or positing a dichotomy between white colonizer and Indian victim. Thus, the body as a meeting place becomes instrumental in an analysis of intergenerational trauma. The meeting place, as conceived in Hogan's novel, mirrors Doreen Massey's conception of place as not just "areas with boundaries around [them]" but as bodies in place as that which "can be imagined as articulated moments in networks of social relations and understandings."[23] If we use a geographer's sense of place and spatial justice, understanding the Canadian-U.S. boundary waters as at once produced by and productive of the violence inflicted on the geography of the body, what might the Wings evince as bodies moving through multilayered and connected spaces?

Hogan is similarly speaking to the material effect of colonization at the scale of the body through figurative language that emphasizes the *gendered* body. While the brutality of the Wing women's lives affects Agnes, and she does have compassion and understanding, she is still afraid of what lurks behind Loretta's dissociation from the world around her. Agnes's fear of Loretta and, eventually, of Hannah is similar to the fear felt by the rest of the community: it is a fear of falling prey to the same wounding. Agnes and the community see in the Wings their own weaknesses and the pain that they represent. In his introduction to *Violence and the Body*, Arturo Aldama identifies how fear operates to affirm structures of oppression and inhibit insurrection—it is the purpose of violence and making present the wounded subject. In what might be applied to the community at Adam's Rib, Aldama states, "Fear is both the metanarrative that drives the disciplinary apparatus of the nation-state . . . and the intended effects on the body politic. Fear drives the repression, containment, coopting, torture, and annihilation of the 'unruly' subjects whose class, race, sex, and ideology identity differences, and indigenous land claims . . . are threats to bourgeois, capitalist, patriarchal, and neocolonial orders."[24] The community fears the Wings—even Angel, to some extent—because there is a material reality of physical violence and the trauma, with few ways to intervene. Violence and the threat of violence are both experienced and witnessed firsthand by Indigenous women. Aldama positions the state spectacle of violence—that which is written on each of the women's bodies—as both "terminal and regenerative acts."[25] Rape, mutilation, and starvation of both the human and the nonhuman further the discursive connections between violence and the body and go beyond mere acts that occur during colonialism to produce regenerative structures.

The Meeting Place

Hannah's act of biting away her own daughter's face symbolizes the cannibalism, the location of the dissociative disorder, that the community is fighting. The scars not only mark Angel throughout her journeys; they also are the scars of the dispossessed people who live at Adam's Rib. Even in this dispossession through time and through varied places, Hogan makes clear that the people work to create a home. Home in *Solar Storms* is a site of contestation, as it is for many Native peoples in a colonial context, whether they are in their homelands, dislocated, or have made new homes in other geographies. Hogan makes explicit how Hannah's dislocation of home—that is, her inability to identify with the human and nonhuman that define home, which lead her to run, to move, to commit acts of violence against others—informs how home, as the "site of personal and familial reproduction, . . . a physical location and perhaps a structure—permanent or temporary,"[26] operates in a settler colonial context.

Hannah's inability to love—to feel a connection to her daughter or even to the world around her, for that matter—poses a terrible threat. Hannah has been changed through the forces of history. She has been starved, beaten, sexually tortured, and exploited, and the accumulation of this force is represented as "hungry," an image of immeasurable pain that threatens to swallow Native people, animals, and land in the novel. The distance Agnes and others keep from Loretta and Hannah, the strange red-headed girls, is similar to the distance they try to keep from the Hungry Mouth of Water, an area that destroys people, animals, and especially man-made technology. It is a place of thin ice with water properties that cannot be explained and that provides the source of power and fear. Like the Hungry Mouth of Water, Hannah embodies the "meeting place," just as her mother, Loretta, did. Hannah is devoid of affective relationships; she is detached, but not with maliciousness.[27] Hannah represents the extraordinary sum of torture, rape, displacement, and exploitation. She is the history that lingers in current generations and in the national consciousness, or, respectively, a history of sexuality, insemination, and rape that becomes erased in dominant histories and laws.[28] This physical embodiment of history is neither a literary tactic nor happenstance, however, as Native women's bodies have been a site of struggle since early in the colonization of the Americas.[29] In fact, in the conquering of precolonial America, the land was often depicted as female or virgin territory waiting to be fertilized and inscribed in European encounters; a look at early maps in colonial America demonstrates the gendering of the Native subject.[30]

Colonial forms of amnesia that regulate Native women as absent bodies or as victimized or degenerative subjects depend on Native bodies' being out of place—that is, shadows and haunting presences of political and symbolic economies. Part of the structure of settler colonialism is to create amnesia around geographies and purport criteria of difference across vertical, as well as horizontal, scales. That is, colonialism in the context of the United States, Canada, and their provinces and states demands a temporal process of re-membering a nostalgic past and places of pristine virgin land. Settler colonial structures must imagine a homogenous stable present space developed for the good of the majority, even while they rely on forgetting the violence it took to produce the nation-state and the violence and fear it takes to sustain the current sociopolitical order, which necessitates a lack of ac-knowledging the ongoing structures of the colonial moment. The memory and history written on the bodies of these women is referred to in perfor-mance studies as "living memory," passed down "through the transmission of gestures, habits, and skills."[31] I argue that it is also passed down through the continued onslaught of colonizing land and reconstituting Native bodies. These transmissions of living memory are loaded with meaning in the context of Native people and are a vital component in how national imaginings have had a material impact on Native communities and conceptions of self. The training of the perceived "savage" body became a main objective of colo-nization, from missionizing Indians to enforcing boarding schools.[32] It is the settler imaginary of Native savagery that legitimates conditions through which bodies were and are continually disciplined. This move in the struc-tures of colonialism, however, is read as "civilizing" or, in today's language, as helping to "develop" Native nations so that they can "share" in progress. The traces of this history linger and fester and manifest themselves on the bodies of Native women. Hogan's depiction of Native bodies as scarred undermines the erasure of this violence and posits these scars and embodiments as Native women's resilience, healing, and alternative conception of history and futurity.

Hannah's, Loretta's, and Angel's bodies are described in a sublime lan-guage as beautiful, dark, red-haired, and terrifying. The three women are depicted as mixed-raced people with a tragic and seductive beauty. The signifying of their mixed-blood status is not what separates them from the community, however; nor does it move them away from their "original" roots, as structures of settler colonialism would have us believe. By focus-ing on the scaled violence on the body, we can think through Neil Smith's operation of scale yet again: "This suggests the double-edged nature of scale. By setting boundaries, scale can be constructed as a means of constraint and exclusion, a means of imposing identity, but a politics of scale can also become a weapon of expansion and inclusion, a means of enlarging identities. Scale offers guideposts in the recovery of space from annihilation."[33] Hogan is rewriting the common narrative of the tragic mixed-blood on the outskirts of her community—a body out of place. Rather than being excluded, the Wings' bodies become the meeting place that opens up to various spatial and temporal dimensions: "One day she told me that the earth had more than one dimension. The one we see is only the first layer" (123). Also dispelled is the suspended subject of the "man between two worlds" (or, in this case, the tragic mixed-blood between worlds) discourse.[34] The bodies encountered in the novel open up an alternative space in which to engage with complicated conceptions of what spatial justice may look like. Death of the Native subject does not come in this case through dissolution of Native blood; most often, it comes through gendered violence and resource exploitation. The women do not inhabit an outside space. Instead, they are intimately tied to a wounded inner space of their communities.

The fear and magnetism the women evoke is intimately part of the community—the space these women engage in the text is pivotal to understanding community formation and re-creation. When Hannah washes up on shore with the same sickeningly sweet smell as her mother, Loretta, Agnes tells us, "No matter how we scrubbed, the smell never came off that poor girl. It was deeper than skin. It was blood-deep. It was history-deep, Old Man said" (40). Hannah is part of the community—a part of them and of the land; thus, the continued attempt to wash off the smell. The metaphor of blood holds significant meaning in Native American literature. As Chadwick Allen writes, "Like Momaday's trope, the blood/land/memory complex articulates acts of indigenous minority recuperation that attempt to seize control of the symbolic and metaphorical meanings of indigenous 'blood,' 'land,' and 'memory' and that seek to liberate indigenous minority identities from definitions of authenticity imposed by dominant settler cultures."[35] In Hogan's case, blood also refers quite literally to the blood spilled through violence. Hannah and Loretta have been literally tortured, communities have been massacred, and violence is still committed in the daily lives of Native people. While I examine the *symbolic* meanings of blood, body, and scars, the *material* reality of tortured, beaten, and murdered people should not be easily forgotten. This embodied experience that Hogan offers us, that reflects "real life" but is not meant to be mimetic in its representation, serves not only to represent or fill in the gaps of violent history. It also intervenes in a dominant ideological formation that disavows and thus legitimates ongoing violence. It is also what makes the symbolism so poignant in *Solar Storms* and Angel's narrative so significant, because it exists even while it is overlooked in economies of abandonment, to use Elizabeth Povinelli's phrase. Povinelli articulates how "framing social difference through specific configurations of tense . . . legitimate differential belonging," and, I argue here, it is this parsing of gendered forms, particularly in settler structures, that "make these forms of killing and letting die seem right, reasonable, and good."[36]

In speaking of death, citizenship, and forms of nation making, Sharon Holland pushes forward Benedict Anderson's theory of narrative state making by addressing the material and racialized body in relation to the structures of the nation-state:

> Anderson still relies, as noted earlier, on the fatality in language rather than on actual fatality as represented by a literal body. In his earlier discussion the body's absence, not presence, figures the nation and its awakening. The study of death in relationship to nationalist discourse proves all the more fascinating when we recall that scores of nationalist literatures rely on a very central image—that of the "nation" being embodied. And this national body is overwhelmingly imagined and inscribed as *female*. This would seem to stand in direct contradistinction to the kind of disembodied anonymity sought after to sustain the nation-state.[37]

I extend Holland's critique here and would further allude to the body in the colonial nation-state as most often gendered and differentiated as Native women; thus, I emphasize the meaning of the scale of the body in the gendered forms of colonial violence. The conquering of the Native body, both figuratively and literally, was the object of many national policies regarding Native people in North America. The death and silencing of Native women are particularly important components of how the United States wrongly imagines itself as a democratic nation of immigrants—a nation of freedom and equality, progressive in its politics, that built itself from scratch and with hard work rather than through exploitation, massacre, theft, and stolen land. It is Loretta's, Hannah's, and Angel's *presence*, in both the fatality of language and the actual fatality of body, that disrupts these imaginings of U.S. citizenship, borders, and nation. Holland emphasizes, "In fact, if hyperbole were my forte, I might want to suggest that the dead and their relations are perhaps the most lawless, unruly and potentially revolutionary inhabitants of any imagined territory, national, or otherwise. Moreover, I would add that the disenfranchised and oppressed often join the dead in this quixotic space."[38]

Hogan's characters are not dead, however; they occupy an even more danger-ous space: they are living registers of diasporic politics and histories of the dispossession that continues to remove them forcibly from their lands and mark their bodies for death. The Wings stand for a meeting place between life and death, a space of in-between and of body as a memory jogger not only of fear, but also of loss and the need for ongoing resistance.

Examinations of gendered bodies as a meeting space intensifies the in-terconnectedness of the various scales and breaks down the distances con-structed by colonial knowledge production. For instance, the protagonist un-ravels her identity through a process of linking history and the body. Agnes tells us, "The curse on that poor girl's [Loretta's] life came from watching the desperate people of her tribe die." It is this curse that Angel is seeking to re-dress and that her community also hopes to lay to rest. Agnes reminds Angel, "When [Loretta] was still a girl she had been taken and used by men who fed her and beat her and forced her. That was how one day she became the one who hurt others. It was passed down. . . . We wanted to blame someone like her. . . . But Loretta wasn't the original sin" (39). The original sin begins with the first acts of inhumanity and does not continue in a linear path, as the original sin and its subsequent disavowal continue. Not only is Angel reclaim-ing her place in a community; she is also reclaiming the history and mem-ories meant to be forgotten. Adam's Rib becomes a community of people who bring together their cyclical memories of a way of life that predates their struggles against missionaries, trappers, miners, and fishermen and the memories of how they survived these events. The confluence of memories and innovativeness of Bush and women like her creates a collapsed space in which original sin is reconstituted. By disrupting the linear and patriar-chal narrative of original sin that begins with knowledge produced from her embodiment, a Native feminist praxis can begin to tackle the cycles of de-struction or even to dismantle the narrative that colonization, or conquest is complete. Creation is not a linear progression, but it is foundational to settler logics. In this Native literary text, the temporality of the everyday provides a new chance for creation because "creation is not yet over" (350). Unlike the garden in the biblical image that separates humans from nature, Angel must recognize the connection between the human and the nonhuman and its extension into all scales. In the text, Angel stands at the point of emerg-ing, in the in-between, and moves toward learning to "know the maps inside ourselves," the cycles of creation and re-creation, life and death.

Hogan's play on the concept of original sin, a sin that is produced through knowledge of the body and, in turn, is productive of patriarchy and gender constructions, brings colonial histories and their ongoing effects together in body, place, and time. Hannah is the key to unlocking Angel's past. For Angel, returning home first means meeting with the beginning of her creation and finding answers to her displacement, again interconnecting mother and motherland. She soon learns that Hannah is the key to much more than her own life story. When Angel was little, Bush, who was taking care of her after the attack, took Hannah to Old Man, an elder who is known for his spiritual strength, wisdom, and knowledge. Old Man told Bush that Hannah was "the House. . . . She is the meeting place" (101). This embodiment of history and space occurs most often and most poignantly in the depiction of Hannah as a house. "I didn't know what he meant at first," Bush tells Angel, "but I saw it in time, her life going backward to where time and history and genocide gather and move like a cloud above the spilled oceans of blood. That little girl's body was the place where all this met" (101).

Although Bush tries to help Hannah, she is unable to call Hannah back to an interconnected world. This is counter to the progressive narrative of development of Native lands and bodies—the narratives used by Quebec, Canada, and corporations to incorporate Native land and erase Native bodies. The songs to call Hannah back are lost in the continued destruction of Native life and culture. Bush, the innovator, sings to Hannah so she can understand her and help rid her of the ghosts inside: "Inside were the ruins of humans. Burned children were in there, as well as fire. It pulled me toward it, like gravity, like dust to earth" (103). But unlike a linear or temporal positioning of an event that is attached to the lived experience of the body that reverberates trauma through generations, it is the historical constructions of the body that become ongoing and make women's bodies expendable.

Hannah resides in the place of in-between, unable to emerge because the terror that lives inside her is larger than the frame of her small, injured body. Bush encounters this occupied space and understands that it is "an inescapable place with no map for it . . . whatever it was, I had to call on all my strength to get away" (103). The terror in Hannah's life goes beyond that of the individual or her family and lends itself to a group trauma. Unlike in a neoliberal approach to trauma or violence, however, it is necessary to see the scale of the body not as a separate space but as connected to others.[39] Occupying this horrific space of pain does not relegate Hannah to a place outside the community; in fact, she provides valuable insight into the community's imagining of itself. The insight that the "meeting place" provides is immeasurable. It is a site of struggle, not one of amnesia or denial: "She was a body under siege, a battleground" (99). Bush tells Angel that Hannah was like a door, "Always closed. But sometimes I thought she was a window, instead, because through her I glimpsed scenes of suffering" (112). Her house is her body, and in the body of this beautiful Indian girl, unspoken atrocities and abnormal strength reside. In witnessing the maimed body of Hannah, other atrocities are recalled, and the body of history becomes alive.

Rebuilding Foundations, Tearing Down Colonial Structures

The women in her community guide Angel through their stories and telling of memories. In her first days at Adam's Rib and throughout her journey to the north, Angel is given the tools she needs to meet her mother. Storytelling is part of the remembering process that is undertaken not only by Angel, but also by the women from Adam's Rib, to break the linearity and material accumulation of colonial dispossession. This speaking is a significant aspect of understanding Angel's relationship to the boundless waters of her origins. Yet Hannah embodies that liminal space of speech akin to the sparseness of documents regarding the gendered violence of settler colonialism and the present-day lack of attention to Native issues. In the first meeting between daughter and mother at a site of impending environmental destruction, silence fills the space of Hannah's sparse and depriving house. It is not coincidental that Hannah is in this meeting place of state destruction, a Native territory that the state is transforming into domesticated service for current and future settler nations. Angel recognizes that the answers for which she searches cannot be found in what she believed was the moment of her creation, and she looks beyond Hannah's body, connecting it to multiple scales. She forgoes the Western map of chronology that would have her pinpoint the events that cause her pain. Literally standing on the doorstep of her mother's death, Angel realizes that "Hannah's house, like her body, even from my beginning, had the same little or nothing to offer" (243). Recalling the narratives, Angel realizes she has the tools to be compassionate at this moment: "I understood already from what the women said that my mother was stairs with no destination. She was a burning house, feeding on the air of others." Angel reminds us of the symbiotic relationship between the injured body and the rest of the community, saying, "She had no more foundation, no struts, and no beams. Always a person would think she was one step away from collapsing. But she remained standing" (96). In examining the scale of the body, we are able to conceive of Native women's bodies not merely as trapped in victimization, genetically inheriting the pain. Rather, they are affected by the constant pressure of a settler colonial environment around them. Yet it is the women's stories that also remap body geographies to show connections. Bush tells Angel about another return to Adam's Rib—this time, Hannah's return from the unspoken and unacknowledged sex boats to the community as a young, pregnant, and dangerous woman: "She would kill you. Husk said it was a law of probability. He also said that a glacier gives off what it can't absorb, blue light and beauty, and that you were the light given off by your mother" (105).

Although Hannah is the place between forgotten and remembered, spoken and unspoken, she is also the meeting place to unmoor the economic, political, and colonial structures that the community continues to endure.[40] She is the acknowledgment of economies of abandonment and their simultaneous disavowal of that violence. In finding her mother, Angel soon realizes what Bush meant about not always being able to recuperate the lost body: "Like Bush traveling north, I wanted a map, something fixed, a road in. I wanted to see what was between this woman and me, a landmark, a bond. I had imagined this meeting so many times, but none of them had been like this. Any path between us had long since been closed. She was as Bush said, a wall, a place to go with no foundation" (230). Hannah is the wounded, the closed-off subject who cannot experience pleasure or pain and can only inflict it on others. Yet as she receives the stories of trauma and colonization, Angel does not have to react in the same manner as her predecessors; she is "embodied potentiality insofar as embodied potentiality is the prime material of moral reflection and evaluation."[41] The moment of Hannah's death leads to one of refiguring geographies not as territory, borders, or impermeable bodies, nor does it resolve Angel to a strict social order or closing off of possibilities. In fact, the picture of Hannah's death is one that opens up growth, forgiveness, and compassion: "It was like a seed of something that opened and grew inside her, as if it had known the territory for a long time, plotting its way through flesh and bone, waiting for the moment of its unfolding" (250). Instead of using the needed cloth to bury Hannah, they place her on newspapers: "How appropriate it was to place her on words of war, obituaries, stories of carnage and misery, and true stories that had been changed to lies" (253). Hannah's body becomes the literal manifestation of history and defining geographies at various scales: "Some of the words stuck to her body, dark ink, but we did not wash them off; it was suitable skin." Unlike Bush's attempt to wash the almond scent off Hannah's body years ago, at Hannah's death, the women confront and make peace with the body of history (double-entendre intended). Hannah is simultaneously crucial for the community and to historical memory and impossible and untenable—so much so that Angel has to both encounter and put to rest her mother, which she does both figuratively and literally as she buries her, in order to belong to the social life of the community and sustain its future. From out of the closed-off body of Hannah comes Angel, who clings to life and desires to know not only who she *is* but where she comes from and who she is becoming.

The covering of Hannah marks a new point in Angel's life in which the dynamics of place are set in terms of the relationships she has formed with Bush, Agnes, Dora-Rouge, and other women at Adam's Rib. Angel goes from the land around her, the displaced to the placed, cemented by the new life given to her. The death signifies the end of Angel's pubescent, diasporic journey and a beginning. As if looking in a mirror, she says, "I was uneasy about being in the house with the body, so I looked at Hannah one more time, at the skin of my skin, the face that had given shape to mine, and then I covered her" (251). She is now the caretaker of a small child, Aurora, signifying the dawning of new day and giving her responsibility for a relationship that she did not expect: one that is formed from kinship, not just biology. As she walks to town, Angel looks at the land around her, referring to the instability: "The land was dried and white-edged, like the alkali flats of Oklahoma. Oil drums sat outside little buildings. Everything looked temporary" (252). The narrative returns to the opening of the book, where Angel journeys on the Greyhound bus from Oklahoma but is not sure how long she will stay once she reaches her destination. She understands in the moment of Hannah's death and the unexpected arrival of Aurora the processes and links between creation and re-creation and possibility. Although speaking specifically to the practices of the Lakota, Brave Heart's words ring true of many tribal cultures not only in which empowerment is brought about by individual healing but also in which part of that healing must be "to function as an integral part of creation." Unlike the idea of healing of the individual self, which all too often becomes how sexual and gendered violence is handled, or the idea of a human-nonhuman binary, becoming a part of creation is the cornerstone that enables Angel to confront the past and the present. Understanding where she belongs in the social world—that of the human and the nonhuman world—enables her to provide alternative futures to the destruction she witnesses in the past and present. While settler spatial construction has not ended, and continues to produce power over Indigenous bodies and land, there continue to be slippages and possibilities.

The terror of history and the sweet smell of desperate survival continue to mark the bodies of Loretta, Hannah, and Angel, representing a violent and ongoing history, as well as its material consequences for dispossessed and disposed-of lands and peoples. The process of remembering, or making sense out of chaos, and creating are pivotal to the survival of those who live at Adam's Rib and all areas it signifies. The scars, however, are permanent. But just as Angel emerges to see a positive reflection of self, so, too, might the answers to Dora-Rouge's question be for Native people to find that "something wonderful lives inside me" (351). This inside, though the smallest of the scale, is intricately connected to generations and ongoing relationships to land and peoples.

At first, the community pulls away from the dangerous bodies of the Wing family, where past and present meet and hold a terrifying power. Much of the symbolism in the novel connects the various scales, demonstrating that the criteria that marks different kinds of spaces are not only Cartesian-based but also reliant on the gendered logics of elimination of the Native and the disavowal of that elimination. Hannah, Loretta, and Angel have faced systematic cycles of colonization in which their bodies have been subjected to erasure and violence. These stories must not be avoided but told, as Million makes clear in talking about the survivors of residential schools: "Indigenous women participated in creating new language for communities to address the real multilayered facets of their histories and concerns by insisting on the inclusion of our lived experience, rich with emotional knowledge of what pain and grief and hope meant or mean now in our pasts and futures."[42] Recuperating the importance of the body and registering it as an embodiment connected to the human and nonhuman becomes a step toward healing the scars of colonization: "What mattered, simply and powerfully, was knowing the current of water and living in the body where land spoke what a woman must do to survive" (204).

Angel's ability to follow her instincts, to identify the hungry maps inside her, not only becomes vital in repositioning herself as a colonized person; she becomes a vital part of the community at Adam's Rib. In Angel's search for answers and journey to "home," she not only encounters the present moment that envelops the preceding quote, but she also takes into account the body of history and makes clear its importance: "I'd searched all my life for this older world that was lost to me, this world only my body remembered. In that moment I understood I was part of the same equation as birds and rain" (79). The bodies of Native women are dangerous because they produce knowledge and demand accountability, whether at the scale of their individual bodily integrity, of their communities' ability to remain on their bodies of land and water, or as citizens of their nations. The sites of these "meeting places" and scales of geographies are key to contesting colonial structures that limit spatial alternatives and thus continue to create spatial injustices. Thus, I end with profound words spoken by Angel: "The problem has always been this: that the only possibility for survival has been resistance. Not to strike back has meant certain loss and death. To strike back has also meant loss and death, only with a fighting chance" (325).

NOTES

1. Linda Hogan, *Solar Storms: A Novel* (New York: Scribner, 1995), 226. (Hereafter, page numbers for direct quotes from this work are cited in parentheses in the text.)

2. Noelani Goodyear-Ka'opua, *The Seeds We Planted: Portraits of a Native Hawaiian Charter School* (Minneapolis: University of Minnesota Press, 2013).

3. Neil Smith, "Homeless/Global: Scaling Places," in *Mapping the Futures: Local Cultures, Global Change*, eds. John Bird, Barry Curtis, Tim Putnam, and Lisa Tickner (London: Routledge, 1993), 101.

4. Smith, "Homeless/Global," 99.

5. Many current environmental policies reflect this "criteria" of spaces that are deemed expendable, as in the case of the Navajo Nation's water rights and potential theft of water by the State of Arizona to expand; the case of tar sands, which affect First Nations communities in Canada and American Indian communities in the United States; the constant threat of oil drilling on Inuit lands. These incidents are just a few ways an exertion of settler definitions of space enables ongoing settler spatial injustice. For a look at grounded normativities as a site of resistance, see Glen Coulthard, "Place against Empire: Understanding Indigenous Anti-Colonialism," *Affinities* 4, no. 2 (Fall 2010): 79–83.

6. Patrick Wolfe, *Settler Colonialism and the Transformation of Anthropology: The Politics and Poetics of an Ethnographic Event* (London: Cassell, 1999), 163.

7. Victoria Sweet, "Rising Waters, Rising Threats: The Human Trafficking of Indigenous Women in the Circumpolar Region of the United States and Canada," Michigan State University Legal Studies Research Paper no. 12–01, February 20, 2014.

8. Here I would like to make clear that I separate sex trafficking from sex work, as conflating the two could lead to increased criminalization of Native women. Jessica Yee importantly states, "Many people uncritically accept the conflation of trafficking and sex work. The same people who think it is taboo to talk about sex are the first to suggest that this is the number one issue of forced labour, but it's not. And people who are actually being trafficked and moved against their will receive no attention because the state is so focused on raiding massage parlours and arresting women who are sex workers. This neglect occurs in the name of righteousness and 'saving' women, yet it is merely

the further colonization of women's bodies, women's spaces, and women's choices": see Robyn Maynard's interview with Jessica Yee in "Sex Work, Migration and Anti-trafficking." *Briarpatch Magazine*, June 6, 2014, http://briarpatchmagazine.com/articles /view/sex-work-migration-anti-trafficking. Yet in the novel, the situation of Hannah and Loretta is not clear (as in many nonfictional cases) and needs to be addressed in the context of colonization. For more information, see Sarah Deer, "Relocation Revisited: Sex Trafficking of Native Women in the United States," *William Mitchell Law Review* 36, no. 2 (2010), http://ssrn.com/abstract=1567144; Melissa Farley, Nicole Matthews, Sarah Deer, Guadalupe Lopez, Christine Stark and Eileen Hudon, "Garden of Truth: The Prostitution and Trafficking of Native Women in Minnesota," report, Minnesota Indian Women's Sexual Assault Coalition and Prostitution Research and Education, William Mitchell College of Law, Saint Paul, October 2011.

9. The Inuit community actually uses maps based on oral stories and Native conceptions of space to document their traditional territory to legally fight the project. For an account of the Inuit place name maps and how they aided in establishing the rights of Inuit people in Nunavik, see Marc Warhus, *Another America* (New York: St. Martin's Press, 1997), 222–29.

10. See Dennis McPherson, "A Definition of Culture" in *Native American Religious Identity: Unforgotten Gods* for an in-depth discussion of how the differing concepts of culture affect the ability of Canada and Aboriginal nations to work through complex historical relationship. Coulthard, "Place against Empire," 79–83.

11. Part of Hogan's project is piecing together the history, people, and cultural ties that exist in the area. It is not a new mapping that takes place but one that is rooted in the past and conditioned by the future. The parentheses perform the act of drawing invention and continuity together. For a larger discussion on this, see Mishuana Goeman, *Mark My Words: Native Women Mapping Our Nations* (Minneapolis: University of Minnesota Press, 2013).

12. Edward W. Soja, *Seeking Spatial Justice* (Minneapolis: University of Minnesota Press, 2010), 24.

13. Judith Butler. "Variations on Sex and Gender: Beauvoir, Witting, and Foucault," in *Praxis International*, no. 4 (January 1986): 505–16, 505.

14. Maria Yellow Horse Brave Heart, "The Impact of Historical Trauma: The Example of the Native Community," in *Trauma Transformed: An Empowerment Response*, eds. Marian Bussey and Judity Bula Wise (New York: Columbia University Press, 2012), 176–93.

15. Irene Vernon provides a useful analysis of the relationship among the three women and the role of trauma in the novel, particularly conveying the use of story as a mechanism for healing: see Irene S. Vernon, " 'We Were Those Who Walked out of Bullets and Hunger': Representation of Trauma and Healing in *Solar Storms*," *American Indian Quarterly* 36, no. 1 (Winter 2012): 34–49.

16. Joseph Gone, "Colonial Genocide and Historical Trauma in Native North America: Complicating Contemporary Attributions," in *Colonial Genocide in Indigenous North America*, eds. A. Woolford, J. Benvenuto, & A. L. Hinton (Durham: Duke University Press. 2014), 273–91.

17. Dian Million, "Felt Theory: An Indigenous Feminist Approach to Affect and History," *Wicazō Ṣa Review* 24, no. 2 (2009): 72.

18. Million, "Felt Theory," 55.

19. Gone, "Colonial Genocide and Historical Trauma in Native North America," 273–91.

20. See Mark Rifkin, *When Did Indians Become Straight? Kinship, the History of Sexuality, and Native Sovereignty* (New York: University of Oxford Press, 2011). Rifkin provides a methodical analysis of how gendered and sexualized practices of subjugation were not just a part of colonization and setting up settler structures but fundamental to it.

21. Cherríe Moraga, "Preface," in *This Bridge Called My Back: Writings by Radical Women of Color*, eds. Cherríe Moraga and Gloria Anzaldúa (New York: Kitchen Table Women of Color Press, 1983), xvii.

22. See Yvonne Yarbro-Bejarano, "The Lesbian Body in Latina Cultural Production," in *Entiendes? Queer Readings, Hispanic Writings*, ed. Emilie L. Bergmann and Paul Julian Smith (Durham, NC: Duke University Press, 1995); Yvonne Yarbro-Bejarano, *The Wounded Heart: Writing on Cherríe Moraga* (Austin: University of Texas Press, 2001).

23. Doreen Massey, "Power-Geometry and a Progressive Sense of Place" in Bird et al., *Mapping the Futures*, 67.

24. Arturo J. Aldama, "Violence, Bodies, and the Color of Fear," in *Violence and the Body: Race, Gender, and the State*, ed. Arturo J. Aldama (Bloomington: Indiana University Press, 2003), 2.

25. Aldama, "Violence, Bodies, and the Color of Fear," 5.

26. Neil Smith, "Homeless/Global: Scaling Places," in *Mapping the Futures: Local Cultures, Global Change*, ed. John Bird, Barry Curtis, Tim Putnam, and Lisa Tickner (London: Routledge, 1993), 101.

27. A comparison between Morrison's character of Beloved and Hannah can be drawn here. A history of violence has led to the physical embodiment of history. Although Hannah is not a ghost, she does appear as a being possessed by ghosts that occupy her at night. Another factor that intimately ties *Beloved* and *Solar Storms* together is the pivotal role of infanticide in the text. Hannah is actually depicted as a cannibal, a woman who ate her own child.

28. Elaine Scarry's *The Body in Pain: The Making and Unmaking of the World* (New York: Oxford University Press, 1985) discusses the ideologies and semiotics of torture and examines the body as a site manipulated by direct extension of power relations in a particular society.

29. In the early formation of nation-states in the Americas, control of women's sexuality, interracial mixing, women as domestic servants, and many other such sites of control over women's bodies existed. In fact, in the early colonial period a woman's autonomy over her body became a site of struggle for priests, educators, and other administrators of colonialism.

30. See Malcolm Lewis, *Cartographic Encounters: Perspectives on Native American Mapmaking and Map Use* (Chicago: University of Chicago Press, 1998).

31. Joseph Roach, *Cities of the Dead: Circum-Atlantic Performance* (New York: Columbia University Press, 1996), 26.

32. K. Tsianina Lomawaima's Foucauldian reading of the practices at *Chilocco* Indian School presents just one example of how Native bodies were trained so that they could become "good citizens": K. Tsianina Lomawaima, *They Called It Prairie Light: The Story of Chilocco Indian School* (Lincoln: University of Nebraska Press, 1994).

33. Smith, "Homeless/Global," 114.

34. For an in-depth study of mixed-blood status in American Indian cultural production, see Louis Owen, *Mixed Blood Messages* (Norman: University of Oklahoma Press, 1998).

35. Chadwick Allen, *Blood Narrative: Indigenous Identity in American Indian and Maori Literary and Activist Texts* (Durham, NC: Duke University Press, 2002), 16.

36. Elizabeth Povinelli, *Economies of Abandonment: Social Belonging and Endurance in Late Liberalism* (Durham, NC: Duke University Press, 2011), 29.

37. Sharon Holland, *Raising the Dead: Readings of Death and (Black) Subjectivity* (Durham, NC: Duke University Press, 2000), 23.

38. Holland, *Raising the Dead*, 23.

39. Sarah Deer's "Decolonizing Rape Law: A Native Feminist Synthesis of Safety and Sovereignty" (*Wicazō Ša* 24, no. 2 [2009]: 149–67) unpacks the relationship between law, which is driven by punishing the individual, and not accounting for a community that becomes disrupted in the wake of sexual violence.

40. Hortense Spillers refers to flesh in the context of the terror slavery inflicted on women's bodies. Spillers is concerned and the continuing construction of blackness through the female black body, which she terms as "the interstices." While her argument adds insight to the connection between bodies and flesh, unspoken and spoken, and living and dead with the making of national subjects, it relies on the historical moment of the Middle Passage—the unmaking and making of black subjectivity. For Hogan, creation and re-creation are continual, occurring as land becomes occupied through the physical and ideological detriments of national narratives: Hortense J. Spillers, "Mama's Baby, Papa's Maybe: An American Grammar Book," *Diacritics* 17, no. 2 (1987): 64–81.

41. Povinelli, *Economies of Abandonment*, 16.

42. Million, "Felt Theory," 54.

4

AUDIOVISUALIZING IÑUPIAQ MEN AND MASCULINITIES *ON THE ICE*

JESSICA BISSETT PEREA

As I listened to numerous legends I would sometimes be pleasantly rewarded with a song. Much of our literature is interspersed with songs. The songs are powerful. There are songs to call animals. Songs that heal. Songs that harm. And songs to relate oneself to the land.—**Edna Ahgeak MacLean (Iñupiaq),** "Role of Literature as a Source of History, Values and Identity"

The Arctic is far from being a remote place disconnected to our daily lives. Instead, we're all connected to the northern landscape . . . we tell many stories of local, regional, and global interconnectedness—both celebratory and tragic.—**Subhankar Banerjee,** *Arctic Voices*

A core aim of the field of men's studies is to better understand a historically recurring "crisis of masculinity," spurred by a diverse range of factors such as modernization, industrialization, urbanization, and bureaucratization.[1] Yet this type of crisis-led inquiry tends to assume that there was once one universal and honorable way to be a man, a loss that reinforces a deficit model that is assumed in questions such as, "Where are the men?"[2] When questioning the absence or presence of men within Native American and Indigenous studies, one must consider intersecting historical crises caused by colonization—namely, settler society's "Indian problem" and its accompanying myth of the "vanishing Indian." When dominant American narratives do imagine or acknowledge Native American and Indigenous presence, that presence is typically male, albeit in very narrow and stereotyped representations of maleness. In relation to representations of Native American and Indigenous men in popular culture, Sam McKegney's term "masculindians" productively encapsulates how colonial mass-produced images "rehearse hypermasculine stereotypes of the noble savage and the bloodthirsty warrior (as well as their ideological progeny—the ecological medicine man, the corrupt band councilor, and the drunken absentee)."[3] One need only consider the deeply problematic discourse surrounding the Washington Redskins' mascot: neoliberal and capitalist interests defend it as "honoring" Native North American people, and Native North American people argue it is exploitative and valorizes colonial expectations of the savage Indian.[4] Here and elsewhere, Native American and Indigenous men are represented as an "impossibly masculine race," as always already removed from their tribal- or community-specific identities and roles.[5] To be sure, these stereotypical representations are rooted in ideologies held and concrete policies enacted by heteronormative and patriarchal settler societies, including: religious conversion and missionization; compulsory Western education via boarding and residential school systems; and economic exploitation via agricultural and industrial labor. Over time these colonial forces have caused a range of imbalances and dislocations for Native American and Indigenous families and communities.

Thus, an emerging cadre of scholars, artists, and activists are working to move beyond emphases on the universality and marginality of man (singular) by calling for more nuanced and culturally responsive emphases on the complexities and diversities of tribal- or community-specific identities and roles for male-identified Native American and Indigenous people. In response, a growing body of research in Native American and Indigenous men and masculinities studies has documented the importance of relearning or recovering of precolonial and precapitalist male identities ("who they are") and masculine roles ("what they do") that reject the long histories of settler colonial dominance and violence.[6] Part of this recovery process necessarily involves decolonizing mass-produced stereotypes and expectations by instead documenting and archiving the diversity of tribal- or community-specific male identities and masculine roles, responsibilities that are culture- and place-based *in relation to* language, land, family, and community.[7] Given this scholarly turn toward culture- and place-based studies of Native American and Indigenous men and masculinities, my goals for this chapter are twofold. First, since very few Inuit voices are featured in the existing scholarship, I seek to address the following questions: "Where are the *Inuit* men?"[8] What historical and ongoing colonial forces unique to the Arctic/ Subarctic region affect how male-identified Inuit people deal with the contemporary challenges of defining "who they are" on the basis of "what they do"?[9] To amplify Inuit perspectives within the emerging field of Native American and Indigenous masculinities studies, this chapter listens critically to contemporary Inuit-produced media to better understand a range of Inuit articulations of male identities and masculine roles and the ways in which they have been shaped by both mass-produced stereotypes and ongoing histories of colonization and decolonization unique to the Arctic.

In turning to contemporary Inuit-produced media, my second goal for this chapter is to demonstrate the value of equalizing the realms of sight and sound when analyzing mediascapes that contain socially engineered stereotypes about Native American and Indigenous men and masculinities.[10] In other words, I want to expand existing ocular-centric critiques of colonial "regimes of images" by emphasizing the auditory significance of colonial regimes of *sounds*.[11] I argue that rejoining visual and aural analyses, a process one might call "audiovisualizing," media scholars could more fully historicize the origins of socially engineered stereotypes and thus productively contribute to a dismantling of harmful expectations of Native American and Indigenous people and cultures.

To achieve these two goals, I begin by discussing the ways in which the Inuit filmmakers Zacharias Kunuk and Andrew Okpeaha MacLean are subverting sonic stereotypes, or what I call the "Sound of Eskimo," used to represent Inuit people and culture in twentieth-century film, which, as I and others have noted, are devoid of actual Inuit practices of sound making, hearing, and listening.[12] I then offer an analysis of the role soundscapes and soundtracks play in the Iñupiaq filmmaker Andrew Okpeaha MacLean's award-winning feature film *On the Ice* (2010), listening closely to three musical scenes featured in the film and the ways in which their diegetic sounds, or actual performances where the sound's source is visible on-screen, subtly convey complicated gendered and racialized histories of colonization in Utqiaġvik (from *Ukpeaġvik*, 'place where snowy owls are hunted'), the Iñupiaq village formerly known as Barrow, from the late nineteenth century to the present day.[13] For modern

Iñupiaq people specifically, and for Native American people more broadly, articulations and performances of gender remain a core component in how we negotiate the false choice between traditional Indigenous lifeways and modern Western lifeways.[14] I argue that MacLean's culture- and place-based portrayals of Inuit men and masculinities unsettle easy notions of what it can mean to be an Inuk—the singular for "Inuit" and a gender-neutral term for "person"—in the present day by audiovisualizing a range of modern cultural tensions and entanglements that continue to vex young Iñupiaq men's negotiations of who they are in relation to what they do.

Notes on Naming and Terminology

Indigenous languages systems are inextricably linked to Indigenous knowledge systems, a fact that leads many Indigenous scholars and community members to privilege language revitalization as an integral part of recovering precolonial and precapitalist Indigenous identities and roles. Regarding the role of language within Native American and Indigenous masculinities studies, Kim Anderson, Robert Alexander Innes, and John Swift remind us that "masculinity" itself is an English word burdened with Western ideologies and that a driving force underlying the recovery work of their male-identified collaborators aims to "eliminate the masculinity out of [their lives and behaviors]."[15] In the Far North, Indigenous language and knowledge revitalization efforts have benefited greatly from the Alaska Native Language Center (ANLC), a research institute housed at the University of Alaska, Fairbanks (UAF) since 1972. For more than four decades, Native and non-Native linguistics scholars and regional specialists from the ANLC have engaged in community-based participatory research to recover, document, and revitalize Indigenous languages *with, by, and for* the Alaska Native communities from whence they come. The ANLC hosts language courses and workshops and publishes a range of language materials, including research papers, dictionaries, story collections, and maps. Its most widely cited map, titled "Indigenous Peoples and Languages of Alaska" (map 4.1), is a useful place to start in terms of illustrating the state's cultural and linguistic diversity. Most significantly, the revised 2011 version of the ANLC map privileges Indigenous naming practices, as in the case of the "Eskimo" language family renamed the "Inuit-Yupik-Aleut" language family, and sheds light on historical and contemporary naming practices.[16]

The multiple and diverse Indigenous communities in Alaska are recognized most broadly by the cover term "Alaska Natives," who historically have been understood to comprise three the equally broad subgroups "Indians,"

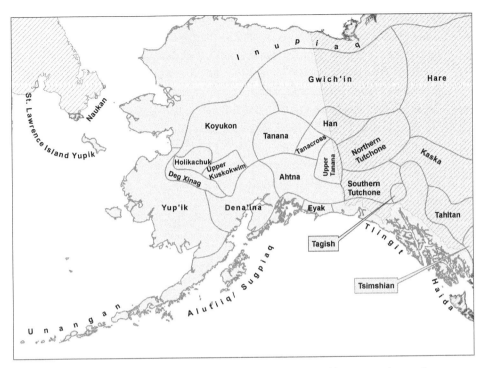

MAP 4.1. Indigenous peoples and languages of Alaska. Adapted by Gary Holton and Brett Parks, Alaska Native Language Center and Institute of Social and Economic Research. Copyright © 2011. Courtesy of the Alaska Native Language Center.

"Eskimos," and "Aleuts."[17] The term "Eskimo" did not originate from within Inuit communities, and because it is widely understood to carry pejorative connotations, it has long since fallen out of use in Canada. While it appears to be falling out of favor among today's Alaska Native youth, many Natives of Iñupiaq and Yup'ik descent have used, and continue to use, the term publicly (and playfully) to identify themselves.[18] Although these terms are always already tethered to a colonial politics of representation in academic fields such as linguistics, ethnology, and anthropology, it remains important to acknowledge the ways in which they continue to circulate.[19] By and large, most Alaska Native people today identify their broad cultural affiliations using the language names illustrated in map 4.1 (e.g., Dena'ina, Unangax̂, Iñupiaq), names that translate to "person" or "the (real) people."

For more specific cultural affiliations, one must consider the particularities of place-based families and communities. The anthropologist Ann Fienup-Riordan, who has collaborated with Arctic communities for more than three decades, explains that when European colonizers began encroaching on Alaska more than two hundred years ago, Yup'ik and Iñupiaq identities "reflected the society into which they were born. They did not identify themselves as Alaska Eskimos, and only in very specific contexts, such as contacts with speakers of another language, did they see themselves as Iñupiat or Yup'ik. Their primary allegiance was to their families and tribal groups. . . . Language, family membership, and local residence determined personal and group identity."[20] Fienup-Riordan reminds us of the importance of remembering to historicize and contextualize the particularities of language in relation to community and family, and for the purposes of this chapter, and as I argue later, the sounds of Native languages themselves have become important auditory signifiers of one's Native affiliations and alliances in the present day.

The "Sound of Eskimo" to Audiovisualizing Inuit

Despite its considerable size, the existing archive of films about Inuit people raises several questions in term of its auditory significance over time. What role has sound design played in twentieth-century films about Inuit people? And how can in-depth analyses of contemporary films produced by Inuit people contribute to studies of Native American and Indigenous men and masculinities studies? Colonial regimes of sounds used to represent Inuit peoples can be traced back to cue sheets, scores, and soundtracks that accompanied Robert J. Flaherty's *Nanook of the North* (1922). The lack of musical specificity granted to Inuit people in popular culture is not wholly surprising, given that much of America's "Nanookmania" was based on selective representations of central and eastern Canadian and Greenlandic Inuit peoples, whose lifeways and performance practices differ from those of their Siberian and Alaskan counterparts in several important ways.[21] Over the past few decades, scholars have begun to pay closer attention to the differences among circumpolar Inuit people, and like Fienup-Riordan they have begun to recognize Alaskan Inuit lifeways as markedly different from Canadian and Greenlandic Inuit lifeways, particularly in the realms of colonial history and political realities and their effects on historical and contemporary Inuit musical life. Until the 1970s, the field of Inuit music studies also lacked comparative scholarship that acknowledged the particularities among and between Inuit performance practices throughout the Arctic.[22] Yet Fienup-Riordan's *Freeze Frame* (1995) provides the only comprehensive and focused analysis of representations of Alaskan Eskimos in film. She describes Yup'ik and

Iñupiaq people's presence in ethnographic, documentary, and feature film productions from the 1900s to the 1990s and asks, "What stories about Eskimos do these films tell us?"[23] Most critical to this study, her work differentiates between colonial popular-culture expectations of American Indians and Alaskan Eskimos: "Whereas the Indian stood in the path of civilization, the Eskimo stood at its foundation—'essential man' enduring in the face of a harsh and unforgiving environment. . . . The portrayal of the American Indian as the paradigmatic 'bad guy' has been devastating. The reverse image of Eskimos as inescapably good is equally harmful."[24] To be sure, representations of Eskimos as "'pure primitives': peaceful, happy, childlike, noble, independent, free" reflect American patriarchy and White supremacy in ways that continue to fuel social injustices experienced by Inuit people.[25]

In terms of contemporary Inuit films that seek to reclaim Inuit auditory cultures in film, scholars have written extensively about Canadian Inuit media phenomena such as Igloolik Isuma Productions and its best-known producer and director, Zacharias Kunuk. His "Fast Runner Trilogy" consists of *Atanarjuat* (The Fast Runner; 2001), *The Journals of Knud Rasmussen* (2006), and *Before Tomorrow* (2009).[26] *Atanarjuat*, perhaps the best-known film in the trilogy, has done critical work in terms of reclaiming visible and audible aspects of Inuit people as represented on film. Critics have noted that *Atanarjuat* "probably has one-third as much soundtrack as any other feature film recently released and relies much more heavily on the actual sounds of the Arctic action . . . We view the audio landscape of the Arctic as a soundscape, and try to convey the same emotional impact normally reserved for violins and drums by sounds of winds, footsteps on frozen snow, and silence."[27] To be sure, the comparatively extreme landscapes have deeply informed Inuit lived experiences since time immemorial. One sees and hears this in *Atanarjuat*, about which Michelle Raheja observes, "[The] 'intense attention' paid to frozen landscapes and seascapes throughout [the film] positions them as 'uncredited protagonists.'"[28] Kunuk's use of actual Arctic sounds is complemented by on-screen performances of traditional Inuit drum songs and vocal games—one of the first non-documentary feature films to feature actual Inuit musicking.

Kunuk's work has unquestionably inspired a new generation of Inuit filmmakers. In a 2015 essay, Fienup-Riordan reflects on the state of Alaskan Inuit presence in the film industry since *Freeze Frame* (1995) and offers a list of Alaska Native filmmakers who emerged after the inaugural Indigenous World Film Festival, hosted by the Alaska Native Heritage Center in 2005.[29] Andrew

Okpeaha MacLean is the only male Inuit filmmaker on this list and one of the few who has produced films that offer a glimpse into contemporary Alaskan Inuit life.

Andrew Okpeaha MacLean was born in 1972 on the Fort Wainwright Army base in central Alaska (near Fairbanks) and was raised in between his ancestral home Utqiaġvik and Fairbanks, where his parents both worked as professors at the UAF. Andrew's mother Edna Ahgeak MacLean (Iñupiaq), an esteemed educator and recognized leader in the revitalization of the North Slope dialect of the Iñupiaq language, has played an integral role in shaping her son's worldview and aesthetics. She was born in Utqiaġvik to Maria (née Brower) and Joseph A. Ahgeak in 1944 and raised in a bilingual environment—both parents were native speakers, yet Edna notes that her mother obeyed the school district's then English only mandate while her father preferred to speak Iñupiaq only.[30] In the winter of 1964 Edna met her future husband, Stephen MacLean in Utqiaġvik; she was an enrolled student at UAF home on break and he was working at the Naval Arctic Research Center. The couple married in 1967 and left Alaska to complete degrees at the University of California, Berkeley—a doctorate in zoology for Steve and a teaching credential for Edna. They returned to Fairbanks and UAF in 1970, where Steve worked as a biology professor and Edna began coursework in linguistics. From 1976 to 1987 she taught courses on the Iñupiaq language and developed the baccalaureate degree program at UAF. She earned a masters in bilingual education from the University of Washington in 1991 and a doctorate in education from Stanford University in 1995. She then returned home where she served as president of Ilisaġvik College, Alaska's only tribally controlled college located in Utqiaġvik, from 1995 to 2005. In 2014 she completed one of her life's major works: a comprehensive North Slope Iñupiaq dictionary in collaboration with over a dozen local elders and native speakers.[31]

MacLean's work shares his mother's imperative to strengthen the presence of their ancestral language, particularly for Iñupiaq people his age: "We are the first generation not to learn to speak the Inupiat language. . . . It's a big hole in our lives and something we feel responsible to correct."[32] MacLean began writing and directing plays at a young age and after graduating high school he left Alaska to study theater at the University of Washington. After earning a bachelor's degree in 1995, MacLean moved back to Utqiaġvik and co-founded the Iñupiat Theatre, a company dedicated to performing solely in the Iñupiaq language. From his work with the Iñupiat Theatre, MacLean decided to pursue a master's in fine arts in film production at New York University. His relationships with and responsibilities to his ancestral Iñupiaq land, language, and family serve as his primary motives for entering the realm of filmmaking. MacLean deliberately aims to unsettle problematic colonial expectations surrounding mass-produced representations of Inuit in media: "We're in a kind of strange position that everybody in the world has heard of Eskimos. Most people have some kind of strange notions—they rely on stereotypes they've heard. . . . We're like a punchline or something. Nobody really knows us. I want to make art that is reflective of a more genuine aspect of our experience."[33] To tell more genuine stories, he therefore takes a culture- and place-based approach to the majority of his projects to date: he films on location in Utqiaġvik and draws on his family's lived experiences and Iñupiaq stories to portray his male protagonists as rooted in community struggles and triumphs.[34]

MacLean also endeavors to bring his culture- and place-based projects to a global audience: "I [wanted] to do something on a larger scale and reach a wider audience, and films seemed a way to do that. I could be making things that were centered in Barrow or that really spoke to who I was and where I was from, and be able to reach out to people that were beyond the communities where I was living."[35] To be sure, Utqiaġvik is unlike any place found in the contiguous United States, leaving MacLean with the challenge to make audible, visible, and legible the differences and similarities of his home community to global audiences. Yet he has been inspired by and benefits from work already in circulation by the Canadian Inuit filmmaker Zacharias Kunuk.

For example, MacLean's dramatic fifteen-minute short film *Sikumi* (2008) marks one of the most significant turns in his career as a filmmaker and, for a number of reasons, invites comparison with Kunuk's *Atanarjuat*. To begin, Kunuk and MacLean are considered the first Indigenous filmmakers from their Arctic regions: Igloolik and Utqiaġvik, respectively. *Atanarjuat* and *Sikumi* hold the distinction of being the first films made entirely in their Indigenous languages (Inuktitut and Inupiatun, respectively, the latter engaging the expertise of MacLean's mother).[36] Temporally, the films are considered "period pieces" in that they are set in pre-development times before Anglo-Canadians and Anglo-Americans began settling the Arctic in the 1950s and 1960s. Thematically, both films are dramatic thrillers drawn from the filmmakers' lived experiences as Inuit men and based on Inuit morals and stories. Yet because Kunuk and MacLean were born a generation apart—the former in 1957, and the latter in 1972—and under different colonial nation-state structures, they came of age under drastically different circumstances. Whereas *Atanarjuat* retells an Inuit legend "from the inside and through Inuit eyes," *Sikumi* was conceived as an "Arctic western" inspired by Sergio Leone and other makers of films in the western genre from the 1950s and 1970s, whose entertaining storylines often focused on issues of morality.[37] *Sikumi* is the story of Apuna,

> an Inuit hunter who drives his dog team out on the frozen Arctic Ocean in search of seals and inadvertently becomes a witness to murder. In the microscopic communities of Arctic Alaska there is no anonymity, thus the hunter knows both the victim and the murderer. The murderer, Miqu, claiming self-defense and desperate to avoid punishment, tries to persuade his friend to forget what he has seen, and help dispose of the body. Apuna is then forced to navigate the uneasy morality between honoring the body and memory of one friend and destroying the life of another.

In *Sikumi*, MacLean seeks to explore how his characters would react to the situation as Iñupiaq people, "taking into consideration our concepts, values,"[38] paying special attention to reactions rooted in a "culture as Iñupiat men."[39] For MacLean, this means that the witness would aim for an "avoidance of conflict": "He wouldn't try to subdue the killer but tries to find a way to bring the killer to realize the magnitude of what he's done—bring justice within himself."[40] The sound design featured in *Sikumi* relies on a collaboratively produced sound-scape created by the Colombian composer Andres Martinez and MacLean. "It is an interesting process because you have to show [in the music] all these nice landscapes and the cold atmosphere," Martinez says about his experience com-posing the score with MacLean. "[The atmosphere] needs a sound, so that's the approach. [MacLean] explained to me a little bit of this atmosphere of these landscape, I tried to transmit that in music."[41] As in Kunuk's *Atanarjuat*, *Sikumi*'s cinematography and accompanying soundscape draw the eye and ear toward the film's "uncredited protagonist," the vast frozen Arctic Ocean.

It is also important to note that Kunuk's and MacLean's film projects rou-tinely feature a mix of experienced and amateur Inuit and Iñupiaq actors to portray their community-based stories. MacLean knew *Sikumi*'s three actors from his Iñupiat Theatre company days: Apuna, the witness, is played by Brad Weyiouanna of Sishmaref, who holds a bachelor of arts in anthropol-ogy from UAF; Miqu, the murderer, is played by Tony Bryant from Point Hope/Point Barrow; and Taqi, the victim, is played by Olemaun Rexford from Utqiaġvik, who is a co-captain of the Atkaan Whaling Crew.

Sikumi has won numerous awards—most notably, the Sundance Film Festival's Jury Prize in Short Filmmaking in 2008—and its storyline served as the basis for MacLean's feature film debut, *On the Ice* (2010).[42] MacLean notes Kunuk's direct influence on his feature film adaptation: noting his love for *Atanarjuat*, MacLean has explained that he set out to differentiate *On the Ice* from the beginning:

> I wanted to do something different, in that I wanted it to be very con-
> temporary story. *Atanarjuat* is awesome. It's a necessary voice, but at
> the same time it's a look at our past. It's set pre-contact. There tends to
> be an assumption amongst audiences that that was somehow a more
> culturally legitimate time. Like we were somehow more pure then. I
> wanted to make something that's a bit of an answer to that. Culture
> survives and cultures change and they don't go away. We've adapted to
> the world that we're in. We don't live up to the stereotypes that people
> might have when they think of people living in igloos and out hunting,
> completely in tune with nature. I wanted to provide a more realistic
> portrayal of like—this is who we are.[43]

Loosely based on *Sikumi*, *On the Ice* replaces the adult men with teenagers, moves forward temporally from the 1950s to today, and trades dogsleds for snow machines. The plot retains the drama or suspense of *Sikumi*, but the feature film takes time to develop into a thriller and focuses on the relationship between its two teenage male protagonists, Qalli (the witness, played by Josiah Patkotak) and Aivaaq (the murderer, played by Frank Qutuq Irelan), whose argument with James (the victim, played by John Miller) results in a tragic accident. MacLean's "Director's Statement" further explains his deliberate choice to contemporize his *Sikumi* storyline:

> Alaska is one of the last mythic places in the world. Nearly everyone
> has heard of it, but very few have any real understanding of what life
> in the Arctic is really like. The majority of the population are Iñupiat,
> as am I. Centuries old traditions are still a bedrock of life. Hunting
> seals, walrus, and whales provides much of the food the town lives on.
> This is a unique setting for a film.
>
> The main characters, Qalli and Aivaaq, are from Barrow. They have
> grown up there, much as I did. As such their lives have been far from
> what is considered normal in other parts of the country. And yet they
> are also much like 17 year-olds anywhere in North America. Their day-
> to-day dramas of status and identity can be found in any small town.
> *On the Ice* is a character-driven thriller about getting away with murder
> and a morality tale about the limits of friendship and forgiveness.
>
> It is a story that can happen anywhere, but only happens as it does
> here, in the Arctic.[44]

MacLean's storyline expansion also includes portrayals of ongoing social problems such as poverty, alcoholism, substance abuse, and teen pregnancy, portrayals of modern Iñupiaq tensions and entanglements that have led critics to hail the film as an exemplar of an "underprivileged-teen drama" or "ethnodocumentary noir" beloved by Sundance audiences.[45] Although *On the Ice* also won numerous awards, critical reception both inside and outside Alaska has been mixed, due in large part to MacLean's commitment to casting primarily amateur Iñupiaq and Inuit actors (not everyone agrees that amateurs serve as ideal conduits for community-based storytelling on the big screen).[46] Nonetheless, MacLean's films build on and are in conversation with a growing archive of Inuit-produced film that seek to move beyond an imagined "Sound of Eskimo," originating from Flaherty's *Nanook of the North* (1922), and toward a more genuine audiovisualization of Inuit lived experiences, most widely circulated by Kunuk's *Atanarjuat* (2001).

MacLean's use of place-based (Utqiaġvik) and culture-based (Iñupiaq) soundscapes and soundtracks audiovisualize a range of modern Iñupiaq tensions and entanglements underlying tribal- and community-based articulations of male identities and masculine roles in ways that illustrate contemporary challenges of defining who young Iñupiaq men are in relation to what they do. Like *Sikumi*, MacLean's *On the Ice* features another collaboratively produced soundscape, this time with the Czech-born composer iZLER, who explains, "[The music] is inspired by the landscape; it's a very stark otherworldly sort of place. . . . Most of it takes place on the ice, in the middle of nowhere, and I really wanted to give that sense of epic scale and loneliness . . . that these boys are completely alone in what they've done."[47] Whereas MacLean's vision for the film's soundscape involved sounding both a "claustrophobic and [an] epic" feel, his choice of soundtracks revolve around his three diverse on-screen musical performances, including traditional Iñupiaq *sayuun* (choreographed motion dances that share stories); an "Eskimo flow" freestyle rap; and a harmonized "singspiration" hymn (a Presbyterian gospel song translated into the Iñupiaq language). MacLean has explained the importance of the three performances this way:

> [*On the Ice*] starts with this traditional dance, and that's our tradition; this is what we've been doing and this is our roots, you know? And then it's got hip-hop. That one scene on top of the water tower and the party scene are really like the "brand new." And then there's also this singspiration scene, which is when they take a hymn—something that came from the outside a hundred years ago and came from Christianity—that

was translated into the Iñupiaq language. So it's these three things: the purely traditional and then these two other forms of musical expression that have either been adapted or appropriated into the culture. It was like the old, the kind of old, and the brand new.[48]

I discuss each of these musical moments, or tracks, to contextualize MacLean's characterizations of them as "the old" and "purely traditional" (sayuun); the "brand new" and "appropriated" (Eskimo flow); and the "kind of old" and "adapted" (singspiration hymn). As I demonstrate, his characterizations are rooted and routed through the particularities of his relationships to his ancestral Iñupiaq language and land, as well as his observations of the status of modern culture- and place-based identities and roles.

Audiovisualizing Modern Iñupiaq Identities and Roles in Utqiaġvik

TRACK 1: SAYUUN (TRADITIONAL DRUM DANCE). *On the Ice opens with aerial shots of Utqiaġvik, a vast sea of ice- and snow-covered tundra; a relatively flat and treeless landscape, with rows of modern, Western-style frame houses, all accompanied by a soundscape of wind and close chords sustained by strings. Gradually, the steady beat of Iñupiaq qilaun (a traditional tambourine drum made of animal hide stretched over a bent wood frame) rises into the foreground, and the camera cuts to a row of seated male drummers midway through a traditional Iñupiaq sayuun. Men and women are then heard singing in a unison melody along with the drumming as the camera cuts to two dancers, one male and one female, performing the final motions to a song about "me and my friend."[49] This performance is taking place in a large and crowded indoor space, and the seated audience members facing the performers applaud and cheer as the drum-dance group prepares to perform its next song. As the leader of the group begins to sing the first line of the second song, Qalli and Aivaaq, the film's two male protagonists, walk to the center of the space to perform a dance depicting a polar bear.*

Utqiaġvik is located on the shores of the Arctic Ocean (more than three hundred miles north of the Arctic Circle) and is often referred to as the "top of the world" because it is the northernmost inhabited point in North America. Regarding southern perceptions of high Arctic landscapes as mysterious or inhospitably barren, Iñupiaq people have thrived in this region since time immemorial, sustained largely by hunting marine mammals such as bowhead

FIGURE 4.1. Qalli and Aivaaq with the Barrow Dancers in MacLean's *On the Ice*.
Photograph by Lol Crawley, courtesy of On the Ice LLC.

whales, beluga whales, bearded seals, and walrus. The centrality of hunting and subsistence activities in general, and of whaling specifically, are deeply embedded in the worldviews, beliefs, and language of Utqiaġvikmiut (Utqiaġvik villagers). Referring to themselves as "people of the whale," Utqiaġvikmiut possess cultural identities and philosophies about the cycle of life that revolve around the bowhead whale, as depicted in one of their origin stories that links the death of a whale with the birth of the Iñupiaq.

Interestingly, there are varying degrees to which gender has been emphasized or deemphasized as a useful frame for understanding divisions of labor in Inuit culture. Lisa Frink notes that "gender has been and continues to be a 'structuring principle' of Arctic people's daily lives and tasks" and that "there is a notably real and ideal pan-Arctic gendered division of labor" in which "men are the primary bulk subsistence harvesters of sea mammals, fish, and game. Women, too, harvest subsistence foods but generally in smaller packages; they collect berries and river greens and jig for fish under the river ice."[50] Barbara Bodenhorn argues that Iñupiaq people consider generation or age as more important than gender, but that gender continues to act as an important marker not only for relations between Iñupiaq women and men, but also for relations between humans and animals.[51] Fienup-Riordan has also found that the relationships between animals and humans—*not genders*—make up the fundamental structuring principles of Yup'ik daily life.[52] On the subject of labor, Bodenhorn explains that while some labor division could be conceived of as gendered, they are not restricted by simplistic notions of biological sex: "There is nothing in [the Iñupiaq gender] model that assigns a 'natural' meaning to the tasks that men and women perform."[53] Moreover, whaling activities involve a very intricate understanding of complementarity and interrelatedness, as suggested in the sentiment from Bodenhorn's title, "I'm Not the Great Hunter, My Wife Is." Cosmologies of marriage in Iñupiaq culture illuminate the problematics of anthropological models of gender in which "men hunt; men dominate Inuit societies; men control the public sphere; men 'work.'"[54] For Iñupiaq people, whaling cannot be reduced to the "event" of catching and killing the whale, and must instead account for a deeply embedded understanding of gender complementarity in the ongoing preparations for the time when a whale gives itself to the community. That said, women's participation in whaling crews has increased in recent years, and three women reportedly have held the critical role of harpooner or "striker."[55]

The practice of whaling is best understood as a yearlong cyclical process that centers on preparing the gear and supplies that will sustain a crew of up to a dozen men and boys living on the ice for a month during the hunt. Preparations for the spring whaling cycle begin over the summer months of July and August when men hunt bearded seals (*ugruk*), the skins of which will cover the crew's *umiaq*, a lightweight handmade skin boat used in the pursuit of a whale.[56] During the fall season—August through October—a whaling captain hunts for fish and game that will be preserved until spring to feed his crew during the month-long hunt. In February, the community prepares the whaling crew's equipment and repairs or builds boat frames. Men clean the ugruk skins so the women can sew them together with a waterproof stitch and cover the boats; guns are cleaned; and essential clothing items (parkas, mukluks, and so on) are sewn or repaired. November through March are spent trapping, fishing, and hunting seal and (rarely) polar bears.

In early to mid-April, the bowhead whales migrate back to the Far North, marking the beginning of the spring whaling season. Whaling crews begin to cut through the sea ice to create a lead, or trail of open water next to the frozen ocean, which attracts marine mammals looking to feed on other sea creatures. In May, once the gear and supplies have been transported to the camp adjacent to the ocean via freight sleds and snow machines, the crews will spread out and camp along the lead in canvas tents, waiting and watching for whales. Drum-dance performances in Iñupiaq culture are closely tied to the whaling cycle and almost always follow a feast. Nalukataq is a day-long feast held in June, at the end of a successful whaling season, and drum dancing and games are performed throughout. Given the centrality of the whaling cycle, it is perhaps not surprising that the most common sayuun themes are whaling, specifically, and hunting, more generally.[57]

The drum dancers featured in this scene are a well-known real-life community group called the Barrow Dancers, an all-ages group with more than sixty members who serve various roles as drummers, singers, dancers, composers, and choreographers. In this on-scene performance, the dance group offers a more formal presentation, given the choice of choreographed sayuun dances (as opposed to *atuutipiaq*, or common/invitational dances) and matching regalia (hooded purple *atikluks*, or summer parkas made of lightweight fabric pulled over white, button-up dress shirts, gloves, dark pants, and *kamŋit* or fur boots).

As a member of the Egasak whaling crew, MacLean has firsthand knowledge of the whaling season cycles, which was respected and attended to during filming of *On the Ice*. Filming began on April 9, 2010, during which time local whaling crews began cutting leads in the sea ice to attract whales. The producer Cara Marcous described how the film crew worked the night before in fashion similar to that of the whaling crews to create leads to transport equipment and supplies to the film camp near the ocean. Marcous notes, "We were given permission by the whaling captains to film by the lead over the next few days, but we [were] under a lot of pressure to get it done quickly so as not to negatively affect any whaling."[58] Despite both whaling and film crew efforts, however, the leads froze over and did not reopen until April 28. Such unexpected changes are indeed part of the cycle, but North Slope residents are also intimately aware of how Utqiaġvik is often cited as a barometer or as "ground zero" for the climate crisis.[59] The realities of a rapidly changing environment caused by global warming hold concrete implications for Indigenous Arctic peoples, especially regarding performances of cultural identity that are inextricably intertwined with traditional whaling cycles.[60]

Historically, dances would be held for both ceremonial and social reasons to foster goodwill between the human performers and their nonhuman and more-than-human relations. Edna MacLean explains that "songs are composed around the hunt, songs and ceremony to entice the whale. Individual songs are very powerful. Hunters could own songs to help them in their hunting. If a person sang a certain song to lure a certain animal, that was his hunting song."[61] For example, in a ceremonial context, spiritual leaders would use drum dances to call the animal spirits, imploring them for a successful hunting season. In a social context, drum dances would be shared with people from neighboring villages to forge relationships imbued with responsibilities and obligations to one another—a process of making relations that encompasses an expansive Indigenous understanding of family as including immediate, extended, adopted, and imagined relations.[62]

The drum is central to traditional Inuit cultural practices across the circumpolar Arctic and materially embodies Inuit worldviews about the interrelatedness of human, nonhuman, and more-than-human realms. Sean Asiqłuq Topkok (Iñupiaq), a professor of education at UAF and founder and leader of the Pavva Iñupiaq Dancers, explains, "[When there is] an animal that's given himself to you, you use every part of the animal, and you make a drum.... It needs to go out and needs to be heard.... We need to use every part of [the animal]."[63] Iñupiaq people's honoring of animals and materials that create the drums in turn directly impact the efficacy of the songs created by them. According to oral histories drum songs embodied peace-keeping powers to end wars between tribes.[64]

Until very recently, Iñupiaq drums were played solely by men (or by female spiritual leaders during ceremonies), while women's primary role in social performances involve singing alongside or dancing in front of the drummers. From a gender studies perspective, it is critical to note how the two primary realms of circumpolar Inuit musicking—drum songs and vocal games (commonly referred to as throat singing)—are to some degree understood as men's and women's genres, respectively. While there are, of course, exceptions, female drummers and male throat singers are indeed in the minority. In terms of song composition, however, Paula Conlon's research in Eastern Canada found "of the 147 drum-dance songs (of known authorship) from Igloolik, Ikpiarjuk, and Mittimatalik, only 4 are attributed to female composers."[65] Although drum-dance songs are the most widely practiced genre across the Arctic, vocal games—a predominantly eastern Canadian Inuit practice— have received the lion's share of scholarly and mainstream attention. Canadian ethnomusicologist Beverley Diamond explains that vocal games receive more attention because of a larger "patron discourse" that fetishizes or privileges musical practices that have "'unusual' timbres, spiritual beliefs, or distinctive social practices.... Only indigenous music that exhibits the expected linkage between radical sound production and indigeneity is widely known internationally."[66] To be sure, Inuit vocal games are heard as exotic or distinctive mostly because the "[harsh and strange] sounds challenge conventional notions of what a woman's voice, and perhaps even what a human voice could sound like."[67] By contrast, Inuit drum songs receive very little attention from the international music and media industrial complex because, one might argue, they are not as "radical" sounding as, say, the high-pitched Northern Plains vocal style made popular through international powwow circuits.

Thus, MacLean's decision to open the film with a traditional Iñupiaq sayuun is significant in at least two ways. First, he features a thriving co-ed community practice that is often misrecognized or silenced by mass-produced imaginations of Arctic people. And second, he foregrounds a community group that has long endeavored to draw on traditional drum-dance practices as a means to revitalize Iñupiaq language, and thus culture- and place-based identities and roles. Following Tengan, these sayuun performances could function as a form of "'re-membering' masculinities, a type of gendered memory work that facilitates the formation of group subjectivities through the coordination of personal memories, historical narratives, and bodily experiences and representations."[68]

TRACK 2, "ESKIMO FLOW" FREESTYLE RAP. *The camera cuts to a house party and an in-progress freestyle rap jam session. High school students crowd the living room, beer and liquor in hand, to watch a timid young man arhythmically stumble through a freestyle rap atop a laptop-generated instrumental track. As his lyrics begin to lose steam, exposing a busy accompanying track of drums, bass, ascending synthesized melodic patterns, and sustained background vocals (on the "ooo" vowel), the din of the audience increases to audible laughter and other playful noises of disparagement, ultimately causing the young man to give up. As the track stops, he playfully yells "hey, fuck you guys" several times, and with both middle fingers upraised he leaves the stage area. His exit route through a crowd of young men crosses Qalli and Aivaaq, all of whom pat the first performer on the back and head to show their encouragement for the effort. Aivaaq then breaks for the stage as the crowd hollers encouragement. He steps up to the mic and calls for Qalli to join him, mid-handshake whispers "bump that Arctic Thug," and tells the crowd that his "main man Qalli came up with this beat." Qalli takes control of the laptop and starts his track—a solid drum-only groove that moves the two performers and numerous onlookers to start nodding their heads or dancing in time with the groove, as Aivaaq confidently and rhythmically delivers the following freestyle rap.*

"Arctic Thug," lyrics by Frank Qutuq Irelan and Torin Jacobs
Performed by Frank Qutuq Irelan

Professional eskimo / gangster in the snow
Aught-six / three clips
Drop you like the temperature
Well below zero / frostbite on your nose
Misigaaq is my flow
In the boat / rock it fast then slow
On the drums / keep the beat keep it slow
Northern lights up above / green as bud
Show some love for these arctic thugs
Hollah! [Ooo . . . Wee!]
Throw your hands up.

Although the Arctic region is conventionally understood in popular culture as remote, isolated, and disconnected from the daily lives of southerners, Iñupiaq people have engaged in trade with British and American whaling and expedition ships, traders, and missionaries since the late eighteenth century. Through these intermittent encounters, Iñupiaq people actively engaged and participated in "a globalized society and economy where ideas and material goods transcend former cultural barriers."[69] As Paul Krejci notes, Iñupiaq people from both Point Hope and Point Barrow (two of the oldest Iñupiaq communities) possessed technology such as phonographs and records by the first decade of the twentieth century. Thus is it plausible to rank the Arctic Ocean coastal region among the notably more cosmopolitan areas in Alaska.

Interestingly, this intermittent history of cultural encounters brought only minimal cultural changes to Iñupiaq cultural and musical life up until the years following the Second World War. During her trip to Utqiaġvik in 1946, Laura Boulton observed and recorded robust traditional drum-dance practices "in spite of the fact that missionary hymns and popular songs picked up from traders, soldiers, and government men ha[d] been brought in from the outside."[70] In fact, Boulton's landmark phonographic release *The Eskimos of Hudson Bay and Alaska* (1954) features field recordings of only traditional drum-dance songs and excludes performances that belie cultural contact with European and American cultures.

However, for most communities located in the Far North, it is our mothers' and fathers' generation—those born in the mid-twentieth century—who witnessed the most dramatic changes to the land and our communities caused by a post–Second World War population boom across the State of Alaska. Native families in the Far North were physically relocated, often by force, to domesticated settler colonial villages. The enforcement of compulsory education removed young children farther from their land and families by relocating them to government-run residential schools. To be sure, these dislocations, to name just two, have contributed to language and identity loss and have caused generational divides within and among Native families and communities. Yet the discovery of oil in Prudhoe Bay in 1968 had the most dramatic effect on North Slope Iñupiaq people specifically and Alaska Native people more broadly.

The drive of non-Native southerners to develop Arctic and Subarctic landscapes for resource extraction has irrevocably changed Native social, cultural, linguistic, political, and economic infrastructures, most notably via the Alaska Native Claims Settlement Act (ANCSA). In brief, ANCSA was signed into law on December 18, 1971, to fast-track the development of oil fields in the North Slope region. It diminished Native claims to the land in exchange for forty-four million acres (approximately 11 percent of the total land) and nearly $1 billion.[71] In addition to twelve regional corporations (which were created using a map of preexisting cultural areas [see map 4.1]), ANCSA established approximately 220 village corporations, and together the regional and village corporations operate as a two-tiered governing system for resource distribution.[72] A clear departure from the Native American reservation system of the Lower 48, ANCSA stipulated a corporate-to-government relationship between enrolled Alaska Natives shareholders and the U.S. federal government. Fashioned after Western business models, Alaska Native Corporations mandated an abrupt modernization of sorts: tribal leaders became presidents in charge of enrolled shareholders, and land and natural resources became corporate investments.

Approximately eighty thousand Alaska Natives were alive on December 18, 1971, and thus eligible to enroll as full shareholders (one hundred shares of stock) in both a regional and a village corporation.[73] In general terms, Alaska Native people chose to enroll in corporations assigned to the areas where they were born or that they considered home at the time the act was passed.[74] Yet with enrollment, ANCSA established a new definition of a "Native" person that is based on ownership of corporate stock and consequently created different classes of Natives—enfranchised "original enrollees" and disenfranchised "descendants" (those born after December 18, 1971).[75] Commonly referred to as "after-borns" or "new Natives," ANCSA descendants can become shareholders only if enfranchised relatives "give" or bequeath some or all of their shares to them. On one hand, the passage of ANCSA gave the broader Alaska Native community some degree of agency and control over land and resources with which to develop political, economic, and cultural capital. On the other hand, scholars argue, ANCSA's exclusionary framework "has had a tremendous and ongoing impact on Alaska Native identity."[76]

Born in 1972, MacLean grew up as part of this post-ANCSA generation surrounded by the boom of development and resource extraction that continues to vex the twenty-first-century realities of Alaska Native youth—a population facing alarmingly high suicide and substance abuse rates, due in large part to ongoing identity crises and intergenerational traumas faced by their families and communities. As MacLean intimated earlier, the second musical moment, a freestyle rap "Arctic Thug," sounds the ostensibly "brand-new" sensibilities of modern Iñupiaq youth and, one might argue, amplifies a so-called generational divide manufactured by colonial legislation such as ANCSA. MacLean was deliberate in his choice to feature modern Iñupiaq youth cultures due in large part to his fascination with the particularities of how they articulate affiliations and identifications inside and outside of Iñupiaq culture. "I'm a generation removed from [them]," he has said. "I grew up in a different era than the one they're growing up in. When I was in Alaska, when I was in Barrow, it was more isolated. It felt smaller. Now the kids up there have this incredible access to the outside world that forces them to confront who they are in a way that I kind of didn't have to as much growing up."[77]

Most Indigenous hip hop studies tend to focus solely on the liberatory potential of Indigenous youth writing and producing their own anticolonial lyrics and beats, and how their appropriation of this genre enables them to reclaim aspects of their identity (in the singular) as thoroughly modern in the face of primitive stereotypes. Colonial powers in the Americas have long aimed to silence Indigenous musical modernities via an active agnotology regarding cultural change, insisting instead that authentic markers of audible Indigeneity are decidedly premodern or ancient. Critics note how the settler nation's inculcation of shame has become a primary mechanism of colonial invasion, alienation, and erasure of Indigenous modernities more broadly: "The policing of tradition as an essence expressive of *real* indigeneity, initially used to shame Indigenous peoples into forcibly abandoning their 'savage' practices, now serves the oppression of multiculturalism."[78] In this way, Indigenous individuals and communities are continually faced with the zero sum game of colonial silencing and shame: one chooses either to internalize or to resist marginalization.

Given the long histories and traditions of cosmopolitanism in the Far North, its continuation by Iñupiaq youth as freestyle rap musicians can hardly be viewed as surprising. Iñupiaq youth living in Utqiaġvik have smartphones, streaming music and video services, and Facebook and Twitter accounts. Given the wide accessibility of these twenty-first-century technological advances, critics note that the person-to-person interactions and encounters that shaped the origins of hip hop and rap music are no longer necessary; for many of today's youth "hip-hop is a corporate legacy, not a lived one," and no encounters other than virtual ones are required to access or disseminate hip-hop culture.[79] MacLean explains, "I think, like kids everywhere, kids in the Arctic . . . take on aspects of popular culture, and hip hop is one of those things. They take that sort of attitude on, but they're not gangsters, they're not out there killing people. There's a kind of machoism. At the same time, they're also using hip hop to express their own pride in being Inupiat, expressing their love of the culture. They're not trying to be Lil' Wayne, but it says something about them."[80]

As the lyrics illustrate, the juxtapositions between and among Iñupiaq and Black-identified rap cultures are both subtle and not so subtle. On the one hand, many would argue that *misigaaq* (seal oil or seal blubber that is typically rendered into a liquid state for dipping frozen meat and fish) is a reference to a foodway that is central to one's sense of Inuitness. On the other hand, linking the green hues of the aurora borealis—a largely Arctic and Subarctic phenomenon—to the "green as bud" color of marijuana seems obvious or clichéd. Likewise, the posturing of violent machoism through the invocation of guns is an interesting point of departure, considering that gun culture in the Arctic is notably different from that in inner-city New York. For example, the legacy of *Nanook of the North* leads one to expect "real Eskimos" to hunt with harpoons, even though most Inuit hunters have used guns for more than a century. The "aught-six" (.30–06 caliber rifle) is a standard hunting rifle initially introduced to the U.S. Army in 1906 and still used today by Yup'ik and Iñupiaq hunters across Alaska.

Yet among the many alliances seen and heard at this otherwise typical high school party, perhaps the most interesting relationship of all is the one *sounded* by "Arctic Thug" itself—namely, the involvement of DJ RiverFlowz (Torin Jacobs), who co-wrote the lyrics and produced the instrumental track heard in the scene. Jacobs's compositions almost always combine artificial or computer-generated instrumental sounds with samples of actual Inuit music and soundscapes (from the sounds of Inuit drumming and singing to the sounds of walking on the snow). As I have argued elsewhere, this innovative type of musical mixture is significant because it reflects "what Alaska Native people, according to colonial expectations, are not supposed to be: modern, educated, urban, and 'mixed-blood.'"[81] Jacobs self-identifies as of mixed Inuit and African descent and, more specifically, as Iñupiaq, Yup'ik, Sami, Cherokee, and African American. He honed his DJing skills while serving in the U.S. Marine Corps in the late 1990s. He is well known in Inuit and Native American music circuits and often performs with his twin brother, DJ He-Took (Julien Jacobs), or as a guest artist with the award-winning Inuit world music band Pamyua, based in Anchorage. His music has been part of several recent multimedia projects in addition to *On the Ice*, including an Inuit dancing flash mob staged in 2012 by the now infamous 1491s, a "Lower 48" Native American sketch comedy group, and *Games of the North: Playing for Survival*, a documentary about the World Eskimo Indian Olympics.[82] Like many other independent musicians, Native and non-Native, Jacobs uses an array of social media, including MySpace, Facebook, YouTube, and Vimeo, to post updates, videos, and concert footage, all of which have attracted a sizeable fan base. In 2015, he released his debut, two-disc album, *RiverFlowz Rural Recordings Atauciq* (disc 1) and *Malruk* (disc 2).

Like MacLean, Jacobs is positioned within the first generation of new Natives who came of age in a post-ANCSA era, which, scholars have shown, witnessed a flourishing of musical revitalization movements for Alaska Native communities.[83] Jacobs and other new Natives benefited from a late twentieth-century Alaska Native Solidarity movement that increased the visibility of traditional Alaska Native music and dance, most significantly in public schools, via national Indian Education reform initiatives and innovative programs.

Many Alaska Native youth in general, and mixed Inuit-African youth such as Pamyua's Blanchett brothers and the Jacobs brothers in particular, also came of age listening to Sly and the Family Stone, Bob Marley and the Wailers, and Afrika Bambaataa and Soulsonic Force. For some music studies scholars, their aesthetic alliances correspond with the "hip-hop generation," which has been described as a cohort of multiethnic individuals born between 1965 and 1977 whose lives have been shaped by factors such as globalization and economic disenfranchisement, incarceration and racial profiling, inner-city disinvestment, and gender wars.[84] Whereas Jeff Chang's work characterizes a "politics of abandonment" of the 1970s, in which government and business entities divested themselves of inner-city spaces such as the Bronx, as having created the conditions for the emergence of hip-hop culture, Anchorage of the 1970s saw a particular wave of non-Native immigration and urbanization driven by the oil industry.[85] Moreover, ANCSA contributed to the increasing visibility of cultural change for Alaska Native communities and led many Native men and women to relocate to urban areas for school, employment, and health care. This led to segregation and marginalization of Alaska Natives within urban spaces, made visible through the stark contrast between oil wealth and Native poverty and homelessness. While inner-city New York and Anchorage present different scenarios, a similar "politics of containment" (curfews, anti-cruising and anti-loitering ordinances) and racial profiling emerged in Alaska in the 1970s.

Regarding interracial and cross-cultural hip-hop cultures emerging in unexpected places, such as Utqiaġvik, I have argued elsewhere, the presence of these mixtures are not incongruent with Inuit worldviews and are often metaphorically aligned with *Akutuq*, or "Eskimo Ice Cream."[86] Today Utqiaġvik serves as the major hub of the North Slope Borough, an Iñupiaq-controlled home-rule government (incorporated in 1972) that encompasses approximately eighty-eight thousand square miles. According to the 2010 census, the borough is home to an estimated 9,430 people, more than half of whom identify as Alaska Native.[87] Further, of the 4,212 people living within the city limits of Utqiaġvik, 2,889 (68.6 percent) self-identify as "American Indian and Alaska Native" alone or in combination with one or more races, and 83 (2 percent) self-identify as "Black or African American" alone or in combination with one or more races. Grappling with the legacies of such systemic micro-aggressions manifest in wide-reaching cultural displacement, poverty, suicide, substance abuse, and violence, young men of color are particularly vulnerable, facing multiple trajectories of intergenerational trauma inflicted by processes of settler colonialism. Knowing that the stakes of erasure are particularly high for young Afro-Inuit men, artists such as the Jacobs brothers have innovated distinctive visions of modern audiovisual media as a means through which to articulate a changing paradigm in terms of how we understand identity formation and notions of belonging and citizenship.[88]

Ultimately, "Arctic Thug" makes audible some of the intersections between and within politics of Blackness and Indigeneity in Alaska and offers a geographical extension northward for studies about the lived experiences and creative expressions of individuals of mixed Inuit and African American descent.[89] Through this distinctively Iñupiaq freestyle musical moment and the Afro-Inuit alliances embodied in it, MacLean and Jacobs challenge racialized expectations of Native American and African American performance practices, particularly with regard to form, process, and agency, laying bare the dual limitations of what I refer to as "sound quantum" ideology.[90] On one hand, sound quantum parallels the colonial and eugenicist logic that underlies racialized or ethnicized understandings of what "counts" as Native music that is endemic to blood quantum ideology—a pseudoscientific measure of one's Nativeness. Like blood quantum, sound quantum is what the music-industrial complex uses as a biopolitical tool of governmentality. Although the performance of blood politics can often perpetuate racial ideology, as Kimberly Tallbear's work shows, these Afro-Inuit soundscapes challenge understandings of blood and race as fixed and divided.[91] On the other hand, sound quantum refers to a quotient of non-Native presence, which in the case of Afro-Inuit mixtures refers to the musicological equivalent of the "one drop" rule that, to paraphrase George Lewis, revokes rather than celebrates mobility and self-determination.[92] The eugenicist politics of sound quantum continues to pervade popular music scholarship and holds implications for how we teach and study "ethnic" music of North America, particularly in the case of mixed-race musicians. MacLean, Jacobs, and their contemporaries are fully cognizant of the racial codings of American popular music, and as young male activists and public intellectuals they dedicate their work to interrupting static notions of cultural music.

TRACK 3, HARMONIZED "SINGSPIRATION" HYMN: *Qalli and Aivaaq arrive at the James's family's home for a singspiration, a community gathering to mourn the dead centered around singing Presbyterian gospel songs translated into the Iñupiaq language and reading scripture. As the camera pans the crowded living room, a mix of old and young community members are shown seated and singing, reading sheet music out of spiral-bound versions of the Iñupiat Eskimo Hymnbook. Their singing is accompanied by an older man and woman strumming chords on their acoustic guitars while another older man plucks a bass line of root and fifth chord tones on an amplified electric guitar. The mixture of raw grief with the organic feel of the singspiration amplifies the tension of the drama on screen.*

The roots and routes of the Presbyterian hymn "He Leadeth Me" and its translation into an Iñupiaq-language hymnal can be traced back to what is known as the Comity Agreement of 1874, a coordinated plan devised and enacted by Protestant church leaders to divide and assign specific regions of Alaska among an array of Protestant denominations, all to avoid any overlap in their missionization activities.[93] In the case of Utqiaġvik, the Presbyterian Church was assigned the vast Arctic rim, among several other regions, in which it began to establish and concentrate its work in 1890. According to church histories, by 1920 the majority of adults living in Utqiaġvik had been converted to Christianity, and that same decade Iñupiaq men began training to become ordained priests. Many of them assisted with translations of Bible passages and hymnody from English into the Iñupiaq language.[94] With regard to the relationship between hymn singing and Christian conversion, Krejci's work on Arctic musical life reinforces two important points: that "hymn singing was a crucial factor in drawing and sustaining church participation" and Iñupiaq congregation members and church officials had a significant impact on the dissemination and revisioning of Christian religious and musical practices both with and without the presence of non-Native missionaries.[95] Yet as Krejci and others have pointed out, the early 1900s witnessed immense traumas wrought by measles and flu epidemics that decimated entire villages. One explanation of the high conversion rate is that these traumas led Iñupiaq people to question their daily rituals and beliefs and, ultimately, to turn away from traditional spiritual practices and toward the Presbyterian Church in their time of immense grief.

The hymn "He Leadeth Me" was written in 1863 by Joseph Henry Gilmore (1834–1918), who was inspired by a passage from Psalm 23:3 in the King James Bible: "He restoreth my soul: he leadeth me in the paths of righteousness for his name's sake." The music was composed a year later by William B. Bradbury. A cursory comparison of the Presbyterian Hymnbook and the Iñupiat Eskimo Hymnbook finds that the key, meter, time signatures, and phrasing are identical. The differences lay in the languages (English and Iñupiat) and the fact that the version from the *Iñupiat Eskimo Hymnbook* provides only two-part harmonies for soprano and alto (or women's) voices in the treble clef and omits the lower tenor and bass (or men's) parts in the bass clef. Traditional Iñupiaq drum-dance songs are typically monophonic strophic and contain repeated sections, stylistic factors that made for an easy adoption of hymn-singing practices.

For the singspiration scene, MacLean again featured local musicians who are members of the Utqiaġvik Presbyterian Church choir. He has explained the scene by saying, "At the wake—which is called a 'Singspiration'—we see the people of Barrow singing together as a means to deal their grief. But the boys are unable to participate because of the lie they're carrying within themselves—and this lie ends up completely alienating them from what is essentially their entire world."[96] When Qalli and Aviaaq arrive at the house of the murdered teen's family, the scene begins with the family and community members singing the hymn's chorus ("*Ilaan urriksuutigaaŋa* / He leadeth me"), which then proceeds to the second verse, insinuating that the first verse

FIGURE 4.2. Barrow Presbyterian Church Choir circa 1946, courtesy of the
Laura Boulton Collection, Archives of Traditional Music, Indiana University.

had already been performed before the boys' arrival. For audiences unfamil-
iar with hymn singing in the Arctic, the *sound* or timbre of the voices is often
the most striking feature. The majority of scholars writing about what one
could call Inuit timbre specifically, or the "Sound of Eskimo" more broadly,
employ descriptors reminiscent of Alan Lomax's classification of "folk song
styles" of 1959, which describe the vocal styles of "others" as "harsh," "stri-
dent," "shrill," "vibrato-less," "high-pitched," and "slightly off-pitch."[97]

There is, however, one noticeable absence: the drum. In many villages
across Alaska, Christian missionaries prohibited the use of drums because
of their perceived association with heathen or pagan rituals and ceremonies. Some Native communities were able to hold on to their languages in
cases where missionaries saw its usefulness in recruitment and conversion.
Although the singspiration performance in *On the Ice* does not take place
in a church, the musicians are in a home or domestic sphere, which was

privileged by missionaries and schoolteachers above the traditional *qargi*, or public meeting places where the opening *sayuun* is performed. One need only consider the gendered implications of how missionaries and residential schools trained Indigenous men and women to operate and exist in separate spheres via gendered labor and how built environments (e.g., houses and churches) in many cases have irrevocably transformed Indigenous lifeways and musical life.

To be sure, further research is needed in terms of the musical consequences of neo-culturated or Indigenized religious practices and organizations. Scholars have paid scant attention to the music making of Alaska Native Christian musicians, perhaps because Christianity seems incongruous with notions of "pure" Nativeness. Or perhaps this stems from a scholarly disavowal of Christianity in Alaska Native life due to misguided assumptions that colonial religious encounters are always violent. This sentiment seems to be at work when Kirk Dombrowski argues that Native people in Alaska "join churches to save their souls, and they join traditional dance groups to discover their identity."[98] In Dombrowski's formulation, Native people face a false choice of being either "against God" or "against culture." Andrea Smith's critique of the politics of decolonial authenticity provides an alternative perspective. She points out that decolonization as a political project has the potential to become mired in identity politics of cultural authenticity, which requires Native peoples to "demonstrate their decolonization by rejecting Christianity, not eating fry bread, living on reservations, and so on."[99] Yet singspirations provide an important counterexample to a false opposition between Native authenticity and Native Christianity by emphasizing the agency of Native individuals and collectives to choose which aspects of their inherited and allied communities they find meaningful and relevant for the future.

A recent example bears repeating: in the early morning hours of February 10, 2016, thirty-six-year-old Utqiaġvik Fire Chief Vincent Pamiuq Nageak III was shot and killed by a police officer responding to a domestic disturbance. Amid the shock and outrage that followed Pamiuq's death, the circumstances of which are still under investigation, Utqiaġvikmiut came together ten days later for a singspiration following Pamiuq's burial. His father, Roy Nageak, spoke extemporaneously before offering a prayer: "Our Iñupiaq culture says 'forgiveness.' Live in harmony, solve problems together, don't be alone. We've got to be together, always. I love singspiration. I love to sing. Have you seen my son's tattooed arm? 'Forgive me . . . Forgive me.' We need to have forgiveness, move forward and not have anger or bitterness."[100] Bill Hess, a longtime Alaskan photographer who documented the funeral proceedings, caught scenes of the singspiration that followed, which mirrored the scene portrayed in MacLean's film. A mix of old and young community members are shown seated and standing on-stage, singing and reading sheet music out of spiral-bound versions of the *Iñupiat Eskimo Hymnbook*. The singing is accompanied by older men and women playing banjos and amplified acoustic guitars, as well as electric guitars and electric basses. To juxtapose—connect and keep apart—Christian and Iñupiaq ways of grieving through Indigenized hymn singing is akin to modes of survival within structures of colonialism documented elsewhere in North America.[101]

Why Audiovisualizing Iñupiaq Musical Modernities Matters Now

The dehumanizing effects of racialized and gendered violence against Native American and Indigenous communities reverberates across generations. Whether through unconscious or conscious bias, negative stereotypes hold concrete consequences for how Native men are perceived by others and how they perceive themselves. In reference to high incarceration rates for Alaska Native people, Ethan Schutt (Athabascan), who served as general counsel for the Tanana Chiefs' Conference (an Athabascan Native rights organization), noted that it is "easier to convict Native people than other defendants or ethnic groups. Police and prosecutors seem to be more vigorous in pursuing Native defendants, and jurors seem more willing to believe the authorities and disbelieve the defense when Native defendants are on trial."[102] These biases are also reflected in Native deaths by shootings that involve law-enforcement officers. Commenting on his friend Pamiuq's death, E. J. R. David, a psychology professor who was born in the Philippines and raised in Utqiaġvik, observes that even a Native's "respectability" cannot save Native lives:

> Vincent "Pamiuq" Nageak III, a proud Inupiaq man, was a U.S. Army veteran. He was the nephew of an Alaska State Representative, and his family is well-known and well-regarded in their hometown of Barrow. Pamiuq served as an officer for the Department of Corrections, working closely with the North Slope Borough Police Department for over 10 years, then transitioned into working for the North Slope Borough Fire Department, being named "Firefighter of the Year," and eventually becoming Fire Chief. He also ran for a City Assembly Seat and won. He also obtained a college degree while serving his community. All of these things he did while also hunting and whaling, staying true to his Inupiaq heritage and further making him a well-respected community

member. Pamiuq did not criticize the justice system; he was part of the system. He did not campaign for the improvement of police work especially with regard to racial inequalities. In fact, he liked t-shirts that said "I can breathe, because I don't break the law."[103]

Lisa Wexler's research with Iñupiaq communities on youth suicide prevention finds that Indigenous youth living in circumpolar regions suffer disproportionately from suicide compared with national averages—alarmingly high rates due to perceived culture loss narratives perpetuated by colonial narratives and discourse.[104] Youth suicides across the Arctic garnered national attention in April 2016 following Rebecca Hersher's special report, "The Arctic Suicides: It's Not the Dark That Kills You," in which she outlines the long colonial histories underlying a series an alarming series of recent deaths in Greenland.[105] This report prompted a follow-up response that notes "there is a suicide 'season'—a time when the most people die by suicide. It's well-known among public health officials and priests and teachers and other people who professionally worry about people in the community. The suicide season is spring. When the dark and the cold finally lift, and the sun is up and the ice is melting. That's when people end their lives. It's not the dark or the cold."[106] Julian Brave NoiseCat (Canim Lake Band Tsq'escen) reported on eleven suicides, illustrating how the suicide season affects communities across the North America's Arctic and Subarctic regions. He described "broke and broken people with little to no opportunities [who] live in cold, run-down homes and suffer from generations of sexual, physical and psychological abuse. They look on as hundreds of millions of dollars worth of resources are mined from their ancestral homelands. This is not an emergency—a catastrophe for which Canada was unprepared and never saw coming. No, this is and always has been part of the design and devastation that colonization wrought."[107]

Given the many issues threatening the well-being of Iñupiaq youth, researchers have been designing therapy or treatment programs that align with American Indian and Alaska Native cultural values, traditions, and customs. Since 2012, Daniel Dickerson (Iñupiaq), an addiction psychiatrist and assistant research psychiatrist with the Integrated Substance Abuse Programs at the University of California, Los Angeles, served as the principal investigator for the grant-funded and culturally based behavioral therapy program Drum-Assisted Recovery Therapy for Native Americans (DARTNA), which analyzed the benefits of drumming for Native Americans who live in Los Angeles and struggle with substance use disorders. The core components of

DARTNA analyzed included (1) drumming education, (2) drumming activities, (3) gender roles, (4) The Medicine Wheel and 12 Steps education, and (5) linkages to drumming within the community.[108] Ultimately at stake here are the presence (sound) or absence (silence) of Indigenous people in the ongoing debates surrounding issues of identity, representation, diversity, and difference, especially in relation to the politics of who can and cannot lay legitimate claim to Native American and Indigenous identities and cultural or intellectual property. Two questions are at the core of these debates: who is Native American, and who gets to decide? As any number of sports mascots make clear, debates over Native identities and property most often play out in the realm of visual representation and tend to be decided in favor of those with the most power—for example, the Washington Redskins can marshal an arsenal of fans claiming Native American ancestry to legitimate keeping the team's offensive mascot.[109] A dominant underlying assumption here is that Native peoples lack presence and therefore power; that we have always already disappeared, along with our ability to substantiate our claims to our identities and our cultural or intellectual property. While these assumptions of absence and invisibility are rarely extended to the realm of audibility, a growing archive of Indigenous-produced mediascapes expand an existing ocular-centrism by emphasizing the significance of audiovisualizations of place-based and culture-based articulations of Indigenous past, present, and future realities.

Through his deliberate juxtaposition of old (traditional), kind of new (adapted), and brand-new (appropriated) Iñupiaq soundtracks, MacLean unsettles colonial representations of "Eskimos" by instead audiovisualizing the many historic and contemporary layers underlying place-based (Utqiaġvik) and culture-based (Iñupiaq) articulations of male identities and masculine roles in the present day. His representations of Iñupiaq modernities are, of course, always already subject to a diverse range of perspectives on how successfully young Iñupiaq men both navigate intergenerational cultural tensions and entanglements and incorporate aspects of tradition and modernity into their lives in ways that meaningfully (re)define who they are in relation to what they do. While the dynamics of these negotiations and incorporations are indeed messy and pragmatic, it is important to emphasize here that Indigenous understandings of tradition and modernity are not separate or linear but interrelated and cyclical.

MacLean's *On the Ice* is but one of many examples of how Alaska Native artists are actively processing and reconciling the long histories of settler colonialism and its ongoing effects on the mental and physical well-being of their families and communities. In the end, assessments of what is gained and what is lost are also always already changing in the face of ongoing development and extraction in the Arctic, coupled with a climate-change crisis and the race to dominate Northwest Passage routes. Iñupiaq families in general, and Iñupiaq men in particular, are poised to face challenges yet unseen. So what can be done in the present moment? In the realm of cultural expression, one could argue that Native American and Indigenous people must continue to produce their own audiovisualizations as a critical and vital corrective to the colonial regimes of sound and image that continue to vex our pathways forward to healing and regeneration.

NOTES

Epigraphs: Edna Ahgeak MacLean, "Role of Literature as a Source of History, Values and Identity," in *Distant Voices, Shared Dreams: Proceedings from the 14th Annual Alaska Bilingual/Multicultural Education Conference* (Anchorage: Alaska State Department of Education, 1988); Subhankar Banerjee, ed., *Arctic Voices: Resistance at the Tipping Point* (New York: Seven Stories, 2013), 9.

1. Key studies include Michael S. Kimmel, Jeff Hearn, and Robert W. Connell, eds., *Handbook of Studies on Men and Masculinities* (Thousand Oaks, CA: Sage, 2005); Robert W. Connell, *Masculinities* (Cambridge: Polity, 1995); Gail Bederman, *Manliness and Civilization: A Cultural History of Gender and Race in the United States, 1880–1917* (Chicago: University of Chicago Press, 1995).

2. Ase Ottosson, "Where Are the Men? Indigeneity and Masculinity Realigned," *Asia Pacific Journal of Anthropology* 11, no. 1 (2010): 75–83; Janice C. Hill Kanonhsyonni, "Where Are the Men?" in *Masculindians: Conversations about Indigenous Manhood,* ed. Sam McKegney (East Lansing: Michigan State University Press, 2014). See also Ty P. Kawika Tengan, *Native Men Remade: Gender and Nation in Contemporary Hawai'i* (Durham, NC: Duke University Press, 2008), 77.

3. McKegney, *Masculindians,* 1.

4. John Keim, "Dan Snyder Defends 'Redskins,'" ESPN, October 10, 2013, http://espn.go.com/nfl/story/_/id/9797628/dan-snyder-defends-washington-redskins-name; Theresa Vargas, "Anti-Redskins Ad Airing during NBA Finals," *Washington Post,* June 10, 2014, http://wapo.st/10869c9. See also the National Council of American Indians' anti-Redskins commercial "Proud to Be," http://youtu.be/mR-tbOxlhvE.

5. Brian Klopotek, "'I Guess Your Warrior Look Doesn't Work Every Time': Challenging Indian Masculinity in the Cinema," in *Across the Great Divide: Cultures of Manhood in the American West,* eds. Matthew Basso, Laura McCall, and Dee Garceau (New York: Routledge, 2001), 251.

6. Kim Anderson, Robert Alexander Innes, and John Swift, "Indigenous Masculinities: Carrying the Bones of the Ancestors," in *Canadian Men and Masculinities: Historical and Contemporary Perspectives,* eds. Wayne Martino and Christopher J. Greig (Toronto: Canadian Scholars' Press, 2012), 271. Key studies in Native American and

Indigenous masculinities studies include Kim Anderson and Robert Alexander Innes, eds., *Indigenous Men and Masculinities: Legacies, Identities, Regeneration* (Winnipeg, Manitoba: University of Manitoba Press, 2015); Tengan, *Native Men Remade*; Brendan Hokowhitu, "Producing Elite Indigenous Masculinities," *Settler Colonial Studies* 2, no. 2 (2012): 23–48; Brendan Hokowhitu, "Māori Rugby and Subversion: Creativity, Domestication and Decolonization," *International Journal of the History of Sport* 26, no. 16 (2009): 2314–34; Brendan Hokowhitu, "Authenticating Māori Physicality: Translations of 'Games' and 'Pastimes' by Early Travellers and Missionaries to New Zealand," *International Journal of the History of Sport* 25, no. 10 (2008): 1355–73; Brendan Hokowhitu, "The Death of Koro Paka: 'Traditional' Māori Patriarchy," *Contemporary Pacific* 20, no. 1 (2008): 115–41; Brendan Hokowhitu, "Tackling Māori Masculinity: A Colonial Genealogy of Savagery and Sport," *Contemporary Pacific* 16, no. 2 (2004): 265–68; Klopotek, "I Guess Your Warrior Look Doesn't Work Every Time"; Richard King, "On Being a Warrior: Race, Gender and American Indian Imagery in Sport," *International Journal of the History of Sport* 23, no. 2 (2006): 315–30; Lloyd L. Lee, *Diné Masculinities: Conceptualizations and Reflections* (North Charleston, SC: Createspace Independent Publishing Platform, 2013).

7. Kim Anderson, John Swift, and Robert Alexander Innes, "To Arrive Speaking: Voices from the Bidwewidam Indigenous Masculinities Project," in Anderson and Innes, *Indigenous Men and Masculinities*, 283–307.

8. It is worth noting that the twelve elders interviewed for Anderson, Innes, and Swift, "Indigenous Masculinities," did not include any Inuit elders; neither did Anderson and Innes's edited collection *Indigenous Men and Masculinities*. Essays that address Inuit men and masculinities include Thomas Kimeksun Thrasher, "A Man beside My Father," in McKegney, *Masculindians*, 65–73; and Norman Vorano, "Inuit Men, Erotic Art: 'Certain Indecencies That Need Not Here Be Mentioned,'" 124–49; Marius P. Tungilik, "The Dark Side of Sex," 50–58; and Makka Kleist, "Inuit Pre-Christian Sexuality," 15–19; all in *Me Sexy: An Exploration of Native Sex and Sexuality*, ed. Drew Hayden Taylor (Vancouver, BC: Douglas and McIntyre, 2008).

9. Although more detailed analyses of female-identified and gender-nonconforming Inuit identities and roles are beyond the scope of this chapter, they are, of course, equally vital to the overall sociocultural balance of contemporary Inuit life.

10. Reference to various "-scapes" originate from Arjun Appadurai, *Modernity at Large: Cultural Dimensions of Globalization* (Minneapolis: University of Minnesota Press, 1996).

11. McKegney, *Masculindians*, 2.

12. I hear the "Sound of Eskimo" as the Arctic complement to Philip Deloria's "Sound of Indian" (e.g., the "tomahawk chop" chant that surfaces at mainstream sporting events): see Philip J. Deloria, *Indians in Unexpected Places* (Lawrence: University Press of Kansas, 2004).

13. Prominent anthropologists of sound explain the Canadian scholar R. Murray Schafer's framing of "soundscape" as "a publicly circulating entity that is a produced effect of social practices, politics, and ideologies while also being implicated in the shaping of those practices, politics, and ideologies": see David W. Samuels, Louise Meintjes, Ana Maria Ochoa, and Thomas Porcello, "Soundscapes: Toward a Sounded Anthropology,"

Annual Review of Anthropology 39, no. 1 (September 2010): 330; R. Murray Schafer, *The Soundscape: Our Sonic Environment and the Tuning of the World*, repr. ed. (Rochester, NY: Destiny Books, 1994). I also want to note that I refer to MacLean's ancestral village by its Iñupiaq name Utqiaġvik, as opposed to the English-language and colonial name Barrow, throughout this chapter (unless I directly quote someone who used the name Barrow) to reflect local efforts to reclaim Iñupiaq naming practices by making this change official. On Dec. 1, 2016, an official ordinance to change the city's name took effect; see Lisa Demer, "Barrow's New Name Is Its Old One, Utqiaġvik," *Anchorage Daily News*, Oct. 29, 2016.

14. Nancy Fogel-Chance's research addresses the ways in which Iñupiaq women living in urban Anchorage endeavor selectively and meaningfully to incorporate aspects from their rural village lifeways with their newly acquired urban lifeways: see Nancy Fogel-Chance, "Living in Both Worlds: 'Modernity' and 'Tradition' among North Slope Iñupiaq Women in Anchorage," *Arctic Anthropology* 30, no. 1 (1993): 95.

15. Anderson, Swift, and Innes, "To Arrive Speaking," 288–289.

16. Gary Holton and Brett Parks, "Indigenous Peoples and Languages of Alaska," grayscale adaptation, Fairbanks: Alaska Native Language Center and University of Alaska Anchorage Institute of Social Economic Research, 2011, http://www.uaf.edu/anla/collections/map/IPLA_simple_gray.pdf. Scholars and Native community members understand the various boundaries drawn in this map as approximating areas of mutual intelligibility circa 1900 (i.e., how well neighboring speakers could understand one another).

It is also worth noting the difference between Yupik (no apostrophe) and Yup'ik. I follow the institutionalized ANLC standard orthography that observes the apostrophe as distinguishing the specific Central Yup'ik language from the larger Yupik (no apostrophe) branch of the Inuit-Yup'ik-Aleut language family.

17. The wide use of the "Alaska Native" designation is evident in the naming of many prominent Indigenous organizations (e.g., Alaska Native Heritage Center, Alaska Native Justice Center, Alaska Native Medical Center).

18. As Shari M. Huhndorf (Yup'ik) explained at the Inuit Circumpolar Conference (ICC) gathering in 1977, participants officially "rejected 'Eskimo' and adopted the term 'Inuit' as the preferred designation for all Eskimo peoples. This decision was both a recognition of the politics of naming and part of a political platform aimed at self-determination": see Shari M. Huhndorf, *Going Native: Indians in the American Cultural Imagination* (Ithaca, NY: Cornell University Press, 2001), 79, n. 2. Despite this official rejection, "Eskimo" is still used today by social and political groups and institutions, including in the logo for the Alaska Federation of Natives (AFN), the largest statewide Native organization. Thus, I use the term "Eskimo" (as opposed to the more specific designations Yup'ik, Iñupiaq, Alutiiq, and Unangan) only in instances in which individuals or groups identify themselves that way or when discussing historical media, print and audiovisual, that employ the term.

19. For a brief etymology of "Eskimo," see David Damas, "Introduction," in *Handbook of the North American Indians, Volume 5: The Arctic*, ed. David Damas (Washington, DC: Smithsonian Institution Press, 1984), 1–7. Arguments over whether "Eskimo" should, or even can, be stricken from usage are ongoing, and most recently surfaced in relation

to the highly controversial and nationwide debates about the name of the Washington Redskins. Those against the use of "Eskimo" cite Canadian efforts to change the name of the Edmonton Eskimos football team. See Alex DeMarban, "As Washington Redskins Controversy Ramps up, Complicated Term 'Eskimo' Is Reconsidered," *Alaska Dispatch News*, June 26, 2014.

20. Ann Fienup-Riordan, *Freeze Frame*, 18.

21. "Nanookmania" was coined by Asen Balikci in "Anthropology, Film, and the Arctic Peoples," *Anthropology Today* 5, no. April (1989): 7.

22. Some key studies that emerged in the 1970s include Nicole Beaudry, "Le katajjaq, un jeu inuit traditionnel," *Études Inuit Studies* 2, no. 1 (1978): 35–54; Nicole Beaudry, "Toward Transcription and Analysis of Inuit Throat Games: Macro-Structure," *Ethnomusicology* 22, no. 2 (1978): 261–73; Beverley Cavanagh, "Annotated Bibliography: Eskimo Music," *Ethnomusicology* 16, no. 3 (1972): 479–87; Beverley Cavanagh, *Music of the Netsilik Eskimo: A Study of Stability and Change*, Mercury Series no. 82, vol. 1 (Ottawa: National Museum of Man, 1982); Claude Y. Charron, "Le tambour magique: Un instrument autrefois útile pour le qûete d'un conjoint." *Études Inuit Studies* 2, no. 1 (1978): 3–20; Claude Y. Charron, "Toward Transcription and Analysis of Inuit Throat-Games: Micro-Structure," *Ethnomusicology* 22, no. 2 (1978): 245–59; Bernard Saladin d'Anglure, "Entre cri et chant: Les katajjait, un genre musical feminin," *Études Inuit Studies* 2, no. 1 (1978): 85–94; Thomas F. Johnston, *Eskimo Music by Region: A Comparative Circumpolar Study* (Ottawa: National Museums of Canada, 1976); Maija M. Lutz, *The Effects of Acculturation on Eskimo Music of Cumberland Peninsula* (Ottawa: National Museums of Canada, 1978); Maija M. Lutz, *Musical Traditions of the Labrador Coast Inuit* (Ottawa: National Museums of Canada, 1982); Jean-Jacques Nattiez, "Comparison within a Culture: The Katajjaq of the Inuit," in *Cross-Cultural Perspectives on Music*, eds. Robert Flack and Timothy Rice (Toronto: University of Toronto Press, 1982), 134–40; Jean-Jacques Nattiez, "La danse à tambour chez les Inuit Igloolik (Nord de la Terre-de-Baffin)" (The Drum Dance in Igloolik Inuit [Northern Baffin Land]), *Recherches Amérindiennes au Québec* 18, no. 4 (1988): 37–48; Jean-Jacques Nattiez, "Inuit Throat-Games and Siberian Throat Singing: A Comparative, Historical, and Semiological Approach," *Ethnomusicology* 43, no. 3 (1999): 399–418; Jean-Jacques Nattiez, "Some Aspects of Inuit Vocal Games," *Ethnomusicology* 27, no. 3 (1983): 457–75; Ramón Pelinski, *La musique des Inuit du Caribou: Cinq perspectives méthodologiques* (Montreal: Presses de l'Université de Montréal, 1981); Ramón Pelinski, Luke Suluk, and Lucy Amarook, *Inuit Songs from Eskimo Point* (Ottawa: National Museums of Canada, 1979).

23. Fienup-Riordan, *Freeze Frame*, xii.

24. Fienup-Riordan, *Freeze Frame*, 207.

25. Fienup-Riordan, *Freeze Frame*, xi.

26. See "The Fast Runner Trilogy" video on demand, IsumaTV, http://www.isuma .tv/fr/fastrunnertrilogy. See also Michelle H. Raheja, "Reading Nanook's Smile: Visual Sovereignty, Indigenous Revisions of Ethnography, and *Atanarjuat* (The Fast Runner)," *American Quarterly* 59, no. 4 (December 2007): 1159–85; Shari M. Huhndorf, "*Atanarjuat, the Fast Runner*: Culture, History, and Politics in Inuit Media," *American Anthropologist* 105, no. 4 (December 2003): 822–26; Michael Robert Evans, *The Fast Runner: Filming*

the Legend of Atanarjuat (Lincoln: University of Nebraska Press, 2010); Faye Ginsburg, "*Atanarjuat* Off-Screen: From 'Media Reservations' to the World Stage," *American Anthropologist* 105, no. 4 (December 2003): 827–831; Paul Apak Angilirq et al., *Atanarjuat 'the Fast Runner'* (Culver City, CA: Columbia TriStar Home Entertainment); Shari M. Huhndorf, "'From the Inside and through Inuit Eyes': Igloolik Isuma Productions and the Cultural Politics of Inuit Media," in *Mapping the Americas: The Transnational Politics of Contemporary Native Culture* (Ithaca, NY: Cornell University Press, 2009).

27. Norman Cohn, quoted in Mark Slobin, *Global Soundtracks: Worlds of Film Music* (Middletown, CT: Wesleyan University Press, 2008), xviii.

28. Michelle H. Raheja, *Reservation Reelism: Redfacing, Visual Sovereignty, and Representations of Native Americans in Film* (Lincoln: University of Nebraska Press, 2011), 210.

29. Ann Fienup-Riordan, "Frozen in Film: Alaska Eskimos in the Movies," in *Films on Ice: Cinemas of the Arctic*, eds. Scott MacKenzie and Anna Westerståhl Stenport (Edinburgh: Edinburgh University Press, 2015).

30. "Uqaluksrat: Something to Say," interview with Edna MacLean, *Aurora*, Spring 2015, http://news.uaf.edu/something-to-say.

31. Edna Ahgeak MacLean, ed., *Iñupiatun Uqaluit Taniktun Sivuninit/Iñupiaq to English Dictionary* (Fairbanks: University of Alaska Press, 2014).

32. Andrew MacLean, quoted in "Twenty-five New Faces of Independent Film," *Filmmaker Magazine Online*, n.d., http://www.filmmakermagazine.com/archives/issues/summer2008/25faces.php.

33. Quoted in Paulette Beete, "Answering Back: Andrew Okpeaha MacLean Captures Life on the Ice," NEA *Arts*, no. 1 (2011), http://arts.gov/NEARTS/2011v1-and-comers-arts/answering-back.

34. MacLean's first short film, *Natchiliagniaqtuguk Aapagalu* (Seal Hunting with Dad; 2006), is about an Inuit hunter teaching his son to hunt on the frozen Arctic Ocean. The film was screened at the Sundance Film Festival in 2005 and was featured at New York's Museum of Modern Art.

35. Quoted in Beete, "Answering Back."

36. *Sikumi* was written in English by MacLean, who then enlisted his mother, Edna, to help translate it into Iñupiatun: see Tamar Ben-Yosef, "Film Brings Traditions of Inupiaq to Screen," *Juneau Empire*, June 24, 2008, http://juneauempire.com/stories/062408/sta_294766366.shtml#.VhVv9dZUteM.

37. See https://www.isuma.tv/atanarjuat.

38. *Sikumi* website: http://sikumifilm.net; Ben-Yosef, "Film Brings Traditions of Inupiaq to Screen."

39. "Twenty-five New Faces of Independent Film," http://www.filmmakermagazine.com/archives/issues/summer2008/25faces.php#.VgB4brRUteM.

40. Ben-Yosef, "Film Brings Traditions of Inupiaq to Screen."

41. Andrés Martínez Ojeda, "A Composer's Experience with Film Forward," Sundance Film Forward website, July 26, 2012, http://www2.sundance.org/filmforward/article/a-composers-experience-with-film-forward.

42. Other awards for *Sikumi* include the British Academy of Film and Television Arts/Los Angeles Award for Excellence at the 2008 Aspen Shortsfest; the King Award

for Excellence in Filmmaking, Wasserman Award for Best Directing, and King Award for Best Screenwriting at the 2008 First Run Film Festival at New York University; the 2008 National Board of Review Award; Best Dramatic Short at the 2008 Arizona International Film Festival; Best Student Short at the 2008 Woodstock Film Festival; Best Narrative Short at the 2008 Austin Film Festival; Best Short Drama at the 2008 ImagineNATIVE Film Festival; Best Snowdance Film at the 2008 Anchorage International Film Festival; Best Overall Film at the 2009 Weeneebeg Aboriginal Film and Video Festival; Best Short Film at the 2009 Montreal First Peoples' Film Festival.

43. Nigel Smith, "Futures: 'On the Ice' Director Andrew Okpeaha MacLean Talks about Shooting in Alaska, and Polar Bears," Indiewire Online, February 16, 2012, http://www.indiewire.com/article/futures-02–16-andrew-okpeaha-maclean-on-the-ice.

44. Andrew Okpeaha MacLean, "Directors Statement," *On the Ice Press Notes*, December 7, 2011: 3. http://www.ontheicethemovie.com.

45. Ella Taylor, "'On The Ice': Boys with a Secret, and a Chill Inside," NPR.org, February 16, 2012, http://www.npr.org/2012/02/16/146830392/on-the-ice-boys-with-a-secret-and-a-chill-inside; Brian Miller, "On the Ice," *Village Voice*, February 15, 2012, http://www.villagevoice.com/film/on-the-ice-6434140.

46. Awards for *On the Ice* include Best First Feature Prize and Crystal Bear for Generations 14 plus at the 2011 Berlinale; International Federation of Film Critics Prize for Best New American Film at the 2011 Seattle International Film Festival; Best Narrative Award and Best Cinematography Award at the 2011 Woodstock Film Festival; Best Director at the 2011 American Indian Film Festival; and Honorable Mention for Best Film at the 2011 Cine Las Americas.

47. "Andrew MacLean and iZLER at Sundance Film Festival," video, http://www.bmi.com/video/entry/andrew_maclean_and_izler_at_sundance_film_festival.

48. MacLean, quoted in "Sundance Exclusive: Andrew Okpeaha MacLean's 'On the Ice,'" interview by Jack Price, January 31, 2011, http://anthemmagazine.com/sundance-exclusive-andrew-okpeaha-macleans-on-the-ice.

49. I thank Fannie Akpik for identifying the opening sayuun songs: Fannie Akpik, personal communication, July 29, 2013.

50. Lisa Frink, "The Identity Division of Labor in Alaska," *American Anthropologist* 111, no. 1 (2009): 23. See also Lee Guemple, "Gender in Inuit Society," in *Women and Power in Native North America*, eds. Laura F. Klein and Lillian A. Ackerman (Norman: University of Oklahoma Press, 1995); Lillian Ackerman, "Gender Status in Yup'ik Society," *Études Inuit Studies* 14, no. 1 (1990).

51. Barbara Bodenhorn, "I'm Not the Great Hunter, My Wife Is: Iñupiat and Anthropological Models of Gender," *Études Inuit Studies* 14, nos. 1–2 (1990): 57, 59.

52. Ann Fienup-Riordan, "The Bird and the Bladder: The Cosmology of Central Yup'ik Seal Hunting," *Études Inuit Studies* 14, nos. 1–2 (1990).

53. Fienup-Riordan, "The Bird and the Bladder," 60.

54. Bodenhorn, "I'm Not the Great Hunter, My Wife Is," 55.

55. "Along Alaska's Arctic Coast, Female Whalers Are Breaking the 'Ice Ceiling,'" *Alaska Dispatch News*, October 9, 2015, http://adn-pb.internal.arc2.nile.works/pb/arctic/article/women-whalers-are-breaking-ice-ceiling/2015/10/10.

56. Utqiaġvik whaling crews also pursue bowhead whales in the fall when the ocean is free of ice, a scenario that is more accessible to people outside the whaling crew. Yet spring whales are considered ideal because of the increased degree of difficulty hunting on the ice, which also translates into different criteria for crew membership and division of meat shares. For more information on Iñupiaq whaling practices, see Harry Brower Brewster and Karen Brewster, *The Whales, They Give Themselves: Conversations with Harry Brower, Sr.* (Fairbanks: University of Alaska Press, 2004), 135; Chie Sakakibara, " 'No Whale, No Music': Contemporary Iñupiaq Drumming and Global Warming," *Polar Record* 45, no. 4 (2009): 289; Norman A. Chance, *The Iñupiat and Arctic Alaska: An Ethnography of Development* (Fort Worth, TX: Holt, Rinehart and Winston, 1990).

57. Chie Sakakibara, "Cetaceousness and Global Warming among the Iñupiat of Arctic Alaska," PhD diss., University of Oklahoma, Norman, 2007, 156.

58. Cara Marcous, "Filming Starts Tomorrow!" blog post, April 8, 2010, http://ontheicethemovie.blogspot.com.

59. Banerjee, *Arctic Voices*.

60. Chie, "No Whale, No Music."

61. Edna Maclean, "Keeping the Songs Alive," in *Surviving in Two Worlds: Contemporary Native American Voices*, eds. Lois Crozier-Hogle, Darryl Babe Wilson, and Ferne Jensen (Austin: University of Texas Press, 2010): 180.

62. For Iñupiaq perspectives on drum-dance performances and Iñupiaq values, see John A. Kakaruk and William A. Oquilluk, *The Eagle Wolf Dance (Messenger Feast)*, privately printed pamphlet, 1964; Deanna M. Kingston, "Siberian Songs and Siberian Kin: Indirect Assertions of King Islander Dominance in the Bering Strait Region," *Arctic Anthropology* 37, no. 2 (2000): 38–51; Deanna Marie Kingston and Elizabeth Marino, "Twice Removed: King Islanders' Experience of 'Community' through Two Relocations," *Human Organization* 69, no. 2 (2010): 119–28; Deanna Paniataaq Kingston, "Ugiuvangmiut Illugiit Atuut: Teasing Cousins Songs of the King Island Iñupiat," in *The Alaska Native Reader: History, Culture, Politics*, ed. Maria Shaa Tláa Williams (Durham, NC: Duke University Press, 2009), 261–71; Charles Sean Asiqłuq Topkok, "Iñupiat Ilitqusiat: Inner Views of Our Iñupiaq Values," PhD diss., University of Alaska, Fairbanks, 2015).

63. Topkok, "Iñupiat Ilitqusiat," 147.

64. The drum's honored place is evident in the decision to feature a stylized Inuit drum and drumstick as the central icons for the ICC's logo: see http://www.inuitcircumpolar.com.

65. See Paula Conlon, "Iglulik Inuit Drum-Dance Songs," in *Music of the First Nations: Tradition and Innovation in Native North America*, ed. Tara Browner (Urbana: University of Illinois Press, 2009), 9.

66. Beverley Diamond, "The Music of Modern Indigeneity: From Identity to Alliance Studies," *European Meetings in Ethnomusicology* 12, no. 22 (2007): 173.

67. Diamond, "The Music of Modern Indigeneity," 175.

68. Tengan, *Native Men Remade*.

69. Paul Krejci, "Skin Drums, Squeeze Boxes, Fiddles, and Phonographs: Musical Interaction in the Western Arctic, Late 18th through Early 20th Centuries," PhD diss., University of Alaska, Fairbanks, 2010, 457.

70. Laura Boulton, *The Music Hunter, the Autobiography of a Career* (Garden City, NY: Doubleday, 1969), 390. Boulton provides one of the earliest collections of Inuit music, if not the first publicly accessible recording of a vocal game, on her phonographic release *The Eskimos of Hudson Bay and Alaska* (Folkways Records FE 4444, 1954).

71. For a more detailed history, see A. J. McClanahan, *Alaska Native Corporations: Sakuuktugut, "We Are Working Incredibly Hard"* (Anchorage: CIRI Foundation, 2006).

72. A thirteenth corporation was later created to account for Alaska Natives living outside the state.

73. The only limitation placed on village corporation enrollment was that Natives had to choose just one (i.e., no double enrollments).

74. If an individual was born in a city, such as Anchorage, however, she or he typically was not enrolled in a village corporation and became classified as an "at-large" shareholder. For example, as of December 2010, 83 percent of the shareholders in Cook Inlet Region Inc. (CIRI) were designated at-large.

75. In 1969, the AFN sought to have a "Native" defined as any citizen who is an Alaskan Indian, Eskimo, or Aleut of one-fourth degree or more, or, lacking proof of race, who is regarded as a Native by the village of which he claims to be a member and one of whose parents was considered a member.

76. In particular, the equation of corporate shares with money and dividends continues to exacerbate a generational divide. To date, only four corporations have opted to enfranchise after-borns, and each has implemented different strategies for doing so, such as the conveyance of restricted or unrestricted stock, which may or may not include voting rights and the allotment of dividends. As of 2010, approximately 60 percent of Alaska Natives are not shareholders: Phyllis Fast, "Alaska Native Language, Culture and Identity," 2008, http://www.uaa.alaska.edu/books-of-the-year/year08–09/supplemental_readings.cfm.

77. MacLean, quoted in *"On the Ice* Director Andrew Okpeaha MacLean Examines Tradition versus Hip-Hop Culture in Alaska," interview by Jen Yamato, June 20, 2011, http://movieline.com/2011/06/20/on-the-ice-director-andrew-okpeaha-maclean-examines-tradition-vs-hip-hop-culture-in-alaska.

78. Lauren Jessica Amsterdam, "All the Eagles and the Ravens in the House Say Yeah: (Ab)original Hip-Hop, Heritage, and Love," *American Indian Culture and Research Journal* 37, no. 2 (2013): 55.

79. Ann Powers, "When Pop Stars Flirt with Bad Taste," blog post, National Public Radio, July 3, 2013, http://www.npr.org/blogs/therecord/2013/07/02/198097817/the-record-when-pop-stars-flirt-with-danger; Adam Krims, *Rap Music and the Poetics of Identity* (Cambridge: Cambridge University Press, 2000).

80. MacLean, quoted in Victor Moreno, "Andrew Okpeaha MacLean: *On the Ice,"* *Dazed Digital* newsletter, n.d., http://www.dazeddigital.com/artsandculture/article/12120/1/andrew-okpeaha-maclean-on-the-ice.

81. Jessica Bissett Perea, "Pamyua's Akutaq: Traditions of Modern Inuit Modalities in Alaska," *MUSICultures* 39, no. 1 (2012): 9.

82. See DJ He Took, "Represent," http://youtu.be/Vivc76uOV24. The flash mob dancers are grooving to the notably modern "Eskimo Flow" hip hop, which consists of

an instrumental track, or "beat," produced by DJ RiverFlowz and the virtuosic turntablism of DJ He Took. See also Jonathon Stanton and Steven Wounded Deer Alvarez, dirs., *Games of the North: Playing for Survival*, Vision Maker Media, Lincoln, NE, 2011.

83. Jessica Perea, "The Politics of Inuit Musical Modernities in Alaska," PhD diss., University of California, Los Angeles, 2011; Maria Del Pilar Williams, "Alaska Native Music and Dance: The Spirit of Survival," PhD diss., University of California, Los Angeles, 1996; James H. Barker, Theresa John, and Ann Fienup-Riordan, *Yupiit Yuraryarait: Yup'ik Ways of Dancing* (Fairbanks: University of Alaska Press, 2010).

84. To be sure, there are some who would limit inclusion in the "hip hop generation" to African Americans: see Bakari Kitwana, *The Hip Hop Generation: Young Blacks and the Crisis in African American Culture* (New York: Basic Civitas, 2002).

85. Jeff Chang, *Can't Stop, Won't Stop: A History of the Hip-Hop Generation* (New York: St. Martin's Press, 2005).

86. *Akutuq* is the Iñupiaq spelling. For discussions of layers of mixing in Yup'ik drum-dance, see Perea, "Pamyua's Akutaq."

87. The 2010 census accounted for 52.9 percent of people self-identified as American Indian and Alaska Native alone in the North Slope Borough. See http://quickfacts.census.gov/qfd/states/02/02185.html.

88. See Jack D. Forbes, *Africans and Native Americans: The Language of Race and the Evolution of Red-Black Peoples*, 2nd ed. (Urbana: University of Illinois Press, 1993); Robert Keith Collins, "What Is a Black Indian? Misplaced Expectations and Lived Realities," in *Indivisible: African-Native American Lives in the Americas*, ed. Gabrielle Tayac (Washington, DC: Smithsonian Books, 2009): 182–95; Robert Keith Collins, "*Katimih O Sa Chata Kiyou* (Why Am I Not Choctaw?): Race in the Lived Experiences of Two Black Choctaw Mixed-Bloods," in *Crossing Waters, Crossing Worlds: The African Diaspora in Indian Country*, eds. Tiya Miles and Sharon Holland (Durham, NC: Duke University Press, 2006): 260–272.

89. See two large-scale National Museum of the American Indian (NMAI) exhibitions: "IndiVisible: African–Native American Lives in the Americas," 2009, collaboratively produced by the NMAI, the National Museum of African American History and Culture, and the Smithsonian Institution, http://nmai.si.edu/exhibitions/indivisible, and "Up Where We Belong: Native Musicians in Popular Culture," 2010. The latter exhibition expands narratives of American music to include the lasting contributions of Native American musicians, especially within genres identified as Black, such as blues, jazz, hip hop, and rap.

90. Perea, "Pamyua's Akutaq," 9.

91. Kimberly Tallbear, "DNA, Blood, and Racializing the Tribe," *Wicazō Śa Review* 18, no. 1 (Spring 2003): 81–107.

92. Christopher Waterman, "Race Music: Bo Chatmon, 'Corrine Corrina,' and the Excluded Middle," in *Music and the Racial Imagination*, eds. Philip Bohlman and Ronald Radano (Chicago: University of Chicago Press, 2000), 166; George Lewis, "Afterword to 'Improvised Music after 1950': The Changing Same," in *The Other Side of Nowhere: Jazz, Improvisation, and Communities in Dialogue*, eds. Daniel Fischlin and Ajay Heble (Middletown, CT: Wesleyan University Press, 2004).

93. See Maria Sháa Tláa Williams, "The Comity Agreement: Missionization of Alaska Native People," in Williams, *The Alaska Native Reader*: 151–62.

94. H. Gene Straatmeyer, "A Model for a Cross-Cultural Church: The White/Eskimo Experience of First Presbyterian Church, Fairbanks, Alaska," D. Min. diss., Iliff School of Theology, Denver, CO, 1979.

95. Krejci names Roy Ahmaogak (1898–1968) as a central figure in linking these processes, for he became an ordained Presbyterian minister in 1947 and is credited with translating hymns from English into the Iñupiaq language: Krejci, "Skin Drums, Squeeze Boxes, Fiddles, and Phonographs," 192, 202–4.

96. Andrew Okpeaha MacLean, *On the Ice Press Notes*, 5–6, http://www.ontheice themovie.com.

97. Alan Lomax, "Folk Song Style," *American Anthropologist* 61, no. 6 (1959): 927–54. See also Thomas F. Johnston, "Eskimo Music: A Comparative Survey," *Anthropologica* 17, no. 2 (1975): 217–32; Krejci, "Skin Drums, Squeeze Boxes, Fiddles, and Phonographs."

98. Kirk Dombrowski, *Against Culture: Development, Politics, and Religion in Indian Alaska* (Lincoln: University of Nebraska Press, 2001), 9.

99. Andrea Smith, "Decolonization in Unexpected Places: Native Evangelicalism and the Rearticulation of Mission," *American Quarterly* 62, no. 3 (2010): 587. See also Andrea Smith, *Native Americans and the Christian Right: The Gendered Politics of Unlikely Alliances* (Durham, NC: Duke University Press, 2008).

100. Quoted in the photographer Bill Hess's documentation of Pamiuq's funeral proceedings: see https://www.facebook.com/bill.hess.313/media_set?set=a.10153791637965546 .1073741842.567585545&type=3.

101. Michael David McNally, *Ojibwe Singers: Hymns, Grief, and a Native Culture in Motion* (Oxford: Oxford University Press, 2000). Luke E. Lassiter, Clyde Ellis, and Ralph Kotay, *The Jesus Road: Kiowas, Christianity, and Indian Hymns* (Lincoln: University of Nebraska Press, 2002); Chad Hamill, *Songs of Power and Prayer in the Columbia Plateau: The Jesuit, the Medicine Man, and the Indian Hymn Singer* (Corvallis: Oregon State University Press, 2012).

102. Dave Stephenson, "For Alaska Natives: Extermination by Incarceration," June 26, 2003, http://indiancountrytodaymedianetwork.com/2003/06/26/alaska-natives -extermination-incarceration-88943.

103. E. J. R. David, "Five Facts on Native Lives and the (In)Justice System," *Psychology Today*, March 7, 2016, https://www.psychologytoday.com/blog/unseen-and-unheard /201603/five-facts-native-lives-and-the-injustice-system.

104. See Lisa Wexler, "Inupiat Youth Suicide and Culture Loss: Changing Community Conversations," *Social Science and Medicine* 63 (2006): 2938–48; Lisa Wexler, "Identifying Colonial Discourses in Inupiat Young People's Narratives as a Way to Understand the No Future of Inupiat Youth Suicide," *Journal of American Indian and Alaska Native Mental Health Research* 16, no. 1 (2009): 1–24; Lisa Wexler, "Looking across Three Generations of Alaska Natives to Explore How Culture Fosters Indigenous Resilience," *Transcultural Psychiatry* 51, no. 1 (2014): 73–92.

105. Rebecca Hersher, "The Arctic Suicides: It's Not the Dark that Kills You," NPR.org, April 21, 2016, http://www.npr.org/sections/goatsandsoda/2016/04/21/474847921/the-arctic-suicides-its-not-the-dark-that-kills-you.

106. "The Arctic Suicides: Your Questions Answered," NPR.org, May 1, 2016, http://www.npr.org/sections/goatsandsoda/2016/05/01/476168761/the-arctic-suicides-your-questions-answered.

107. Julian Brave NoiseCat, "The Canadian First Nation Suicide Epidemic Has Been Generations in the Making," *The Guardian*, April 12, 2016, https://www.theguardian.com/commentisfree/2016/apr/12/canadian-first-nation-suicide-epidemic-attawapiskat-indigenous-people.

108. Daniel L. Dickerson, Kamilla L. Venner, Bonnie Duran, Jeffrey J. Annon, Benjamin Hale, and George Funmaker, "Drum-Assisted Recovery Therapy for Native Americans (DARTNA): Results from a Pretest and Focus Groups," *American Indian and Alaska Native Mental Health Research (Online)* 21, no. 1 (2014): 37.

109. See https://www.washingtonpost.com/local/new-poll-finds-9-in-10-native-americans-arent-offended-by-redskins-name/2016/05/18/3ea11cfa-161a-11e6–924d-838753295f9a_story.html.

5

AROUND 1978

*Family, Culture, and Race in
the Federal Production of Indianness*

MARK RIFKIN

In the lead-up to the reauthorization of the Violence against Women Act (VAWA) in March 2013, the U.S. Senate and House of Representatives both passed versions with very different provisions with respect to sexual assault and domestic violence by non-Natives on reservations.[1] The law originally was adopted in 1994 and was previously reauthorized in 2005. In its various iterations, it has, among other things, created categories for interstate domestic violence, dating violence, and stalking in federal law and provided funding (for which periodic reauthorization is needed) for the prevention and prosecution of violent crimes against women. Specifically, the language of the Senate version, which was included in the enacted law, allowed for tribes to have limited criminal jurisdiction in cases involving dating and domestic violence over the non-Indian "romantic" and "intimate" partners of women living in Indian country and enabled tribal governments to issue and enforce protection orders. These provisions were absent in the House bill, which instead required that Native women seek protection from federal courts. The Republican resistance to this section in the Senate bill (S. 1925), and the effort to have it removed from the legislation, offers some sense of why it was not included in the House bill (H.R. 4970). In a speech on the Senate floor, Republican Senator John Kyl of Arizona described these provisions as "blatantly unconstitutional," adding that the section "breaks with 200 years of American legal tradition that tribes cannot exercise criminal jurisdiction over non-Indians." He went on to say, "All tribes require either Indian ancestry or a specific quantum of Indian blood in order to be a tribal member. Even a person who has lived his entire life on the reservation cannot be a tribal member if he does not have Indian blood." In a similar vein, Republican Senator Chuck Grassley of Iowa argued, "Constitutional problems are made worse because the bill gives tribes criminal jurisdiction as part of their claimed inherent sovereignty."[2]

These comments speak to a much larger problem within contemporary federal Indian policy—namely, the issue of precisely how to determine the contours and content of Native sovereignty. Kyl suggests that tribal authority can be defined by reference to Indianness, the reproductive transmission of an otherwise undefined racial substance via "ancestry" or the passage of "blood." To attempt to extend the jurisdiction of Native nations further, to include those who are "non-Indian," then, would unconstitutionally subject them to the rule of a racialized clique to which they can never belong. The opposition to the "Indian" provisions of the Senate bill, then, seemed to depend on treating Native political authority as self-evidently equivalent to Indian identity, presuming the United States has the right to regulate the jurisdiction of Native polities, and claiming that the racial limits of Indigenous governance are constitutionally mandated. Maintaining the distinction between Indians and non-Indians as the central axis by which to define the limits of Native sovereignty substitutes the reproductive transmission of racialized substance—having "Indian blood" or "Indian ancestry"—for the geopolitical dynamic of Indigenous peoples continuing to exist on territory forcibly incorporated into/ as the settler state. In this frame, Indians are a special kind of group within the overall structure of U.S. constitutionalism, as opposed to Indigenous polities whose status as such precedes and exceeds the U.S. Constitution. The political anxieties generated by Native peoples' continued survival emerges perhaps most directly in the VAWA debate in hesitations around the "claimed inherent sovereignty" of tribal nations. While the assertion that Native peoples have not exercised criminal jurisdiction over non-Indians at any point in the past two hundred years is simply inaccurate,[3] it bespeaks a worry that acknowledging the legitimacy of such power puts in jeopardy central aspects of the "American legal tradition"—that the right claimed by the United States to exercise authority over the territory said to compose the nation may be put in doubt. Turning the matter of the bounds of Native governmental authority into the question of who counts as Indian transposes the issue into a different register, one that makes Native sovereignty dependent on biological difference and a heteronormative logic of reproduction.

However, even though the final act does offer possibilities for tribal jurisdiction over "non-Indians" unavailable in the House bill (replicating the language that had been in the Senate version), it does not escape the orbit of the racializing reproductive assumptions guiding the arguments made by the Senate bill's detractors. The law notes that the persons who would be prosecutable under this act must be "in a social relationship of a romantic or intimate nature" with the alleged victim or "a current or former spouse or intimate partner." While such categories do not fit exactly the contours of the nuclear family unit, especially since the act pertains to "dating" as well as to "domestic" violence, the model here still appears to be that of marital pairing, extended backward to courting and forward through divorce. This delimitation of the potential authority exerted over "non-Indians," then, seems to take couplehood as the axiomatic frame. Why, though, would romantic partnering provide the prism for thinking about how legally to redress violence against Native women by non-natives?[4] The key to answering this question may lie in the repeated description of the powers of Native governments under this law as "special domestic violence criminal jurisdiction." What makes it "special" is that the statute offers forms of authority "that a participating tribe may exercise under this section but could not otherwise exercise."[5] In other words, this law creates a limited exception for kinds of violence that can be understood in relation to the nuclear family unit. In this way, the statute preserves the presumptively reproductive distinction between non-Indian and Indian (a term that itself is nowhere defined in the statute) while allowing for cases in which non-Indians enter into the romantic-familial orbit of the propagation of Indianness.[6] Thus, the reauthorized VAWA also indicates an understanding of Native sovereignty as control over the genealogical process of transmitting Indianness. More than signaling a particular Republican reluctance to expand tribal jurisdiction or a Democratic championing of Native self-determination, the debate over VAWA reveals the lineaments, and limits, of the ostensible U.S. commitment to recognizing Native sovereignty. Specifically, it indicates the ways seemingly antithetical positions continue to operate within a heteronormative assemblage in which the reproduction of the body of the Indian provides the frame for conceptualizing Indigenous governance.[7]

In this way, the recent controversy over the legal status of domestic abuse and sexual assault against Native women foregrounds an ongoing set of dynamics in federal Indian law and policy that can be traced back at least thirty years. In particular, the claims about the inapplicability of tribal criminal law to "non-Indians" follow from the decision offered in *Oliphant v. Suquamish* (1978), in which the Supreme Court first articulated that principle.[8] The decision bases this determination on the diminished "status" of Native nations that supposedly necessarily follows from their incorporation into the domestic territory of the United States. In reaching this conclusion, the court circumvents the problems for U.S. sovereignty posed by the extraconstitutional and prior existence of Indigenous polities (what Joanne Barker refers to as "the polity of the Indigenous" in the introduction to this volume). Instead, it construes Indianness as a kind of extrapolitical attribute that attaches to particular kinds of bodies and not others, presenting "non-Indian" (presumptively white) bodies as both innately bearing a constitutionally sacrosanct status and needing to be protected from contamination/assault in enclaves ordered around "Indian" propensities. In translating the geopolitics of Indigenous self-determination into the itinerary of racial reproduction, the case provides a key precedent that helps structure the current debate, but it also reveals the prominent tendency within contemporary U.S. Indian policy to define the political dimensions of Native sovereignty through reference to a reprosexual logic,[9] in which an implicit emphasis on the generational inheritance of biological Indianness despatializes Native identity and, thus, translates place-based indigeneity into a matter of lineage.

That representation of Indigenous peoples as if they were extended families, and therefore necessarily something other than full polities, though, extends to endorsements and even expansions of Native sovereignty. Looking at Congress's passage of the Indian Child Welfare Act (ICWA), which also occurred in 1978, one might interpret this measure as moving in the opposite direction from *Oliphant* in its effort to increase the scope of Native authority by giving tribal courts jurisdiction over the placement of Indian children. If measured against a "race" versus "politics" binary, ICWA would seem firmly in the second category, but the law also relies on an understanding of Native identity figured in reproductive terms, even if not in the more incipiently racializing ways *Oliphant* does so. Instead, "culture" and "community" serve as the gradients for assessing, affirming, and protecting Native distinctness and continuity. In developing these ways of indexing indigeneity, ICWA foregrounds what might be termed kinship as the matrix through which to determine the boundaries of Nativeness. However, while kinship and race cannot and should not be equated by seeing the former as merely a stand-in for the latter,[10] the familialization of Native peoples does not so much repudiate the principles of Oliphant as supplement them. ICWA produces a vision of Indigenous belonging still based on calculating "Indian" descent, segregating the content and determination of such genealogical relation from the sphere of politics proper, and excluding "non-Indians."[11] Although perhaps more capacious, and certainly less dismissive, this approach to Indian policy shares in the kind of heteronormative orientation guiding *Oliphant*, a connection we can see at play in the VAWA debate in which the progressive option is to extend the boundaries of family rather than to recast the terms of U.S. recognition and regulation of Native peoples.

Rather than suggesting that all of contemporary Indian policy follows a singular logic or set of principles, I seek to demonstrate how approaching it through a critique of heteronormativity can help in tracking patterns of translation and forced relation that cut across seemingly opposed political positions, thereby indicating some of the ways the possibilities for Indigenous self-determination are managed and stymied in the current conjuncture. More than simply referring to the privileging of heterosexual relationships over same-sex ones, the concept of heteronormativity captures a range of simultaneous and interarticulated forms of normalization that pivot around, in Elizabeth Povinelli's terms, the "intimate event" of conjugal couplehood and bourgeois homemaking.[12] In addition to pointing toward the ideological and institutional dynamics that naturalize the nuclear family unit as the self-evident atom of social existence, the term speaks to the ways processes of privatization, racialization, and depoliticization cross-reference one another in the alignment of procreation with the replication of social identities understood as inherently beyond governmental creation or control, as having a quasi-organic existence properly free from political interference. In this way, heteronormative discourses and policies generate the impression of a sphere of life whose contours are biologically determined (since they supposedly are necessary for human reproduction itself) that exists independently of all forms of political determination, negotiation, and contestation. The concepts of Indianness as the transmission of racial substance and of Native kinship systems as unique forms of family both take part within a heteronormative understanding of Native identity and of Indigeneity itself as a form of genetic or genealogical inheritance that, therefore, is intrinsically distinct from anything that could constitute true political sovereignty. In interpellating Native peoples into the terms of Euro-American discourses of sexuality, and thus also of racial reproduction, U.S. Indian policy translates polities into populations whose "special" recognition by the settler government can be diminished or retracted at any time, seeking to manage and displace the anxieties generated by the fundamental illegitimacy of absorbing Indigenous territories into/as the settler state. Using this framework to analyze two of the watershed policy changes in different branches occurring in the same year, which seem in many ways rather disparate, then, helps illustrate one of the central strategies by which the U.S. acknowledges continuing Native collective presence while seeking to accommodate it to—and to validate the persistence of—the geopolitics and jurisdiction of settlement.

Mapping the Indian

The decision in *Oliphant* turns on the question of what constitutes an Indian tribe as such. The case involves the prosecution of Mark David Oliphant for assaulting a Suquamish police officer on the Port Madison Indian Reservation on August 19, 1973.[13] After being released on his own recognizance from the tribal jail, Oliphant petitioned the U.S. District Court for a writ of habeas corpus, arguing that the tribal court had no jurisdiction over him as a non-Indian. The District Court denied the writ; the Appellate Court affirmed that decision; and the Supreme Court reversed it. While putatively focused on defining the position of "non-Indians" in relation to Native governments, the majority opinion, written by William Rehnquist, rehearses a version of the history of federal Indian policy in order to present the exertion of criminal jurisdiction over those outside the category of "Indian" as fundamentally incommensurable with the "tribe" as a kind of entity under U.S. law.[14] The decision uses Indianness as a placeholder to bridge forms of political and conceptual incoherence, positioning it as a quality that self-evidently attaches to certain bodies and not to others. It provides a principle of uniqueness that depends on a kind of belonging that can be differentiated from the fact of inhabitance in a given space. As Philip Frickey observes, "in *Oliphant* there was no contention that the reservation had been diminished," therefore, "the Court had to limit tribal territorial sovereignty by limiting the sovereignty rather than the territory," and N. Bruce Duthu argues that the case "gutted the notion of full territorial sovereignty as it applied to Indian tribes."[15] Indian and non-Indian appear as categories that precede and exceed the law, as bearing inherent orientations and qualities that the court merely recognizes and that provide an immanent and obvious set of limitations to the scope of tribal authority. The decision, then, articulates a vision of Native sovereignty as itself turning on the possession of a purposively ill-defined Indianness, whose contours and character are implicitly racial.

In addressing the question of tribal jurisdiction, the decision does not so much examine existing precedent as offer a broad (re)assessment of the character of tribes in relation to the U.S. government. As against well-established judicial and administrative principles for understanding Native nations as continuing to possess an inherent sovereignty over all matters not explicitly ceded to or prohibited by the federal government, *Oliphant* creates the doctrine of what would come to be known as "implicit divestiture"—that tribes' occupation of lands within U.S. borders necessarily means that they cannot exercise certain kinds of authority.[16] Approaching the question of whether tribes have the power to try non-Indians in this way, though, leaves the decision with something of a logical and ethical conundrum. How precisely did Indigenous peoples who occupied their lands prior to the emergence of the U.S. nation-state and in ways not subject to U.S. control come to be under the jurisdiction of the federal government? The opinion insists, "Upon incorporation into the territory of the United States, the Indian tribes thereby come under the territorial sovereignty of the United States and their exercise of separate power is constrained so as not to conflict with the interests of this overriding sovereignty."[17] The supposed obviousness of the contours of U.S. domestic space leads to the conclusion that everything within national boundaries must be subject to the "territorial sovereignty" of the nation, and no form of "separate power" that *conflicts* with that "overriding" jurisdiction can be deemed valid. In other words, the unilateral declaration by the settler state that Native peoples and their lands have been *incorporated* into an alien political entity without their consent counts as the means for determining the legitimacy of Indigenous governance.[18] Later, the decision ameliorates this description a bit by indicating that the constriction of Native peoples' authority arises as a result of "the tribes' forfeiture of full sovereignty in return for the protection of the United States,"[19] suggesting that the diminishment of sovereignty results from decisions made by "the tribes" rather than the enforced, colonial inscription of settler territoriality on top of Indigenous polities.[20] However, this narrative remains in tension with the decision's earlier derivation of the U.S. government's "overriding sovereignty" as necessarily following from its projection of political contiguity "within" its borders, a process that functions independently of Native choice. The claim that tribes *forfeited full sovereignty*, then, seems retrospectively to posit a moment of Native agency in order to provide a legitimizing gloss for the a priori imposition of "territorial sovereignty" by the settler state over the lands it claims as its domestic space. In seeking to argue that the bare fact of tribes' inhabitance of territory "within" the United States necessarily limits their sovereignty,[21] the decision runs headlong into the central aporia of federal Indian policy— namely, that the "conflict" between the "separate power" of Native peoples and the settler state's effort to superintend them cannot be resolved in con- stitutional terms and that the geopolitical existence of the state rests on an extraconstitutional and ongoing process of imperial arrogation.[22]

The decision seeks to manage this fundamental and irresolvable problem by recasting the specific impasses in legitimizing U.S. jurisdiction as the con- tent of Indianness. Citing the language of the Appellate Court's decision, the opinion finds tribes' exertion of criminal jurisdiction over non-Indians to be "*inconsistent with their status.*"[23] What precisely is that "status"? If tribes lack "full sovereignty," are they polities? If they are not, how could they consent to forfeit sovereignty (including through land cessions in the treaty system)? Moreover, if they were polities for the purposes of ceding authority to the United States, are they something else now? If so, what, and how exactly did they become so? *Oliphant* displaces these troubling questions by treat- ing Indianness as a kind of status that can provide continuity across time and that can have sovereignty-effects without being understood as properly political (as competing or in "conflict" with the geopolitical claims of the settler-state). While acknowledging that Indians form collectives that possess sovereignty in some fashion, such that it can be ceded to the United States, the decision argues that the very kinds of juridical processes that would indi- cate their ability to try non-Indians have been lacking historically. Rehnquist asserts, "Until the middle of this century, few Indian tribes maintained any semblance of a formal court system. Offenses by one Indian against another were usually handled by social and religious pressure and not by formal judi- cial processes."[24] Rehnquist's language here certainly presents Native peoples as "relatively lawless, unsophisticated, and uncivilized,"[25] but perhaps more notable than the general cast of his comments, and their racist intimations of Indian barbarism, is the way they indicate not so much tribes' inability to produce order as the absence of specifically *legal* means to do so. If tribes address "offenses" by exerting "social and religious pressure," the principles guiding that effort and the formations through which such discipline is en- acted do not constitute "a formal court system." The opinion suggests that whatever specific configurations and processes the terms "social" and "reli- gious" might designate, they are not of the same kind as the political and constitutional structure of the United States and other recognized nation-states. Rather, they illustrate a communality that cannot make comparable geopolitical or legal claims to that of the "territorial sovereignty" of the U.S. The term "Indian" serves as a mediator in naming the kind of entity they are and the (limited) "separate power" they exercise, providing a way to substantialize the incommensurability of settler and Indigenous framings as a set of attributes that characterizes the latter. The inherently diminished "status" of tribes, then, appears to derive from their Indianness.

However, in this formulation, is Indian a racial category? Can it be juxtaposed to a more properly political way of designating Native peoplehood under U.S. law? As part of developing its argument about the necessary immunity of non-Indians from tribal justice systems, *Oliphant* cites an earlier case, *Ex Parte Crow Dog* (1883), to bolster its claim about the difference that Indianness makes in the construction and operation of systems of governance, including criminal jurisdiction. In that case, federal authorities had prosecuted and convicted a Lakota man for killing another Lakota man; he appealed to the Supreme Court, arguing that the U.S. government had no jurisdiction over Native-on-Native crime in Indian country. The court found in his favor, leading to the enactment of the Major Crimes Act (1885), which formally created such jurisdiction.[26] Quoting from the Supreme Court opinion in that case, Rehnquist says that, in it, "The United States was seeking to extend United States 'law, by argument and inference only, . . . over aliens and strangers; over the members of a community separated by race [and] tradition, . . . from the authority and power which seeks to impose upon them the restraints of an external and unknown code.'" He continues, quoting from *Ex Parte Crow* Dog, "It tries them, not by their peers, nor by the customs of their people, nor the law of their land, but by . . . a different race, according to the law of a social state of which they have an imperfect conception."[27] The decision in *Ex Parte Crow Dog* actually found for inherent Native sovereignty, but *Oliphant* inverts it to illustrate that non-Indians should not be subjected to rule by "a different race" and "tradition" about which "they have an imperfect conception." More specifically, the particular way the opinion invokes *Ex Parte Crow Dog* suggests that the understanding of Indianness as a racial category crucially supplements *Oliphant*'s portrayal of tribal identity, endowing that identity with a sense of innateness and generational continuity over time that makes it impermeable and unintelligible to those who do not always-already belong while casting that belonging as something other than due to the exercise of full political sovereignty. Being subjected to a tribe's "tradition," "code," or "social state" entails bearing a "status" that immanently prequalifies one for such incorporation into the "community." The geopolitical torsions involved in narrating Indigenous peoples' "status" in relation to U.S. jurisdiction are transposed as the inherent/racial terms of belonging to a tribe—having "status" as a member.

Although precedent at the time of *Oliphant* defined "Indian" as a *political* rather than a *racial* designation (specifically, *Morton v. Mancari* [1974] and *U.S. v. Antelope* [1977]), those decisions and *Oliphant* cannot maintain that distinction, as the two seemingly distinct kinds of categorizations fold into each other in articulating the reason for the "special" status tribes bear under the overarching sovereignty of the United States.[28] In *Morton*, non-Indian employees of the Bureau of Indian Affairs (BIA) claimed that the clause of the Indian Reorganization Act (1934) providing for Indian preferences in BIA hiring maintained an illegal and unconstitutional form of race preference. The court found, "The preference, as applied, is granted to Indians not as a discrete racial group, but, rather, as members of quasi-sovereign tribal entities whose lives and activities are governed by the BIA in a unique fashion," adding that "the preference is reasonably and directly related to a legitimate, nonracially based goal."[29] The decision has been understood as indicating that designations of Indianness in federal law do not prima facie refer to racial identity, instead presumptively indicating a "tribal" relation.[30] *Antelope* addressed the claim by two enrolled Coeur d'Alenes that their prosecution for murder under the Major Crimes Act as Indians constituted racial discrimination. Following *Morton*, the court found that "federal legislation with respect to Indian tribes, although relating to Indians as such, is not based upon impermissible racial classifications," instead noting that "classifications expressly singling out Indian tribes as subjects of legislation are expressly provided for in the Constitution and supported by the ensuing history of the Federal Government's relation with Indians."[31] While opposing racial identity to tribal belonging, the concept "tribal entities" itself fudges the question of what exact status Native peoples occupy in relation to U.S. law. *Morton* grounds the supposed displacement of racial meaning in "the unique legal status of Indian tribes under federal law and upon the plenary power of Congress, based on a history of treaties and the assumption of a 'guardian-ward' status, to legislate on behalf of federally recognized tribes."[32] Tribes have a "legal status" that previously entailed the negotiation of diplomatic agreements having the highest constitutional status—treaties—*and* that status now licenses the exertion of virtually unlimited congressional authority—plenary power. Here we see again the legitimacy problem raised by the construction of the settler state on top of existing Indigenous polities, presented as a *uniqueness* that attaches to "tribes" as a "special" kind of entity within U.S. law.

However, both decisions defer the question of what defines "tribal" identity. If tribes are not fully sovereign polities (referred to in the decisions as "quasi-sovereign" and "once sovereign"),[33] what are they? *Antelope* refers to "Indian tribes" as "unique aggregations." What precisely do they "aggregate"? *Antelope* speaks of the U.S. "relation with Indians," and *Morton* invokes the federal government's "unique obligation toward the Indians."[34] In attempting to signify the kind of "entity" tribes are, all these decisions (including *Oliphant*) end up citing Indianness as determinative. If "tribe" names a polity, what makes that polity "special" (somehow less sovereign than the United States and necessarily subordinated to its "overriding" authority), unless the tribes' definitional Indianness partakes of something that is not quite political and that must give way, in *Oliphant*'s terms, in the face of the apparently self-evident "territorial sovereignty" of the United States as the polity exerting jurisdiction over Native peoples' lands. Brian L. Lewis suggests that "*Morton* and *Antelope* created a legal fiction that Indian status is not based on race or ancestry."[35] Rather than arguing that these decisions invent a "political" category for what was previously "based on race"—or, conversely, that "political" identification is preferable to "racial"—I suggest that a racial imaginary crucially supplements the legal notion of tribe by offering Indianness as an innate and immutable characteristic that is not itself political in character. Racial Indianness, then, provides a means of differentiating tribes from other populations but in ways that do not undermine the authority of the U.S. government to superintend them and to assert the a priori internality of Indigenous territory with respect to the settler state.

This ostensibly "nonracial" mobilization of racially conceived Indianness as a way to tether tribes' authority to U.S. sovereignty appears perhaps most insidiously in *Oliphant*'s claims about the need to protect non-Indians. More than simply recirculating a racist image of needing to save whites from the dangers of Indian savagery, the opinion develops an implicit account of what non-Indianness is that has broad ramifications for understanding the character of Native sovereignty. The opinion observes, "Protection of territory within its external boundaries is, of course, as central to the sovereign interests of the Unites States as it is to any other sovereign nation." Further, it states, "the United States has manifested an equally great solicitude that its citizens be protected by the United States from unwarranted intrusions on their personal liberty" and that "[b]y submitting to the overriding sovereignty of the United States, Indian tribes therefore necessarily give up their power to try non-Indian citizens of the United States except in a manner acceptable to Congress."[36] A series of transferals and translations occur here, with the court asserting that the "external boundaries" of the nation are clear, and Native peoples lie within them; the "sovereign interests" of the nation in that exclusive jurisdiction manifest as the "personal liberty" of its citizens; and non-Indians must be insulated from "intrusion" on such liberty, because making such intrusions, absent congressional plenary permission, would be tantamount to refuting U.S. sovereignty within national borders. *Protection* transits from national territory to non-Indian persons, appearing as an embodied quality of the latter. As Duthu suggests, the decision posits a "nationality that clung like a protective cloak to these settlers."[37] It may be helpful, though, to approach non-Indian status less as a cloak than as a form of innate and immutable inheritance. Rehnquist indicates that "many of the dangers that might have accompanied the exercise by tribal courts of criminal jurisdiction over non-Indians only a few decades ago have disappeared,"[38] further heightening the sense of a preexisting bodily coherence potentially *endangered* (even if less so now) by Native presence and governance.[39] In this way, the decision restages the question of national territoriality as a set of somatic properties, thereby displacing the legitimacy crisis that subtends its jurisdictional claims over Indigenous peoples.

Yet in referring to Mark David Oliphant, as well as Daniel B. Belgrade (whose case was folded into the consideration of Oliphant's), the decision notes, "Both petitioners are non-Indian residents."[40] What does it mean to *reside* in Native territory? Or, more precisely, how is such residence emptied of significance by the decision's portrayal of non-Indianness as a constitutive *lack of relation* that defines non-Indian legal personhood? How is non-Indianness cast as a given and unchangeable insulation from Indian spatiality?[41] Within the decision's logic, non-Indian persons bear their non-Indianness as an extralegal quality of which the state takes notice, particularly in *protecting* them from capture by Indian institutions. This somatization of non-Indianness can be understood as the inverse of what Barker refers to as the transposition of Indigenous peoples into minority people in the introduction to this volume. If the non-Indian body gains its meaning from its difference from the Indian place it occupies, that (kind of) body is understood as bearing qualities or an identity that emanates from somewhere other than the space of residence and the relations and imbrications that follow from it. From whence does non-Indianness arise? To say that the issue is that non-Indians cannot become members of a tribe because tribal members must be

Indians does not address this question; instead, such a claim defers the issue through the supplemental and unacknowledged citation of racial genealogy as the de facto framing principle for conceptualizing Indianness and tribal belonging. Seeking to provide a context for the decision's argument that exceeds the strict language of treaties, statutes, and congressional documents,[47] Rehnquist insists that "the intricate web of judicially made Indian law, cannot be interpreted in isolation but must be read in light of the common notions of the day and the assumptions of those who drafted them."[43] While certainly not cited, one of those "common notions" stretching from the nineteenth century through today and given greater judicial force by *Oliphant* would be the notion of Indianness as a reproductively transmitted substance that can be gained only through birth to an Indian parent or parents.[44] In discussing the relation between the (re)construction of racial identity and notions of reproductive union and inheritance, Sara Ahmed addresses "the production of whiteness as a straight line rather than whiteness as a characteristic of bodies," observing, "we can talk of how whiteness is 'attributed' to bodies *as if* it were a property of bodies; one way of describing this process is to describe whiteness as a straightening device. We can ask how whiteness gets reproduced through acts of alignment, which are forgotten when we receive its line." She adds, "Genealogy itself could be understood as a straightening device, which creates the illusion of descent as a line."[45] Non-Indianness in the decision is not described as itself a kind of racial identity (namely, whiteness), but it does appear in the decision as a form of descent. Non-Indians appear to inherit their non-Indianness in ways that precede and exceed any judicial determination, aligning that body with other-than-Indian bodies and spaces. The non-Indian body supposedly bears such an orientation/tendency immanently rather than as a result of the *straightening* effects of the decision. The opinion implicitly construes the vertical line of racial lineage as necessarily insulating the non-Indian from the horizontal spatiality of tribal jurisdiction. Ahmed further observes, "a white body might be barred from access to nonwhite bodies given the 'reachability' of such bodies: a prohibition only makes sense when something can be reached."[46] In this case, the issue is the "reachability" of non-Indian—specifically white—bodies to Native jurisdiction. In prohibiting tribal prosecution of non-Indians, the court presents non-Indianness as if it were "a property of bodies" rather than a legal device by which to carve out zones of jurisdictional incapacity within Native political space.

This implicit heteronormative citation of racial reproduction as the means of characterizing the limits of tribal authority reciprocally contributes to defining the positive contours and content of that authority and tribal identity itself. The positing of an exemption for non-Indians denies the territorial and geopolitical coherence of Native peoples, positioning them as less than fully sovereign and as not-quite-properly-political entities. It does so by invoking and evoking "common notions" of race as reproductively transmitted in defining "tribe" as a "special" category. Unlike other polities understood as having a determinate territory over which they exercise sovereign authority, tribes are a "unique" kind of legal entity, and if they at times exert "quasi-sovereign" powers, they ultimately have a "status" that is not "inconsistent" with U.S. claims to "overriding sovereignty" within its "external boundaries." The decision achieves that non-contradiction by denying tribal authority over non-Indians, a finding that appears as if it were somehow something other than the further exertion of settler colonial superintendence based on imperial arrogation. This insulation of the non-Indian appears as if it were merely a recognition of the ultimately genealogical and extrapolitical character of *Indianness* as an inherited status.

Reproducing Indian Culture

Oliphant clearly engages in an assault on tribal sovereignty. By contrast, ICWA has been hailed as a victory for Native peoples in seeking acknowledgment of their inherent right to self-governance and redress for the ongoing effects of a history of genocidal policies designed to eliminate tribal existence as such.[47] The law's passage was a response to the astronomical rates of states' social-service interventions in Native families and of Native children's adoption by non-Natives, including a rate of adoption twenty times the national average and the fact that one-quarter to one-third of Native children were taken from their families.[48] In keeping with the overall tenor of the "era of self-determination," as announced by President Richard Nixon in 1970,[49] Congress sought to remedy this most current instantiation of persistent patterns and projects of displacement, in which generations of Indigenous youth had been alienated from their peoples in various ways—all justified as supposedly for their betterment and in their best interests. The statute gives tribes exclusive jurisdiction over all child custody proceedings for Indian children domiciled in Indian country, gives tribes the right of refusal for jurisdiction in such proceedings for Native children outside Indian country, puts in place tribal notification requirements and procedures in cases where Indian children are involved, creates greater protections for Indian parents against termination of their parental rights, requires that states use tribally-set priorities for foster care and adoptive placement, and provides a set of placement priorities absent the indication of tribal preferences.[50] While the act has been attacked as adopting an unconstitutionally race-based scheme, its defenders argue that it falls squarely within Congress's authority over Indian affairs and that its application to Indians (pace *Morton v. Mancari*) turns on their political status as members of tribal entities rather than their belonging to a racial group, and both of these claims have been supported by courts at all levels.[51] However, what vision of sovereignty does ICWA offer? In linking sovereignty to "family" and offering a narrative of tribal identity as a "cultural" affiliation that follows from genealogical connection, the law ties Indigenous self-determination to Indianness, understood in implicitly reproductive terms. Although ICWA's aims and application differ markedly from those in *Oliphant*,[52] its alignment of Indigeneity with lineage helps further the construction of Native peoplehood as an other-than-geopolitical status, while also in many ways fueling efforts made to undermine the law (and tribal sovereignty) via arguments about various ways Indianness can become generationally attenuated.[53]

The legislation frames itself as an effort to respond to difficulties faced by tribes, particularly seeking to thwart intrusions by others on a vital area of tribal life. In its listing of congressional findings that provides the context for the statute, ICWA states, "Congress, through statutes, treaties, and the general course of dealing with Indian tribes, has assumed the responsibility for the protection and preservation of Indian tribes and their resources" (2.2). It also indicates that "an alarmingly high percentage of Indian families are broken up by the removal, often unwarranted, of the children from them by non-tribal public and private agencies and that an alarmingly high percentage of such children are placed in non-Indian foster and adoption homes and institutions" (2.5). As opposed to trying to eliminate tribes' existence, the official policy of the U.S. government during both the allotment (1887–1934) and termination (1948–70) periods, Congress has the duty of *protecting* and *preserving* Indian tribes as such, and since "there is no resource that is more vital to the continued existence and integrity of Indian tribes than their children" (2.3), the government must act to undo the "alarming" actions by various agencies that work to dismantle tribes in slow motion through the seizure of their children and placement of them in non-Indian settings. Beyond acknowledging the primary jurisdiction of tribes over such matters in Indian country (101.a), the law makes clear that in proceedings conducted by states with respect to children domiciled elsewhere, the child's tribe has "a right to intervene at any point in the proceeding" (101.c). Moreover, the field of potential caregivers, and the priorities among them, should conform to "the law or custom of the Indian child's tribe" (4.2, 105.c), and the act expands those who have standing in a parent-like relation to include the "Indian custodian," meaning "any Indian person who has legal custody of an Indian child under tribal law or custom" (4.6). Cumulatively, these provisions indicate Congress's intention to affirm and extend tribes' ability to operate as self-determining entities with respect to children who are members or are "eligible for membership" (4.4). The statute pegs Indianness to official criteria for citizenship adopted by the Native nation in question, with the caveat that since children have no choice over enrollment the presumption should be in favor of tribal belonging if they are not members at the time of the judicial proceedings but fit the tribe's criteria for membership. ICWA further enables tribes to reclaim jurisdiction that was transferred to the states via Public Law 280 during the termination era. Passed in 1953, that act gave six states complete civil and criminal jurisdiction over tribes within their boundaries, except for a few named exceptions, and was a vital part of the broader effort to remove federal funding and recognition from Native peoples.[54] ICWA authorizes "[a]ny Indian tribe which became subject to State jurisdiction pursuant to the provisions" of Public Law 280, "or pursuant to any other Federal law," to "resume jurisdiction over child custody proceedings" through petitioning the Secretary of the Interior (108.a), also providing criteria for consideration of such petitions (108.b.1.a).

However, if Congress wants to indicate its commitment to affirming preserving, protecting, and supporting the "self-determination" of Indigenous peoples on land claimed by the United States, why carve out only this limited exception to the prior transferal of jurisdiction to the states? Why not simply repeal Public Law 280 and similar acts or make their provisions optional for tribes?[55] The focus on Native families enables an implicit account of tribal identity and sovereignty that orients away from the kinds of knotty tensions around jurisdiction, Indigenous territoriality, and political legitimacy running through *Oliphant*. As noted earlier, ICWA indicates that it applies to Indians only as members of tribes or as potentially eligible members, rather than as a racial group, and this approach correlates with the logic of the decision in *Morton* and with the Supreme Court's determination in *Santa Clara Pueblo v. Martinez*, also decided in 1978, that tribes have complete authority over determining membership criteria.[56] However, when speaking of tribal belonging, jurisdiction, and prerogatives in the child custody process, the law often employs language in a register different from that usually used to designate matters of citizenship and the scope and character of political sovereignty. In chastising the states, it notes that their "administrative and judicial bodies" often have "failed to recognize the essential tribal relations of Indian people and the cultural and social standards prevailing in Indian communities and families" (2.5). This phrasing is repeated later in the discussion of how to set priorities for placement, indicating that court decisions should reflect the "prevailing social and cultural standards of the Indian community in which the parent or extended family resides or with which the parent or extended family members maintain social and cultural ties" (105.d). While "tribal relations" might simply refer to relations among members of a tribe and with the tribal government, it seems to bear a meaning different from tribes' acts of governance as political entities. Instead, it comprises "standards" and "ties" of a nature that the law implies usually would be beyond the ken of state courts but that need to be attended to in this instance due to the particular population involved. As with *Oliphant's* juxtaposition of "social and religious pressure" with "formal judicial processes," the use of the phrase "social and cultural" here marks something other than that which normally enters the field of properly "administrative and judicial" consideration, and the acknowledgment of such "relations" is part of an attempt to reckon with and "reflect the unique values of Indian culture" (3). "Culture" and "community" designate a kind of *tribal* entity that the United States has the duty to *protect* and *preserve*, and the accession to tribal wishes with respect to children is central to doing so.

The designation of tribal jurisdiction and decision making criteria as *uniquely* Indian is of a piece with the practice of characterizing the recognition of Native policy determinations as part of "the special relationship between the United States and the Indian tribes" (2). This framing suggests that engagement with tribes marks a "special" exception from the usual structure of U.S. law and legal geography. ICWA transposes Native polities' exertion of authority over their citizens and the effort to protect them from various modes of settler intervention and invasion into the expression of Indianness, as a set of qualities and inclinations that attaches to particular "communities and families." One might interpret a phrase like "social and cultural" as trying to designate forms of political relation not usually understood as such within U.S. legal discourses, seeking to encompass and give legal force in state courts to exertions of Indigenous sovereignty that might otherwise be treated as extraneous to judicial determinations. The language of ICWA, then, could be read as trying to index a process of translation whereby modes of governance that do not conform to the framework of (neo)liberalism get (mis)apprehended as "culture," as opposed to the exercise of political sovereignty.[57] However, the act's repeated characterization of Native people-hood in terms of "culture" and "community," and its further tying of both of these concepts to family formation as the privileged sphere of transmission, casts Indianness in its *social* and *cultural* dimensions as a function of biological reproduction. In the act, Indianness appears to emanate from a sphere that is not itself political but that should be acknowledged due to the "special" connection between the United States and tribes.

This depiction of Indigenous peoples as having a "unique" form of sociality that inheres in "families," often presented as recognizing Native practices of *kinship*, functions as the flip side to the broader privatizing nuclear conception of family at play in U.S. legal and popular discourses. As Povinelli suggests, heteronormativity has a "genealogical underbelly," and the celebration of the monogamous, marital couple-form as the apotheosis of individual freedom and self-elaboration, which she terms "the intimate event," "derives much of its ideological force from something that co-emerged with it—discourses about the genealogical society."[58] She adds, "The self-evident value of liberal adult love depends on instantiating as its opposite a particular kind of illiberal, tribal, customary, and ancestral love."[59] The *specialness* of Native "communities" and "culture" arises out of an implicit, and implicitly invidious, comparison to the nuclear family form, which serves as the de facto norm. Moreover, both of these visions of family, liberal and tribal, depend on being measured against a reprosexual standard: "A couple of assumptions about human beings, sex difference and heterosexual reproduction—assumptions that could be claimed to be the universal preconditions of human life—provided just enough structure for the maximal comparison among societies."[60] Thus, the genealogical relations that supposedly made Native peoples "unique" are constituted as such—are rendered as a tribal version of family—through interpellation into a heteronormative framework in which such relations are tied to biological reproduction, thereby casting them as occupying a social sphere that is distinct from that of politics per se.

Although the (dis)placement of Native children certainly has served as a major vehicle for settler projects of assimilation, dispossession, and detribalization, and the insistence on tribal authority over childcare does work to redress that (ongoing) history,[61] positioning childcare as the principal means of defining Indigeneity aligns and justifies Native jurisdiction as a form of genealogical preservation instead of presenting control over matters concerning children as merely part and parcel of Native peoples' legitimate exercise of authority as polities. The law makes clear that tribes can set virtually whatever priorities they wish for child placement.[62] However, it designates that authority through the phrase "extended family member," which "shall be defined by the law or custom of the Indian child's tribe," but, "in the absence of such law or custom," is taken to mean an adult "who is the Indian child's grandparent, aunt or uncle, brother or sister, brother-in-law or sister-in-law, niece or nephew, first or second cousin, or stepparent" (4.2). The presumptive model is the nuclear family form, with relatives radiating outward from the unit of the marital couple and their children, which is taken as the axiomatic core. The very terms used here seem to treat that pattern as the universally referential basis for defining familial connection, despite the fact that in many forms of Native sociality persons share the same familial title who do not occupy the same position within the Euro-American genealogical grid (for example, where one's "mother" and "mother's sister," or "aunt," are referred to by the same term). In addition, the "family" does not appear to have any political function, despite the historical and, in many places, continuing role of corporate entities—often anthropologically known as "clans"—in Native governance and policy setting. In this way, the act implicitly preserves the distinction between the familial and the governmental that is one of the constitutive features of liberal statehood.[63] Whatever "culture" and "community" might entail, then, they seem to be bound to a set of "tribal relations" de facto understood as circulating around the family unit, heteronormatively conceived, as the site for the manifestation and perpetuation of Indian *uniqueness*.[64]

"Culture," then, does similar work to "race" in positioning Indigeneity as a set of relations that follows from the procreative transmission of Indianness.[65] This configuration of how to *protect* and *preserve* Indian tribes specifically does not pose a challenge to the continuing insistence of the settler state on its unquestionable authority over its domestic space. In elaborating its aims and their validity, ICWA lists as its first item that "Congress has plenary power over Indian affairs" (2.1),[66] which is tied in *Oliphant* and earlier court decisions to the self-evidence of national boundaries and the supposedly necessary corollary that the federal government must have "overriding sovereignty" in that space. Moreover, if the placement of Indian children has jurisdictional components to it, the emphasis on tribal governments' role in Native family matters both inside and outside Indian country makes the inheritance of Indianness the primary criterion for assessing such jurisdiction, rather than highlighting the rightful authority of Indigenous polities over their territories and citizens. A dialectic emerges in and around ICWA in which "culture" and its correlates seek to name something that exceeds the administrative scope and character of U.S. political and legal processes with respect to non-Natives. That disjunction, though, gets linked to family as its sphere of realization in ways that allow whatever "culture" might name to be cast as commensurate with the self-evidence of congressional superintendence of Indigenous peoples as "dependent communities."[67] In this way, "culture" coordinates with "family," the one gaining its explanatory force from its linkage to the other. As Povinelli suggests, "True indigenous culture is characterized, in the ideology of law and society, as iterative, as disciplined by the descending object," and the ostensibly unbroken continuity signaled by genealogy can both surrogate for and be surrogated by figurations of Indian racial descent.[68] She further observes, "[I]ndigenous groups . . . are not families of choice any more than they are cultures of invention, because a status of common descent stands in the background. And this difference provides social traction for people like the land commissioner who need some distinction to operate the legal machinery of the politics of cultural difference."[69] In providing a nonpolitical basis around which to collect and define cultural difference, common descent offers a mode of distinction that neither appears to be about racial identity nor simply functions as race in disguise. Rather, as a familialized/familializing legal fiction, "culture" constellates with race as related (and often intertwined) means of articulating Indianness as something reproduced and transmitted generationally in ways that can be segregated from Indigeneity—the geopolitics of self-determination as peoples based on prior landedness.

That process of translation and transposition can be seen in the House of Representatives report that preceded the passage of the act (often cited in scholarly and judicial discussions of the law), *Mississippi Band of Choctaw Indians v. Holyfield* (1989), and *Adoptive Couple v. Baby Girl* (2013).[70] These texts help illustrate the tendencies present within the act itself. The House report insists, "The wholesale separation of Indian children from their families is perhaps the most tragic and destructive aspect of American Indian life today." However, in articulating the nature of the destruction wrought by that mass alienation, the report observes, "In judging the fitness of a particular family, many social workers, ignorant of Indian cultural values and social norms, make decisions that are wholly inappropriate in the context of Indian family life and so they frequently discover neglect or abandonment where none exists," adding, "Many social workers, untutored in the ways of Indian family life or assuming them to be socially irresponsible, consider leaving the child with persons outside the nuclear family as neglect and thus as grounds for terminating parental rights."[71] The systemic pattern— "wholesale separation"—appears here to be due to social worker ignorance and prejudice. They have a notion of proper childcare modeled on "the nuclear family," described elsewhere in the report as "a white, middle-class standard,"[72] and that orientation blinds them to other possibilities for family and household formation. The issue is one of failed "cultural" translation, an inability to recognize extant "values" and "norms" In particular communities—a specifically *Indian* way of ordering "family life." ICWA, then, will force state workers and institutions to acknowledge and respect those patterns. On what basis, though, will it do so? The report invokes Congress's "plenary power" and its "broad, unique powers with respect to Indian tribes,"[73] indicating the federal legislature's right to make rules for tribes based on their *special* relationship to the U.S. government. In articulating this authority, it also cites *U.S. v. Kagama* and *U.S. v. Nice*, Supreme Court decisions from the late nineteenth century and early twentieth century that cast Native peoples as *dependents* whose need for protection (especially from the states) licenses federal actions and exceptions on their behalf.[74] Furthermore, defending the choice to include children who are eligible to be tribal members under the act, rather than solely those who already are members, the report asserts, "Blood relationship is the very touchstone of a person's right to share in the cultural and property benefits of an Indian tribe."[75] In this way, the "values" and "norms" that the legislation is meant to protect appear as themselves a function of a "blood" relation, which provides the "touchstone" for the "cultural" bond that defines belonging to a tribe.[76]

Thus, although also citing *Morton* as a means of indicating that the proposed law's parameters are political rather than racial,[77] the House Committee on Interior and Insular Affairs approaches ICWA as a means of institutionalizing the acknowledgment of the "unique" modes of Indian kinship, which themselves correlate with the reproduction of Indianness as such. Racial heritage is what prequalifies one for participation in the nexus of tribal "cultural" life, and such culture functions as an extension of the inheritance of biological Indianness. This emphasis on a nexus of culture, family, and blood, though, arises despite the report's documentation of the ways the seizure of Indian children usually occurs "without due process of law" and is lubricated through pressure by welfare agencies on whom Native people rely for "survival."[78] Such tracking of the jurisdictional violence of states' exertion of control over Native citizens and lands and the impoverishing effects of prior and ongoing settler policies of intervention and appropriation does not lead to an analysis of the need for a broad-based engagement with Indigenous sovereignty and self-determination. Rather, it confirms "the special problems and circumstances of Indian families and the legitimate interest of the Indian tribe in preserving and protecting the Indian family,"[79] reaffirming the jurisdictional placeholder of *specialness* and pegging its content to "the Indian family."

In *Holyfield*, the Supreme Court goes further in explicating the politics of tribes' relation to their citizens than the House report, as well as in detailing the broader implications for Native sovereignty of ICWA's recognition of such an "interest." Yet in addressing the reason for and reasoning of the law, the court displaces the issue of Indigenous self-determination in favor of affirming the importance of engaging with familially-based Indian cultural inclinations. The case concerns the question of whether the Mississippi Choctaw tribal court has primary jurisdiction over the placement of two Indian children who were born off-reservation to tribal members who reside on the reservation and who specifically arranged before the birth for the children to be adopted by a non-Indian couple. The central issue is what constitutes "domicile" for the purposes of the act. In arguing that the children were domiciled on the reservation (although they were never physically present there) for the purposes of jurisdiction, thus finding that the Choctaw court did have authority in determining custody, the decision rejects the idea that domicile could be dependent on each state's own precedents in defining it for state purposes.[80] Rather, the court finds that Congress sought to impose a uniform federal principle specifically to shield Indian affairs from the states' interests and invidious intrusions, and that intent to protect tribal autonomy extends to Native nations' relation to their own citizens: "Tribal jurisdiction . . . was not meant to be defeated by the actions of individual members of the tribe, for Congress was concerned not solely about the interests of Indian children and families, but also about the impact on the tribes themselves of the large numbers of Indian children adopted by non-Indians."[81] Thus, the opinion articulates what scholars have characterized as a tribe's interest in the welfare of its children as part of its maintenance of itself as a viable collectivity, as well as the attendant need to distinguish "tribal jurisdiction" from that of the states without subjecting tribal jurisdiction to the rules, definitions, and qualifications found in state laws.[82] Further, the decision quotes from the testimony of Calvin Isaac (tribal chief of the Mississippi Band of Choctaw Indians) before Congress in the hearings prior to ICWA's passage, in which he says of the taking of Native children by state agencies, "these practices seriously undercut the tribes' ability to continue as self-governing communities. Probably, in no area is it more important that tribal sovereignty be respected than in an area as socially and culturally determinative as family relationships."[83] His comments frame Native nations' jurisdiction in child welfare as part of the larger project of Indigenous self-governance, justifying it on that basis and condemning state intervention for its attenuation of that broader sovereignty. In citing Chief Isaac's argument, the court implicitly endorses that understanding of the legitimacy and aims of the law.

At other moments, though, *Holyfield* focuses less on Indigenous self-determination than the process of avoiding endemic misinterpretations by the states. The opinion approvingly quotes from a decision on ICWA by the Supreme Court of Utah: "The protection of this tribal interest is at the core of the ICWA, which recognizes that the tribe has an interest in the child which is distinct from but on a parity with the interest of the parents. This relationship between Indian tribes and Indian children domiciled on the reservation finds no parallel in other ethnic cultures found in the United States. It is a relationship that many non-Indians find difficult to understand and that non-Indian courts are slow to recognize."[84] The question of "domicile," and thus of the territoriality of Native sovereignty and the relation between Indigenous governance and land, becomes the expression of an "ethnic culture," exhibiting a uniqueness ("no parallel") that itself needs to be respected. Why, though? This statement implies that non-Indians act in ways that illustrate a lack of comprehension of Indian "culture" and do damage based on that misunderstanding. *Holyfield* confirms this perspective in finding that "it is clear that Congress' concern over the placement of Indian children in non-Indian homes was based in part on evidence of the detrimental impact on the children themselves of such placements outside their culture."[85] The right to self-governance for Native polities found in Chief Isaac's statement, presumably based on their status as Indigenous peoples whose existence precedes and exceeds that of the settler government established around and on top of them, morphs into the need for children to maintain a continuity of "culture" lest they face the "detrimental" effects of a disorienting dislocation into non-Indian sociality.

This formulation stages the law as primarily protecting a kind of familiarity and familiality due to the *specialness* of Indians, presenting Indianness as transmitted within the scene of "extended" family relations. This very sense of Indianness as a quality that inheres in families becomes the guiding logic of *Adoptive Couple v. Baby Girl* in ways that efface entirely the question of Native sovereignty at play in *Holyfield*. The case is about the daughter of a man who is a citizen of the Cherokee Nation whose mother put her up for adoption to a couple from South Carolina. The man had waived his parental rights but under what he asserted were false pretenses—namely, that the baby would be raised by the biological mother. In addition, on documents sent to the Cherokee Nation by the adoptive couple, the biological father's name was misspelled and an incorrect birthdate was given, so the Cherokee Nation asserted that he was not a citizen, allowing the adoption to proceed. Rather than commenting on the numerous, grievous procedural errors that occurred in the process of the adoption, or what lower courts had found to be the explicit effort of the adoptive couple's lawyers to obfuscate the issue of Native national citizenship in order to facilitate the adoption,[86] the Supreme Court's majority decision focuses on the racial limits of Cherokeeness and the question of what constitutes familial attachment. In the first sentence of the opinion, Justice Samuel Alito notes that the case "is about a little girl ... who is classified as an Indian because she is 1.2% (3/256) Cherokee," at the end describing her relation to Indianness as "a remote one," despite her father's enrollment as a Cherokee citizen.[87] These phrasings that book-end the opinion frame the issue of Native identity, or of belonging to the Cherokee people in particular, as one of a relative amount of inherited Indian racial substance. The percentage clearly is meant to suggest that the girl has too little Indian blood meaningfully to count as Native, an insinuation that effaces not only the specificities of citizenship in the Cherokee Nation of Oklahoma in particular (defined by lineal descent from anyone on the Dawes Rolls) but the sense of Native nations as polities whose sovereignty derives from their indigeneity rather than the generational transmission of particular bodily properties.[88] In addition, the decision continually returns to ICWA's stated aim of preventing the "breakup of the Indian family," which serves as the unit for "preserv[ing] the cultural identity and heritage of Indian tribes."[89] The court claims that since the biological father "*never* had custody of the Indian child," the law's goal "to stem the unwarranted removal of Indian children from intact Indian families" is not relevant in this case.[90] The legal scope and character of Native peoples' sovereignty fades entirely from view, replaced by an attenuated sense of racial Indianness that cannot constitute an "Indian family" and thus cannot be the bearer of "cultural identity."

When confronting critics' portrayal of ICWA as a constitutionally suspect use of racial criteria, defenders of the law have emphasized its function as a form of political recognition. As I have been suggesting, however, such a reading underexamines the deep ambivalence in the law itself (and in the surrounding supportive legislative and judicial explanations of it) about the status of Native peoples. Specifically, supporters overlook the ways the attempt to manage the jurisdictional and ethical conundrums posed by the geopolitics of the settler state gets displaced onto "family" and "culture" as cross-referencing, not-quite-political bearers of Indianness. In particular, supporters of ICWA have argued against the "existing Indian family exception" that has been carved out by some state courts, in which children of parents who are deemed not to have a substantive relation with a particular tribe (even if they themselves are enrolled) do not fall under the purview of the law. One of the best known and commented on cases in this vein is *In re Bridget* (1996), decided by the California Appellate Court. Its argument in favor of the exception highlights the conceptual and juridical impasses animated by the U.S. government's heteronormative invocation of culture and family.[91] The case involves twins whose parents chose to put them up for adoption, having purposefully failed to indicate their own Indian status on the relevant documents. The father was a member of the Dry Creek Rancheria, although he was not formally enrolled until after the children were placed up for adoption (having been born before the institution of a tribal constitution in 1973 but having met the former criteria for membership and been included as a member under the constitution). The court finds that unless a parent retains "a significant social, cultural or political relationship" with a tribe, the application of ICWA to the adoption of that parent's child is unconstitutional on three grounds: "(1) it impermissibly intrudes upon a power ordinarily reserved to the states, (2) it improperly interferes with Indian children's fundamental due process rights respecting family relationships; and (3) on the sole basis of race, it deprives them of equal opportunities to be adopted that are available to non-Indian children."[92] With respect to the first point, the decision reads ICWA as an exercise or extension of federal power rather than an acknowledgment of Native peoples' inherent sovereignty.[93] The opinion asserts, "The interests of the Tribe in this dispute are likewise based solely upon ICWA. There neither is nor can be any claim that the Tribe's interests are constitutionally protected."[94] Finding that those federally-borne "interests" conflict with the children's constitutional right to due process, in terms of having a stable home and family (with their soon-to-be-adoptive parents), the court decides that ICWA's terms must be subjected to "strict scrutiny," measuring the intrusion on constitutional rights against the compelling state interest behind the law. However, this double-sided logical maneuver (weighing federal versus state powers under the Tenth Amendment and the tribe's federally constructed interest versus the constitutional rights of the children under the Fifth Amendment and Fourteenth Amendment) implicitly vacates Native sovereignty of any legal status except inasmuch as it is delegated to tribes by the federal government; otherwise, the issue at stake is less federal intrusion on the state or on the constitutional rights of U.S. citizens than the recognition of a prior and unceded authority by Native nations over their own citizens.

Thus, while the decision includes "political" as one of the items in its list of "significant" kinds of relation to the tribe, the definition of that term depends for its substantive meaning on kinds of association that attach to the notion of "culture," and the opinion's reading of tribal political identity as indexing an extrapolitical content—a special or unique Indianness that is not itself legal in character—reiterates the kinds of ambiguities and translations circulating around and through the law itself. The decision notes, "We have no quarrel with the proposition that preserving American Indian culture is a legitimate, even compelling, governmental interest," adding, "It is almost too obvious to require articulation that 'the unique values of Indian culture' (25 U.S.C. §1902) will not be preserved in the homes of parents who have become fully assimilated into non-Indian culture."[95] In quoting this particular provision of ICWA, the court picks up on the law's tendency to translate sovereignty as the preservation of "culture" through Indian familial association. Following from this tendency, the opinion reads "preserving American Indian culture" as something other than the presence and action of Indigenous governance. Instead, culture appears as an extragovernmental topic (like citizens' health and welfare) that can reasonably be understood as a "legitimate" object of (federal) "governmental interest" and policy. However, the "tribal relations," in ICWA's terms, of Native peoples are in this way conceptualized as a matrix of voluntary action and affection that can attenuate through time, particularly through the drift of families away from the sites, practices, and associations through which a specifically Indian kind of culture is maintained. To become "assimilated into non-Indian culture" entails a loss of Indian *cultural* distinctiveness, whereas the governance of a polity and belonging to it usually are presumed to have a durability and relevance that exceeds the question of the individual choices and changing practices of members.[96] Moreover, ICWA construes cultural "values" as a separate, special sphere implicitly distinct from governance or politics per se, one that resides principally in family life and that is given standing and force in the law by Congress's "plenary" will. In this way, the law evades the overriding question of Indigenous self-determination in ways that give rise to *In re Bridget*'s claim that ICWA "can properly apply only where it is necessary and actually to accomplish its stated, and plainly compelling, purpose of preserving Indian culture through the preservation of Indian families."[97] The decision presents culture as inherently constellated with family and with parental choice; in doing so, the opinion limits the legal scope of the project of "preserving" Indianness. Within the frame set up by ICWA, Indianness can be interpreted as a cultural/familial inheritance rather than as indicating belonging to a kind of polity that antecedes the United States and thereby exceeds, and challenges, its jurisdictional structures. Thus, while *In re Bridget* rightly can be critiqued as deviating from the emphasis and aims of ICWA, the decision activates and expands inclinations and aporias found in the statute (and supportive legislative and judicial accounts of it). The case highlights the stakes of the reproductive drift of "culture" within the logic of the law and the implications of having Indianness (as something that is envisioned as generationally transmitted within families) surrogate for a broader conception of Indigenous self-determination.

  In re Bridget indicates how the invocation of "culture" necessarily falls back on racial reproduction in delimiting an Indian uniqueness that deserves to be recognized by the U.S. government, and this dynamic can be understood as the flip side of the need to limit the reach of Indianness in *Oliphant*. The opinion in *In re Bridget* observes, "wheresuch social, cultural or political relationships do not exist or are very attenuated, the only remaining basis for applying ICWA rather than state law in proceedings affecting an Indian child's custody is the child's genetic heritage—in other words, race," thereby triggering Fourteenth Amendment concerns and requiring "strict scrutiny."[98] Absent evidence of parents' robust "relationships" to a tribe, a child's putative Indianness appears as nothing but a racial attribution. In addition, the very definition of tribal membership threatens to raise constitutional questions: "If tribal determinations are indeed conclusive for purposes of applying ICWA, and if, as appears to be the case here, a particular tribe recognizes as members all persons who are biologically descended from historic tribal members, then children who are related by blood to such a tribe may be claimed by the tribe, and thus made subject to the provisions of ICWA, solely on the basis of their biological heritage. Only children who are racially Indians face this possibility."[99] The concept and legal category of Indianness mediates Indigeneity by transposing it into a biological relation across time, as opposed to a geopolitical relation to and exertion of authority over place. In doing so, Indianness displaces and manages the anxieties generated by the impossibility of articulating a viable constitutional or normative account of the settler state's jurisdiction over its "domestic" space. Condensing the (geo)politics of Indigeneity and its erasure/regulation by the settler state into the figure of the Indian recasts the paradoxes and bad faith of settler mappings as the unique, special, or peculiar characteristics of Indianness it-self, conceived as a kind of reproductive transmission of "blood" that oper-ates in a sphere distinct from and prior to (U.S.) governance.

The attempt to separate the "political" from the "racial" effaces the ways that, within contemporary U.S. Indian law and policy, the political becomes utterly incoherent without supplementation by the racial as the horizon of *Indian* particularity, and the effort to redeem settler policy through a sup-posed purging of its vestigial racializing and racist tendencies ignores how "racial" determinations of Indianness bear within them the history of settler-Indigenous conflict and negotiation, including the legacies of U.S. determi-nations about the proper form, scope, and character of Indigeneity.[100] In this way, jettisoning the "racial" as a false mode of designation does not address the knotty conceptual and legal process of (re)producing Indianness as a cat-egory. Rather, we need to trace the heteronormative matrix through which Indigeneity 1) becomes understood as a function of the genealogical passage of Indianness and 2) gets segregated from the sphere of politics as such. In this way, Indigenous governance is made to pivot around some version of the family as its definitional core (including for the purposes of casting it as "culture" and exempting non-Indians from it), and that process delimits the scope of Native peoplehood by repeatedly linking it to the scene of (racial) procreation—even in policies whose goals and trajectories appear quite dis-crepant, as in *Oliphant* and ICWA. The debate over VAWA restages this im-passe, exempting non-Indians from control by a racial enclave or endorsing such "special" and limited jurisdiction due to its proximity to dating, mar-riage, and procreation. We can see in such continuities the ongoing modes of Indianization that facilitate the (non)justification of the settler state's jurisdiction, a persistent dynamic made manifest when one attends to the seemingly contradictory legacy of 1978. In this way, an analysis organized around the critique of heteronormativity can highlight the political work performed by interdependent and cross-referencing figurations of race, culture, and family in the settler project of acknowledging Indian *unique-ness*, as opposed to engaging with the self-determination of Indigenous peoples.

NOTES

1. See Brian Bennett, "House Narrows Scope of Anti-violence Bill," *Los Angeles Times*, May 17, 2012, 8; Robert Pear, "House Sets up Battle on Domestic Violence Bill," *New York Times*, May 17, 2012, 19; Laurie Kellman, "GOP Revises Anti-violence Bill, Draws

White House Veto Threat," *Washington Post*, May 16, 2012, 19; Jonathan Weisman, "Senate Votes to Reauthorize Domestic Violence Act," *New York Times*, April 27, 2012, 13.

2. See 158 Cong. Rec. S 2761, 2772, 2786 (2012).

3. As noted in *Oliphant v. Suquamish*, the case that established the principle that tribes do not have criminal jurisdiction over "non-Indians," "Of the 127 reservation court systems that currently exercise criminal jurisdiction in the United States, 33 purport to extend that jurisdiction to non-Indians": *Oliphant v. Suquamish*, 435 U.S. 191 (1978), 196. This fact means that dozens of tribes, at least, were exercising such jurisdiction as of thirty-five years ago. Moreover, given that for at least the first century of the existence of the United States federal and state governments had little meaningful jurisdiction over many, if not most, Native peoples within the "domestic" boundaries of the nation, it seems absurd to claim axiomatically that Native peoples did not exert authority over non-Indians engaged in activity that violated the laws and social standards of the particular peoples with whom they resided. To do so is to imagine the boundaries of the United States as static (which they most certainly were not), to treat circumstances in Indian policy at the end of the nineteenth century as if they defined the status quo from the Revolutionary War onward (denying the actual history of the treaty-system, as well as the fact of ongoing wars with Native peoples, largely over settler incursions), and to take the U.S. government's claims about the extent of its own jurisdiction as actually descriptive of what was occurring in Indian country.

4. Notably, the controversy about adding provisions to protect women in same-sex relationships as part of the VAWA reauthorization and that over extending Native nations' criminal jurisdiction to non-Natives were not connected in legislative, popular, or academic discussion of the bill, so that violence against Native women comes to appear de facto as a straight issue and Native lesbians become somewhat invisible. Thanks to Kēhaulani Kauanui for highlighting this dynamic.

5. 113 PL 4 (2013), sec. 204. For the Senate's version, see S. 1925, 112th Cong., 2nd sess. (2012), sec. 904.

6. In sec. 204.a.4, the statute indicates that it applies to "an Indian tribe that elects to exercise special domestic violence criminal jurisdiction over the Indian country of that Indian tribe," and in sec. 204.b.3.B.I-II, it indicates that it applies to any victim who is "a member of the participating tribe" or "an Indian who resides in the Indian country of the participating tribe." Indianness, therefore, cannot be defined exclusively by membership in the tribe.

7. To be clear, though, I am critiquing the ways that Native people and peoples are hemmed into particular strategies and framings when seeking to have forms of sovereignty and self-determination recognized by the U.S. government, but I also want to acknowledge the incredibly difficult work of Native activists in trying to get initiatives such as the extension of tribal jurisdiction in the VAWA reauthorization passed. On the difficulties of negotiating this process, the hurdles of having to make change in this "piecemeal" fashion, and the effort to get the federal government out of Native national governance, see J. Kēhaulani Kauanui, interview with Sarah Deer, February 2, 2013, http://indigenouspolitics.org/audiofiles/2013/IP%20Feb%2022%202013%20PodCast.mp3.

8. For arguments that a congressional repudiation of *Oliphant* is necessary to redress rampant sexual violence in Indian country, see Sarah Deer, "Decolonizing Rape Law: A Native Feminist Synthesis of Safety and Sovereignty," *Wicazo Sa Review* 24, no. 2 (2009): 149–67; Amanda M. K. Pacheco, "Broken Traditions: Overcoming the Jurisdictional Maze to Protect Native American Women from Sexual Violence," *University of San Francisco Journal of Law and Social Challenges* 11 (2009): 1–42; Laura E. Pisarello, "Lawless by Design: Jurisdiction, Gender, and Justice in Indian Country," *Emory Law Journal* 59 (2010): 1515–52; Marie Quasius, "Native American Rape Victims: Desperately Seeking an Oliphant-Fix," *Minnesota Law Review* 93 (2009): 1902–1941.

9. On the term "reprosexual," see Dana Luciano, *Arranging Grief: Sacred Time and the Body in Nineteenth-Century America* (New York: New York University Press, 2007).

10. Here, I am speaking mainly of the ways that "kinship" potentially can designate forms of Native governance, diplomacy, and ethics of care that exceed the scene of genealogical transmission designated by "race." See Joanne Barker, *Native Acts: Law, Recognition, and Cultural Authenticity* (Durham: Duke University Press, 2011); Daniel Heath Justice, "'Go Away, Water!' Kinship Criticism and the Decolonization Imperative," in *Reasoning Together*, ed. Native Critics Collective (Norman: University of Oklahoma Press, 2008): 147–68; J. Kēhaulani Kauanui, *Hawaiian Blood: Colonialism and the Politics of Sovereignty and Indigeneity* (Durham, NC: Duke University Press, 2008); Mark Rifkin, *When Did Indians Become Straight? Kinship, the History of Sexuality, and Native Sovereignty* (New York: Oxford University Press, 2011); Pauline Turner Strong and Barrik Van Winkle, "'Indian Blood': Reflections on the Reckoning and Refiguring of Native North American Identity," *Cultural Anthropology* 11, no. 4 (1996): 547–76; Kimberly TallBear, "DNA, Blood, and Racializing the Tribe," *Wicazo Sa Review* 18, no. 1 (2003): 81–107.

11. On the ways settler policy does not simply displace the supposedly familial from the political but regulates what kinds of reproductive and martial relations will be understood as conveying Indianness and in what circumstances such transmission will become legally relevant, see Jodi Byrd's essay in this volume.

12. See Elizabeth Povinelli, *The Empire of Love: Toward a Theory of Intimacy, Genealogy, and Carnality* (Durham, NC: Duke University Press, 2006). For differently configured definitions of heteronormativity, see Lauren Berlant and Michael Warner, "Sex in Public," *Critical Inquiry* 24, no. 2 (1998): 548–66; Cathy J. Cohen, "Punks, Bulldaggers, and Welfare Queens: The Radical Potential of Queer Politics?" *GLQ* 3, no. 4 (1997): 437–65; Roderick A. Ferguson, *Aberrations in Black: Toward a Queer of Color Critique* (Minneapolis: University of Minnesota Press, 2004); Jasbir K. Puar, *Terrorist Assemblages: Homonationalism in Queer Times* (Durham, NC: Duke University Press, 2007); Rifkin, *When Did Indians Become Straight?*; Michael Warner, "Introduction," in *Fear of a Queer Planet: Queer Politics and Social Theory*, ed. Michael Warner (Minneapolis: University of Minnesota Press, 1993), vii–xxxi.

13. For this background, see the Appellate Court decision in *Oliphant v. Schlie et al.*, 544 F.2d (1976), 1007.

14. The decision was endorsed by six justices, with two dissenting in an opinion written by Thurgood Marshall; one justice did not participate in the decision at all.

At this point, I will cease to put Indian, non-Indian, and tribe in scare quotes, but readers should continue to bear in mind the political semiotics of the seemingly straightforward reference implied by these terms.

15. Philip P. Frickey, "A Common Law for Our Age of Colonialism: The Judicial Divestiture of Indian Tribal Authority over Nonmembers," *Yale Law Journal* 109 (1999): 38; N. Bruce Duthu, *American Indians and the Law* (New York: Penguin, 2009), 21.

16. See Duthu, *American Indians and the Law*, 19–24; Steven Russell, "Making Peace with Crow Dog's Ghost: Racialized Prosecution in Federal Indian Law," *Wicazo Sa Review* 21, no. 1 (2006): 64–66; David E. Wilkins, *American Indian Sovereignty and the U.S. Supreme Court: The Masking of Justice* (Austin: University of Texas Press, 1997), 187–213; Robert A. Williams, Jr., *Like a Loaded Weapon: The Rehnquist Court, Indian Rights, and the Legal History of Racism in America* (Minneapolis: University of Minnesota Press, 2005), 98–113.

17. *Oliphant v. Suquamish*, 209.

18. I should make it clear that I am referring here to the decision's narrative of U.S. authority rather than describing how such authority/jurisdiction/diplomacy actually operated historically.

19. *Oliphant v. Suquamish*, 211.

20. Russell observes, "If Indian nations were not separate sovereigns in the sense of criminal law then it is unclear how they could have the sovereignty" to cede land to the United States via the treaty-system ("Making Peace with Crow Dog's Ghost," 62). On the history of producing legal subjectivities for Native peoples that indicate their putative consent to U.S. legal mappings, see Mark Rifkin, *Manifesting America: The Imperial Construction of U.S. National Space* (New York: Oxford University Press, 2009).

21. In this way, though, the Supreme Court decision does not go as far as the dissent at the appellate level in *Oliphant v. Schlie*, even though Rehnquist borrows language from it. Written by Anthony Kennedy, who would be appointed to the Supreme Court a decade later, the dissent suggests that the notion of tribal inherent sovereignty is nothing but dicta from the case of *Worcester v. Georgia* (1832) and that "[t]he term 'sovereignty,' then, is merely a veil used where the issue is, in fact, one of federal preemption [of states] in the field of Indian affairs" (*Oliphant v. Schlie et. al.*, 1014–15). From this perspective, Native peoples have no autonomous sovereignty; they have only delegated authority from the federal government.

22. Philip P. Frickey suggests, "The place of federal Indian law in American public law can be understood by imagining layers of law, with American constitutionalism built on top of American colonialism," adding, "We have every right to be confused about what we should make of our origins, our evolution, our sense of nationhood, and our creation of a constitutional democracy through colonialism." See Philip P. Frickey, "(Native) American Exceptionalism in Federal Public Law," *Harvard Law Review* 119 (2005): 467, 489. See also Kevin Bruyneel, *The Third Space of Sovereignty: The Postcolonial Politics of U.S.-Indigenous Relations* (Minneapolis: University of Minnesota Press, 2007); Jodi Byrd, *The Transit of Empire: Indigenous Critiques of Colonialism* (Minneapolis: University of Minnesota Press, 2011); Eric Cheyfitz, "The (Post)Colonial Construction of Indian Country: U.S. American Indian Literatures and Federal Indian

Law," in *The Columbia Guide to American Indian Literatures of the United States Since 1945*, ed. Eric Cheyfitz (New York: Columbia University Press, 2006), 1–124; Duthu, *American Indians and the Law*; Mark Rifkin, "Indigenizing Agamben: Rethinking Sovereignty in Light of the 'Peculiar' Status of Native Peoples," *Cultural Critique* 72 (Fall 2009): 88–124.

23. The Appellate Court's decision actually uses this phrase as part of its argument that tribes "retain the powers of autonomous states" except under very specific circumstances (*Oliphant v. Schlie et al.*, 1009). The Supreme Court decision demurs from the prior judicial convention of viewing Native nations as autonomous entities save for the explicit limitations placed on their sovereignty by specific treaty provisions and acts of Congress. On the growing displacement of that canon of construction in the later decades of the twentieth century, see Frickey, "A Common Law for Our Age of Colonialism."

24. *Oliphant v. Suquamish*, 197. The opinion also quotes an 1834 report from the House of Representatives, noting, "This principle would have been obvious a century ago when most Indian tribes were characterized by 'a want of fixed laws [and] of competent tribunals of justice'" (*Oliphant v. Suquamish*, 210).

25. Williams, *Like a Loaded Weapon*, 101.

26. On *Ex Parte Crow Dog*, see Sidney L. Harring, *Crow Dog's Case: American Indian Sovereignty, Tribal Law, and United States Law in the Nineteenth Century* (New York: Cambridge University Press, 1994), 100–41; Russell, "Making Peace with Crow Dog's Ghost."

27. *Oliphant v. Suquamish*, 210–211. The ellipses and interpolations are reproduced here as they appear in the *Oliphant* opinion. On the ways Rehnquist uses ellipses in this decision to edit out the most severely racist expressions of his source material, thereby making nineteenth-century legal conclusions more presentable for a 1970s audience, see Williams, *Like a Loaded Weapon*, 109–10.

28. See *Morton v. Mancari*, 417 U.S. 535 (1974); *U.S. v. Antelope*, 430 U.S. 641 (1977). Both *Morton* and *Antelope* were unanimous decisions, and virtually all of the justices taking part in *Oliphant* also participated in the prior two cases.

29. *Morton v. Mancari*, 554.

30. A corollary raised by the decision is that determinations not directly tied to tribal membership may be constitutionally suspect, disallowing "Indian" status for a variety of purposes. On this possible implication of *Morton*, see Brian L. Lewis, "Do You Know What You Are? You Are What You Is; You Is What You Am: Indian Status for the Purpose of Federal Criminal Jurisdiction and the Current Split in the Court of Appeals," *Harvard Journal on Racial and Ethnic Justice* 26 (2010); Katharine C. Oakley, "Defining Indian Status for the Purpose of Federal Criminal Jurisdiction," *American Indian Law Review* 35 (2010): 177–209; Rose Cuison Villazor, "Blood Quantum Land Laws and the Race versus Political Identity Dilemma," *California Law Review* 96 (2008): 801–37.

31. *U.S. v. Antelope*, 645.

32. *Morton v. Mancari*, 551. The reference to a guardian-ward relation refers to the decision in *Cherokee Nation v. Georgia* (30 U.S. 1 [1831]), and the finding that Congress has "plenary power" in Indian affairs can be traced substantively to *U.S. v. Kagama* (118 U.S. 375 [1886]).

33. *Morton v. Mancari*, 554; *U.S. v. Antelope*, 646.

34. *U.S. v. Antelope*, 645; *Morton v. Mancari*, 554.

35. Lewis, "Do You Know What You Are?", 252. Lewis addresses how determining Indianness for prosecution under the Major Crimes Act has never depended exclusively on formal tribal membership, arguing that it should not. For a counterargument that doing so would clarify currently conflicting ways of determining Indianness for prosecutorial purposes, see Oakley, "Defining Indian Status for the Purpose of Federal Criminal Jurisdiction."

36. *Oliphant v. Suquamish*, 209–10.

37. Duthu, *American Indians and the Law*, 22.

38. *Oliphant v. Suquamish*, 212.

39. This formulation also presents the prosecution of non-Indian defendants in Native courts as if it were a captivity narrative. On the legacy of the captivity narrative, see Christopher Castiglia, *Bound and Determined: Captivity, Culture-Crossing, and White Womanhood from Mary Rowlandson to Patty Hearst* (Chicago: University of Chicago Press, 1996); Audra Simpson, "Captivating Eunice: Membership, Colonialism, and Gendered Citizenships of Grief," *Wicazo Sa Review* 24, no. 2 (2009): 105–29; Pauline Turner Strong, *Captive Selves, Captivating Others: The Politics and Poetics of Colonial American Captivity Narratives* (Boulder, CO: Westview, 1999).

40. *Oliphant v. Suquamish*, 194.

41. While *Oliphant* argues for such insulation solely for the purposes of criminal prosecution, the principle of non-Indian immunity has been extended into a series of civil and regulatory matters by later decisions. See Duthu, *American Indians and the Law*, 36–51; Frickey, "A Common Law for Our Age of Colonialism," 43–45.

42. On the paucity of precedent in the decision, see Quasius, "Native American Rape Victims," 1915, 1935–37; Wilkins, *American Indian Sovereignty and the U.S. Supreme Court*, 204; Williams, *Like a Loaded Weapon*, 107–11.

43. *Oliphant v. Suquamish*, 206.

44. On the presence of such an understanding in the nineteenth century, see Cheyfitz, "The (Post)Colonial Construction"; Maureen Konkle, *Writing Indian Nations: Native Intellectuals and the Politics of Historiography, 1827–1863* (Chapel Hill: University of North Carolina Press, 2004); Rifkin, *When Did Indians Become Straight?*; Paul Spruhan, "A Legal History of Blood Quantum in Federal Indian Law to 1935," *South Dakota Law Review* 51 (2006): 1–50. In particular, in *U.S. v. Rogers* (1846), about a murder committed by a white man who belonged to the Cherokee Nation and who sought immunity from federal prosecution as an "Indian," the Supreme Court found that Indianness and tribal belonging are not equivalent, understanding the former as an inborn racial quality. See Bethany R. Berger, "'Power over This Unfortunate Race': Race, Politics, and Indian Law in *United States v. Rogers*," *William and Mary Law Review* 45 (2004): 1957–2052; Mark Rifkin, "Making Peoples into Populations: The Racial Limits of Tribal Sovereignty," *Theorizing Native Studies*, eds. Audra Simpson and Andrea Smith (Durham, NC: Duke University Press, 2014), 149–87; Wilkins, *American Indian Sovereignty and the U.S. Supreme Court*, 38–51.

45. Sara Ahmed, *Queer Phenomenology: Orientations, Objects, Others* (Durham, NC: Duke University Press, 2006), 121–22.

46. Ahmed, *Queer Phenomenology*, 128.

47. See Terry L. Cross and Robert J. Miller, "The Indian Child Welfare Act of 1978 and Its Impact on Tribal Sovereignty and Governance," in *Facing the Future: The Indian Child Welfare Act at 30*, eds. Matthew L. M. Fletcher, Wenone T. Singel, and Kathryn E. Fort (East Lansing: Michigan State University, 2008), 13–28; Lorie M. Graham, "Reparations, Self-Determination, and the Seventh Generation," in Fletcher et al., *Facing the Future*, 50–110; Pauline Turner Strong, "What Is an Indian Family? The Indian Child Welfare Act and the Renascence of Tribal Sovereignty," *American Studies* 46, nos. 3–4 (2005): 205–31.

48. Strong, "What Is an Indian Family," 205.

49. See George Pierre Castile, *To Show Heart: Native American Self-Determination and Federal Indian Policy, 1960–1975* (Tucson: University of Arizona Press, 1998).

50. The original text of the law is in the *United States Statutes at Large* as P.L. 95–608, 92 Stat. 3069. Hereafter, section and clause numbers for quotations from the law are cited in parentheses in the text.

51. See *Mississippi Band of Choctaws v. Holyfield*, 490 U.S. 30 (1989); Lorinda Mall, "Keeping It in the Family: The Legal and Social Evolution of ICWA in State and Tribal Jurisprudence," in Fletcher et al., *Facing the Future*, 164–220; Strong, "What Is an Indian Family." State courts have raised challenges to the application of the act in given circumstances, particularly in terms of the "existing family exception," which I address later.

52. The discussion of ICWA as employing similar assumptions to *Oliphant* refuses the notion of a clear break between periods of federal Indian policy that affirm Native sovereignty and self-determination and those that do not. My point here is, in many ways, similar to the critique Barker offers in the introduction to this volume about dividing up feminist and sexuality movements into "waves."

53. My critique of how ICWA's affirmation of the integrity of Indian families reiterates the pervasive familialization of Native polities within Indian policy resonates with Kauanui's chapter in this volume in its discussion of the difference between the inclusion of same-sex couples in a vision of Hawaiian "recognition" by the federal and state governments and earlier Hawaiian anti-heteronormative analysis in its challenge to the legitimacy of U.S. rule in Hawai'i more broadly.

54. On policy during the termination period, including the passage of Public Law 280, see Donald L. Fixico, *Termination and Relocation: Federal Indian Policy, 1945–1960* (Albuquerque: University of New Mexico Press, 1986); Kenneth R. Philp, *Termination Revisited: American Indians on the Trail to Self-Determination, 1933–1953* (Lincoln: University of Nebraska Press, 1999). On the legacy of that law and changes in its sphere of application due largely to court decisions, see Carole Goldberg-Ambrose, *Planting Tail Feathers: Tribal Survival and Public Law 280* (Los Angeles: American Indian Studies Center, University of California, 1997).

55. The Indian Civil Rights Act (1968) made any future extension of civil and criminal jurisdiction by states over tribes dependent on the tribes' consent. It also enabled states that previously had been given or had chosen such jurisdiction to retrocede it in part or in its entirety by petitioning the federal government, which many states have done. See Cross and Miller, "The Indian Child Welfare Act of 1978 and Its Impact on Tribal Sover-

eignty and Governance," 17–18; Pacheco, "Broken Traditions," 33; Pisarello, "Lawless by Design," 1516. However, no mechanism exists for tribes placed under state jurisdiction by federal action prior to 1968 to choose to have it returned to them, and since 1968 no tribe has chosen voluntarily to have state jurisdiction extended over it.

56. The case concerned a woman who was Santa Clara Pueblo and whose children had grown on the reservation but whose husband was not. The tribal code defined membership patrilineally, so her children were barred from membership. She sued under the provisions of the Indian Civil Rights Act. The court found that it had no jurisdiction to hear the case, because the matter was purely a matter internal to the tribe. See *Santa Clara Pueblo v. Martinez*, 436 U.S. 49 (1978).

57. On the attempt to insert Native "culture" into U.S. legal discourse as a way of marking alternative modes and means of enacting Indigenous sovereignty, see Wallace Coffey and Rebecca Tsosie, "Rethinking the Tribal Sovereignty Doctrine: Cultural Sovereignty and the Collective Future of Indian Nations," *Stanford Law and Policy Review* 12 (2001): 191–210. On the problems raised in the context of Indigenous politics by the increasing prominence of a discourse of "culture," see Jessica Cattelino, *High Stakes: Florida Seminole Gaming and Sovereignty* (Durham, NC: Duke University Press, 2008); Karen Engle, *The Elusive Promise of Indigenous Development: Rights, Culture, Strategy* (Durham, NC: Duke University Press, 2010); Ronald Niezen, *The Origins of Indigenism: Human Rights and the Politics of Identity* (Berkeley: University of California Press, 2003); Elizabeth Povinelli, *The Cunning of Recognition: Indigenous Alterities and the Making of Australian Multiculturalism* (Durham, NC: Duke University Press, 2002); Patrick Wolfe, *Settler Colonialism and the Transformation of Anthropology: The Politics and Poetics of an Ethnographic Event* (New York: Cassell, 1999).

58. Povinelli, *The Empire of Love*, 198–99.

59. Povinelli, *The Empire of Love*, 225–26. Povinelli's ethnographic work concerns peoples in Australia. However, she extends her claims to include other (Anglophone) settler states, and they work quite well as a way to characterize the contours of post-1970 U.S. federal Indian policy.

60. Povinelli, *The Empire of Love*, 219.

61. On the relation between ICWA and customary international law with respect to children's right to remain with their peoples, see Graham, "Reparations."

62. Such authority, though, does need to meet several conditions: it needs to be "in the least restrictive setting which most approximates a family" (105.b); "Where appropriate, the preference of the Indian child or parent shall be considered" (105.c); and the authority may be altered when "the continued custody of the child by the parent or Indian custodian is likely to result in serious emotional or physical damage to the child" (102.e).

63. On the ways the familial and the governmental are not as distinct in practices of liberal governance as suggested in its narratives of itself, see Janet R. Jakobsen, "Can Homosexuals End Western Civilization as We Know It?" in *Queer Globalizations: Citizenship and the Afterlife of Colonialism*, eds. Arnaldo Cruz-Malavé and Martin F. Manalansan IV (New York: New York University Press, 2002), 49–69; Povinelli, *The Empire of Love*; Jacqueline Stevens, *Reproducing the State* (Princeton, NJ: Princeton University Press, 1999); Alys Eve Weinbaum, *Wayward Reproduction: Genealogies of*

Race and Nation in Transatlantic Modern Thought (Durham, NC: Duke University Press, 2004). On the history in anthropology of translating non–European American social systems (including those of Indigenous peoples) into a logic of "kinship" implicitly conceptualized as a set of "cultural" deviations from the "natural" standard of the nuclear family, see Rifkin, *When Did Indians Become Straight?*; David M. Schneider, *A Critique of the Study of Kinship* (Ann Arbor: University of Michigan Press, 1984); Thomas R. Trautmann, *Lewis Henry Morgan and the Invention of Kinship* (Berkeley: University of California Press, 1987).

64. For a discussion of how the U.S. Supreme Court decision in *Santa Clara Pueblo v. Martinez* (often cited as the basis for non-racialist, tribally defined notions of membership) implicitly defines belonging in terms of familially transmitted Indianness, see Rifkin, "Making Peoples into Populations."

65. On how culture and race can supplement each other in political and popular discourses, see Étienne Balibar, "Is There a 'Neo-Racism'?" (1988), in Étienne Balibar and Immanuel Wallerstein, *Race, Nation, Class: Ambiguous Identities*, trans. Chris Turner (New York: Verso, 1991), 17–28; Kamala Visweswaran, *Un/common Cultures: Racism and the Rearticulation of Cultural Difference* (Durham, NC: Duke University Press, 2010); Weinbaum, *Wayward Reproduction.*

66. In doing so, it cites the part of the commerce clause in the U.S. Constitution that gives Congress power to "regulate Commerce with foreign Nations, and among the several States, and with the Indian Tribes." On the ICWA and the commerce clause, see Matthew L. M. Fletcher, "ICWA and the Commerce Clause," in Fletcher et al., *Facing the Future*, 28–49.

67. See *U.S. v. Kagama.*

68. Povinelli, *The Empire of Love*, 134. On the role of racial descent as a means of figuring a continuity in Indianness for various federal purposes, most of which present themselves as not in fact about race, see Margo S. Brownwell, "Who Is an Indian? Searching for an Answer to the Question at the Core of Federal Indian Law," *University of Michigan Journal of Law Reform* 34 (2000–2001): 275–320; Kirsty Gover, "Genealogy as Continuity: Explaining the Growing Tribal Preference for Descent Rules in Membership Governance in the United States," *American Indian Law Review* 33 (2008–2009): 243–309; Carole Goldberg, "Members Only? Designing Citizenship Requirements for Indian Nations," *Kansas Law Review* 50 (2002): 437–71; TallBear, "DNA, Blood, and Racializing the Tribe."

69. Povinelli, *The Empire of Love*, 140.

70. See "Establishing Standards for the Placement of Indian Children in Foster or Adoptive Homes, to Prevent the Breakup of Indian Families, and for Other Purposes," H.R. Rpt. 1386, 95th Cong., 2nd sess. (1978); *Mississippi Band of Choctaw Indians v. Holyfield; Adoptive Couple v. Baby Girl*, 133 S. Ct. 2552 (2013).

71. "Establishing Standards for the Placement of Indian Children in Foster or Adoptive Homes," 9–10.

72. "Establishing Standards for the Placement of Indian Children in Foster or Adoptive Homes," 24.

73. "Establishing Standards for the Placement of Indian Children in Foster or Adoptive Homes," 13–14.

74. On *U.S. v. Nice*, see Wilkins, *American Indian Sovereignty and the U.S. Supreme Court*, 119–36.

75. "Establishing Standards for the Placement of Indian Children in Foster or Adoptive Homes," 20.

76. This syllogistic chain again suggests the limits—or, at least, dangers—of seeking to gain leverage on settler superintendence by employing the concept of "kinship."

77. "Establishing Standards for the Placement of Indian Children in Foster or Adoptive Homes," 16.

78. "Establishing Standards for the Placement of Indian Children in Foster or Adoptive Homes," 11.

79. "Establishing Standards for the Placement of Indian Children in Foster or Adoptive Homes," 19.

80. *Mississippi Band of Choctaw Indians v. Holyfield*, 47.

81. *Mississippi Band of Choctaw Indians v. Holyfield*, 49.

82. Mall observes that ICWA "sets out the basic premise that the best interest of an Indian child runs parallel to the best interests of the tribe" ("Keeping It in the Family," 167). See also Graham, "Reparations"; Cheyanna L. Jaffke, "The 'Existing Indian Family' Exception to the Indian Child Welfare Act: The States' Attempt to Slaughter Tribal Interests in Indian Children," *Louisiana Law Review* 66 (2006): 733–61; Aliza G. Organick, "Holding Back the Tide: The Existing Indian Family Doctrine and Its Continued Denial of the Right to Culture for Indigenous Children," in Fletcher et al., *Facing the Future*, 221–34; Strong, "What Is an Indian Family."

83. *Mississippi Band of Choctaw Indians v. Holyfield*, 34.

84. *Mississippi Band of Choctaw Indians v. Holyfield*, 52.

85. *Mississippi Band of Choctaw Indians v. Holyfield*, 49–50.

86. Joanne Barker, "Adoptive Couple versus Baby Girl: On the Disarticulation of Native Self-Determination," paper presented at the Native American and Indigenous Studies Association, Austin, May 2014.

87. *Adoptive Couple v. Baby Girl*, 2556, 2565.

88. On the history and politics of Cherokee citizenship determinations, see Circe Sturm, *Blood Politics: Race, Culture, and Identity in the Cherokee Nation of Oklahoma* (Berkeley: University of California Press, 2002).

89. *Adoptive Couple v. Baby Girl*, 2557, 2565.

90. *Adoptive Couple v. Baby Girl*, 2560–61.

91. On this exception, including discussion of *In re Bridget*, see Jaffke, "The 'Existing Indian Family' Exception to the Indian Child Welfare Act"; Organick, "Holding Back the Tide"; Strong, "What Is an Indian Family," 215–18; Susan Waszak, "Contemporary Hurdles in the Application of the Indian Child Welfare Act," *American Indian Culture and Research* 34, no. 1 (2010): 124–27.

92. *In re Bridget* 41 Cal. App. 4th 1483 (1996), 1511.

93. The opinion subjects the law to Tenth Amendment scrutiny, which is inappropriate given the fact that tribes and Congress's relation to them exist outside the terms of that amendment's limitations. See Fletcher, "ICWA and the Commerce Clause."

94. *In re Bridget*, 1507.

95. *In re Bridget*, 1507.

96. This train of thought/definition in the decision explains how the twins' father's membership in the Dry Creek Rancheria would not count as legally salient absent some active performance of connection that could code as a choice to participate in Indian culture. The decision asserts, "more is required to justify an application of ICWA than a biological parent's mere formal enrollment in a tribe, or a self-serving after-the-fact tribal recognition of such a parent's membership. Such token attestations of cultural identity fall short of establishing the existence of those *significant* cultural traditions and affiliations which ICWA exists to preserve, and which are consequently necessary to invoke a constitutionally permissible application of the Act" (*In re Bridget*, 1512). Membership in a tribe functions as a "cultural identity," subject to assessment of active participation and association, rather than a mode of belonging to a polity—a relation whose terms, content, and scope remain assessable only by that polity, since they are of a "political" nature that puts them beyond the jurisdiction of another polity.

97. *In re Bridget*, 1511.

98. *In re Bridget*, 1508.

99. *In re Bridget*, 1509.

100. See Barker, *Native Acts*; Brownwell, "Who Is an Indian?"; Eva Marie Garroutte, *Real Indians: Identity and the Survival of Native America* (Berkeley: University of California Press, 2003); Goldberg, "Members Only?"; Gover, "Genealogy as Continuity"; Steven Russell, "The Racial Paradox of Tribal Citizenship," *American Studies* 46, nos. 3–4 (2005): 163–85; Strong and Winkle, "Indian Blood"; Sturm, *Blood Politics*; TallBear, "DNA, Blood, and Racializing the Tribe"; Villazor, "Blood Quantum Land Laws and the Race versus Political Identity Dilemma."

6

LOVING UNBECOMING

The Queer Politics of the Transitive Native

JODI A. BYRD

I'm not sure how the change in the social status of homosexuality, sadomasochism, and the like have changed the way we read the story today. Ask me what the story is about now, however, and I'll probably say it's somehow about the desire for desire.—**Samuel R. Delany,** "Aye, and Gomorrah"

To think about desire is to arrive at a queer place. But I do not mean for that queer place to become overdetermined by its association with desire, with the erotic. In essence, I am opening the door to a notion of the "erotic" that oversteps the category of the autonomous so valued in queer theory so as to place the erotic—the personal and political dimension of desire—at the threshold of ideas about quotidian racist practice.—**Sharon Patricia Holland,** *The Erotic Life of Racism*

The last week of June 2013 saw the perfect storm of U.S. Supreme Court landmark decisions. On June 25, the justices handed down their ruling in *Shelby County, Alabama v. Holder* and in the process effectively dismantled key protections in sections 4–5 of the Voting Rights Amendment of 1965. On the same day, and with the same 5–4 majority, the court attacked tribal sovereignty and the Indian Child Welfare Act of 1978 in *Adoptive Couple v. Baby Girl.* The following day, the court struck down the Defense of Marriage Act (DOMA) of 1996 as a violation of the Fifth Amendment in *United States v. Windsor* and decided that proponents of California's Proposition 8 to ban gay marriage had no grounds to appeal the district court's ruling. That the pair of cases that purportedly advanced gay marriage as a homonormative civil right were issued on the tenth anniversary of *Lawrence v. Texas* (June 26, 2003) drove home the weighted intentionality of the court's procedural deliberations. Indeed, the significance of such anniversary alignments also helped predict exactly how, in the context of current neoliberal refortifications of possessive white heteropatriarchy, arguments about the Equal Protection Clause of the Fourteenth Amendment could and would unfold. In each case, the court ruled consistently to maintain the logics of racial liberalism, which, as Jodi Melamed observes, "allow violence to advance precisely through a formally antiracist, rational apparatus."[1]

While it may be tempting to read these cases as isolated, what emerges in their temporal synchronicity are the machinations of a well-scripted liberalism designed to maintain settler colonialism through dialectical and competing modes of inclusion and exclusion. Indeed, the trifecta of political issues surrounding these cases, with the undermining of Indigenous sovereignty and voting rights for minorities on the one hand, and the tepid affirmation of same-sex couples' rights to federal benefits and marriage recognition on the other, demonstrates the trenchant need for queer, Indigenous, feminist, and critical race theories to continue hammering home how U.S. neoliberal biopolitics govern bodies, rights, and access through state-sanctioned normativities that expand access only to ensure incorporation as non-transformation. These four cases, taken altogether as a unit of U.S. juridical biopower, exemplify the state-endorsed modes of liberal tolerance that contemporary settler colonial governments use to manage racial, gender, sexual, and Indigenous differences.

The consolidation of normative hetero- and non- families, especially at the sites of transnational and transracial adoption, as well as gay marriage, signals, then, the degree to which discourses of integration, tolerance, and rights serve to tender equality within the U.S. settler nation-state at the price of assimilation, erasure, and violence. Using equal protection to expand the notion of individual rights over and against collective group rights, the Supreme Court advances a rather chilling hegemonic liberalism: that rich, white heterosexual couples make the best parents for "vulnerable children at a great disadvantage solely because an ancestor—even a remote one—was an Indian";[2] that race has been severed from the historical and material conditions of racism; and that same-sex couples, if white, propertied, and wealthy, might become surrogates for white heterosexual couples. In the zero-sum contest that pits gay rights against Indigenous sovereignty against civil rights for all arrivants within the institutions built through settler colonial occupation of Indigenous lands, equivalences and precedents reign as the vertical and horizontal axes of intersectionality. Within such economies of normativity, vulnerability, and accommodation, as Lisa Duggan might argue, we are left with a "politics that does not contest dominant heteronormative assumptions and institutions, but upholds and sustains them."[3] Given the conditions of the United States' postwar imperial and expansive gesture toward integration and naturalization as remedy to the injury of exclusion, the Supreme Court's rulings of summer 2013 augur the maintenance—and, in fact, the sustenance—of the status quo.

In the social media celebrations that followed the Supreme Court's decisions on the two cases affecting same-sex marriage recognition and benefits, at least, there was a triumphal air reminiscent of a mission finally accomplished. By December, journalists had declared that 2013 "was a really gay year," with the top of the "best of" lists including the striking down of DOMA, the extension of federal benefits to married same-sex couples, and the resumption of same-sex marriages in California.[4] States including Delaware, Hawai'i, Illinois, Minnesota, New Jersey, New Mexico, and, at least temporarily and provisionally, Utah legalized same-sex marriage throughout the months following the Supreme Court's decision in *United States v. Windsor*. In delivering the opinion of the court, Justice Anthony Kennedy observed that "DOMA's avowed purpose and practical effect are to impose a disadvantage, a separate status, and so a stigma on all who enter into same-sex marriages made lawful by the unquestioned authority of the States."[5] Evoking *Loving v. Virginia* (1967), as well as *Lawrence v. Texas* (2003), to provide precedence for "constitutional guarantees" within and against the states' responsibilities for "defining and regulating the marital relation," Justice Kennedy explained that DOMA "uses the state-defined class for the opposite purpose—to impose restrictions and disabilities."[6] Finally, he wrote, "DOMA's principal effect is to identify and make unequal a subset of state-sanctioned marriages. It contrives to deprive some couples married under the laws of their State, but not others, of both rights and responsibilities, creating two contradictory marriage regimes within the same State."[7]

While Kennedy's opinion does not directly draw on the precedence of race within its framing of the injury DOMA inflicts on same-sex married couples, his use of phrases such as "separate status," "disadvantage," "restrictions," and "two contradictory marriage regimes" are inflected with what has now become the conventional narratives used to frame same-sex marriage rights as disenfranchised minority civil rights. In essence, Kennedy's word choices bear the trace of *Brown v. Board of Education* (1954), with the implication that civil unions and same-sex marriages under DOMA are separate and unequal. In what has become known as the "*Loving* analogy," or what Siobhan Somerville identifies as the "miscegenation analogy," same-sex couples, and LGBTQ2 people in general, are figured as one of the last groups in the United States to receive equal rights, recognition and incorporation within the nation-state as full citizens.[8] Such arguments hinge on a further palimpsest: gender and sexuality become "like race" or "black equivalents" within popular and activist discourses, while racial violence and oppression are rendered somehow already settled within the juridical and civil arenas of the nation-state.[9]

Tellingly, even before the new millennium arrived, it had already been proclaimed as the achievement of a much desired "postracial" society, and certainly the juridical governance structures of the United States have embraced such declarative fantasies with aplomb over the past fifteen years. The legacies of the past five centuries of first European domination and then U.S. imperial domination, however, persist within the juridical categories of property, identity, citizenship, marriage, inheritance, and freedom that undergird such beloved notions as rights, equality, and democracy. The quartet of decisions issued by the Supreme Court in June 2013 draws on analogies of prior rulings to legitimate the violent imaginary of postracial incorporation into what was always intended to remain a white heteropatriarchal occupation of Indigenous lands, and each case relies on a narrative of incremental progress that, as Somerville points out, "creates and maintains comparisons among different historically excluded groups, such that the rights gained by one group establish a precedent for another group's entitlement to the same rights."[10] Chandan Reddy provocatively argues in his analysis of the structuring force of *Loving v. Virginia* that the "miscegenation analogy" of gay marriage mobilizations "becomes the *form* by which such questions are structured and temporarily resolved." Further, he points out, within such postracial and analogous modes of the accrual of rights is an implicit desire for a post-queer future in which "advocates seek something like a gay marriage analogy that would benefit the very others seeking to emerge from the shadows of legal illegitimacy that the assertion of formal equality at this moment casts."[11] Race, in other words, is the harbinger of gender, sexual, class, immigrant, disabled, trans, and other rights within U.S. settler colonial imaginings. Race, as the baseline historical sign of injury and its reparation, becomes the condition of possibility through which the threshold of rights becomes discernible for all other groups.

Such temporal hauntings of the historical consequences of race, subjectivity, property, and identity collide with anticipated futures in which such matters will finally have been resolved in repeating waves of increasing, if halting, accrual of rights and acceptance within the nation-state for all those who may have yet to struggle against adversity to achieve full equality. There is, however, no possibility of an end point to what Reddy identifies as a *form*, because, by its very genre, it becomes the structuring force through which the United States establishes its own legitimacy for the continued occupation of Indigenous lands. This narrative, if reduced to its plot device, is just another metonymic refrain of Frederick Jackson Turner's "Frontier Thesis of 1893," in which he argued that, for others to cast off their origins and achieve American identity, they had to wrest it out of the adversity of the wilderness and in struggle with its prior inhabitants. It is a narrative that, as Reddy argues, serves a "powerful regulative fiction" that coheres territoriality, identity, and culture.[12] The generic form of the "miscegenation analogy" embodies this regulative power at the site of a movable frontier now figured as the cauldron of integration. Matters of race, subjectivity, and citizenship are only temporarily resolved so that boundaries and borders can be established, violated, and exceeded in a never-ending push toward a civil and civilizing horizon. In this process, however, indigeneity collapses into race and is then supposedly remediated through a racial liberalism that offers incorporation into the imperial nation as the fulfillment of humanity's struggle against oppression.

What becomes clear in the aggregate of these four cases, however, is that ongoing U.S. settler colonialism substantiates itself through concomitant processes that extend and deny rights and equal protections at the site of a fetishized disavowal of an Indigenous as well as a racialized presence. That disavowal simultaneously desires authenticity even as it abjects indigeneity as categorically illiberal and unjust within the horizons of colonial governance. In the process, indigeneity by its very nature presents current modes of theorizing race and belonging, identity and possession, rights and freedoms with a fundamental and often incommensurable conundrum within the dialectics of recognition. As the Supreme Court rendered its opinions on adoption, voting rights, and gay marriage, indigeneity continues to circulate as a site of intelligibility and of delimitation, a site that is both required to establish the field through which rights are wrested from the wilderness and the threshold through which those rights are differentiated for the individual and the state. At minimum, these simultaneous and contradictory significations of indigeneity raise considerable stakes for activating intersectional analyses grounded in queer, feminist, critical ethnic, and Indigenous studies as a way to disrupt the colonialist logics of erotics, desire, subjectivity, and identity that underwrite the normative equivalences of civil and gendered protections within U.S. settler colonial racial liberalism. How scholars take up such questions between and among the queer and Indigenous offer instructive, if sometimes vexing, directions for interrogating the subject of rights within U.S. juridical governance.

Undoing the Subject

One of the persistent and recurrent themes of Indigenous critical theory centers on the autonomy Indigenous peoples have, or often do not have, to affect and determine the scales of debate and urgency within the well-heeled modes of liberal critiques of colonialism, racism, sexism, and homophobia. Certainly, indigeneity has provisionally now arrived as a newly revitalized category of analysis, although its efficacy and distinguishability are often circumscribed within the larger intellectual routes of settler colonialism. As an analytic, though, indigeneity is still most often apprehended at the disciplinary boundaries of anthropology, history, literature, and law. Such bedfellows have operationalized indigeneity as a site of intervention to how culture, temporality, narrative, recognition, identity, and legal discourses have constituted U.S. liberal settler colonialism, but they have also tended to capture indigeneity within the expected temporal assemblages of recovery, archive, authenticity, resistance, and performative enunciation of the speaking Native. Put another way, in the first instance the United States has juridically, socially, and politically figured indigenous peoples as disadvantaged children in need of U.S. white protestant tutelage to become, as Mark Rifkin might argue, "straight" at some yet unknown future moment; in the second instance, indigenous peoples are expected to serve as ventriloquist conduits to culture, nature, and progressive modes of sociality and sexuality that might then offer alternatives to a world in crisis in what Scott Morgensen has diagnosed as at least one form of "settler homonationalism."[13]

   In this vein, recent scholarship in Indigenous studies has begun to open up the colonially inflected relations among identity, kinship, erotics, sociality, recognition, sovereignty, and belonging, particularly as they arise within the context of the nation-state formations in which federally recognized tribes are interpellated as "domestic dependent nations." That enforced dependence, as well as the concomitant domesticity Chief Justice John Marshall's ruling connotes in its relational construction, has always borne the trace of sexuality and gender as wildness and savagery are civilized, abjected, or disavowed. Scholarship in the field continues to grapple with the consequences of such resonances. Desire—for legibility, for futurity, for intimacy, for authority, and for priority—raises questions about how vulnerability, embodiment, and erotics might challenge or transform assumptions about resistance and accommodation within U.S. colonial and racial regimes. For Rifkin, it is the possible reconfiguration of indigeneity *as* erotics that "takes the kinds of physicality, intersubjectivity, and vulnerability categorized and cordoned off as 'sexuality' within dominant discourses as a starting point for mapping both the ongoing management of Indigenous polities and the forms of collective perception and experience settler policy has sought to foreclose."[14] Such a sovereign erotics, Rifkin continues, reimagines "peoplehood and placemaking in ways that register the complex entwinement of unacknowledged survivals, unofficial aspirations, and the persistence of pain."[15] Coupling queer to desire and sexuality to erotic sovereignty, scholars have begun to chart a queer Indigenous theory of resistance that manifests with and against fetishizations of exceptional Indigenous difference.

As an emergent field in its own right, then, queer Indigenous studies has begun to stage difficult and important questions about the nature of identity and its discontents, posing quandaries about the possibilities and limits of the transformative politics of gender and sexuality especially where they intersect with race, transnationalism, and colonialism. As queer Indigenous studies begins to articulate some of the stakes for culturally and tribally inflected counter-practices of gender and sexuality, kinship, governance, and relationally, one of the remaining challenges for the field is to interrogate whether the queer in Indigenous studies is the same as the queer in queer studies. At first blush, it might be tempting to assume that the answer is self-evident, the question slightly coy. The question, however, might trouble some of the methodological, theoretical, and quotidian horizons that intersectionality and interdisciplinarity seek to make visible within the fields of Indigenous, gender, and sexuality studies. The queer within Indigenous studies has already come to signify a range of prescribed practices attached to decolonizing desire, gender performance, kinship socialities, and relationities to land and community.

On the flip side, queer has had a longer trajectory within critical theoretical conversations, although its meaning continues to expand, transcend, and escape expectations of causal subjectivity. According to Cathy J. Cohen, "Queer theory stands in direct contrast to the normalizing tendencies of hegemonic sexuality rooted in ideas of static, stable sexual identities and behaviors. In queer theorizing the sexual subject is understood to be constructed and contained by multiple practices of categorization and regulation that systematically marginalize and oppress those subjects thereby defined as deviant and 'other.' "[16] As queer theory has developed from its early iterations in performance studies in the 1990s, and especially in the context of queer-of-color interventions that mediated against normative whiteness and the respectability of certain subjects and not others, the field of inquiry has proliferated the sites of engagement. The definition of queer, David Eng, Jack Halberstam, and José Esteban Muñoz suggest, "can neither be decided on in advance nor be depended on in the future. The reinvention of the term is contingent on its potential obsolescence, one necessarily at odds with any fortification of its critical reach in advance or any static notion of its presumed audience and participant."[17] It is a word whose time has come and whose time is already past. Queer is an analytic, and it is one, as Sharon Holland observes, whose "methodology for thinking through the queer body can be cited along three registers: the psychoanalytic, the critique of global capital, and the biopolitical."[18]

At its best, queer theory interrogates the stakes of recognition, as well as the bargains embedded within identitarian-based politics that proclaim injury and demand redress from the state. The queer pushes against static and stable notions of identity and toward reinvention, often refusing and resisting the affective placations of liberalism that center rights and recognitions, structured through the historical violence of sexism, racism, and homophobia, as biopolitical reparations in the form of marriage, military service, health-care benefits, citizenship, and livability. That mode of reinvention, that refusal of a presumed audience and participant that Eng, Halberstam, and Muñoz hail, though, also presents us with a fundamentally incommensurable transitive figure within the theory, particularly as it intersects with the Indigenous. Suggesting that queer studies might better serve diasporic, queer-of-color, and Indigenous critique through an engagement with normalization as a field of social and historical forces, Eng, Halberstam and Muñoz offer subjectlessness as an epistemological denial that "disallows any positing of a proper subject *of* or object *for* the field by insisting that queer has no fixed political referent." Subjectless critique, in other words, "orients queer epistemology . . . as a continuous deconstruction of the tenets of positivism at the heart of identity politics."[19] In a similar vein, Judith Butler has suggested that queer studies entails, in part, an undoing by grief, rupture, and desire: "And so when we speak about *my* sexuality or *my* gender, as we do (and we must) we mean something complicated by it. Neither of these is precisely a possession, but both are to be understood as *modes of being dispossessed*, ways of being for another or, indeed, by virtue of another."[20] Each of these moves—subjectlessness and undoing, possession and dispossession—serves to orient the field of the queer toward the ethical, the being for the other, by challenging the possessive logics inherent in liberalism, subjectivity, and personhood.

Within queer Indigenous studies, questions of subjectlessness have taken a slightly different turn as some scholars in the field have suggested that the intersections of queer and Indigenous studies might enable alternative modes of identity formation against the identity politics of Indigenous communities, including enrollment, citizenship, and community recognition. Subjectlessness as an analytic also transforms the scale of inquiry for the field. As Andrea Smith suggests, "A subjectless critique can help Native studies (as well as ethnic studies) escape the ethnographic entrapment. A subjectless critique helps demonstrate that Native studies is an intellectual project that has broad applicability not only for Native peoples but for everyone."[21] Such orientations, which diverge from queer theory's notion of subjectlessness as a decentering of a cohesive and authoritative subject of inquiry, reify indigeneity into a practiced positionality produced at and through colonialism. Haunted by the land rushes of the late nineteenth century, Indigenous possessions, in Smith's formulation, are understood to be for everyone except Indians. Indigeneity itself becomes transient, unmoored, and appropriable in procedural narratives through which, as Jean M. O'Brien explicates, Native peoples "are made to disappear, sometimes through precise declarations that the 'last' of them has passed, and the colonial regime is constructed as the 'first' to bring 'civilization' and authentic history to the region. Non-Indians stake a claim to being Native—Indigenous—through this process."[22] O'Brien names this process "firsting and lasting," and it is the method through which Enlightenment liberalism formed its investments in possessive logics as the keys to personal autonomy, individualism, and freedom. White possession, Aileen Moreton-Robinson argues, operates at an ontological level in which "the structure of subjective possession occurs through the imposition of one's will-to-be on the thing which is perceived to lack will, thus it is open to being possessed. This enables the formally free subject to make the thing its own."[23]

Faced with the quandaries that the colonial, racial, gendered, and historical disjunctions of encounter, contact, and orientation have left us, what can desire and grief mean to the colonized if they signal, at their core, modes of dispossession, undoing, firsting, and lasting? What might the subjectlessness that Andrea Smith suggests as intervention to ethnographic entrapment offer queer Indigenous critique if it disallows anything fixed, grounded, located, or, most important, accountable to community, relationality, and connection? As a concept, indigeneity admittedly has had and has required a political referent that is tied to land, relation, and community, even if such referents are fluid and mutable. But at the same time, and as an ideological referent that is always up for grabs, indigeneity remains elusive, ontologically ephemeral, temporally challenged, and captured within the discourses of discovery, enlightenment, and sovereignty. Caught within modes of possession and its lack, Indigenous subjectlessness at the site of the queer simultaneously straddles the threshold between the colonialist practices of replacing the Indigenous, on the one hand, and emptying the Indigenous of any prior signification, on the other. In the grammars of empire where subject formation occurs through the Hegelian dialectics of freedom and enslavement, ownership and property, civilized and savage, sovereign and beast, the Indigenous might be understood as the domain or register in which the tensions between and among these antagonisms become sensible.

Indigeneity's challenge to settler colonial subjectivity and its loss, then, requires us to shift the frame slightly askew to apprehend how the processes of subjectivity—be they queer or normative—cohere, entangle, and unravel in relation to what Elizabeth Povinelli has identified as the *governance of the prior*. That governance, defined as "the priority of the prior person (or people) as a natural right of all persons and the people as such emerged as an impediment to the previous logics of kingly seizure and to the emergent logic of colonial governance," hinges on an unresolvable temporal paradox that produces the conditions of indigeneity as prior to and a priority of the law at the same time that the law abjects indigeneity from having any priority at all.[24]

Returning to a distinction within the conceptualization of subjectless critique may help parse some of these tensions that exist within and between the queer and the Indigenous that have made questions of subjectivity and its temporality so fraught. In *Imagine Otherwise*, Kandice Chuh advocates for the creation of subjectlessness as a way to "prioritize difference by foregrounding the discursive constructedness of subjectivity," where the subject "only becomes recognizable and can act as such by conforming to certain regulatory matrices."[25] I want to pry open this space of subjectivity, its regulatory matrices, and its queer refusals to posit that a prior presence, whether we name it Indigenous or something else, retains key transitive properties that enable and, in fact, are required to adhere relationality within the intimacies and violence of empire. According to Karen Elizabeth Gordon, transitive verbs "are those that *cannot* complete their meaning without the help of a direct object."[26] Like vampires, such verbs feed off an object to sustain, fulfill, and extend themselves in embodied orientations that require the object in order to exist. Such orientations, after Sara Ahmed, "are about the intimacy of bodies and their dwelling places"; they "allow us then to rethink the phenomenality of space—that is, how space is dependent on bodily inhabitance."[27] Caught in a transitive relationality with indigeneity, settlers cannot achieve their sovereign subjectivities and embodiments without the help of the Native as object to orient them. In other words, the discursive frameworks and "regulatory matrices" of the subject have already been formulated in response to the colonization of American Indians. Within the structuring elements of settler colonialism, subjectivity, claiming to be, and speaking for have gone hand in hand with the theft of lands, the politics of replacement, and the forced normativities of compulsory heterosexuality and lineal descent.

The fraught and contradictory desires for and against subjectivities embedded within the ontological orientations of empire are located within the diversity of experiences that have shaped such positionalities as settler, arrivant, and Native. These colonial contexts inform modern claims to Indigenous identity within the racial regimes of U.S. neoliberal multiculturalism and intersect with those queer politics that disrupt static, essential, and normalized privileges of race, class, and gender, on the one hand, and Indigenous identities that are tied to community recognition, sovereignty, and land, on the other. How might desire—which, as Holland has argued, is imbricated within quotidian racist practices—function to reproduce the logics of dispossession at the site of reinvention and becoming for the other? The U.S. Supreme Court, building on an interlocking foundation of precedence for its juridical authority, issued four rulings in June 2013 that hinged on equal protection to arbitrate the triad of sexuality, race, and indigeneity. In the process of maintaining white normativity within heterosexual—and now, by extension, same-sex—family units, the court inveighed on Indigenous identity, fearing the possibility of a remote Indian ancestor to be a disability hampering a child's full incorporation into the rights due her as a transracial Indian-into-white subject. That fear not only demonstrates the degree to which the legal normativities of embodied ability depend on racializing and colonizing logics to produce the righted subject, but also highlights the transitive form through which the law interpellates indigeneity as difference and recourse. But how did indigeneity become transitive within the regulative fictions of rights and liberties? That answer might be found within the racial integrity acts of the nineteenth and twentieth centuries that the *Loving v. Virginia* landmark ruling in 1967 purportedly overturned. By framing these concerns at a slight slant, it is my hope that we might be able to begin to apprehend how desire and identity function within the context of an ongoing colonialism that adjudicates inclusion and exclusion through a transitive relationality that requires the Native other to make visible the biopolitical structures of race, sexuality, gender, and sovereignty.

Spacers between Us

In his short story "Aye, and Gomorrah " (1967), African American science fiction author Samuel R. Delany attends to the queer terrains of desire and colonialism by constructing a futuristic world traversed by "come downs" and "went ups"—the story's slang for shore leave on Earth and the return to space—where spacers, astronauts who have been neutered at puberty, and the frelks obsessed with them mark the longing abjections of transgressive fetish at the edges of Earth-bound normativity and exchange values. Caught in the Hegelian master-slave dialectics of desire, disgust, and need, the first-person narrator of the story is a spacer taunted by possibilities that are forever teased and frustrated. Over the course of the story, the nameless narrator maneuvers an intricate and dangerous world of coded come-ons and hustles in a lurid cruise for a frelk encounter amid the homosexual and heterosexual pairings of human desire. And "frelk," to be clear, is a derogatory term that spacers use for those people, male and female, straight and gay, on Earth who have a "free-fall-sexual-displacement complex" that manifests as mad love for the spacers.[28] It is not erotic desire that the spacer-frelk intimacy charts but, rather, its displacement and deferral into the silences and ellipses of space. As the story progresses, the reader learns that spacers, in this sci-fi world Delany creates, represent the failure of identification and gender. They are the absence of desire as they are simultaneously a desire surplus that is evident in key moments throughout the story. " 'You look as though you might have once been a man,' " a blond young man tells the narrator. " 'But now . . .' He smiled. 'You have nothing for me now.' " From the man, the spacer learns that in French, *frelk* is a feminine noun, and that the spacer would need to look elsewhere to find fulfillment (91). A page later, and during another come down in Mexico, the narrator grabs the wrist of a Mexican woman and whispers, *"Usted es una frelka?"* She smiles and responds, *"Frelko en español.* . . . Sorry. But you have nothing that . . . would be useful to me. It is too bad, for you look like you were once a woman, no? And I like women, too'" (92). Delany queers the naturalization of desire and in so doing relocates the queer at the intersection of the self-same and its abjective refusal.

In many ways, the story is Delany's reflection on the plasticity of the body; the genocidal constraints enacted through normativities and their trans; the aberrations of embodied race, class, ability, and gender; and the resilience of bodies to enact resistance and survival. Desire itself is not biological, and sexuality is socially constructed through the enunciative force of the law of the father that announces its presence at the level of grammar to interpellate gender norms that have now been denied a biological determiner. Toward that end, Delany imagines a world delineated through exceptions, perversions, disruptions, and surveillances, and the narrative slowly reveals spacers to be government employees surgically engineered to work in the precarious conditions of interplanetary exploration and development. Spending all their time in deep space, on Mars, on the moon, or on the satellites of Jupiter, with only occasional Earthside shore leave to drink and reenter the gravitational pull of capital and human contact, spacers are exposed to dangerous levels of radiation that would guarantee that their offspring would be, were they not already rendered impossible, deformed. Instantly recognized by the inhabitants of Earth for the work they perform—and the material conditions that enable it that have been written onto their de-sexed bodies and into their blue uniforms—spacers were "altered" as children because they were identified as having sexual responses that were "hopelessly retarded at puberty" (97). In this futuristic world, they, rather than gays and lesbians, are the strangers with no future. In many ways, the title itself, with its affirmative "Aye" in the place of Sodom, signals the story's concern with the ethics of alterity as it anticipates the liberal investments of homonationalism from the historical context of the Civil Rights Movement of the late 1960s.

In their constant movement, the spacers are always in transit between here and there, and the frelks who worship them are, according to a woman the spacer meets in Istanbul, perverted necrophiliacs "in love with a bunch of corpses in free fall!" (97). As abjected sexuality, the spacers produce in their physical neutering and undoing a casting off, an antimony of desire for those earthbound people who have developed a deep and abiding attachment to the deferral of sexual possibility the spacers have been constructed to perform.

Frelks worship spacers because spacers cannot want them back. And the spacers hustle frelks for money in exchange for proximity and access. "Aye, and Gomorrah" is, ultimately, a meditation on the psychic reproduction of desire that proliferates the queer in the face of norms outside the embodied mechanics of sexuality and within the material exchanges of labor, capital, and exploration. The core of the text ponders a central conundrum of the production of desire. "If spacers had never been, then we could not be . . . the way we are," a frelk observes as she reflects on her need for the narrator (96). In the invention of frelks as a response to spacers, future queerings prolifer-ate and function in the story as rumor and anecdote: "Say, last time I was in Istanbul—about a year before I joined with this platoon—I remember we were coming out of Taksim Square down Istiqlal. Just past all the cheap movies we found a little passage lined with flowers. . . . Anyway, we noticed something funny about the spacers. It wasn't their uniforms: they were per-fect. The haircuts: fine. It wasn't til we heard them talking—they were a man and woman dressed up like spacers, trying *to pick up frelks!* Imagine, queer for frelks!" (93).

The possibility of queer for frelks occurs at the site of passing, mimicry, and ventriloquism and in the face of the repudiation of the ways the spac-ers' undone gender has been conscripted into their bodies. Frelks, the reader learns, are experts on spacers, and their fetish manifests in the Orientalist mode of knowledge production and in the desire to finally and fully become that which they desire so that they can then desire themselves.

Delany's ten-paged story might be said to function as a parable of differ-ence produced and desired within the historiography of embodied racial and colonial normativities that interpellate and police aberrations through heterosexuality and the expression of fulfillable desires. Circulating at the transnational borders between the United States and Mexico and within the terrorist assemblages of Istanbul and Muslim countries where it is difficult for spacers to find and consume alcohol, Delany's story delves into the fractures of race and empire as they collide with sexuality and the state. Along with an-ticipating the self-identifications that enable queer transgressions, Delany's 1967 story signals something incredibly profound about liberal investments with progress and rights as they play out in the heart of colonialism. Gays and lesbians in the story are fully accepted in this world: the police do not bother them, although they might, it is implied, bother spacers because they are now the strangers, the shadows cast beyond gay incorporation who may one day also achieve full equality and subjectivity. The clandestine meetings between spacers and frelks enable the deferred rights for gays and lesbians by fulfilling the exception that demarcates the thresholds of equality. And it is all done through evocations of Indianness and disability—Delaney's narrator, we finally learn, was an "American red Indian" boy before he was captured and altered at puberty (95).

The presence of the Indian, evoked here by Delany in the future as both "hopelessly retarded at puberty" and forever excluded from the futurity of reproduction, is not chance; nor is it an isolated event. The Kid in his novel *Dhalgren* (1975) is Cherokee and white although many authors often assume other identifications for the character in their readings of the racial politics of the text. In "Aye, and Gomorrah," Delany's evocation of Indian identity at the site of the impermanence of gender, sexuality, ability, embodiment, and desire bears something of that register or domain function that I discussed earlier. Precisely because of Indianness, the nameless spacer embodies the logics of desire that the short story constellates within the biopolitical structures of racial capitalism. Forced into abject labor and bodily transformed in the process, Delany's "American red Indian" spacer charts an erotic life of colonialism that desires desire for the other as a redemptive politic. The story, however, frustrates any positive outcome for such an erotic exchange, and the only ones fulfilled within the story are the frelks themselves when they pose as spacers to seduce other frelks. The presence of the Indian in the story serves a transitive function and reorients desire and erotics, race and nationality, ability and disability, within the larger historical and normative implications of empire and colonialism. The "American red Indian," dis/figured as exceptional other foreclosed within the circuits of intimacy, renders sensible the allegory of the story and in the process reveals something profound about not only the function of desire within the context of ongoing colonialist violence, but also the function of identification that requires the Indian as a mode of refraction to perceive the self.

Queer for Frelks

"Aye, and Gomorrah," was first published in December 1967, before the Stonewall Riots of 1969, and the story's inquiries into how desire and normativities traffic through elision and occlusion were informed by and through the material conditions of the Civil Rights Movement that culminated in the Supreme Court's ruling in *Loving v. Virginia* (1967). That case, as I have discussed, gained notoriety as a watershed moment especially within the gay marriage rights movement, where it continues to serve as precedent because it purportedly promises state recognition of marriage equality for all those who historically have been, and who continued to be, excluded from the institution. The racial and miscegenation analogies of the case continue to inflect homonormative claims to equal protection, civil rights, and marriage equality, and such analogies reify the trajectories of race into recognizable mnemonics of black-white oppositions that align the neoliberal projects of institutionalized multiculturalism around questions of inclusion, participation, and equality.

The details of the case at this point have been codified into a particular narrative that may be familiar. In June 1958, Mildred Jeter, a Black woman with Amerindian ancestry, married Richard Loving, a white man, in the District of Columbia. Not long after the wedding, the newlyweds returned to Virginia and their community in Caroline County. In 1924, the State of Virginia had passed an Act to Preserve Racial Integrity, which required citizens to file a registration certifying his or her racial composition "as Caucasian, negro, Mongolian, American Indian, Asiatic Indian, Malay, or any mixture thereof." Further, if any racial admixture was discernible, the registrant had to "show in what generation such mixture occurred." That act made falsifying a registration a felony punishable by up to one year in jail and outlawed any marriage between a white person and a person of color.

In October 1958, the Lovings were indicted for violating sections of the Virginia Code that made it illegal to leave the state to evade the law and included punishments for interracial marriage. In January 1959, they pled guilty to the charges and were sentenced to one year in jail. That sentence was suspended for twenty-five years, with the stipulation that the Lovings leave the state and never return. The case reached the Supreme Court after a series of hearings that took the issue from a class action suit the Lovings had filed in the U.S. District Court for the Eastern District of Virginia to the Supreme Court of Appeals of Virginia. Arguing that the antimiscegenation statutes were unconstitutional, the Lovings filed motions to vacate the original judgment under the grounds that Virginia's Racial Integrity Act violated the Fourteenth Amendment including due process and equal protection. After having the racial integrity statutes upheld in the lower courts, Chief Justice Warren, in a landmark opinion of the Supreme Court, delivered that "marriage is one of the 'basic civil rights of man,' fundamental to our very existence and survival. . . . To deny this fundamental freedom on so unsupportable a basis as the racial classifications embodied in these statutes, classifications so directly subversive of the principle of equality at the heart of the Fourteenth Amendment, is surely to deprive all the State's citizens of liberty without due process of law."[29]

Loving v. Virginia, according to Somerville, was inflected at the time by the debates within the court not just about race but also about homosexuality, and the expansion of marriage rights the case instituted "effectively consolidated heterosexuality as a privileged prerequisite for recognition by the state as a national subject and citizen. An alternative lesson of *Loving*, in fact, is that 'free men' may be identified by any race, but their entitlement to that claim is based on their presumed heterosexuality."[30] Reddy has additionally linked the *Loving v. Virginia* case to a number of court cases that grappled with interracial marriage and immigrant rights, assessing that "perhaps we can read in the desire to further extend marriage as a right the preservation of a modern feeling of personhood founded in racial typology."[31] Citing prior cases including *Pace v. Alabama* (1883), *Perez v. Sharp* (1948), *Naim v. Naim* (1955), and *McLaughlin v. Florida* (1964), as well as *Boutilier v. Immigration Service* (1967), Somerville and Reddy compellingly argue for a reframing of the *Loving* case through the larger state investments in racial liberalism, xenophobia, and normative strictures of citizenship.

As queer theorists grapple with the transnational implications of gay marriage in light of the deeply engrained histories of racism, on the one hand, and the implications of racial typologies of diasporic transnationalism, on the other, the larger frame of U.S. colonialism embedded in Virginia's original "racial integrity" is often overlooked within ongoing considerations of the intersectionality of race, sexuality, and civil rights. Part of the work the *Loving v. Virginia* case accomplished was to instantiate particular narratives about race within the United States, and, as Arica L. Coleman explains, "[The] lawyers Bernard Cohen and Philip J. Hirschkop's representation of the case as overturning the last of the odious laws of slavery and segregation once again reified the racial dichotomy of White and Black within American racial discourse. Consequently, the arguments presented before the court and later the majority opinion obscured racial issues beyond the Black-White boundary, namely the Afro-Indian identity of Mildred Loving."[32] The effects of such elisions are multiple and likely expected, including the typical narrative that American Indians are vanished within the binaries of race deployed during segregation that eclipsed colonialism in emphasizing racial antagonisms. Coleman's argument, however, suggests an alternative reading that situates *Loving v. Virginia* within a series of cases such as *Atha Sorrells v. A. T. Shields* (1925) that challenged white supremacist investments in eugenicist language to pry apart the racial distinctions of African American and American Indian identities at a moment when the State of Virginia had a vested interest in collapsing both into the category of "colored."

In evoking the "American red Indian" as "retardation," dislocation, and the failure of desire, Delany's "Aye, and Gomorrah" wrestles multidirectionally with the colonial logics that underwrite the racial politics of Jim Crow and liberal multiculturalism embedded in *Loving v. Virginia* and the Racial Integrity Act that necessitated the ruling as it draws the transitive logics of Indianness into the terrains of queer identities and desires that refuse static notions of bodies, biology, erotics, and even racial positionality.[33] Not only did Virginia's "Racial Integrity" occlude Mildred Loving's Cherokee and Rappahannock ancestry by rendering her intelligible in the archive as African American, it ensured that Indianness was reserved solely for whiteness. As Virginia's white supremacist "first families" sought to codify racial exclusions into law, they faced the racial complexity of their own, faux or factual, New World origin story that called into question their integrity through a claim of descent through Thomas Rolfe, son of John Rolfe and Pocahontas. Their solution was to implement the so-called Pocahontas Exception to preserve their whiteness through a claim to a hyperdescent Indianness: "It shall hereafter be unlawful for any white person in this State to marry any save a white person, or a person with no other admixture of blood than white and American Indian. For the purpose of this act, the term 'white person' shall apply only to the person who has no trace whatsoever of any blood other than Caucasian; but persons who have one-sixteenth or less the blood of the American Indian and have no other non-Caucasic blood shall be deemed to be white persons."[34]

This exception, according to Kevin Maillard, "regulate[s] Indians to existence only in a distant past, creating a temporal disjuncture to free Indians from a contemporary discourse of racial politics."[35] Arguing that "such exemptions assess Indians as abstractions rather than practicalities, or as fictive temporalities characterized by romantic ideals," Maillard highlights how Indianness is essentialized while simultaneously rendered an inconsequential ethnicity within the racial topographies of U.S. liberal multiculturalism in which many now claim an Indian great-great-grandmother.[36] For Coleman, however, the Pocahontas Exception retained an added alchemical function within Virginia's racializing regimes, and it helped cohere American Indian investments in blood purity that allow only white and Indian admixture and refuse any possible African American ancestry for tribes still residing in the Commonwealth. As Coleman observes, "Mildred's Indian identity as inscribed on her marriage certificate and her marriage to Richard, a White man, appears to have been more an endorsement of the tenets of racial purity rather than a validation of White/Black intermarriage as many have supposed."[37] Mildred Jeter, in other words, may have used the Pocahontas Exception to assert an Indian identity to achieve whiteness through the logics of miscegenation that would have disallowed her marriage to a white man if she had, in fact, understood her own identity to be African American *and* Rappahannock and Cherokee.

Rather than fulfilling the logic of elimination that Patrick Wolfe portrays as the organizing task of settler colonialism whereby settler colonialism "destroys to replace," the Pocahontas exception manages to proliferate the Indigenous within the prior terrains of antecedent and forebear as whiteness comes to depend on a recidivist nativism that reproduces itself at the site of a self-same Indianness.[38] It creates, in other words, a transitive relationality that, like the queer-for-frelk that Delany's story imagines, assumes an Orientalist mien of Indianness to pick up whiteness. Such transracial transformations do not transgress colonialism so much as they enable colonialism through usurpation, and although the queer remains always contingent and provisional as a planned obsolescence or a radical undoing, it seems worth interrogating further how the colonization of American Indians encodes itself into the technologies and imaginaries used to constitute subjects, rights, desires, and recognitions, especially where they emerge in service to maintaining the continued colonial privileges of normativity and whiteness.

By the time the U.S. Supreme Court delivered its opinions in the quartet of cases at the end of June 2013, the presence of the *Adoptive Couple v. Baby Girl* case alongside cases adjudicating voting rights and marriage rights signals a simultaneity that matters beyond the "pink-washing" performances of settler nation-states. And questions of transitive Indianness are hardly settled as the Supreme Court determined the possibility that the presence of an Indian ancestor—even a remote one—might in fact now prove a disability to the full achievement of whiteness for a baby girl in transition. As Justice Sonia Sotomayor observed in her dissent, "The majority's repeated, analytically unnecessary references to the fact that Baby Girl is 3/256 Cherokee by ancestry do nothing to elucidate its intimation that the statute may violate the Equal Protection Clause. . . . The majority's treatment of this issue, in the end, does no more than create a lingering mood of disapprobation of the criteria for membership adopted by the Cherokee Nation, that in turn, make Baby Girl and 'Indian Child' under the statute."[39] Indian identity continues to be the register through which possessive subjectivities construct and deconstruct themselves within the context of ongoing colonialism. Within such erotic terrains, desire for indigeneity manifests as a quotidian struggle to maintain whiteness as hegemonic possession, and there can be no decolonization until such transitive logics are disrupted, refused, and failed. The queer in Indigenous studies, then, challenges the queer of queer studies by offering not an identity or a figure necessarily, but rather an analytic that helps us relocate subjectivity and its refusals back into the vectors of ongoing settler colonialism.

NOTES

Epigraphs: Samuel R. Delany, "Aye, and Gomorrah" (1967), in *Off Limits: Tales of Alien Sex*, ed. by Ellen Datlow (New York: St. Martin's Press, 1996), 226; Sharon Patricia Holland, *The Erotic Life of Racism* (Durham, NC: Duke University Press, 2012).

1. Jodi Melamed, *Represent and Destroy: Rationalizing Violence in the New Racial Capitalism* (Minneapolis: University of Minnesota Press, 2011), xiii.

2. *Adoptive Couple v. Baby Girl*, 570 U.S. (2013), 16.

3. Lisa Duggan, *Twilight of Equality: Neoliberalism, Cultural Politics, and the Attack on Democracy* (Boston: Beacon Press, 2003), 50.

4. "Queer Year in Review 2013: DOMA, Transgender Victories and More," February December 20, 2013, http://www.huffingtonpost.com/2013/12/20/gay-year-in-review_n_4482440.html.

5. *United States v. Windsor*, 570 U.S. (2013), 3–4.

6. *United States v. Windsor*, 3.

7. *United States v. Windsor*, 4.

8. Siobhan B. Somerville, "Queer *Loving*," GLQ 11, no. 3 (2005): 335.

9. For more discussions on how racial analogies function within same-sex marriage debates, see Somerville, "Queer *Loving*"; Catherine Smith, "Queer as Black Folk?" *Wisconsin Law Review* 2 (2007): 379–407; Chandan Reddy, "Time for Rights? *Loving*, Gay Marriage, and the Limits of Legal Justice," *Fordham Law Review* 76, no. 6 (2008): 2849–72; Adele M. Morrison, "Black v. Gay? Centering LBGT People of Color in Civil-Marriage Debates," in *Loving v. Virginia in a Post-Racial World: Rethinking Race, Sex, and Marriage*, ed. Kevin Noble Maillard and Rose Cuison Villazor (Cambridge: Cambridge University Press, 2012), 235–41.

10. Somerville, "Queer *Loving*," 335.

11. Reddy, "Time for Rights?," 76.

12. Chandan Reddy, *Freedom with Violence: Race, Sexuality, and the U.S. State* (Durham, NC: Duke University Press, 2011), 62.

13. Mark Rifkin, *When Did Indians Become Straight? Kinship, the History of Sexuality, and Native Sovereignty* (New York: Oxford University Press, 2011), 8.

14. Mark Rifkin, *The Erotics of Sovereignty: Queer Native Writing in the Era of Self-Determination* (Minneapolis: University of Minnesota Press, 2012), 28–29.

15. Rifkin, *The Erotics of Sovereignty*, 31.

16. Cathy J. Cohen, "Punks, Bulldaggers, and Welfare Queens: The Radical Potential of Queer Politics?," GLQ 3, no. 4 (1997): 438–39.

17. David Eng, Judith Halberstam, and José Esteban Muñoz, "What's Queer about Queer Studies Now?," *Social Text* 84–85, vol. 23, nos. 3–4 (Fall–Winter 2005).

18. Holland, *The Erotic Life of Racism*, 13.

19. Eng et al., "What's Queer about Queer Studies Now?," *Social Text* 84–85, vol. 23, nos. 3–4 (Fall–Winter 2005).

20. Judith Butler, *Undoing Gender* (New York: Routledge, 2004), 19.

21. Andrea Smith, "Queer Theory and Native Studies: The Heteronormativity of Settler Colonialism," GLQ 16, nos. 1–2 (2010): 44.

22. Jean M. O'Brien, *Firsting and Lasting: Writing Indians out of Existence in New England* (Minneapolis: University of Minnesota Press, 2010), xv.

23. Aileen Moreton-Robinson, "White Possession: The Legacy of Cook's Choice," in *Imagined Australia: Reflections around the Reciprocal Construction of Identity between Australia and Europe*, ed. Renata Summo-O'Connell (Bern, Switzerland: Peter Lang, 2009), 31–32.

24. Elizabeth Povinelli, "The Governance of the Prior," *Interventions* 13, no. 1 (2011): 17.

25. Kandice Chuh, *Imagine Otherwise: On Asian Americanist Critique* (Durham, NC: Duke University Press, 2003), 9.

26. Karen Elizabeth Gordon, *The Deluxe Transitive Vampire: The Ultimate Handbook of Grammar for the Innocent, The Eager, and the Doomed* (New York: Pantheon, 1993), 42.

27. Sara Ahmed, *Queer Phenomenology: Orientations, Objects, Others* (Durham, NC: Duke University Press, 2006), 6, 8.

28. Delany, "Aye, and Gomorrah," 98. (Hereafter, page numbers for direct quotes from this work are cited in parentheses in the text.)

29. *Loving v. Virginia* 388 U.S. 1 (1967).

30. Somerville, "Queer *Loving*," 357.

31. Reddy, *Freedom with Violence*, 209.

32. Arica L. Coleman, *That the Blood Stay Pure: African Americans, Native Americans, and the Predicament of Race and Identity in Virginia* (Bloomington: University of Indiana Press, 2013), 152.

33. I deploy the idea of multidirectional here after Michael Rothberg, *Multidirectional Memory: Remembering the Holocaust in the Age of Decolonization* (Stanford, CA: Stanford University Press, 2009).

34. Racial Integrity Act of 1924, Virginia, SB 219, HB 311 https://lva.omeka.net/items/show/128.

35. Kevin Noble Maillard, "The Pocahontas Exception: The Exemption of American Indian Ancestry from Racial Purity Law," *Michigan Journal of Race and Law* 12, no. 351 (2006–2007): 357.

36. Maillard, "The Pocahontas Exception."

37. Coleman, *That the Blood Stay Pure*, 175.

38. Patrick Wolfe, "Settler Colonialism and the Elimination of the Native," *Journal of Genocide Research* 8, no. 4 (2006): 387–409.

39. *Adoptive Couple v. Baby Girl*, Sotomayor, dissenting opinion, 24.

7

GETTING DIRTY

The Eco-Eroticism of Women in Indigenous Oral Literatures

MELISSA K. NELSON

Physical bodies can beckon us toward a more complex understanding of how the personal, the political, and the material are braided together.—**Stacy Alaimo**, *Material Feminisms*

We do not come into this world; we come out of it, as leaves from a tree.—**Alan Watts**, *The Book*

Prelude

Some of my first memories are of eating dirt. Eating dirt with great joy. I felt an intimate, sensuous, and, dare I say, "erotic" relationship with the physical earth I consumed.[1] Red rock on red tongue, slick, earth clay slowly sliding down my throat, the tart tingle of metallic gravity and the delicious irony of iron resonating with the core of my blood cells, like a lightning bolt to my flesh and bones. Ingesting the world, "eating the landscape," and enjoying the original "soil/soul food" is a long and old tradition of many cultures around the world, including many Native American cultures here on Turtle Island, especially among women with eco-erotic proclivities.[2]

I also remember relishing as a child the curves on a piece of driftwood and even later and now feeling wooed by the smell and shape of buckeye blossoms; getting aroused by the splash of ocean waves on granite rock, stirred by the flying movements of a pileated woodpecker, intoxicated by the incessant power of a waterfall, caressed by the warm wind on top of a desert mountain, or feeling a little sleazy by the penetrating clarity, color, and twinkle of the star Sirius. All of these things arouse deep feelings in me still. They stimulate my senses and awaken a desire to be intimate, to be fully alive. These eco-erotic moments make me feel connected to something outside and distant yet connected to my human skin. They remind me that I am a semipermeable membrane and that life is filled with fluid attractions and intimate encounters, if we only allow ourselves to feel and experience them.

In the face of such sensuous ecological encounters, both ordinary and spectacular, I step outside the sense of myself as a contained being. I am no longer a solid center but part of an unending field of entwined energies. I am connecting to another, greater life force, embodied in dirt, the material soil and source of matter. Whether watching a simple brown sparrow bathing in a mud puddle on a street or smelling the aromatic heat off a sage plant, these encounters stimulate, arouse, awaken, and excite me in profoundly meaningful ways. They can break my heart open, take my breath away, make me shed tears, or force me to listen with the ears of my ancestors. In these moments, I often feel dwarfed, in awe, vulnerable, even shocked. And in the act of sex, I feel these same emotions—these vulnerable feelings combined with a strange sense of authentic, surging power.

The French call orgasm la petite mort (the little death), where we can actually be relieved of being ourselves and disappear for an ecstatic moment. The Sanskrit root meaning of the word "nirvana" means "extinction, disappearance (of the individual soul into the universal)."[3] It is in these moments of disappearing and ego extinction in the sexual act that most of us find solace and bliss. This relief from our persona helps us get in touch with a deeper sense of being—some would say, a larger sense of self; an ecological or even a cosmological self.

Likewise, eco-erotics is a type of meta (after, higher)-sexual or trans (over, beyond)-sexual intimate ecological encounter in which we are momentarily and simultaneously taken outside of ourselves by the beauty, or sometimes the horror, of the more-than-human natural world. This means we are potentially aroused by anything, meaning "pan," or all: pansexual. The Anishinaabe writer Louise Erdrich says it so well in *Love Medicine*: "I'll be out there as a piece of endless body of the world feeling pleasures so much larger than skin and bones and blood."[4]

Feeling inside this fluid, living entity of what we call "nature" does have its consequences, as my sensuality often gets in the way of my scholarship. But then again, my scholarship often gets in the way of my sensuality. It is a common conundrum, feeling the difference between the world of thought and the world of my other senses. Do I read through that wetlands ecology essay or that classic piece on Zen Buddhism, or do I work with my hands in the garden repotting lupine and sage and revel in the smell of sweet-smelling medicine plants and fresh dirt? Do I sit and pull black-and-white words from full-spectrum thoughts or walk in a damp redwood forest to feel like a small mammal? There is a profound relationship between these different activities. As I stimulate many senses and decenter thought, I eventually illuminate new cognitive pathways and storylines. I enjoy the challenge of precipitating words from inner imaginings (and sensations) and offering them to the page to share with others for enticement, arousal, and critique: "The writing down of words is a relatively recent practice for the human animal. We two-legged have long been creatures of language, of course, but verbal language lived first in the shaped breath of utterance, it laughed and stuttered on the tongue long before it lay down on the page, and longer still before it arrayed itself in rows across the glowing screen."[5] Language used to be more like music, perhaps, spoken and heard in ephemeral moments rather than recorded as "permanent," future visual references. Here I make these offerings of written words as I grapple with the old stories of Native women loving other-than-humans and the new fields of Indigenous eco-erotics and queer ecologies.

Introduction

In some vocabularies, these encounters would be intersections where emotional and erotic intelligences, biophilia, and eco-literacy come together.[6] These are encounters anyone can have anywhere on the planet; this is one of the reasons people love to travel so much, especially for "peak experiences" at spectacular places. I believe that these fresh, often ahistorical moments of superficial arousal or stimulation are important and interesting but potentially problematic. I see that they can be linked to colonial desire and exotic romanticism in a way that is nearly *opposite* of what I want to explore in terms of stories about Indigenous peoples' long-term, ancestral connections to specific places and particular more-than-human others.

The feminist scholar Stacy Alaimo writes, "Crucial ethical and political possibilities emerge from this literal 'contact zone' between human corporeality and more than human nature."[7] In this chapter, I argue that these encounters at the contact zone of human and more-than-human can provide critical eco-erotic experiences that are conducive to embodying an ethic of kinship so needed in the world today to address ecological and cultural challenges. This "contact zone" is the place that I call "getting dirty"—a messy, visceral, eco-erotic boundary-crossing entanglement of difference that can engender empathy and kinship and a lived environmental ethic. I assert that this contact zone is facilitated and supported by communities that practice oral traditions about territorial attachment to ancestral places and beings. Indigenous eco-erotics are maintained and strengthened through pansexual stories, clan and family identification, and a trans-human concept of nationhood.

I suggest that this eco-erotic impulse is deeply human and part of a co-evolutionary pansexual adaptation not only for survival but also for regeneration. For survival it is key, as it encourages us to understand "carnal knowledge" and the risks and opportunities of intraspecies encounters for mates and interspecies encounters for sustainable food. For regeneration, procreation is key not only for our biological species but also for our imaginative and spiritual capacities to be in intimate relationship with the more-than-human world, on which we are completely dependent for life. We are always inside other beings and inside what the Kogi Mamas of Colombia believe is "the very mind of Nature itself."[8] Other beings are always inside of us—bacteria, viruses. That is basic biology. But to truly feel the sensuous gravity of the life that surrounds us and is within us is an act of profound intimacy, vulnerability, and courage.

Being alive means that in every moment we are involved in the interpenetration of air, water, food, sound, smell, taste, and sight. Humans are completely dependent on these numerous natural processes to give us life, and Indigenous peoples of the Americas tell many stories that describe these intimate encounters with natural phenomenon and other-than-human persons: "Such narratives depict humans, animals, and other nonhuman beings engaged in an astonishing variety of activities and committed to mutually sustaining relationships that ensure the continuing well-being of the world."[9] These stories offer teachings about reciprocity, belonging, communal connections, and essential kinship bonds.

Tragically, these beautiful stories of embodied connection have been demonized and silenced by patriarchal, colonial, and Judeo-Christian ideologies, and these rich eco-erotic experiences have been suppressed and, in many cases, extinguished. The history of colonial and sexual violence against Native peoples and the imperial imperative of severing First Peoples' relations with land have had severe intergenerational consequences for the health of Native peoples and for the "well-being of the world." It could also be said that this profound historical disruption of human-environment relations has led to the ecological and social crises we face today.

I am committed to remembering these stories of relationship and re-awakening and embodying the metaphysics and praxis of Indigenous eco-erotics. I believe it is our human birthright and, as Native people, we have an additional responsibility to decolonize and reignite the spark of these ancestral relations. According to Anishinaabeg prophecy, we are people of the seventh fire (generation) since the time before colonial impact, and we have a cultural obligation to restore our traditional knowledge and sacred ways, not only for ourselves, but also ultimately for all peoples and life. For me as an educator, that translates into seeing how these Indigenous oral stories and the ethical insights they share about human–more-than-human relations can be productively and creatively applied in academia and social movements and, specifically, in addressing the dire need to mend the human split with our sacred Earth.

Out of the Tipi: A Collective Resurgence of Indigenous Erotica

Today the topics of nature, sexuality, and Indigeneity are converging in some very exciting and novel ways and are showing up in academia, popular media, environmental movements, and arts circles. Eco-erotics. Pansexuality. Erotic ecology. Ecofeminism. Queer ecology. Ecosexual. Eco-porn. SexEcology. Queer Indigenous. Sovereign erotic. Erotics of place. Indigenous erotica. The convergence of ecology and sexuality studies may seem like a spurious connection to some. For decades, the two fields have not been analyzed or theorized together except in the simplest Darwinian sense (i.e., notions of evolutionary sexual selection). To many of us, however, it is an obvious and fertile overlap. Nature is sex, sex is nature, and *we* are nature. Add Indigenous studies to the mix and you have a potent and possibly "dirty" fusion of theories and methods. The explicit subject of Indigenous eco-erotics is still on the fringe in academia (and in Native communities); yet the actual *practice* of it is very old and very common, just more tacit and often hidden or silenced due to centuries of colonial oppression.

As Joanne Barker's introduction outlines, this silence is being broke with a plethora of new publications in the area of Native sexualities, with titles such as *Queer Indigenous Studies, Sovereign Erotic,* and *Me Sexy.*[10] These radical, recent texts have opened up profound questions and discussions about previously transgressive subjects in fresh, insightful, and humorous ways. They are a reanimation of the erotic intelligence embedded (and mostly dormant) within Native worldviews, oral literatures, and practices. As Drew Hayden Taylor shares in *Me Sexy,* "Since that fabled age known as Time Immemorial, we, the First Nations people of this country, have all been intimately familiar with our delightful practices of passion, but for reasons unknown, members of the dominant culture have other perceptions about said topics."[11] From the same great text, the Cree writer Tomson Highway provides a "reason" for these other perceptions of Indigenous erotica. Highway claims that it is the Christian myth of the Garden of Eden, with its emphasis on human "eviction from the garden," that disconnects some Eurocentric cultures from the human body and nature: "At that moment, the human body became a thing of evil, and nature became an enemy."[12] Highway claims that under this myth, humans and the English language became disembodied, or only located in the head. Native myths and languages, however, do not cut humans off from nature and our bodily functions. In fact, they celebrate our fun and funny body parts and honor human sexuality as a sacred process. The very notion of "original sin" injects profound notions of shame into one's relationship with bodies and sexualities. This religious teaching, although one of many Christian myths and interpretations, was repeatedly and often zealously promulgated in American Indian boarding schools; thus, the critical emphasis on healing from it for many Native peoples today.[13] Other Native scholars, such as Kim TallBear, are examining how "both 'sex' and 'nature' and their politics are at the heart of narratives and strategies used to colonize Indigenous peoples."[14] TallBear and I share an interest in "greening" Indigenous queer theory and investigating how Indigenous stories portray social relations with nonhumans.

I am a Native ecologist, and I am deeply interested in the interrelationships and theoretical synergy among ecology, sex, and Native cultures—or, put more academically, among the fields of ecology, sexuality studies, and Indigenous studies. I am interested in what an Indigenous environmental sexuality study would look like. I may be presumptuous or horribly naive to think that a "Native eco-erotics for dummies" manual could lead to a more sustainable future for all life. What if every human being—or, at least, a lot more than at present—could awaken to their pansexual nature, to the fact that we are living animals in sensuous interaction with the material fabric of life that provides us with everything we need to survive? The evolutionary biologist Stephen Jay Gould claimed, "We cannot win this battle to save species and environments without forging an emotional bond between ourselves and nature—for we will not fight to save what we do not love."[15]

Walking barefoot on the earth; drinking a cold glass of water; eating a fresh summer peach; breathing in warm air—these basic, often unconscious daily acts are not in fact mundane but are sublime and sensuous eco-erotic connections to the more-than-human world. If we truly felt this, in our guts, in our cells, would we continue to poison our soils and water? Mine our mountains? Genetically alter our seeds? I think not. The metaphysics of eco-erotics teaches us that we are related to everything through a visceral kinship and that our cosmo-genealogical connections to all life demand that we treat our relatives with great reverence and appreciation.[16]

This topic is also important because it is an essential part of the decolonization process. Decolonizing the "self" includes decolonizing our whole beings: body, mind, heart, spirit, and more. Decolonizing requires a fierce reexamination of our colonial, and often sexist and homophobic, conditioning and an honest inventory of our pansexual natures and visceral connections to the more-than-human world. Reclaiming our eco-erotic birthright as human beings and Indigenous citizens requires a peeling away of the colonial and religious impositions of patriarchy, heteronormativity, internalized oppression, original sin, shame, and guilt (among many other idiosyncratic layers), especially in relation to our bodies and our capacity for intimacy and pleasure. These beliefs are based on a fear of the wild and uncontrollable, both in nature and in ourselves. After centuries of oppression, expressing the joy and diversity of our Native sexualities is truly an anticolonial, liberating act. Questioning the internalized authoritarianism that denies and demonizes our psychospiritual and animal closeness to "nature" is a decolonial and revolutionary act of survivance.[17]

Can there be a way to explore Indigenous eco-erotics that embraces the science and poetry of it without falling into the binary of objectivity and subjectivity? To do this, we will need to create and use new theoretical frameworks and decolonize nature itself. Stacy Alaimo has proposed the term "trans-corporeality" as a "theoretical site where corporeal theories and environmental theories meet and mingle in productive ways."[18] Catherine Baumgartner, an independent researcher, is using biocultural neuroscience to explore "embodied ecologies." Her objective is to "investigate and understand the essential role of embodied sensory experience in human relationships to the places and ecosystems we inhabit."[19] Her work is showing how critical it is to integrate sensory, emotional, cultural, symbolic, and other aspects into an embodied sense of place. She is also exploring how place attachment is key to human health and well-being; yet most people in industrial society have attachment *disruption* due to removal, dislocation, migration, diaspora, and general environmental degradation. The cultural critic T. J. Demos says, "To 'decolonize nature' would suggest the cancellation of this subject-object relation between humans and the environment, the removal of the conditions of mastery and appropriation that determine the connection between the two, and the absolution of the multiple levels of violence that mediate the relation of human power over the world."[20]

Given these theoretical frameworks of trans-corporeality, embodied ecologies, and a decolonized nature, I envision an intellectual ecosystem in which these different species of knowledge—ecological, critical Indigenous, and sexual theories and metaphors—can inform and inspire one another for a deeper dialogue and greater understanding of the enmeshed relations humans have with one another and the more-than-human world. I contend that this multivocal dialogue is essential for decolonization, liberation, and even the very survival of our, and other, species. As Barker states in this volume's introduction, this collective work "anticipates a decolonized future of gender and sexual relations."

Pansexuality in Oral Narratives

Human nature is a multispecies relationship.—**Anna Tsing,** "Unruly Edges: Mushrooms as Companion Species"

One significant (and vastly underused) source of insights into eco-erotic questions comes from Native oral literatures, the "original instructions" or metaphysical blueprints for many Indigenous cultures.[21] These oral narratives often appear as fanciful and poetic stories yet contain insightful "scientific" observations about ecological patterns and political insights into social patterns. These stories are deeply significant because, as the Cherokee author Thomas King says, "The truth about stories is that's all we are."[22] Yet, there really is no "original" here, as stories are told, retold, interpreted, changed, and transformed over time and place. There is a strange sameness and difference each time an Indigenous oral story is shared, much like complex bird and whale songs.[23] As the Okanagan writer Jeannette Armstrong has stated, "Words come from many tongues and mouths and the land around them. I am a listener to the language of stories and when my words form I am merely re-telling the same stories in different patterns."[24] Native stories transcend many Western binaries such as past and present, original and derivative, and so on. The Anishinaabe scholar Kimberly Blaeser says it well: "Native stories are seldom about separate parallel existences but about intricately linked relationships and intersections."[25]

Numerous Native stories explore these intersections and erotic contact zones between humans and nonhuman others. The Métis artist and writer Michelle McGeough writes, "Oral traditions often incorporated what Europeans considered erotic elements."[26] In hearing and reading these stories, it is clear that a whole other level of Indigenous sexuality and "carnal knowledge" is happening that is deeply tied to tribally specific understandings of sovereignty, language, relationship, and place. These stories can reveal profoundly diverse Indigenous epistemologies of pansexuality and visceral ontologies of intimacy. I believe that a deeper investigation into these stories can offer fruitful ways to Indigenize queer ecology, "green" Indigenous erotica, and reclaim Indigenous erotic intelligence that recognizes women's (and humans') inheritance as pansexual, eco-erotic beings that have ethical obligations to our more-than-human relatives.

These stories often demonstrate Indigenous women's historically adopted role as mediators of kinship with the more-than human world. In this tricky territory of story re-interpretation and precarious "legibility," Barker reminds us that we must "grapple with the demands of asserting a sovereign, self-determining Indigenous subject without reifying racialized essentialisms and authenticities." Given these complications, many oral narratives describe interspecies and trans-species relationships and speak to both their promise and their dangers.

According to numerous stories in Native American oral literature, Native women have a propensity to fall in love with other-than-human beings. And I truly mean "other than human": animals, plants, stars, even sticks and rocks. Underwater serpents, coyote men, cloud beings, and even the wind have also been gendered and sexualized characters with which Native women have carnal relations. These personified others have masculine and feminine qualities, like humans, and many variations in between this oversimplified gender binary. Within many Indigenous worldviews, it is common—dare I say, "natural"—for young women to fall in love with these other beings: to marry them, make love, and live together as lovers and married couples.

According to modern society's standards, this sounds ludicrous. It sounds fanciful and downright dangerous. According to the late environmental author Theodore Roszak, the person who coined the terms "counter-culture" and "eco-psychology"—the only references to "nature" in the psychologists' bible, the *Diagnostic and Statistical Manual of Mental Disorders* (DSM-IV) are seasonal affect disorder and bestiality.[27] "Funny how psychiatrists are absolutely inspired when it comes to mapping sexual dysfunction," Roszak writes, "but fail to chart the strong emotional bond we have with the natural habitat."[28] Humans' sensuous relationships with "nature" are often considered a mental illness. We see this message again and again from modern literature (e.g., *Equus*) and contemporary comedians who regularly make fun of tree hugging and bestiality.

It is true that these traditional stories often do not end well for the women. Torrid romances with nonhumans are dangerous business. Some women go mad; some die; some are banished to horrible circumstances. Sometimes they live happily ever after or make sacrifices to feed the nation. Often they create relationship agreements and covenants for a nation to follow. Many live as most married couples, experiencing the usual ups and downs of relationship dynamics. So why are these interspecies stories so prevalent in Native cultures, and what are their deeper messages? I assert that these stories provide critical insights about humans' eco-erotic relationship with other than human beings and that stories about falling in love with a star or a beaver should be considered signs of intelligence about the ethics involved with maintaining harmonious and resilient kinship relations.

In *Animal Spaces, Beastly Places*, Chris Philo and Christ Wilbert clearly outline that human-animal relations are very important for human health and often overlooked. They elaborate, "Stories of animals are especially valuable in helping their human tellers and hearers to develop their own moral identities and psychological interiorities."[29] In thinking through her relationship with her dog Cayenne, the maverick scholar Donna Haraway writes about "companion species." In her *Companion Species Manifesto* (2000), she articulates the profound and messy "significant otherness" of human-animal relations to reexamine species boundary constructions and naturecultures in a technoscientific era.[30] The profundity of human-animal relations—and, thus, human-nature relations—is finally getting some thoughtful attention, yet Indigenous oral literature has always featured such multispecies and trans-human interactions.

In Native American and Indigenous communities today—and, I assume, throughout colonial history—there are many boisterous and hushed conversations that hark back to these stories with relished details about naughty pleasures, affairs, and lust. I once tried very earnestly to interview a ninety-six-year-old elder from the Turtle Mountain Chippewa Reservation about traditional foods and language. She and her seventy-year-old daughters started speaking "Michif" and laughing hysterically.[31] Once I got my mom to stop laughing, I asked her to translate for me, and she said that the conversation had quickly turned to puns on oral sex.

References to "oral" traditions have led to many wordplays and jokes about kissing, oral sex, flirting, and the "hunt." Erdrich writes that the word for flirting and hunting is very close in the Ojibwe language.[32] This conjures up the idea that although there are different forms of human desire, the desire for flesh in food and sex may have a similar core root. This alludes to the dangers of the hunt (potentially getting hurt by the "prey") and the ultimate satisfaction of the conquest of the hunted. This connection also gives new meaning to the common term "carnal knowledge," as with anything we eat, consume, or have sex with, we are engaged in a similar interspecies or intraspecies biological transformation of substance and energy with uncertain results: strength or sickness from the quality and metabolism of food; bliss, pregnancy, or sickness from the quality and communicability of the person "consumed" in sex. In eating food and in sex, two become one, even for a moment.

Interspecies and trans-species sex are common occurrences in Native oral literature.[33] These stories often celebrate the various plants, animals, and other living beings of a specific territory as teaching tools for educating the young about the material environment that provides life—water, air, food, medicine, clothing, shelter. Native taxonomies are quite sophisticated and are often more complex than modern biology's binomial system of species identification.[34] These elements of the environment are considered animate, living beings, and important relatives that give life, so they are spoken about with great respect and reverence. Thus, it is natural to refer to them with familiarity and humor as they embody human traits, both sacred and profane.

In many tribal creation stories, these different species connect, converse, fight, and get together as commonly as humans do. In fact, they are considered "people" with their own individual and species sovereignty, yet they are all interrelated through creation or what ecologists call "ecosystem dynamics" or "food webs": eventually, everything eats everything. So much interspecies co-mingling is going on. Other oral narratives speak about strange, zoomorphic, mythic creatures, such as Thunderbirds and other winged creatures; underwater serpents and strange water monsters; the Little People; Rock beings and underground creatures. Even common, natural phenomena such as the elements have agency and personality. These "trans-species" beings are also randy. They, like all these other people, enjoy pleasure and sex.

Add to these types of sex the trickster character with his or her lascivious nature and ability to shape-shift. Tricksters can be transgendered, bisexual, polyamorous, and downright horny creatures. The So:lo scholar Jo-ann Archibald writes, "The English word 'trickster' is a poor one because it cannot portray the diverse range of ideas that First Nations associate with the Trickster, who is sometimes like a magician, an enchanter, an absurd prankster, or a Shaman, who sometimes is a shape-shifter, and who often takes on human characteristics."[35] In many traditions, Trickster takes on a significant spiritual and sacred role. But "trickster's amusing—and sometimes frightening—licentiousness is a significant danger to the social fabric."[36] Given the fact that Trickster holds a sacred role and is also a transgressor of boundaries, including gender and species boundaries, one sees a more open understanding of the fluidity of self, gender, spirituality, and sexuality in these stories. "Getting dirty" is Trickster's business. As King has written, "The Trickster is an important figure. . . . it allows us to create a particular kind of world in which Judeo-Christian obsession with good and evil and order and disorder is replaced with the more native concern of balance and harmony."[37] Given Trickster's wanderlust, gender fluidity, dirty nature, and shape-shifting ability, it is easy to understand how sex with an other-than-human being could occur and could be part of an Indigenous eco-erotic repertoire. With this outline of interspecies, trans-species, and Trickster sexuality themes, we can now dive into some of the oral narratives.

Retellings of Oral Stories

The stories in this [essay] about . . . the birth and death of naanabozho, that figuration of a compassionate tribal trickster, have been heard and remembered by tribal people in many generations; the published versions of these stories are various, and a sense of contradiction is endowed in postcolonial literature.—**Gerald Vizenor**, *Summer in the Spring*, 13

Writing about published oral literature is contradictory, at best. These "postcolonial literatures" have been spoken, performed, recorded, translated, transcribed, published, interpreted, forgotten, reinterpreted, remembered, dismembered, misinterpreted, and re-written many times in different contexts and times. They are fragments of orality re-presented here as stories of Native women's connections to the more-than-human world. I have faith that the seeds of these stories were once spoken and performed and passed on through listening, memory, and voice. Still, they are not unproblematic "traditional" stories but fragments of perspectives that contribute both practical advice and metaphoric value. I invite you into these messy storyscapes to discern your own understanding about the meaning of these offerings.

In re-telling human–more-than-human marriage stories, I first offer a couple of short anecdotal stories to introduce the concepts and some key elements. I then explore the bear marriage stories because it has global implications. Finally, I delve into one extensive narrative: a very specific and popular tribal story from my own Anishinaabeg heritage that has also been retold and published by contemporary Anishinaabe writers.

"STAR HUSBAND"

"Star Husband" is a short story from the Kootenai tradition about a young woman who desires and marries a star.[38] She is enamored with a particular star's beauty and wants the "little, nice" star to marry her. Her desire is so strong that the little star hears her and takes her to the star world. She realizes that the little stars are the old men and the large stars are the young men, and she ends up married to an old man. She finds herself in a cold star world with an old Star Husband away from her home country, and she cries. She "wished upon a star" and literally got what she wanted, to marry the Star Husband. She realizes the foolishness of her desire and wants to return to her human world. She is out digging roots with the Star Women, and they warn her not to dig too deeply by a tree. She does what they tell her *not* to do, and she digs through the thin layer and sees her home and family down below. She makes a ladder and lets herself down to Earth to reunite with her family. Her parents are very happy to see her; they ask about what happened to her, and she tells them. The Star Husband realizes his wife is missing and is not coming back. The young woman and her family go to bed. When they try to wake her in the morning, she is dead. The Star Husband struck her down.

This is clearly a warning story about the potential consequences of women's desire. It dramatically demonstrates the "be careful what you wish for" idiom. The girl is young and naive; she expresses her desire before thinking about it. Her impulsiveness is enacted, but with dire results. It is unclear whether she is punished for wanting something beyond her sphere or not wanting the world she was in. These traditional warning stories often remind us of the consequences of not expressing gratitude for the place one finds oneself in. This story shows us that impulsiveness and the desire for something beyond our current world, something "foreign," can be very dangerous, indeed. It is also a precautionary tale communicating that if one goes to another world (beyond one's boundaries) and tries to come home again, things will never be the same. In fact, "coming home" may not be possible.

Through another lens, this story could speak to the familiarity and even affection this people had for stars and could be a way to get young people to look up into the night sky with curiosity and attention.

"STICK HUSBAND"

There is a particularly fascinating story about a Coast Yuki woman who marries a stick.[39] Yes, a small piece of wood. In the story of "Stick Husband," a young woman lives with her grandmother, who is blind. The young woman helps her grandma by fetching wood and water, gathering food, and generally taking good care of her. One day while out picking up wood the girl notices a special stick. "What a pretty stick," she thinks. Soon after that, the stick rolls up to her and starts following her wherever she goes. She kind of likes it and develops a fondness for the stick. At night when she goes to bed, it rolls into her bed with her. The next morning she sees the stick roll out of bed and come back with a dead deer, a rare and special gift of fresh meat. The girl feeds her grandma this fresh meat and realizes she has to tell her grandma what has happened. The grandma is very happy about the girl's relationship with the stick. At night the stick started to roll all over the girl: on her body, between her legs, everywhere. Soon she is pregnant and has a baby boy. She then gets pregnant again and has a baby girl. The Stick Husband is good to her, keeps her warm at night, and provides good food and shelter.

Here we see a young girl having a satisfying relationship with an animate stick being. The grandmother approves, and they have a happy life together. What is this story telling us about Indigenous eco-erotics, or what is possible for two women in the absence of a man? Is it suggesting that it is normal and healthy for a woman to be autoerotic, to satisfy herself sexually with a stick? Is this an Indigenous precursor to the "vibrator," discovered in England in the 1800s? This story of Stick Husband illustrates woman's autonomy from human man and her ability to live well and satisfy herself on many levels absent a human man in her life. This Yuki narrative also illustrates the profound intimacy a woman can have with a stick, something the modern, industrial world would call an "inanimate" object but that, in the Yuki worldview, is a unique "person" with important qualities worthy of a relationship. The writer and publisher Malcolm Margolin comments on this story, "To live in a world in which everything was animate and had personhood was to live in a world of endless potentiality. The most common objects around one were filled with power, intelligence, and even sexual desire, making for a thoroughly unpredictable and magical world."[40] The unpredictability of nature (even its unknowability in some cases) is an important teaching imbedded in these pansexual stories and contributes to a sense of ordinariness with surprise and the unusual.

"THE WOMAN WHO MARRIED A BEAVER"

There is a well-known Anishinaabeg story about a woman who married a beaver; there are also many other stories about beaver marriages from tribes throughout the Great Lakes, upper Midwest, and Northwest.[41] The woman lived with the beaver for a long time and had four children with him. He eventually died, and she returned to the human world to tell humans about the importance of maintaining loving and respectful relations with the Beaver nation.

Like all of these stories, the story has many layers. It goes something like this: a young woman went out to fast for a vision quest, probably during her puberty time. While on her fast she met a human-looking person who spoke to her and eventually asked her to come live with him. She went to live with him and eventually married him. He treated her very well, with good food, shelter, and clothing. She soon was pregnant and ultimately gave birth to four children. She then started to notice odd things about her husband and finally realized she had married a beaver. She noticed that from time to time her husband and children would leave their home, which she was forbidden to leave, and they would meet with a human being. When they returned from these outings, they were always rich with new items—kettles, bowls, knives, tobacco, "all the things that are used when a beaver is eaten."[42] The woman soon realized that the beavers were going to the humans to get these goods, but also to give them their fur; she understood that they were being killed, but not *really* killed, because they would come back home with their gifts. After much exchange like this, the old Beaver Husband eventually died. The woman returned to the life of human beings and lived to be an old woman. She often told the story of her experience being married to a beaver and always told people to be kind to the beavers and never speak ill of them, because then they would never be able to kill them: "And he who never speaks ill of a beaver is very much loved by it; in the same ways as people often love another, so is one held in the mind of the beaver, particularly lucky then is one at killing beavers."[43]

This story illustrates the important message of "carnal knowledge" of food and the need to treat what we eat with great respect so it will keep sacrificing itself for our nourishment and survival. It speaks to the necessity of reciprocity in our physical consumption of other beings. It points out that to live, we have to eat; to eat, we have to kill. How do we kill with care? With kindness?

How is hunting like flirting? Insights into these questions can be found in these human-animal marriage stories. This story also problematizes the usual narrative of the human predator hunting the beaver prey by opening up the possibility that the beavers were actually using the humans to meet *their* material needs.[44] This, sadly, did not happen historically, as the beavers were driven nearly to extinction by the fur trade. But it is interesting that this story alludes to beavers' agency and this imagined reverse exploitation. This story could also be a rationalization for Native peoples' internalizing and adopting the new materialism of the frontier fur trade and colonial economy for survival—that is, the beaver was a good exchange for the kettles, knives, and other goods supplied by the fur trade. This story also indicates, like so many others, that women have a distinct role as mediators between humans and other beings and that they are fluid boundary crossers who can enter and maintain erotic intimacy and economic trade with nonhumans.

"THE WOMAN WHO MARRIED A BEAR"

The story of "the woman who married a bear" is relatively omnipresent in traditional cultures wherever bears are found, especially in the deep North.[45] Bear mythology, art, literature, and rituals are found around the world, and one can find human-bear marriage stories throughout North America, South America, Russia, Siberia, Japan, Europe, and Asia.[46] I tell a specific Kashaya Pomo bear story in the conclusion to this chapter. There are bear clans, bear dances, bear symbols, bear songs, and many extraordinary stories highlighting humans' deep relationship with bear nations, including Yup'ik and Cree of the north, Maidu in California, Lakota in the Northern Plains, Navajo in the desert, and Seneca in the East. Regardless of culture or tradition, these narratives speak to the profound closeness humans feel with bears historically and the exceptional reverence humans have for this powerful creature.

Some tribes and traditional societies have bear laws that say one can never eat the bear because he or she is so similar to humans it would be like cannibalism. Most have profound messages that outline the moral codes for hunting, coexisting with, and consuming bears in detailed rituals. Most Native bear stories highlight how similar we truly are as mammals: we are omnivores; our skeletal structures are very similar (especially in the hands and feet); we share a walking style (plantigrade locomotion); we are highly intelligent and family-oriented: "The Blackfeet word *o-kits-iks* refers to both the human hand and a bear's paw."[47] Because of this uncanny likeness, some stories say, humans and bears at one time were actually the same. Other narratives say that humans and bears spoke the same language. Due to this likeness, and given Indigenous kin-centric worldviews, the human-bear marriage stories seem fairly obvious, or expected. There are profound differences, of course, between our two species, such as bears' practicing hibernation and regular infanticide, but humans' mythical and spiritual connection with bears is mysterious, strong, and enduring. There are many rich variations on the bear marriage theme, yet most human-bear stories feature a young woman and a male bear. There are some stories, however, that include men who marry female bears.[48]

Bear stories by nature are long, involved, diverse, and complicated. The king of the land deserves such time and respect. The power of the bear and the global diversity of his or her stories is found in many works.[49] I am not going to retell one here.

I do want to share one very interesting aspect of bear stories that I found in many that I have encountered: that bears should not be made fun of, especially their scat or waste. Bears' waste often contains seeds from berries and other forest foods and bones from salmon and other water and land animals and therefore is a critical part of the sacred food web. Bears' "waste" is actually a critical part of life regeneration so should not be stepped in, jumped over, or made fun of in any way. Scat contains seeds and creates soil; seeds and soil contain and create the groundwork of life.

The Birth of Nanaboozhoo

My Anishinaabeg oral tradition has a very important creation story of how our trickster icon Nanaboozhoo was created. Of course, there are many different versions of this story, but the basic narrative goes something like this: this is the story of how Winonah, the mother of our trickster cultural hero Nanaboozhoo, was impregnated by the West Wind Ae-pungishimook. In the North Woods of Anishinaabeg-Aki (Ojibwe territory), a young woman lived with her grandmother. It was berry-picking season, and Nokomis, the grandmother, asked her granddaughter to go to a particular patch to pick a pail or two of June berries. She warned the girl to stick to business and just go there, pick the berries, and return home before dark. In some versions, the grandmother/mother figure is very specific about instructing the young girl never to face the West Wind directly or to turn her back to it while urinating.[50] The daughter politely accepts these instructions and goes out to the forest to collect the berries. She has picked a good pail of berries but knew she should pick more. Just as she sits down for a moment to pause (or pee), she feels a strong wind whip up all around her. It is a very boisterous wind that starts to pull at her clothes and lift her dress. She feels a warm, strong sensation under her dress and then sighs and falls back onto the ground, feeling exposed and vulnerable.

The Ojibwe scholar Gerald Vizenor retells this important story in *Summer in the Spring*. In his version, the girl is living with her mother, not grandmother, and it is the North Wind, not the West Wind, that takes her. As he describes of the scene, "While she was busily engaged gathering berries, the *giiwedin manidoo*, in a very noisily and boisterous manner, came to her, took her in his arms and kissed her, fluttered her garments and then departed from whence he had come. For some time the young girls was overcome with a delicious feeling of joy and happiness and she reclined to rest."[51]

The renowned Ojibwe historian and author Basil Johnson retells a less romantic and more violating version of this scene: "When *Ae-pungishimook* saw Winonah's little moss-covered cleft, the coals of lust glowed in his loins, and without prolonged foreplay or the recitation of sweet nothings, he cast his loincloth aside and humped the girl then and there. When his fire had petered out, *Ae-pungishimook* put his loincloth back on and staggered away, leaving poor Winonah to manage for herself and to face the future alone. Winonah rued the day that she had ever seen the Manitou and never expected to see him again."[52]

The environmental philosophers J. Baird Callicott and Michael P. Nelson also retell an Anglicized version of this story:

> Now such was the way it was, for it was true that at the time heedful was this woman who was a maiden. Never with men had she intimate association. But once on a time unmindful became the maiden; so when out of the doors she went and afterwards sat down facing the west, then heard she the sound of wind coming hitherward. When she felt it, she was chilled there at the place of the passage out. Accordingly she quickly leaped to her feet. "o my mother, behold the state that I am in? It may be that what you told me of is the matter with me."[53]

In some versions of the story the young woman picks more berries and then heads home. She does not tell her grandmother/mother until she starts showing that she is pregnant. In other stories she feels so distraught and sullied she heads straight home and tells her grandmother/mother all about it right away. And in yet other stories, her grandmother/mother already knows what has happened to her. This "immaculate conception" or "trans-human conception" of a young Anishinaabe woman by the West Wind gives birth to one of our most celebrated cultural icons, Nanaboozhoo.

As the examples show, in some versions of this story the girl is nearly raped. This could be a precautionary tale about not listening to your mother's warnings about the dangers of men's lust and power, and their dire consequences. It could also be a reinforcement of certain gender roles, however patriarchal or unjust they may seem to us now. Johnson interprets this encounter in a metaphoric way. He says that the West Direction and the West Wind represent age and destiny. The young woman represents youth and innocence. It is an important life teaching that "age will always ravish youth."[54] In other versions of this story, the girl has more agency and enjoys the experience as a young woman can enjoy being seduced by a powerful man—in this case the West Wind. In Johnson's version, Winonah bears four sons by the West Wind. The Wind, by its nature and definition, is an invisible, immaterial force. Yet wind is deeply visceral and in the stories express attraction, desire, and power in taking the young girl. This communicates that more-than-human natural phenomena have great power and unpredictability and that there are appropriate and wrong ways to interact with them, even if they are invisible.

For contrast, I now share a contemporary version of this Native story that, on one hand, emulates many of the same plot points and character traits of this Nanaboozhoo birthing story, but, on the other hand, flips some of the gender dynamics in what Vizenor called a "sacred reversal." What follows is a summary of one story that is part of the "Potchikoo Stories," a series of short stories by the award-winning contemporary Ojibwe author Louise Erdrich: Potchikoo is an Ojibwe man who is a modern Nanaboozhoo, as he has a difficult time repressing his hunger for food and women and often has to trick or lie to people to get what he wants. But in the end, his heart is good, and he does try to help his community. He had an unusual birth, just like Nanaboozhoo: his mother was taken by the Sun in a potato patch, and nine months later she gave birth to a potato-looking boy, Potchikoo. His mother's "pregnancy" was also unique in that his mother was impregnated by the powerful sunlight, much as Winonah was impregnated by the Wind.

Potchikoo lives on the Chippewa Indian reservation in the Turtle Mountains in postcontact times, probably in the 1950s. He, like any good trickster, goes through many adventures, and Erdrich writes several wonderful short stories and poems about his life and death. In one story, Potchikoo is out walking in the woods when he sees beautiful smooth stones emerging from mud. He finds himself drawn to the stones. He is quite attracted to them and is aroused by their smoothness. To him, the rocks resemble women's breasts. He caresses them, fondles them, and grows sexually excited. The rocks are located in a slough, and the warm mud starts to rise around the rocks. "When the slough rises to his crotch he enters an ambisexual encounter with the mud and rocks."[55] In the end, he "makes love to the slough."[56] As a result of this sexual act, three rock daughters are born. One day they go to visit their father and hug him. They end up crushing him under their weight and accidentally kill him. But then he is magically and miraculously revived.[57]

Here we see a man having pansexual experiences with stones and mud. He takes it beyond a multisensory experience into a definitive eco-sexual— or, more accurately, *geo*-sexual—experience that results in the birth of three hybrid stone daughters. As Callicott and Nelson write, "Sex is not what these marriages (or encounters) are all about."[58] So what are they about? I attempt to answer this question in the conclusion.

Modern Science Confirming Indigenous Sexuality Knowledge

Many Native traditions refer to the Earth as a Mother. The co-sexual activist Annie Sprinkles says we need to start thinking of Earth as a Lover.[59] Western scientists have come up with the "Gaia hypothesis," based on the Greek story of Gaia, which theorizes that the Earth is a living organism that is capable of self-regulation.[60] Regardless of assigned gender or relationship, modern geology tells us that the Earth has a magnetic iron core, and gravity is one of the fundamental laws of nature. Things are attracted to each other; this is an obvious statement but one that is uniquely reinforced by Native oral stories about human–more-than-human marriage stories. As Western science posits, basically the whole universe, including the Earth and us, is based on gravitational attraction and magnetism. It is about getting pulled into someone's orbit or pulling someone into your orbit, whether consciously or not.

Most of us take gravity for granted, yet it is a constant force between any two objects with mass, and it provides our most basic needs and desires: feet to earth (walking), mouth to apple (food), head to pillow (sleep), and so on. As the eco-philosopher David Abram writes, "We now scorn the ground. Gravity, we think, is a drag upon our aspirations; it pulls us down, holds us back, makes life a weight and a burden."[61] But gravity is a fundamental force that affects all of life *all* of the time. I believe that many Native peoples were historically aware of this force but spoke of it in different terms. For example, the Chickasaw law professor and Native science scholar James Sakej Henderson writes, "*Kesalttimkewey* (deep love) or *kesalk* (spirit of love) is a Mi'kmaq concept for gravity, it is like dark matter gravity. Thoughts [*snkita'suti*] are like the stars or white light gravity."[62]

From a Western scientific perspective, specific gravity is highest in rocks or things rich in the element of iron. Blood is red because an iron atom is at the core of our blood cells, just like the iron core of the Earth, making gravity and attraction inescapable. Every free body is falling toward every other; this implies a universal force of gravitation as articulated by Isaac Newton and others. Indigenous and other peoples for millennia knew this modern "law of gravity" as a fundamental "natural law," a life force of kinship, attraction, and, according to Sakej Henderson's understanding of Mi'kmaq, deep love. Abram continues, "The gravitational draw that holds us to the ground was once known as Eros—as Desire!—the lovelorn yearning of our body for the larger Body of the Earth, and of the Earth for us. The old affinity between gravity and desire remains evident, perhaps, when we say that we have fallen in love—as though we were off-balance and tumbling through air, as though it was the steady pull of the planet that somehow lay behind the Eros we feel toward another person."[63] A visceral, proprioceptive awareness of gravity is a critical way to reawaken our eco-erotic nature. For Indigenous peoples marinated in diverse, creative, and sexy stories of "deep love" with nonhumans, this sensuous definition of gravity is familiar.

Similarly, the concept of magnetic force tells us that we are all filled with little magnets (electrons), but they exert a major force on us and others only when they are lined up, or aligned. Also, magnetism, unlike gravity, depends on specific properties of objects. The interesting thing about the magnetic force is that it can either pull two objects together *or* push them apart, depending on the alignment of the magnets. In terms of eco-erotics, all of the Earth (every ecological and cosmological element) has a gravitational pull on us. This is the basic pull of life and fundamental desire for distant bodies; it is a constant, perhaps unquenchable longing. Magnetism, however, is a specifically strong yet fickle attraction that depends on mysterious alignments. It can create an extraordinary allure, or "animal magnetism," that draws unlikely "people" together on an instinctive, unconscious level. It can then equally repel these same two "people" or "objects." This kind of magnetic attraction and repulsion on an erotic level provides the ingredients for torrid love affairs, lust, obsession, and heartbreak, the exciting ingredients often explored in poetry and literature.

Our senses are easily attracted and seduced by physical desire: the smell of fresh baked bread, the sight of luscious strawberries, the rare beauty of a person's smile. In the stories shared in this chapter, we see this gravitational attraction between the young woman and the star, a woman and a stick, the wind and a woman, an old man and smooth stones, and so on. Our senses and the mysterious spark of erotic attraction become an undeniable force that brings people and energies together—sometimes like a light mist; at other times like a crashing wave.

Our minds and creative imaginations are also seduced, but by a different type of attraction: by story and metaphor; by the ability to wonder, imagine, learn, and know. Stories stretch our minds and provide other types of desire and fulfillment. Stories can demonstrate powerful types of yearning in the human spirit and expand our sense of self. One could say that all attractions are based on some form of gravity or urge to connect. The anthropologist Edward T. Hall has said, "The drive to learn is as strong as the sexual drive. It begins earlier and lasts longer."[64] Others have said that the mind is the greatest sex organ.[65] No doubt, humans have an erotic mind, and with this erotic mind we are able to transcend species divisions and find intimacy and connection with countless other-than-human beings. In all fairness to gravity (and many modern people's feeling toward it), it is also important to point out that Nietzsche and other existentialists correlated gravity with "the grave" and even "the Devil," and that there is an equal and opposite existential force to intimacy that can pull us toward emptiness and despair.[66] These poles of intimacy and loneliness are also reflected in the oral narratives shared here, as one experience can quickly lead to the other, and this is the precarious nature of magnetic attraction.

Regarding the topic of women's pansexuality and queerness, the developmental psychologist Lisa Diamond did an extraordinary study following one hundred women over ten years to understand and, if possible, determine their sexual preferences. Her conclusions state that women have an amazing capacity for sexual fluidity within our own species.[67] That is, women can easily flow between the standard categories and identities of heterosexuality and homosexuality over time and include other liminal identities such as bisexual, transsexual, queer and "unlabeled." According to Diamond's study, many women apparently make little distinction between attraction to men and attraction to women, and their love and desire are more context-dependent than gender-specific. Many women also can enjoy long periods of celibacy or autosexuality with much contentment.

Diamond also points out how many women can "fall in love" with other women without having a physical attraction or sexual component. This emotional bonding is quite profound and includes the usual "love drugs" of the brain—dopamine and oxytocin—but does not necessarily spill into a physical or sexual arousal.[68] Recent scientific studies about women's sexual fluidity (and ability to fall in love without a sexual component) confirm some of the fluid erotic relations Native women have in the various stories shared. If women's desires are "person"-dependent rather than gender-dependent,[69] and according to many Indigenous worldviews, other-than-humans are considered "people," it makes complete sense that human women (and, surely, men and other gendered people) could fall in love and have relationships with "other" people such as stars, beavers, bears, wind, and sticks.

These Native stories, and some stories from modern Western science, remind us that humans—as individuals, clans, nations, and species—are always entangled within complex ecologies and cosmologies and that humans are eco-erotic, pansexual animals. This is our birthright and our responsibility: to care for other life forms in respectful, reciprocal, and joyful ways. It is a sign of erotic intelligence that has meaningful implications for decolonizing and re-Indigenizing our relationships with the natural world, one that feeds us literally and metaphorically.

Native oral literature and its many stories about interspecies, trans-species, and pansexual intimacy are not necessarily about the literal act of sex as we experience it, although sometimes it could be. As James Mallet, a biologist at the University of London, has stated, "Sex with another species may be very occasionally quite a good idea."[70] An article published by Mallet in *Nature* in 2007 noted that, on average, 10 percent of animal species and 25 percent of plant species engage in "interspecies sex" in a process known as hybrid speciation.[71] This occurs when two separate species mate and produce sexually fertile hybrid offspring that can evolve into separate species. Butterflies and bears have successfully mated with other species within their own kind, blurring the species boundary and showing that interspecies mating can be successful for producing new life forms. Mallett states, "it might be worth throwing the dice every now and then to try for something really weird and see if it works out."[72] Apparently, nature *does* play dice and experiment with interspecies sex. This is something that Indigenous cultures clearly know about with the theme of the trickster, and they communicated these possibilities through their zoomorphic, shape-shifting, transformative stories and images of eco-erotic affairs. Yet this understanding that some species did literally mix with each other does not mean that humans should entertain this notion of actual sex with other species. These stories tell us we should care for and love these "others"—whether animal, plant, stone, stick, or star—and do so with a sense of ethics and consent. The whole topic of bestiality is beyond the scope of this chapter, but it is clear that, "based on the literature, bestiality—sexual relations with animals has been part of the human race throughout history, in every place and culture in the world."[73] Many cultures, including Native cultures, have strict taboos against sexual relations with animals, yet like all taboos, they often come from bad past experiences. They also spark forbidden curiosity, as erotic desire is often fueled by the opportunity (thought, fantasy) or act of transgression.

Conclusion

If we appreciate the foolishness of human exceptionalism, then we know that becoming is always becoming with—in a contact zone where the outcome, where who is in the world, is at stake.—**Donna Haraway,** *When Species Meet*

In these extraordinary stories, sex with more-than-humans may actually sometimes be about sex as we know it, but most likely, sex is a metaphor. Sex is a symbol for intimate, visceral, embodied kinship relations with other species and with natural phenomenon. The "sex," the "intercourse" (from the Old French *entrecours* "exchange, commerce; and from the Late Latin *intercursus* "a running between, intervention"[74]), is an emotional and ethical transaction, an agreement, a treaty of obligations. These often unspoken agreements arise out of the ecotone between the sovereignty of humans and the sovereignty of other-than-human people. It is the "contact zone" where carnal knowledge is exchanged and codes of behavior are learned or instilled. As the Anishinaabeg political scientist Heidi Kiiwetinepinesiik Stark has noted, "There is a rich body of scholarship that calls for us to seriously consider how narratives, whether encoded in law or circulated throughout the dominant society and embedded in the national consciousness, shape and inform how we understand ourselves and relate to others."[75] In other words, stories create law, and law is a story. Barker affirms that this process is a way of "narrating Indigenous peoples back into their governance, territories, and cultures."

For example, in a lovely short story from Otis Parrish of the Kashaya Pomo Nation in northern California, we learn about the in-depth "treaty" between the bear and the huckleberry and then the humans. This story, like many, is communicated in a song yet outlines a type of territorially and tribally specific interspecies agreement. It is an example of what Barker calls "the polity of the Indigenous." According to the story, when Creator made the world, he made it so that some of the plants and animals were paired off together. He gave "Huckleberry the right to be made for food and the Bear was given the taste for Huckleberries."[76] Creator then gave Bear a beautiful song, and Huckleberry heard it and fell in love with the song. Creator gave Huckleberry its berries and made Bear taste them. Bear fell in love with the taste of the berries. Huckleberry said, "If you want to have my beautiful, tasty berries, you have to sing your most beautiful song for me every time you want my beautiful, tasty berries." Bear had a beautiful voice but got stingy with it and did not always want to sing. Huckleberry warned Bear that if he did not sing his song, the quality of his voice would get worse, and he would not get his berries. Finally, Bear tried to sing his song, but only grunts and ugly sounds came out. Huckleberry had warned him, but he did not listen. Bear started to cry and throw a tantrum, rolling around on the ground and kicking up dust. Huckleberry felt sorry for him and finally gave him the right to eat the berries, but he still had to sing his song, even in his ugly voice. Then humans entered the picture and loved the taste of the berries, too. Bear warned them that they could not eat the berries or he would kill them. They could eat the berries only if they sang his Bear song to Huckleberry. Huckleberry agreed that humans had to sing Bear's song to them before taking any of the berries or else "old lady Bear will drag you into the deep woods, and you'll never come back."

Humans made an agreement with Huckleberry and Bear. From that point on, humans agreed to sing Bear's song for the Huckleberries, and Huckleberry would provide its berries for medicine and food. Bear, too, could still sing his song and access Huckleberries, and since humans sang the Bear song, they could all coexist and benefit from the "beautiful, tasty" Huckleberries.

This story is about "carnal knowledge" in the sense of food rather than sex, but it is still a type of erotic partnership and includes many of the same elements of attraction, desire, "falling in love," consumption, and agreements and rules about how natural "people" are to consume one another. It outlines a sort of interspecies "treaty" among three distinct creatures that ultimately all want the same thing: to eat and be sustained as autonomous beings yet acknowledge their essential interdependence with others. This story, and others, shows us that diverse living beings can enter a contact zone" of reciprocal relations with others in which all benefit. As the Potawatomie botanist Robin Wall Kimmerer has stated, "We are all bound by the moral covenant of reciprocity."[77] Beyond the utilitarian benefits of these interspecies treaties, this story also alludes to the fact that huckleberry bushes and bears can fall in love with songs and taste, both immaterial and material offerings. This explicit acknowledgment of love and attraction to food and song is an essential part of Indigenous eco-erotics. The Jamaican writer and linguist Esther Figueroa proposes that this trope of "romance" is also used strategically as a way for humans to pay attention and remember these instructions.[78]

In terms of women's unique role in forging ahead with these trans-species relationships, the stories certainly remind us that women have great curiosity and complex desires. Cultural and ecological boundaries can be blurry at times, and it is often difficult to know when desires are healthy and beneficial and when they are dangerous and potentially destructive. In many versions of the Haudenasaunee creation story, it is Sky Woman's *curiosity* that leads her to look down the hole in the sky and fall through to Turtle's back, creating Turtle Island. Where would we be if she had not followed her impulses rather than the rules? Native oral narratives show us the adventures, benefits, risks, and consequences of following women's desires, and trickster stories show how ambivalent and complicated our desires can be. In these compassionate and often humorous narratives we are warned about lust, greed, and other overly acquisitive behavior. The woman-other marriages make us aware of the permanency of change when some boundaries are transgressed. There are other stories, however, that go to the extreme to warn against insatiable desire and overconsumption; these are the Windigo/Wetiko, or cannibal, stories. These stories show, in gruesome ways, that unchecked desire will lead to greed and cannibalism and a hunger so desperate and dark that one becomes a monster. The late Lenape scholar Jack D. Forbes linked colonialism to this Windigo spirit.[79]

These rich stories of independent women also allude to the patriarchal control wielded historically in some tribal nations—for example, that women could be the property of their fathers and husbands and that they needed to be watched, controlled, and warned about the consequences of transgressing patriarchal rules and protocols. But many tribal nations were equally matriarchal or women-centered. In these cases, these stories could speak to women's ability to define their own rules and protocols; to test and break taboos (in many cases without severe consequence); and to be self-sufficient, productive, and happy without a human man or with other-than-human husbands and partners. These narratives also illustrate that women have a profound connection with the natural elements—wind, water, soil—and with plant and animal species and sticks and rocks. This is not meant to imply the old, essentialist "woman as nature" trope. It is simply a comment on the diversity of relations women have in these stories. It could also speak to a unique aspect of women's psychology and fluid sexual behavior that (as noted earlier) is currently being researched by contemporary female scientists, with surprising discoveries and intriguing theories.

Human pansexuality is queer and polyamorous within our own species; it is also interspecies and trans-species. It alludes to the fact that our creative imaginations and animal bodies and senses can be aroused and stimulated in erotic ways by other-than-human beings. I call this *re-Indigenizing our senses* by relearning to listen, once again, to the languages of our four-legged, finned, and winged relatives, as well as those of our rooted and stationary kin: the plants and trees and stone grandfathers. Reawakening all of our senses, including the metaphoric mind but especially our kinesthetic, visceral sense, helps us remember our primal intimacy with, and fluency in, the languages of the more-than-human world. It is what Abram calls "becoming animal"—that is, "getting dirty" in a physical and metaphysical way.

"Getting dirty" means we become fully human by remembering and embodying our trans-human animalness. This requires a decolonization process, because we must question and shed the conditioned beliefs that say we are more intelligent than, different from, or better than our animal nature and other natural beings (i.e., human exceptionalism). Our bodies are filled with intelligences that are faster than and beyond the intelligence of our cognitive brains. Reawakening these intelligences and our intuitive and imaginative capacities reconnect us to the natural world in ways that can engender reciprocal coexistence. The Mohawk scholar Dan Roronhiakewen Longboat reminds us that *imagination is a place*. It is not the exclusive domain of human consciousness, and "spiritual and intellectual integrity is achieved on Turtle Island by the interplay of human and more-than-human consciousness."[80] This critical interplay of consciousness is mirrored and expressed in these place-based pansexual stories that outline crucial interspecies agreements and a trans-human concept of nationhood.

These Native stories outline the fertility and fluidity of Indigenous imaginations and remind us that we are always human animal, one of many, made up of dirt and stardust. Gravity is unavoidable. Magnetic attractions are ever present, when the mysterious alignments occur. All life depends on other life for survival, regeneration, and celebration. The Indigenous eco-erotics evident in these oral narratives remind us that humans (and all life forms) are capable of profound intimacies and transformations if we embrace rather than repress our fundamental desires and the permeability of our consciousness. Embracing our eco-erotic nature helps us recognize the generosity of creation, and our part in it, so we can truly embody an ethic of kinship.

Epigraphs: Stacy Alaimo and Susan Hekman, *Material Feminisms* (Bloomington: Indiana University Press, 2008); Alan Watts, *The Book: On the Taboo against Knowing Who You Are* (Visalia, CA: Vintage, 1989), 83; Anna Tsing, "Unruly Edges: Mushrooms as Companion Species," *Environmental Humanities* 1 (November 2012): 141; Gerald Vizenor, *Summer in the Spring: Anishinaabe Lyric Poems and Stories* (Norman: University of Oklahoma, 1993), 13; Donna Haraway, *When Species Meet (Posthumanities)*. Minneapolis: University of Minnesota Press 2007, 244.1.

1. By "erotic" I mean the "ambiguous space between anxiety and fascination" and the heightened holistic arousal of connecting with an "other": Esther Perel, *Mating in Captivity: Unlocking Erotic Intelligence*. New York: Harper Perennial, 2007, 18. Eroticism is playing on the edge of self and other, certainty and uncertainty, security and danger, power and surrender.

2. Eating dirt is a long and old tradition and is technically known as "geophagy." Many Native American cultures historically practiced this, especially women, and still do: Carol Diaz-Granados and James R. Duncan, *Rock-Art of Eastern North America: Capturing Images and Insight* (Tuscaloosa: University of Alabama Press, 2004). See also Marc Lallanilla, "Eating Dirt: It Might Be Good for You," ABC News, October 3, 2005, http://abcnews.go.com/Health/Diet/story?id=1167623&page=1; Enrique Salmon, *Eating the Landscape: American Indian Stories of Food, Identity, and Resilience* (Tucson: University of Arizona Press, 2012).

3. See http://www.etymonline.com/index.php?term=nirvana.

4. Louise Erdrich, *Love Medicine* (New York: HarperCollins, 1993 [1984]), 287.

5. David Abram, *Becoming Animal—An Earthly Cosmology* (New York: Pantheon, 2010), 27.

6. Greg Cajete, *Native Science: Natural Laws of Interdependence* (Santa Fe, NM: Clear Light, 1999); Daniel Goleman, *Emotional Intelligence: Why It Can Matter More than IQ* (New York: Bantam, 2005); Stephen Kellert and E. O. Wilson, *The Biophilia Hypothesis* (Covelo, CA: Island, 1995); David Orr, *Ecoliteracy: Educating Our Children for a Sustainable World* (San Francisco: Sierra Club, 2012).

7. Alaimo and Hekman, *Material Feminisms*, 238.

8. Alan Ereira, dir., *From the Heart of the World*, documentary, BBC Worldwide, London, 1990.

9. Julie Cruikshank, *The Social Life of Stories: Narratives and Knowledge in the Yukon Territory* (Lincoln: University of Nebraska Press, 1998), xii.

10. *Queer Indigenous Studies: Critical Interventions in Theory, Politics, and Literature*. Qwo-Li Driskill, Chris Finley, Brian Gilley, and Scott Morgensen (Tucson: University of Arizona Press, 2011); *Sovereign Erotics: A Collection of Two-Spirit Literature*, Qwo-Li Driskill, Daniel Heath Justice, Deborah Miranda, and Lisa Tatonetti (Tucson: University of Arizona Press, 2011); *Me Sexy: An Exploration of Native Sex and Sexuality*, Drew Hayden Taylor (Vancouver, BC: Douglas and McIntyre, 2008).

11. Taylor, *Me Sexy*, 2.

12. Tomson Highway, "Why Cree is the Sexiest of All Languages," in Taylor, *Me Sexy*, 38.

13. At the urgings of First Nations leaders who demanded the Residential Schools Settlement Agreement, Canada instituted a Truth and Reconciliation Commission to help support the healing "truth and reconciliation" process of Native peoples from the abuses they experienced in residential school. See http://www.trc.ca/websites /trcinstitution/.

14. Kim TallBear, "Indigeneity and Technoscience," blog, http://www.kimtallbear .com.

15. Stephen Jay Gould, *Eight Little Piggies: Reflections in Natural History* (New York: W. W. Norton, 1993), 40.

16. Sadly, this perspective is anathema to the prevalent paradigms of the day. Many political and religious ideologies insist on a type of sexual purity and control of women and reproduction that amputates healthy eroticism from daily life. Repression and denial become the norm, with global capitalism exploiting this void with hypersexualized marketing strategies, pornography, and, worse, criminal sex trafficking and slavery.

17. "Survivance" is a critical term in Indigenous studies. It was used by Gerald Vizenor to emphasize both survival and resistance and emphasize a "renunciation of dominance, tragedy, and victimry" (Vizenor 1999, vii).

18. Alaimo and Hekman, *Material Feminisms,* 238.

19. See http://embodiedecologies.moonfruit.com.

20. T. J. Demos, "Decolonizing Nature: Making the World Matter," *Social Text* (no vol./no. found online (March 8, 2015), http://socialtextjournal.org/periscope_article /decolonizing-nature-making-the-world-matter.

21. Melissa K. Nelson, *Original Instructions: Indigenous Teachings for a Sustainable Future* (Rochester: Bear & Company, 2008).

22. Thomas King, *The Truth about Stories* (Minneapolis: University of Minnesota Press, 2008).

23. See David Rothenberg, *Why Birds Sing: A Journey into the Mystery of Birdsong* (New York: Basic, 2006); David Rothenberg, *Thousand-Mile Song: Whale Music in a Sea of Sound* (New York: Basic, 2010).

24. Jeannette Armstrong, "Land Speaking," in *Speaking for the Generations*, ed. Simon Ortiz (Tucson: University of Arizona Press, 1998), 181.

25. Kimberly M. Blaeser, "Like 'Reeds through the Ribs of a Basket': Native Women Weaving Stories," in *Other Sisterhoods: Literary Theory and U.S. Women of Colour*, ed. Sandra Kumamoto Stanley (Urbana: University of Illinois Press, 1998), 268.

26. Michelle McGeough, "Norval Morrisseau and the Erotic," in Taylor, *Me Sexy*, 59.

27. American Psychiatric Association, *Diagnostic and Statistical Manual of Mental Disorders*, 4th ed. (Washington, DC: American Psychiatric Association, 2000).

28. Theodore Roszak, "The Nature of Sanity." *Psychology Today*, Vol. 29 (1), January 1, 1996, 22.

29. Chris Philo and Christ Wilbert, *Animal Spaces, Beastly Places: New Geographies of Human-Animal Relations* (New York: Routledge, 2000), 24.

30. See Donna Haraway, *Companion Species Manifesto*: Dogs, People, and Significant Otherness (Chicago: Prickly Paradigm Press), 2003.

31. "Michif" is a language spoken and an identity expressed at the Turtle Mountain Chippewa Reservation and other Métis communities in North Dakota, Montana, and Manitoba, Canada. The word comes from "Métis," meaning mixed-blood French Indians, and the language is a mix of Plains Cree, Ojibwe, and French: see Peter Bakker, *A Language of Our Own: The Genesis of Michif, the Mixed Cree-French Language of the Canadian Metis* (Oxford: Oxford University Press, 1997).

32. "The same Chippewa word is used both for flirting and hunting game, while another Chippewa word connotes both using force in intercourse and also killing a bear with one's bare hands": R. W. Dunning, *Social and Economic Change among the Northern Ojibwa* (1959), quoted in Louise Erdrich, *Jacklight* (New York: Henry Holt, 1984).

33. I use the term "species" loosely here because it is a Eurocentric social construct. Although it is usually taken as a solid concept in biology, it has been questioned recently as a fixed category: see Donna Haraway, *The Species Companion Manifesto: Dogs, People, and Significant Otherness* (Chicago: Prickly Paradigm, 2003). On the exciting new field of "multispecies ethnography," see, e.g., Kirksey and Helmreich, "The Emergence of Multispecies Ethnography," *Cultural Anthropology* website, June 14, 2010. https://culanth.org/fieldsights/277-the-emergence-of-multispecies -ethnography.

34. This system was interestingly based on Karl Linneaus, a Swedish botanist in the eighteenth century who learned a lot about plants from the local, Indigenous Saami; see "The Expedition to Lapland," http://www.linnaeus.uu.se/online/life/5_4.html.

35. Jo-ann Archibald, *Indigenous Storywork: Educating the Heart, Mind, Body, and Spirit* (Vancouver: University of British Columbia Press, 2008), 5.

36. Franchot Ballinger, *Living Sideways: Tricksters in American Indian Oral Traditions* (Norman: University of Oklahoma Press, 2006), 88.

37. King, Thomas. *One Good Story, that one: Stories* (New York: HarperPerennial, 1993), xiii.

38. Donald Frey, *Stories That Make the World: Oral Literature of the Indian Peoples of the Inland Northwest* (Norman: University of Oklahoma Press, 1999), 160–62.

39. Malcolm Margolin, *The Way We Lived: California Indian Stories, Songs, and Reminiscences* (Berkeley, CA: Heyday, 1992), 91.

40. Margolin, *The Way We Lived*, 91.

41. See Bruce M. White, "The Woman Who Married a Beaver: Trade Patterns and Gender Roles in the Ojibwa Fur Trade," *Ethnohistory* 46, no. 1 (Winter 1999): 109–47.

42. White, "The Woman Who Married a Beaver," 110.

43. White, "The Woman Who Married a Beaver," 110.

44. White, "The Woman Who Married a Beaver," 111.

45. See A. Hollowell, "Bear ceremonialism in the northern hemisphere" (*American Anthropologist* 28[1]: 1–175, 1926); and Joseph Campbell, *The Masks of God: Primitive Mythology* (New York: Viking Press, 1959), 339.

46. See Bruchac, *Native American Animal Stories* (Golden, CO: Fulcrum Publishing 1992); Michel Pastoureau, *Bear: History of a Fallen King* (Cambridge: Belknap Press: 2011; David Rockwell, *Giving Voice to Bear: North American Indian Rituals, Myths and*

Images of the Bear (Lanham, MA: Roberts Rinehart, 2002); Paul Shepard, *The Sacred Paw: the Bear in Nature, Myth, and Literature* (New York: Penguin Group/Arkana, 1992).

47. See Rockwell, *Giving Voice to Bear*, 2.

48. See Franz Boas, *Folk Tales of Salishan and Sahaptin Tribes* (New York: American Folk-Lore Society, 1917), 198–200, quoted at http://www.pitt.edu/~dash/animalindian .html#sahaptinbear.

49. See, e.g., D. A. Clark and D. S. Slocombe, "Respect for Grizzly Bear: An Aboriginal Approach for Co-existence and Resilience," *Ecology and Society* 14, no. 1 (2009): 42; and Boaz 1917; Rockwell 2002, Pastoureau 2011, Shepard, 1992 cited above.

50. Interestingly, in some interpretations of the birth of the Greek god Eros, he was also born to a West Wind father: see http://www.theoi.com/Ouranios/Eros .html#Birth.

51. Vizenor, *Summer in the Spring*, 101.

52. Basil Johnson, *The Manitous: The Spiritual World of the Ojibway* (Minneapolis: Minnesota Historical Society Press, 2001), 17.

53. J. Baird Callicott and Michael P. Nelson, *American Indian Environmental Ethics—An Ojibwa Case Study*, 79)

54. Johnson, *The Manitous*, 238.

55. Dean Rader, *Engaged Resistance: American Indian Art, Literature, and Film from Alcatraz to NMAI* (Austin: University of Texas Press, 2011), 142.

56. Erdrich, *Jacklight*, 78.

57. See Louise Erdrich, *Original Fire: Selected and New Poems* (New York: Harper Perennial, 2004), 35–54.

58. Callicott and Nelson, *American Indian Environmental Ethics*, 120.

59. See Annie Sprinkles, "Eco-Sexual Manifesto," http://sexecology.org/research -writing/ecosex-manifesto.

60. James Lovelock and Lyn Margulis, "Atmospheric Homeostasis by and for the Biosphere: The Gaia Gypothesis," *Tellus* 26, nos. 1–2 (1974): 2–10.

61. Abram, *Becoming Animal*, 27.

62. James Sakej Henderson to the author, personal e-mail, April 20, 2015.

63. Abram, *Becoming Animal*, 27.

64. Edward T. Hall quoted in Peter Senge, *Schools That Learn: A Fifth Discipline Resource* (Redfern: Australia, Currency, 2000), 4.

65. See Jack Morin, *The Erotic Mind: Unlocking the Inner Sources of Passion and Fulfillment* (New York: Harper Perennial, 1996).

66. Nietzsche connects gravity to the Devil, writing, "Especially . . . I am hostile to the spirit of gravity, that is bird-nature:—verily, deadly hostile, supremely hostile, originally hostile! Oh, whither hath my hostility not flown and misflown! And when I saw my devil, I found him serious, thorough, profound, solemn: he was the spirit of gravity—through him all things fall": Friedrich Nietzsche, *Thus Spake Zarathustra* (New York: Dover, 1999), chap. 55.

67. Lisa Diamond, *Sexual Fluidity: Understanding Women's Love and Desire* (Cambridge, MA: Harvard University Press, 2008).

68. Diamond, *Sexual Fluidity*, 219–20.

69. Diamond, *Sexual Fluidity*, 173.

70. Mallet quoted in James Owen's, "Interspecies Sex: Evolution's Hidden Secret?," *National Geographic News*, March 14, 2007.

71. Mallet, James. Hybrid Speciation. *Nature* 446, 279–83 (March 15, 2007).

72. Owen, "Interspecies Sex."

73. See Hani Meletski, "A History of Bestiality," in *Bestiality and Zoophilia: Sexual Relations with Animals*, edited by Anthony L. Podberscek and Andrea M. Beetz, *Anthrozoos* Series. (Oxford: Berg, 2005): 1–22.

74. See *Etymology Dictionary*, http://www.etymonline.com.

75. Jill Doerfler, Niigaanwewidam James Sinclair, and Heidi Kiiwetinepinesiik Stark, *Centering Anishinaabeg Studies: Understanding the World through Stories* (East Lansing: Michigan State University Press, 2013), 262.

76. Otis Parrish, "Healing the Kashaya Way," in *Healing and Mental Health for Native Americans: Speaking in Red*, eds. Ethan Nebelkopf and Mary Phillips (Walnut Creek, CA: AltaMira, 2004), 123.

77. See Robin Wall Kimmerer, *Braiding Sweetgrass: Scientific Wisdom, Scientific Knowledge and the Teachings of Plants* (Minneapolis, MN: Milkweed, 2013).

78. Personal communication with Esther Figueroa, August 17, 2014. See Figueroa, *Limbo: A Novel About Jamaica*. Arcade Publishing, 2014.

79. See Jack D. Forbes, *Columbus and Other Cannibals* (New York: Seven Stories Press, 2008).

80. See Joe Sheridan and Roronhiakewen, "He Clears the Sky"; Dan Longboat, "The Haudenosaunee Imagination and the Ecology of the Sacred," *Space and Culture* 9 (2006): 365.

260 · Nelson

Contributor Biographies

JOANNE BARKER (Lenape [Delaware Tribe of Indians]) is Professor of American Indian Studies at San Francisco State University. She is author of *Native Acts: Law, Recognition, and Cultural Authenticity* (Duke University Press) and editor of *Sovereignty Matters: Locations of Contestation and Possibility in Indigenous Struggles for Self-Determination* (University of Nebraska Press). She has published several juried articles and book chapters on issues including Indigenous feminism and debt politics and directed/written several educational documentaries on international human rights.

JODI A. BYRD is a citizen of the Chickasaw Nation and an Associate Professor of English and Women's and Gender Studies at the University of Illinois at Urbana-Champaign where she is also a faculty affiliate at the National Center for Supercomputing Applications. Her work has been published in journals including *American Indian Quarterly, Cultural Studies Review, Interventions, College Literature, J19, American Quarterly, Settler Colonial Studies*, and *Wičazo Ša Review*. Her book, *The Transit of Empire: Indigenous Critiques of Colonialism* (Minnesota, 2011) won the 2013 Native American and Indigenous Studies Association Award for best first book. Her current manuscript in process, entitled *Indigenomicon: American Indians, Videogames, and Structures of Genre*, interrogates how the structures of digital code intersect with issues of sovereignty, militarism, and colonialism.

JENNIFER NEZ DENETDALE (Diné) is from Tohatchi, New Mexico and an associate professor of American Studies at the University of New Mexico. She is author of *Reclaiming Diné History: The Legacies of Chief Manuelito and Juanita* (2007), two Navajo histories of young adults, and numerous articles and essays.

MISHUANA R. GOEMAN, Tonawanda Band of Seneca, is Associate Professor of Gender Studies at the University of California, Los Angeles and affiliated faculty of American Indian Studies. Her recent book is *Mark My Words: Native Women Mapping Our Nations* (University of Minnesota Press). She is also a co-principal investigator on a community based digital project, Mapping Indigenous L.A. (www.mila.ss.ucla.edu).

J. KĒHAULANI KAUANUI (Kanaka Maoli) is Professor of American Studies and Anthropology at Wesleyan University. Her first book is *Hawaiian Blood: Colonialism and the Politics of Sovereignty and Indigeneity* (Duke University Press, 2008). Kauanui's second book project, *The Paradoxes of Hawaiian Sovereignty*, is a critical study on land, gender and sexual politics, and the tensions regarding indigeneity in relation to statist Hawaiian nationalism (contracted with Duke University Press). Kauanui serves as a radio producer for an anarchist politics show called "Anarchy on Air," and previously hosted the radio program, "Indigenous Politics; From Native New England and Beyond," which aired for seven years and was broadly syndicated through the Pacifica network. She serves as an advisory board member of the U.S. Campaign for the Academic and Cultural Boycott of Israel.

MELISSA K. NELSON (Anishinaabe/Cree/Métis [Turtle Mountain Chippewa]) is Associate Professor of American Indian Studies at San Francisco State University. A Native ecologist, she is also president of the Cultural Conservancy, an indigenous rights organization. She is editor of *Original Instructions: Indigenous Teachings for a Sustainable Future*, author of many articles and chapters, and has produced several documentary short films on indigenous revitalization and food sovereignty.

JESSICA BISSETT PEREA (Dena'ina [Knik Tribe]) is an interdisciplinary scholar whose work intersects the larger fields of Native American & Indigenous studies and Music & Sound studies. She earned her PhD in Musicology from the University of California, Los Angeles and currently works as an assistant professor in the Department of Native American Studies at the University of California, Davis.

MARK RIFKIN is Director of Women's and Gender Studies and Professor of English at the University of North Carolina at Greensboro. He is the author of five books, including *Beyond Settler Time: Temporal Sovereignty and Indigenous Self-Determination*; *Settler Common Sense: Queerness and Everyday Colonialism in the American Renaissance*; and *When Did Indians Become Straight?: Kinship, the History of Sexuality, and Native Sovereignty*, and he co-edited the award-winning special issue of GLQ, "Sexuality, Nationality, Indigeneity." He also has served as president of the Native American and Indigenous Studies Association.

Note: page numbers in *italics* refer to illustrations; those followed by "n" indicate endnotes.

Abercrombie, Neil, 46

Abram, David, 248–49, 255

adoption of children. *See* Indian Child Welfare Act

Adoptive Couple v. Baby Girl, 188, 191–92, 208, 225

African Americans, Iñupiaq and, 148–49, 150–51

Ahmaogak, Roy, 167n95

Ahmed, Sara, 181, 217

aikāne relationships, 49, 59, 64n17

Aivaaq, *140*, 144, 151, 152

Akiwenzi-Damm, Kateri, 26–27

Alaimo, Stacy, 229, 232, 235

Alaska Federation of Natives (AFN), 160n18, 165n75

Alaska Native Claims Settlement Act (ANCSA), 146–47, 150

Alaska Native Corporations, 146–47, 165nn73–76

Alaska Native Language Center (ANLC), 130

"Alaska Natives" as term, 130–31, 160n17. *See also* Inuit/Alaska Natives

Alaska Native Solidarity movement, 149

Aldama, Arturo, 112

Alito, Samuel, 192

Allen, Chadwick, 115

Allen, Paula Gunn, 18–20

All Our Relations (LaDuke), 26

aloha ʻāina (love for the land), 54–56

Anderson, Benedict, 97n79, 116

Anderson, Gary, 93n9

Anderson, Kim, 130

Anderson, Larry, 90

animal-human relations. *See* eco-eroticism and oral narratives

Animal Spaces, Beastly Places (Philo and Wilbert), 238

Apess, William, 39n41

appropriations, racially gendered and sexualized, 1–5

Archibald, Jo-ann, 240

"Arctic Thug" (Ireland and Jacobs), 145, 147, 150–51

Armstrong, Jeannette, 236

Arny, William F., 86

assimilation: biopolitics and, 74; "cultural distinctiveness" and, 194; as ethnic cleansing, 85; expectations of the "traditional" and, 89; modernist theories of Indigenous inferiority and, 17; New Indian history and, 71; patriarchy colonialism and, 19; *In re Bridget* (CA) on, 194; settler colonialism and, 64n14

Atanarjuat (film; Kunuk), 133, 135–38

attachment disruption, 236

Attawapiskat Nation, 4, 36n12

Austin, Raymond, 76, 89–90

authenticity: Allen on blood/land/memory complex and, 115; Christianity and, 154; decolonial politics of, 154; expectations of, 63n13, 89, 212; family, gender, marriage, and sexuality and, 74; fetishized disavowal of the Indigenous and, 211; hip hop and, 147; Navajo (Diné) and, 89; recognition and, 3

"Aye, and Gomorrah" (Delany), 207, 218–21, 224

Ba'áliilii, 77

Baehr v. Lewin (later *Baehr v. Miike*), 47

Banerjee, Subhankar, 127

Barker, Joanne, 63n13, 74, 89

Barrow, AK. *See* Utqiaġvik

Barrow Dancers, *140, 142*

Baumgartner, Catherine, 235–36

Bear, 244–45, 252–54

Beautiful Mountain "uprising," Navajo (1913), 69–71, 77–84

beaver marriages, 243–44

Belgrade, Daniel B., 180

Beloved (Morrison), 125n27

berdache, 19

Binalli, Niduhullin, 82

biopolitics: 2013 court cases and, 208; assimilation and, 74; Indianness and, 221; neoliberal, 208–9; queer theory and, 214; settler colonialism and queer politics, 64n14; sound quantum and, 151; terrorizing sexual colonization and, 74. *See also* bodies and embodiment; queer politics of the transitive native

biphobia, 63n10

Biyi, Bizhoshi, 81–82, 84

Bizhoshi, 84

Blackhawk, Ned, 91

Blackness, Iñupiaq and, 148–49, 150–51

Blaeser, Kimberly, 237

Blaisdell, Kekuni, 51

blood: Indianness and, 170, 189, 192, 195; as metaphor, 115

Bloodland (film; Tailfeathers), 30

Blue, Martha, 97n71

boat sex workers, 103–4

Bodenhorn, Barbara, 140–41

bodies and embodiment: Christian conceptions of, 110; as cultural locus and locus of gendered meanings, 108; disciplined bodies in colonialism, 113–14; ecologies, embodied, 235–36; gendered, colonized bodies as meeting place, 112, 113–19; gravity and, 249; intelligences of the body, reawakening, 255; material and racialized body in relation to structures of nation-state, 116; nation-state formation and control of women's bodies, 125n29; plasticity of the body, 219; scaled violence on the body, 114–15; settler colonialism and, 102, 108–10; signatures metaphor, 103; theories of the flesh, 110–11; tragic mixed-blood as body out of place, 114–15; trans-corporeality, 235; at various scales, 101; world, body of, 231. *See also* eco-eroticism and oral narratives; *Solar Storms* (Hogan)

Body in Pain, The (Scarry), 125n28

Bolton, Laura, 145

Bosque Redondo reservation, 75, 76, 82, 84

Bradbury, William B., 152

Brant, Beth, 18–20

Brave Heart, Maria Yellow Horse, 109

Bridge Called My Back, A (Moraga), 111

Brown v. Board of Education, 210

Brugge, David, 80

Bryant, Tony, 136

Bureau of Indian Affairs (BIA), 178

Butler, Judith, 12, 108, 215

Callicott, J. Baird, 246, 248
"Captivating Eunice" (Simpson), 15
captivity narratives, 15
Carleton, John, 76
carnal knowledge, 232, 237, 239, 243, 252, 253
Chang, Jeff, 149
Cherokee Nation and same-sex marriage, 90, 91
Cherokee Nation v. Georgia, 200n32
Chicana feminism, 111
child custody and adoption. See Indian Child Welfare Act
Christianity: body conceptions in, 110; Comity Agreement (1874), 151; eco-eroticism and, 232–33, 234; Hawai'i and, 49–50; hymn singing, Iñupiaq, 151–55; missionaries in the Arctic, 151–54; Native authenticity and, 154; reinscription of, by Indigenous writers, 17; Utqiaġvik (Barrow, AK), conversions in, 152
Chuh, Kandice, 216–17
citizenship, captivity narratives and, 15
"civilization" and civilizing/modernizing narratives: audiovisualizing Iñupiaq and musical modernities, 155–58; Christianization and, 110; "developing" Native nations and, 114; Hawai'i and, 50; Navajo (Diné) and, 75–80, 84–91
climate change, 142
Cogewea (Mourning Dove), 16
Cohen, Bernard, 223
Cohen, Cathy J., 214
Coleman, Arica L., 223, 224–25
Collier, John, 75–76, 87
Comity Agreement (1874), 151
congressional apology to the Hawaiian people, 47
Conlon, Paula, 143
containment, 101
corporations, Alaska Native, 146–47, 165nn73–76
Correll, J. Lee, 77
court cases: Adoptive Couple v. Baby Girl, 188, 191–92, 208, 225; Baehr v. Lewin

(later Baehr v. Miike), 47; Brown v. Board of Education, 210; Cherokee Nation v. Georgia, 200n32; Ex Parte Crow Dog, 177; Lawrence v. Texas, 208, 209; Loving v. Virginia, 209, 210–11, 221–25; Mississippi Band of Choctaw Indians v. Holyfield, 188, 190–91; Morton v. Mancari, 178–79, 183, 189; Oliphant v. Schlie, 199n21, 200n23; Oliphant v. Suquamish, 172–73, 174–85, 196, 197n3; In re Bridget (CA), 193–96, 206n96; Rice v. Cayetano, 60, 66n40; Santa Clara Pueblo v. Martinez, 184, 203n56; Shelby Count, Alabama v. Holder, 207; Sorells v. Shields, 223; U.S. v. Kagama, 189, 200n32; U.S. v. Nice, 189; U.S. v. Rogers, 201n44; U.S. v. Windsor, 208, 209–10
creation narratives, 90, 98n88, 254
Cree, 105
critical Indigenous studies (CIS): curriculum vs. scholarship, 9; early writings, 14–18; ethnic and critical race studies and, 8–10; gender, sexuality, and feminist studies, criticisms of and disconnects from, 10–11; on gender and sexuality identificatory categories in Indigenous languages, 13; institutional histories of, 7–11; interdisciplinary circulation, shift in, 18–20
crucible image in historical narrative, 85
"culture": assimilation and "cultural distinctiveness," 194; bodies as cultural locus, 108; Hawaiian cultural concepts used in same-sex marriage debate, 58–60; Indian Child Welfare Act and, 187–89, 194–95; Inuit post-WWII cultural changes, 145–46; self-determination, cultural, 25–26
Curtis, Edward S., 29

Dancing on Our Turtle's Back (Simpson), 25–26
Danforth, Jessica Yee, 27–28
David, E. J. R., 155–56
De Beers, 36n12

decolonization: environmental justice and, 26; erotica, sexuality, and, 26–28; Hawaiian nationalism, inclusion, and, 57, 61–62; masculinities and, 24–25; of nature, 235 36, 255; Navajo (Diné) and, 72–73, 91–92; politics of cultural authenticity and, 154

Deer, Sarah, 126n39

Defense of Marriage Act (DOMA), 47, 63n8, 208, 209–10

Delany, Samuel R., 207, 218–21, 224, 225

Deloria, Ella Cara, 18

Deloria, Phlip, 74–75, 79, 83, 85, 159n12

Deloria, Vine, Jr., 11, 37n26

Demos, T. J., 236

Denetdale, Jennifer Nez, 31, 37n26

Depp, Johnny, 2

desire, 207, 213, 217, 231, 241, 249–50

Dhalgren (Delany), 221

Diamond, Beverley, 143–44

Diamond, Lisa, 250

Dickerson, Daniel, 156

Dickson, Charles H., 86–87

difference, colonial logics of, 101

Diné. See Navajo

Diné Marriage Act (2005), 90–91

divisions of labor, gendered (Inuit), 140–41

DJ HeTook (Julien Jacobs), 149–50

DJ RiverFlowz (Torin Jacobs), 145, 148–51

Dodge, Chee, 79–80, 82

Dodge, Thomas, 87

Dombrowski, Kirk, 154

"domestic dependent nations," 213

domesticity, Navajo (Diné) gender and, 88

domicile, question of, 190, 191

Drum-Assisted Recovery Therapy for Native Americans (DARTNA), 156–57

drum dance performance, Iñupiaq, 139–44, 140

Duggan, Lisa, 209

Duthu, N. Bruce, 174, 180

eco-eroticism and oral narratives: Bear, Huckleberry, and Human treaty, 252–54; Birth of Nanaboozhoo (Anishinaabeg), 245–47; body intelligences and, 255; "carnal knowledge," 232, 237, 239, 243, 252, 253; colonial, patriarchal, and Judeo-Christian suppression of, 232–33; colonial desire, exotic romanticism, and, 231; contact zone, human and more-than-human, 232, 252, 253; human co-evolutionary pansexual adaptation, 232; interspecies and transspecies sexuality, 237–40, 251–52; modern science and, 248–50; moments and experiences of, 229–30; Native oral literatures (overview), 236–37; new theoretical frameworks for, 235–36; pansexuality, 230–31, 232, 234–35, 250–51, 255; patriarchy, matriarchy, and, 254; "Potchikoo" (Ojibwe), 247–48; senses, re-Indigenizing, 255; sexuality studies and, 233–34; Sky Woman in Haudenasaunee creation story, 254; "species" as construct, 258n33; "Star Husband" (Kootenai), 242–43; "Stick Husband" (Coast Yuki), 243–44; "The Woman Who Married a Bear" (multiple traditions), 245–46; "The Woman Who Married a Beaver" (Anishinaabeg), 244–45; trickster characters and, 241, 245; women's capacity for sexual fluidity, 250–51

education, forced (Navajo), 71

Eng, David, 214

environmental justice, 26, 28

Equal Protection Clause, 14th Amendment, 208–9, 225

Erdrich, Louise, 231, 239, 247

erotica and decolonization, 26–27

eroticism, transspecies. See eco-eroticism and oral narratives

"Eskimo" as term, 131–32, 160nn18–19. See also Inuit/Alaska Natives

"Eskimo Flow" hip hop, 165n82

essentialisms, 11–14

ethnic and critical race studies, 8–10

ethnic cleansing, 71–72, 75, 93n9

exceptionalism, American, 70

Ex Parte Crow Dog, 177

Fallin, Christina, 2
Family Homes of Reserve Matrimonial Interests of Rights Act (Bill S-2) (Canada), 35n10
family model, normative, 171, 183, 187–88
fasting protests, 4
"Fast Runner Trilogy" (films; Kunuk), 133
fear, 78–79, 112
feminism: Chicana, 111; Indigenous sovereignty and, 20–21; modernist ideologies and discourses and, 16–17. *See also* gender, sexuality, and feminist studies
Fienup-Riordan, Ann, 131–33, 141
Figueroa, Esther, 254
"firsting and lasting," 215
First Nation Education Act (Canada), 35n10
First Nations Self-Government Recognition Bill (Bill S-212) (Canada), 35n10
Flaherty, Robert J., 132, 138
flesh, theories of the, 110–11
Fogel-Chance, Nancy, 160n14
food and sex, 239, 243–44
Forbes, Jack D., 254
Fort Wingate, 70
Freeze Frame (Fienup-Riordan), 132–33
Frickey, Philip, 174, 199n22
Frink, Lisa, 140
Frontier Thesis, 211

Gaia hypothesis, 248
Gathering of Spirit, A (Brant), 18–20
gender: body as locus of gendered colonial meanings, 108, 119–20; Inuit divisions of labor, gendered, 140–41; Iñupiaq drum songs and vocal games and, 143–44; *nádleehí* (third gender, Navajo), 90, 98n88; race and ethnicity or law and politics, disarticulation from, 11; separation of sex from, 13
gender, sexuality, and feminist studies: critical Indigenous studies and, 10–11; essentialisms and discursive foundations of, 11–14; historical institutionalization of, 7–8; suffragist writings, 16
genealogy: heteronormative framework and, 186; "Indian" and racial logics of, 33–34; matrilineality and patrilineality, 13–16,

59; Nā Mamo (Hawai'i) and, 50–51, 53; as straightening device, 181; Violence against Women Act and, 171
geophagy, 229–30, 256n2
Gill, Sheila, 96n52
Gilmore, Joseph Henry, 152
Goeman, Mishuana, 17, 31
Goldberg-Hiller, Jonathan, 65n25
Gomes, Ku'umeaaloha, 50
Gone, Joseph, 109, 110
Goodyear-Ka'ōpua, Noelani, 100–101
Gordon, Jessica, 3
Gordon, Karen Elizabeth, 217
Gould, Stephen Jay, 235
"governance of the prior," 216
Grassley, Chuck, 170
gravity, 248–50
gynocratism, 19

Halberstam, Jack, 214
Hale Mua (Men's House), 24
Hall, Edward T., 250
Halsey, Theresa, 20
hānai (to feed), 59
Haraway, Donna, 238, 252
Harper, Stephen, 4, 106
Harris, Cheryl, 23
Hawaiian masculinities, Tengan on, 24
Hawaiian Sovereignty Advisory Commission (later Hawaiian Sovereignty Elections Council), 53–54, 66n40
Hawaiian Sovereignty Advisory Council, 66n38
Hawaiian sovereignty and sexual diversity debate: competing sovereignty projects, 60; cultural concepts used in same-sex marriage debate, 58–60; genealogy and Native lineage claims, 50–51; historical background, 49–50; Nā Mamo BLGTM group, 50–51, 53–57; Puwalu 'Ekolu gathering, land base, and antidiscrimination clause debate, 53–57; sovereignty leader interviews on recognition, 51–53; state constitutional amendment, 47, 63n7; True Aloha and Hawaii Marriage Equality Act, 45–47, 46, 58–59

Hawaii's Story by Hawaii's Queen (Liliuoka-lani), 16
"He Leadeth Me" (hymn; Gilmore), 152
Henderson, James Sakej, 248–49
Hersher, Rebecca, 156
Hess, Bill, 154–55
heteronormativity: colonialism and, 3; definitions of, 198n12; genealogical underbelly of, 186; Indianness and, 173–74, 181–82, 196; meaning of, 173; Navajo (Diné) and, 73–74, 91; *In re Bridget* (CA) and, 193; reinscription of, 17; Violence against Women Act and, 171. *See also* marriage equality and same-sex marriage; queer studies and theory
heterosexist ideologies: "heterosexism" as term, 63n10; masculinities, decolonization, and, 24–25; Navajo and heteropatriarchy, 73–74; Navajo (Diné) and hetersexual gender binaries, 87–88. *See also* marriage equality and same-sex marriage
Highway, Tomson, 234
hip hop and rap, 144–51, 165n82
Hirschkop, Philip J., 223
historical trauma, 109–10
Hogan, Linda, 99. See also *Solar Storms* (Hogan)
ho'omanawanui, kuualoha, 58
Holland, Sharon, 116, 207, 214, 217
home, in Hogan's *Solar Storms*, 113
homonormativity, 208, 222
homophobia as term, 63n10
Hopkins, Sarah Winnemucca, 16
Huckleberry, 252–54
Huhndorf, Shari M., 160n18
Hunt, Sarah, 28
Hydro-Québec dams project, 105–7
hymn singing, Iñupiaq, 151–55

identity and identification: gender and sexuality categories in Indigenous languages, 13; inclusion in and exclusion from governance, territorial, and cultural practice rights, 10; transhistorical approach to sexual identities, 65n27; tribal identity in

Morton v. Mancari and *U.S. v. Antelope*, 179. *See also* Indianness, federal production of; indigeneity
Idle No More movement, 3–4, 26, 28
Igloolik Isuma Productions, 133
implicit divestiture, doctrine of, 175
Indian Act Amendment and Replacement Act (Bill C-428) (Canada), 20–21, 35n10
Indian Child Welfare Act (ICWA), 172–73, 182–96, 208
Indian Civil Rights Act (1968), 202n55, 203n56
Indianness, federal production of: *Adoptive Couple v. Baby Girl*, 188, 191–92; blood and, 170, 189, 192, 196; "culture" and, 187–89, 194–95; Delany's "Aye, and Gomorrah" and, 221; *Ex Parte Crow Dog*, 177; as extrapolitical attribute, 172; Indian Child Welfare Act (ICWA), 172–73, 182–96; Indigeneity mediated by, 195–96; kinship, family, and heteronormative discourses, 173–74, 186–90, 193; Major Crimes Act (1885), 177; *Mississippi Band of Choctaw Indians v. Holyfield*, 188, 190–91; *Morton v. Mancari*, 178–79, 183, 189; non-Indian legal personhood, genealogy, and racial reproduction, 180–82; *Oliphant v. Suquamish*, 172–73, 174–85, 196, 197n3; Pocahontas Exception, 224–25; Public Law 280 and state jurisdiction, 184–85; *In re Bridget* (CA), 193–96, 206n96; "special relationship" between U.S. and tribes, 185–87, 189–91; territorial sovereignty limitation, 174–75; tribal identity and Indianness as a kind of status, 176–82; *U.S. v. Antelope*, 178–79; Violence against Women Act (VAWA) reauthorization, 169–71, 173, 196, 197n4
Indian Offenses Act (1883), 76
Indian Reorganization Act (1934), 75, 88, 178
indigeneity: authenticity and, 3, 147, 211; biopolitics of settler colonialism and, 64n14; "culture" and, 187; as difference and recourse in legal discourse, 218; as

erotics, 213; inclusion in and exclusion from category of, 11–12; Indian Child Welfare Act and alignment of lineage or genealogy with, 183, 186; Indianness and, 188, 195–96; ongoing debates about, 6; political referents, 216; settler colonialism and, 211–12, 217; settler colonial subjectivity, challenge to, 216–17; subjectlessness and, 215. *See also specific topics, such as* Loving v. Virginia

"Indigenous Peoples and Languages of Alaska" (map), 130, *131*, 160n16

Indigenous World Film Festival, Alaska Native Heritage Center, 133

Innes, Robert Alexander, 130

In re Bridget (CA), 193–96, 206n96

interspecies sexuality. *See* eco-eroticism and oral narratives

Inuit/Alaska Natives: Alaska Native Solidarity movement, 149; globalized society, participation in, 145; Hydro-Québec dams project and, 105, 124n9; languages, terminology, and politics of naming, 130–32, *131*, 160n16, 160n18; marriage cosmologies, Iñupiaq, 141; oil and Alaska Native Corporations, 146–47, 165nn73–76; post-WWII cultural changes, 145–46; whaling practice and ritual, 141–43, 164n156. *See also* Iñupiaq film, soundscape, and masculinities

Iñupiaq film, soundscape, and masculinities: audibility and inaudibility assumptions, 157; audiovisualization of musical modernities, significance of, 155–58; Drum-Assisted Recovery Therapy for Native Americans (DARTNA), 156–57; "Eskimo Flow" freestyle rap and "Arctic Thug" (MacLean's *On the Ice*), 144–51, 165n82; Flaherty's *Nanook of the North* and colonial sound regimes, 132, 138, 148; *Freeze Frame* (Fienup-Riordan) on, 132–33; hymn "singspiration" (MacLean's *On the Ice*), 151–55, *153*; Kunuk's *Atanarjuat* ("Faster Runner"), 133, 135–38; MacLean, about, 133–35; MacLean's *On the*

Ice (overview), 136–38; MacLean's *Sikumi*, 135–37, 162n42; place-based and culture-based soundscapes and soundtracks (MacLean's *On the Ice*), 138–39, 157–58; *sayuun* drum dance (MacLean's *On the Ice*), 139–44, *140*; sound quantum ideology, 150–51; "soundscape," defined, 159n13; vocal games, 143–44

Iñupiaq Theater, Utqiaġvik, 134

Iñupiat Eskimo Hymnbook, 152

invasion, Wolfe on, 22–23

ʻIoane, Skippy, 56

Irelan, Frank Qutuq, 145

Isaac, Calvin, 190–91

Iverson, Peter, 79, 83, 84–85

iZLER, 138

Jacobs, Julien (DJ HeTook), 149–50

Jacobs, Torin (DJ RiverFlowz), 145, 148–51

Jaimes Guerrero, M. A., 20

Jobs and Growth Act (Bill C-45) (Canada), 4

Johnson, Basil, 246, 247

Johnson, E. Pauline, 16

Johnston, David, 4

Justice, Daniel Heath, 23–24

justice, legal. *See* law and justice

Kailala, Aʻo Pohaku, 51–52

KaLāhui Hawaiʻi, 52–53

Ka Leʻa O Ke Ola: A Forum on Kanaka Maoli Culture, Sexuality, and Spirituality, 67n41

Kameʻeleihiwa, Lilikalā, 49, 56, 65n19

Kamehameha I, 24, 49, 50

Kamehameha III, 60

Kanahele, Dennis "Bumpy," 53

Kanaka Maoli (Native Hawaiians). *See* Hawaiian sovereignty and sexual diversity debate

Kanui, Kawehi, 53

Kaplan, Amy, 70

kʻé (kinship-based relations, Navajo), 73, 92

Kennedy, Anthony, 199n21, 209–10

Kimmerer, Robin Wall, 253

King, Thomas, 236, 240

kinship: Indianness, family, and hetero-normative discourses, 173–74, 186–90, 193; Indianness and, 173–74; *k'é* (Navajo kinship-based relations), 73, 92; with more-than human world, 237

knowledge systems and language systems, 130. *See also* carnal knowledge

Krejci, Paul, 145, 152, 167n95

Kunuk, Zacharias, 133, 135–38

Kyl, John, 170

LaDuke, Winona, 26

Laenui, Pōkā, 66n38

land. *See* territoriality and land

law and justice: Navajo vs. American, 76–77, 80–81, 86, 89; Navajo Witch Purge of 1878, 97n71; non-Indian legal person-hood, 180–82; spatial justice, 106, 123n5. *See also* court cases; Indianness, federal production of

Lawrence v. Texas, 208, 209

Leacock, Eleanor, 39n40

legibility and illegibility, 12

Lewis, Brian J., 201n35

Lewis, George, 151

Life among the Piutes (Hopkins), 16

Liliuokalani, Queen, 16

Linnekin, Jocelynn, 49

Little Singer (Hatalii Yazi), 69, 77, 79–80, 82–84

Live Long and Prosper (Spock Was a Half-Breed) (Yepa-Pappan), 28–30, 29

Living the Spirit (Roscoe), 18–20

Lomax, Alan, 153

Long, Dáilan J., 96n63

Longboat, Dan Roronhiakewen, 255

Long Walk (Navajo), 82, 84

Loving, Mildred Jeter, 222–24

Loving, Richard, 222

Loving analogy, 210

Loving v. Virginia, 209, 210–11, 218, 221–25

Lowaimia, K. Tsianina, 126n32

Machado, Collette, 58

MacLean, Andrew Okpeha: about, 133–35, 147; *Natchiliagniaqtuguk Aapagalu* ("Seal Hunting with Dad") (film), 162n34; *Sikumi* (film), 133–37, 162n42. See also *On the Ice*

MacLean, Edna Ahgeak, 127, 134, 142–43

magnetic force, 249

māhū, 48, 59, 63n11

Maillard, Kevin, 224

Major Crimes Act (1885), 177, 201n35

malama 'āina (caring for the land), 54–56

Mall, Lorinda, 205n82

Mallet, James, 251

Marcous, Cara, 142

Margolin, Malcolm, 242

marriage: as colonial imposition in Hawai'i, 50; human and more-than-human, in oral narratives, 241–45; Iñupiaq cosmologies of, 141; Navajo practices, tradition, and polygamy, 69, 83–84, 86–88, 89–90

marriage equality and same-sex marriage: 2013 as "really gay year," 209; broader queer political organizing overtaken by, 67n51; California Proposition 8 ban, 208; Cherokee and, 90, 91; *Loving and Virginia* and, 221–25; "miscegenation analogy," 210–11; Navajo resolution and law against, 87–88, 90; religious exemptions, 46–47, 62n5; True Aloha and Hawaii Marriage Equality Act, 45–47, 46, 58–59

Marshall, John, 213

Martin, Biddy, 13

Martinez, Andres, 136

Masculindians (McKegney), 25, 128

masculinities: emerging research on, 128–29; hypermasculine stereotypes, 128; "masculine" as Western concept, 130; men's studies and "crisis" of, 127–28; scholarship on racists ideologies of, 24–25. *See also* Iñupiaq film, soundscape, and masculinities

Massey, Doreen, 112

matriarchy, 11, 13, 254

matrilineality, 13–16, 96n63

McAdam, Sylvia, 3

McGeough, Michelle, 237

McKegney, Sam, 25, 128

McKibbin, Davidson, 77–78

McLean, Sheela, 3

Means, Russell, 11

Medicine, Beatrice, 18

Melamed, Jodi, 208

memory and forgetting: blood/land/memory complex, 115; historical memory in Hogan's *Solar Storms*, 120; Inuit hunting and, 136; living memory, 114; masculinities, "re-membering," 144; oral narratives and, 240; past invoked to normalize heteropatriarchy, 74; settler colonialism and nostalgic past, 114; violence, Navajo collective memory of, 79

Me Sexy (Taylor), 26–27, 234

Michif, 239, 258n31

Miller, Susan, 51–53

Million, Dian, 109

Miranda, Deborah, 74, 77

miscegenation, logics of. See *Loving v. Virginia*

"miscegenation analogy," 210–11

missionaries, 151–54

Mississippi Band of Choctaw Indians v. Holyfield, 188, 190–91

Mitchell, Charlie, 82

mixed-blood, tragic, 114–15

modernist ideologies and feminism, 16–17

modernization. See "civilization" and civilizing/modernizing narratives

Mohawk Interruptus (Simpson), 92

Monture-Angus, Patricia, 20

Moraga, Cherríe, 110–11

Moreton-Robinson, Aileen, 23, 215

Morgensen, Scott Lauria, 23–24, 64n14, 74, 96n60, 212

Morrison, Toni, 125n27

Morton v. Mancari, 178–79, 183, 189

Mourning Dove, 16

Muñoz, José Esteban, 214

nádleehí (third gender, Navajo), 90, 98n88

Nageak, Roy, 154

Nageak, Vincent Pamiuq, III, 154–55

Nā Mamo, 50–51, 53–57

Nanaboozhoo, 245–47

Nanook of the North (film; Flaherty), 132, 138, 148

Natchiliagniaqtuguk Aapagalu ("Seal Hunting with Dad") (film; MacLean), 162n34

nationalism, Hawaiian. See Hawaiian sovereignty and sexual diversity debate

National Museum of the American Indian (NMAI), 166n89

National Public Commission of Inquiry on Violence against Indigenous Women (Canada), 5

Nation of Ku, 51–52

Nations Financial Transparency Act (Bill C-27) (Canada), 35n10

Navajo (Diné): Beautiful Mountain "uprising" (1913), 69–71, 77–84; Bosque Redondo, return form, 84–85; Bosque Redondo reservation and the Long Walk, 75, 76, 82, 84; decolonization, 72–73; Diné Marriage Act of 2005 (same-sex marriage ban), 90–91; ethnic cleansing, 71–72, 75; forced education, 71; gender and domesticity, 88; justice and criminal law, Navajo vs. American, 76–77, 80–81, 86, 89; *k'é* (kinship-based relations), 73, 92; marriage regulation and heterosexist gender binaries, 87–88; modernizing and civilizing narrative, 75–80, 84–91; *nádleehí* (third gender), 90; nationhood and authenticity, 88–89; polygamy and marriage customs, 69, 83–84, 86–87, 89–90; settler colonialism and, 72; White fear of Navajo violence, 78–79

Navajo: A Century of Progress, 1868–1968, 88

"Navajos on the Warpath?" (Weber), 78

Navajo Times, 88

Nelson, Alray, 91

Nelson, Melissa K., 26

Nelson, Michael P., 246, 248

neoliberal biopolitics, 208–9

New Indian history, 70–72
Newton, Isaac, 249
Nietzsche, Friedrich, 250, 259n66
Nixon, Richard, 182
NoiseCat, Julian Brave, 156

O'Brien, Jean M., 215
Occom, Samson, 39n41
oil, 146–47
Oliphant v. Schlie, 199n21, 200n23
Oliphant v. Suquamish, 172–73, 174–85, 196, 197n3
Omi, Michael, 23
On the Ice (film; MacLean): audiovisualization of musical modernities, significance of, 155–58; awards, 163n46; "Eskimo Flow" freestyle rap and "Arctic Thug," 144–51; hymn "singspiration," 151–55, 153; Kunuk's *Atanarjuat* and, 136–37; place-based and culture-based soundscapes and soundtracks, 138–39; plot and Director's Statement, 137–38; *sayuun* drum dance, 139–44, 140
oral literatures. *See* eco-eroticism and oral narratives; stories and storytelling
orgasm, 230
Orientalism, 225
Original Instructions (Nelson), 26
original sin, 103, 117–18, 234
Ortiz, Alfonso, 18
"outbreak" as term of colonial power, 79

pansexuality, 230–31, 232, 234–35, 250–51, 255
patriarchy, 19, 73–74, 254
patrilineality, 13–14, 59, 65n27
Perry Reuben, 80
Philo, Chris, 238
Pocahontas, 31
Pocahontas Exception, 224–25
"polity of the indigenous," 5, 18, 172, 252–53. *See also* self-determination; sovereignty, Indigenous
polygamy, Navajo, 69, 83–84, 86–87, 89–90
po'olua (two heads), 59
postcolonialism, 23

Potchikoo, 247–48
Povinelli, Elizabeth, 116, 173, 188, 203n59, 216
Powell, Dana E., 96n63
Presbyterian missionaries, 151–52
Public Law 280 (1953), 184
punalua relationships, 48, 49, 65n18
Puwalu 'Ekolu gathering and Resolution (Phi Bay, Hawai'i, 1996), 53–57

Qalli, 140, 144, 151, 152
queer politics of the transitive native: 2013 U.S. Supreme Court rulings and, 207–12, 217–18, 225; Delany's "Aye, and Gomorrah," 207, 218–21, 224; desire and the subjectlessness, 212–18; gay marriage implications and, 223; *Loving v. Virginia*, 209, 210–11, 218, 221–25; "miscegenation analogy," 210–11; neoliberal biopolitics and, 208–9; same-sex marriage, broader queer political organizing overtaken by, 67n51
queer studies and theory: definition and re-invention of "queer," 214; desire and, 207; greening of Indigenous queer theory, 234; pansexuality and, 250–51; queer, as term, 63n10; queer indigenous studies, 213–14; settler colonialism and, 23–24; subjectless critique, 214–17

race studies, ethnic and critical, 8–10
Racial Integrity Act (VA), 222–24
Raheja, Michelle, 133
rap and hip hop, 144–51, 165n82
"rebellion" as term of colonial power, 79
recognition: authenticity and, 3; First Nations Self-Government Recognition Bill (Bill S-212) (Canada), 35n10; Hawaiian sovereignty leaders on, 51–53; Simpson on rejection of gift of, 92
Reddy, Chandan, 210–11, 223
Red Girl's Reasoning, A (film; Tailfeathers), 31
"Red Hot to the Touch" (Akiwenzi-Damm), 27
Reford, Olemaun, 136
Rehnquist, William, 174, 176, 181, 199n21

"Relative to the Policy of the Indian Office in Dealing with Plural Marriages, Divorce, and Other Customs of Unallotted Indians," 86

reproductive understanding of Native identity, 172–73

reproductive vs. environmental justice, 28

resistance: Beautiful Mountain "uprising," Navajo (1913), 69–71, 77–84; "outbreak," "rebellion," and "uprising" as terms of colonial power, 79; white fear of violence, 78–79

Rice, Harold, 66n40

Rice v. Cayetano, 60, 66n40

Rifkin, Mark, 17, 64n14, 74, 75, 212–13

rights, Indigenous. *See specific case and topics, such as* marriage equality *or* Navajo

Roscoe, Will, 18–20

Roszak, Theodore, 237–38

Russell, Steven, 199n20

Sacred Hoop, The (Allen), 18–20

Safe Drinking Water for First Nations Act (Bill S-8) (Canada), 35n10

same-sex marriage. *See* marriage equality and same-sex marriage

same-sex relations and Hawaiian Native lineage claims, 50–51

Santa Clara Pueblo v. Martinez, 184, 203n56

sayuun (Iñupiaq drum dance), 139–44, 140

scales: in Hogan's *Solar Storms*, 101, 112, 114–15, 119–21; human and non-human bodies at levels of, 107–8; social processes that freeze, 101; vertical and horizontal, 105, 114

Scarry, Elaine, 125n28

scat, 245

Schafer, R. Murray, 159n13

Schneider, Bethany, 23–24

Schutt, Ethan, 155

Scott, Hugh L., 79, 81–82

self-determination: civil rights vs., 20; critical Indigenous studies and, 8–10; cultural, 25–26, 32; in Hogan's *Solar Storms*, 112; Indian Child Welfare Act and, 182–84; Indianness and, 188; in *Mississippi Band of Choctaw Indians v. Holyfield*, 191; Navajo

(Diné) and, 72, 84; New Indian history and, 71; *Oliphant v. Suquamish* and, 33, 202n52; polity of the indigenous, 5, 18, 172, 252–53; *In re Bridget* and, 194–95; sound quantum and, 151; Violence against Women Act and, 171. *See also* Hawaiian sovereignty and sexual diversity debate

senses, re-Indigenizing, 255

settler colonialism: Alaska Native artists and, 157–58; fetishized disavowal of the Indigenous, 211–12; gendered, embodied experiences and, 102, 119–20; geographic amnesia and, 114; interpersonal, community, and state levels of violence, 100; liberalism and, 208; Morgenson on, 64n14; Navajo (Diné) and, 71–72; queer studies and, 23–24; recognition and, 92; redistribution and spatial injustice, settler model of, 106, 123n5; Rifkin on, 64n14; same-sex marriage in Hawaii and, 59–60; scale-based difference and spatial injustice, 101, 123n5; Simpson's *Dancing on Our Turtle's Back* and, 25–26; spatial embodiments in Hogan's *Solar Storms* and, 108–10; subjectlessness ad, 216–17; unjust geographies and, 107; Wolfe on, 22–23, 64n14, 72, 102, 225; women's bodies, pressure on, 119–20

Settler Colonialism and the Transformation of Anthropology (Wolfe), 22–23

"settler homonationalism," 212

sex, anatomical, separated from gender, 13

sex trafficking vs. sex work, 123n8

sexuality: "carnal knowledge," 232, 237, 239, 243, 252, 253; decolonization and, 26–28; ecology and sexuality studies, 233; erotica, 26–27; food and, 239, 243–44; gender, sexuality, and feminism, 11–14; orgasm, 230; pansexuality, 230–31, 232, 234–35, 250–51, 255; race and ethnicity or law and politics, disarticulation from, 11; repression and denial as normative, 257n16; sex as metaphor, 252; trickster sexuality, 240; women's capacity for sexual fluidity, 250–51. *See also* eco-eroticism and oral narratives sexual violence. *See under* violence

sex work, 103–4, 123n8

Shah, Nayan, 65n27

Shelby Count, Alabama v. Holder, 207

Shelton, William T (aka Nat'aani Nez, Tall Leader), 77–79, 81–84, 85–86

Shiprock, 81–82

Shirley, Joe, Jr., 90

Sikumi (film; MacLean), 135–37, 162n42

Silko, Leslie Marmon, 19

Silva, Noenoe K., 49, 51, 54–55, 56, 65n19

Simpson, Audra, 15, 18, 92

Simpson, Leanne Betasamosake, 25–26

Sky Woman, 19, 254

Smith, Andrea, 154, 215, 216

Smith, John, 31

Smith, Laurajane, 16–17

Smith, Neil, 101, 114–15

socio-intellectual evolution, ideology of, 12

Soja, Edward, 107

Solar Storms (Hogan): bodies of land and water and the Hydro-Québec dams project, 105–8; embodiment of brute force of colonization, 111; gendered, colonized bodies as meeting place, 112, 113–19, 120; gendered colonial violence written on the body, 102–5; generational violence and historical trauma, 108–10; Hannah's body and death at various scales, 119–21; home in, 113; ongoing abandonments and resistances, 122–23; regenerative structures of violence, 110–12

Somerville, Siobhan, 210, 223

Sorells v. Shields, 223

Sotomayor, Sonia, 225

sound quantum ideology, 150–51

soundscape, Iñupiaq. *See* Iñupiaq film, soundscape, and masculinities

Sovereign and Independent National-State of Hawai'i, 53

sovereignty, Indigenous: feminist politics and, 20–21; Hawaiian same-sex marriage, cultural concepts, and, 58–60; Hawaiian

sovereignty groups and BLGTM recognition, 51–53; Indianness and, 170–71, 183; limitation on sovereignty vs. territory, 174–75; "separate power" prohibition, 175–76

Spade, Dean, 67n51

Sparks, Carol, 96n61

spatial justice, 106

"special relationship" between U.S. and tribes, 185–87, 189–91

Spence, Chief Theresa, 4

Spider Woman, 19

Spillers, Hortense, 126n40

sports mascots, 128, 157

Sprinkles, Annie, 248

Stark, Heidi Kiiwetinepinesiik, 252

state jurisdiction, 184–85, 202n55

Stefani, Gwen, 2

Stewart, J. M., 87

Stoler, Ann Laura, 72–73

stories and storytelling: Bear, Huckleberry, and Human treaty, 252–54; *Birth of Nanaboozhoo* (Anishinaabeg), 245–47; in Hogan's *Solar Storms*, 119; Old Man and Old Woman (Lenape), 21–22; "Potchikoo" (Ojibwe), 247–48; "Star Husband" (Kootenai), 242–43; "Stick Husband" (Coast Yuki), 243–44; "The Woman Who Married a Bear" (multiple traditions), 245–46; "The Woman Who Married a Beaver" (Anishinaabeg), 244–45; Windigo, 111–12

subjectlessness and the subjectless critique, 214–17

suffragist writings, 16

suicide, 156

Supreme Court cases. *See* court cases

survivance, 235, 257n17

Swift, John, 130

Tailfeathers, Elle-Máijá, 30–31

Tallbear, Kimberly, 151, 234

Tanana Chiefs' Conference, 155

Taylor, Drew Hayden, 26–27, 234

Tengan, Ty P. Kāwika, 24, 144

Tenth Amendment, 193, 205n93

territoriality and land: Hydro-Québec dams project and devouring of Native lands and bodies, 105–7; implicit divestiture, doctrine of, 175; indigenous identification and, 10; *malama 'āina* and *aloha 'āina* and BLGTM in Hawai'i, 54–56; oil discovery in Alaska and, 146–47; settler colonialism and unjust geographies, 107; Turner's Frontier Thesis, 211; *Violence over the Land* (Blackhawk), 91

terrorism, 76, 77, 94n29

therapy and treatment programs for youth, 156–57

Tohe, Laura, 20

Tonto, 2

Topkok, Sean Asiqłuq, 143

trans-corporeality, 235

transspecies sexuality. *See* eco-eroticism and oral narratives

Trask, Haunani-Kay, 20

Trask, Mililani, 52–53

trauma, historical, 109–10

tricksters, 241, 245–47

True Aloha, 45–47, 46, 58–59

Truth and Reconciliation Commission, Canada, 257n13

Tuck, Eve, 72

Turner, Frederick Jackson, 211

Turpel, Mary Ellen, 20

"uprising" as term of colonial power, 79

U.S. v. Kagama, 189, 200n32

U.S. v. Nice, 189

U.S. v. Rogers, 201n44

U.S. v. Windsor, 208, 209–10

Utqiaġvik (Barrow, AK): about, 139–40; as climate crisis "ground zero," 142; hymn singing and Barrow Presbyterian Church Choir, 151–55, 153; MacLean and, 134–35; North Slope Borough, 150; post-WWII cultural changes, 145–46. See also *On the Ice* (MacLean)

Vandever, William, 86

Van Valkenburgh, Richard, 87

Vernon, Irene, 124n15

violence: Blackhawk on terrorizing violence, 91; gendered colonial violence as original sin, 103–4; historical trauma, 109–10; integenerational, in Hogan's *Solar Storms*, 108–10; interpersonal, community, and state levels of, 100; regenerative structures of, 110–12; scaled violence on the body, 114–15; sexual, as integral to colonial projects, 77; terrorism, 76, 77, 94n29; white fear of Navajo violence, 78–79

Violence Against Women Act (VAWA), 169–71, 173, 196, 197n4

Violence over the Land (Blackhawk), 91

Vizenor, Gerald, 240, 246, 247, 257n17

Voting Rights Amendment (1965), 207

Walker, Frank, 79

Warren, Earl, 222

Washington Redskins, 128, 157

Watts, Alan, 229

Wauneka, Annie Dodge, 80

Waziyatawin (Angela Cavender Wilson), 71–72

Weaving Worlds (film), 96n63

Weber, Anselm, 78–83

West Wind, 245–47

Wexler, Lisa, 156

Weyiouanna, Brad, 136

whaling practice and ritual, Iñupiaq, 141–43, 164n156

Wilbert, Christ, 238

Wilkinson, Charles, 98n80

Williams, Eunice, 15

Williams, Joe, 86

Willse, Craig, 67n51

Wilson, Angela Cavender (Waziyatawin), 71–72

Wilson, Nina, 3

Winant, Howard, 23

Windigo/Wetiko, 111–12, 254
Witch Purge of 1878 (Navajo), 97n71
Without Reservation (Akiwenzi-Damm), 26–27
Wolfe, Patrick, 22–23, 64n14, 72, 102, 225
women's eco-eroticism. *See* eroticism and oral narratives
women's studies, 14. *See also* feminism

Wounded Knee, 79, 80
Writer, Jeannette, 94n29

Yang, K. Wayne, 72
Yee, Jessica, 123n8
Yepa-Pappan, Debra, 28–30, 29, 31

Zitkala-Ša, 16